Appalachians All

Appalachians All

East Tennesseans and the Elusive History of an American Region

Mark T. Banker

The University of Tennessee Press • Knoxville

Library of Congress Cataloging-in-Publication Data

Banker, Mark T., 1951–
Appalachians all: East Tennesseans and the elusive history of an American
region / Mark T. Banker. — 1st ed.
p. cm.
Includes bibliographical references and index.
ISBN 13: 978-1-57233-786-2
ISBN 10: 1-57233-786-9
1. Appalachians (People)—Tennessee, East—Ethnic identity.
2. Appalachians (People)—Tennessee, East—History.
3. Tennessee, East—History.
I. Title.

F442.1.B365 2010
976.8'8—dc22
2009045367

Appalachians All

East Tennesseans and the Elusive History of an American Region

Mark T. Banker

The University of Tennessee Press • Knoxville

ぱ

Cloth: 1st printing, 2010.
Paper: 1st printing: 2011

Library of Congress Cataloging-in-Publication Data

Banker, Mark T., 1951–
Appalachians all: East Tennesseans and the elusive history of an American
region / Mark T. Banker. — 1st ed.
p. cm.
Includes bibliographical references and index.
ISBN 13: 978-1-57233-786-2
ISBN 10: 1-57233-786-9
1. Appalachians (People)—Tennessee, East—Ethnic identity.
2. Appalachians (People)—Tennessee, East—History.
3. Tennessee, East—History.
I. Title.

F442.1.B365 2010
976.8'8—dc22
2009045367

In Memory of
Luke Eugene Banker (1913–1986)
and
Katherine Thomas Banker (1919–1997)

Dad's passing and Mom's needs thereafter brought me home to East
Tennessee—making this book both possible and necessary.

Hear what the Lord Says: Arise, plead your case before the mountains, and let the hills hear your voice.... He has showed you, O man, what is good; and what does the Lord require of you but to do justice, and love kindness, and to walk humbly with your God.

—Micah 6:1 and 8 (Revised Standard Version)

If what I have to say, then, does not entirely satisfy your desire for intimate knowledge, the severity of your criticism may be minimized somewhat by the admission that I now make that I do not claim to have compassed the whole truth. I do assert, however, that what I say seems true to me at present writing and necessary to be known.

—John C. Campbell, *The Southern Highlander and His Homeland*

Contents

Illustrations

Illustrations

Preface

....

And the end all of our exploring will be to arrive
where we started and know the place for the first time.

Writing this book confirms for me the truth of T. S. Eliot's often-repeated assertion. Indeed, this book's most fundamental finding eluded my attention for the first two-thirds of my life. Yet glimpses into the insights offered here were never more than a short walk from my actual and proverbial backdoor. This vantage point is a small cemetery sitting high atop a hill overlooking Watts Bar Lake and a vast and beautiful East Tennessee panorama. The cemetery marks the southern property line of the farm my parents purchased in 1950, when Mother was pregnant with me. This farm provided a pleasant and productive setting for the first third of my nearly sixty years, but, when grander horizons beckoned in 1969, this book's concerns were as unknown to me as the farm was familiar. All of this changed when my father died unexpectedly in 1986. Coming home the following summer set in motion a puzzling process of self-discovery that has culminated (for now at least) in this book's unusual take on the history of my home region.

Shortly after I returned to East Tennessee, we placed a marble bench near the center of the cemetery in memory of Dad. For twenty years, that bench—which became Mom's bench as well in 1997—has been my refuge. But the bench is more than a respite from life's wearisome routines and hectic surprises. Regular visits there enable me to look inward and outward in ways I never before imagined. Coming home awakened my interest in family histories deeply rooted in East Tennessee's past. While Mother was still alive, I probed her for information, supplementing her recollections with knowledge from other family members and genealogical records. I have continued this pursuit since her passing. But the historian in me was never content with merely gathering factual information about my forebears. The broader contexts of their lives and the elusive "whys?" that shaped them drew my interest and attention. Gradually my view and understanding of the vast East Tennessee panorama spanning out from my parents' bench broadened and deepened.

Looking north from the bench, the Tennessee and Clinch Rivers converge in the foreground. With headwaters in western North Carolina and southwestern Virginia, these two rivers drain all of East Tennessee and much of greater Appalachia. In their confluence, just beyond my home, three disparate parts of East Tennessee converge. In the far distance beyond the Clinch, craggy waves of the Cumberland Mountains extend northward across Tennessee and into Kentucky and Virginia. In the mid-nineteenth century, a youthful United States uncovered in these rugged mountains an energy source that fueled our nation's emergence into the world's greatest industrial power. For inhabitants of this part of East Tennessee and other Appalachian locales farther north, coal has been both blessing and curse. From my parents' bench, billows of steam and smoke from the towering stacks of TVA's Kingston power plant, and jagged scars from abandoned strip mines in the distance, serve as reminders that feeding a nation's insatiable appetite for energy has many costs.

Directly below and west of the cemetery, the Tennessee River churns slowly. Far upriver and well beyond my vista, a tangle of streams cascade down from the Smokies to form the Holston and French Broad Rivers. Just above present-day Knoxville, those two tributaries converge to form the main channel of the Tennessee. The wide Tennessee Valley and the chain of ever-narrower coves and hollows linking it to the distant Blue Ridge have fed and sustained East Tennesseans since humans arrived in the region. Vast hardwood forests once extended well beyond the crest of the mountains. This timber offered economic opportunities for ambitious entrepreneurs and job seekers and provided affordable building materials for local and distant markets. By the early 1900s, timbering ravaged most of East Tennessee's easternmost slopes. In the years since, the region's resilient flora and scenic vastness have found new life as recreational sites and havens for locals and visitors from around the globe. Much like coal for the Cumberlands, timber and tourism have bestowed mixed blessings on this other distinct East Tennessee mountain hinterland.

A generation before settlers penetrated these more remote parts of East Tennessee, Europeans challenged the Cherokees for control of the greater Tennessee Valley, including the land that became my family's farm. Abundant game and relatively rich soils attracted explorers and land speculators. Permanent settlements appearing around the time of the American Revolution served surrounding farms, becoming way stations for river travelers. Soon after its founding as White's Fort in 1791, Knoxville became the link between the Tennessee Valley's disparate parts and its connection to the greater world. From valley farms, Knoxville drew abundant foodstuffs; from the Cumberlands and the Smokies, it gained access to inexpensive energy resources and construction materials. After a slow start and Civil War setbacks, Knoxville emerged as East

Tennessee's economic and cultural hub in the latter nineteenth century. Processing raw materials, sending farm products, timber, coal, and other regional resources to distant markets, and wholesaling consumer goods to the hinterlands—where those resources had been extracted—brought Knoxvillians a standard of living in many ways more similar to that of the broader, modern Gilded Age America than to the more idyllic, semi-isolated, but more difficult lives of their rural neighbors. From the 1870s to the 1930s, harsh economic realities in East Tennessee's hinterlands—combined with the lure of modernity—pushed and pulled émigrés from those hinterlands into what boosters proudly proclaimed the "Queen City of the Mountains." Knoxville abandoned that title long ago, but it still retains the regional preeminence the name implied. Much like their hinterland ancestors and neighbors from whom they often distinguished themselves, many Knoxvillians discovered by the mid-twentieth century that modernity's fruits could sometimes be unpleasant.

This book explores the intertwined histories of Knoxville—East Tennessee's preeminent valley community—and selected communities from the region's outlying hinterlands in the Cumberlands and the Smokies. Economic and demographic developments have linked East Tennessee's disparate parts together and, in turn, have tied East Tennessee as a whole to broader national and global developments. These relationships—often symbiotic—also produced many strains. Cumulatively they created "Appalachian" conditions in East Tennessee: a stubborn independence, relative isolation, and, for many, a hardscrabble existence. These traits fostered a sense of pride—but also much uncertainty—among our subregion's diverse inhabitants. Ambivalence about this Appalachian identity ebbs and flows throughout East Tennessee's history and, I maintain, is both cause and consequence of the very elusiveness of the idea and place that has come to be known as "Appalachia." Until a generation ago, commentators attributed "Appalachia's" assets—and particularly its alleged ills—to isolation and regional defects, and expected that contact with the cultural mainstream would cause those regional distinctions to disappear. More recent observers, particularly the first wave of Appalachian studies scholars from the 1960s and '70s, blamed outside exploitation for Appalachia's problems, and expressed pride in regional attributes earlier commentators disdained.

Peering out from my parents' bench for the past two decades has enabled me to see beyond the perspectives of earlier observers and to reenvision the histories of East Tennessee and greater Appalachia. In the converging waters of the Clinch and the Tennessee Rivers, I see the intertwined histories of East Tennessee's major city and its hinterland communities; that reality, in turn, illuminates collective and regional identities that have long been elusive.

Acknowledgments

Many influences opened my eyes to this vision of East Tennessee's history and have allowed me to present it in this fashion. I am most grateful to a generous Creator. But I hasten to add that I neither presume to understand the fullness of God's generous designs nor believe that any expression of gratitude for that benevolence is adequate. Like John F. Kennedy, I recognize that here on earth, the Almighty counts on ordinary folk to strive for His purposes. Hence I am grateful to the many mere mortals whose concrete, knowable contributions made this book possible. It is fitting that I begin a revisionist history of a region and people long identified by independence and individualism by emphasizing that scholarship is a collaborative venture. As such, it requires support and good will from a broad array of individuals and institutions. Without encouragement, sound advice, and patience from the University of Tennessee Press, I would simply not be writing these words. Financial support from the National Endowment of the Humanities, Webb School of Knoxville, and several private donors via the East Tennessee Foundation funded a sabbatical from my teaching duties during the 2005–06 school year that enabled me to complete research and compose the first two-thirds of this manuscript. Relatively unimpeded vacations the past three summers enabled me to complete the project. For this, I must again thank Webb School.

Thanks are also due to the generous and competent staffs of the following institutions for making my research productive and pleasant: the McClung Historical Collection of the Knox County Public Library and East Tennessee Historical Society, the John C. Hodges Library at the University of Tennessee, the Archives of Appalachia of East Tennessee State University, the Oak Ridge (Tennessee) Children's Museum, the Berea College (Kentucky) Archives, the Archives and Library of the Great Smoky Mountains National Park, and the Campbell County (Tennessee) Historical Society. At these locations, the following individuals proved particularly helpful to me in gathering the photos presented in this book: Vicky Bills, Ann Bridges, Shannon Wilson, Annette Hartigan, and Jerry Sharp.

Extending appreciation to all the individuals who contributed to an effort such as this can be a challenge. Finding a balance between exaggerating one's own importance by providing a seemingly endless list of influences on his effort and failing to extend credit where it is due can be daunting.

Many persons who contributed to my formal education made foundational contributions to this effort. Prominent among them were the late Rose Ferguson (my second-grade teacher at Kingston Elementary School), Ronald C. Wilson (of Warren Wilson College), and Ferenc M. Szasz (of the University of New Mexico). More direct and absolutely essential contributions to this project came from the three individuals who planned and taught the workshop that introduced me to Appalachian history and literature at Berea College in the summer of 1988: Loyal Jones, Richard Drake, and the late Wilma Dykeman. Two of my fellow students from that summer in Berea, Alan Speer and Rebecca Mobbs, became dear friends who have helped me grapple with many of the puzzling issues that accompanied my return to East Tennessee. That workshop also introduced me to the greater Appalachian studies community. Many individuals from this cordial camp of scholars and activists made vital contributions to my outlook and this book. I am most indebted to the following persons: the late Jim Wayne Miller, Gurney Norman, Jean Haskell, Ron Lewis, Durwood Dunn, Gordon McKinney, David Hsiung, Tyler Blethen, Paul Salstrom, Phil Obermiller, Chad Berry, Emily Satterwhite, Rebecca Bailey, Kristen Kant, and Penny Messinger. Several other scholars who are not directly associated with Appalachian studies, historian Ernest Freeburg, anthropologist Mark Groover, and economist Gregory Smith, also deserve mention here. Finally, two historians whom I only know from their provocative works, William Cronan and Patricia Nelson Limerick, influenced my thinking on issues essential to this study.

We academics, in both the creation and dissemination of our scholarship too often limit ourselves to our own kind. In my sincerest attempt to avoid this pitfall, I have made acquaintances and learned much from countless regional residents whose insights and perspectives have been as vital to this project as those of the aforementioned scholars. These include: community activist Marie Cirillo (and a whole circle of Clearfork Valley friends), retired Campbell County educator and freelance historian Bonnie Page, David Blankenship of TECO Coal Company, Ken Maples (former assistant county executive for Sevier County, Tennessee), Herb Handly of the Townsend (Tennessee) Chamber of Commerce, Knoxville Mayor Bill Haslam, Knoxville journalist Jack Neely, National Park Service rangers Kent Cave and Ian Shanklin, and Elkmont friend and defender Lynn Faust.

Scholarly and personal insights that I gained from twelve years in New Mexico bear a disproportionate influence on this book about a locale that, on the surface at least, appears so markedly different. I am particularly indebted to a number of close friends whose personal examples complemented and enriched own importance by providing a seemingly endless list of influences on his effort and failing to extend credit where it is due can be daunting.

Many persons who contributed to my formal education made foundational contributions to this effort. Prominent among them were the late Rose Ferguson (my second-grade teacher at Kingston Elementary School), Ronald C. Wilson (of Warren Wilson College), and Ferenc M. Szasz (of the University of New Mexico). More direct and absolutely essential contributions to this project came from the three individuals who planned and taught the workshop that introduced me to Appalachian history and literature at Berea College in the summer of 1988: Loyal Jones, Richard Drake, and the late Wilma Dykeman. Two of my fellow students from that summer in Berea, Alan Speer and Rebecca Mobbs, became dear friends who have helped me grapple with many of the puzzling issues that accompanied my return to East Tennessee. That workshop also introduced me to the greater Appalachian studies community. Many individuals from this cordial camp of scholars and activists made vital contributions to my outlook and this book. I am most indebted to the following persons: the late Jim Wayne Miller, Gurney Norman, Jean Haskell, Ron Lewis, Durwood Dunn, Gordon McKinney, David Hsiung, Tyler Blethen, Paul Salstrom, Phil Obermiller, Chad Berry, Emily Satterwhite, Rebecca Bailey, Kristen Kant, and Penny Messinger. Several other scholars who are not directly associated with Appalachian studies, historian Ernest Freeburg, anthropologist Mark Groover, and economist Gregory Smith, also deserve mention here. Finally, two historians whom I only know from their provocative works, William Cronan and Patricia Nelson Limerick, influenced my thinking on issues essential to this study.

We academics, in both the creation and dissemination of our scholarship too often limit ourselves to our own kind. In my sincerest attempt to avoid this pitfall, I have made acquaintances and learned much from countless regional residents whose insights and perspectives have been as vital to this project as those of the aforementioned scholars. These include: community activist Marie Cirillo (and a whole circle of Clearfork Valley friends), retired Campbell County educator and freelance historian Bonnie Page, David Blankenship of TECO Coal Company, Ken Maples (former assistant county executive for Sevier County, Tennessee), Herb Handly of the Townsend (Tennessee) Chamber of Commerce, Knoxville Mayor Bill Haslam, Knoxville journalist Jack Neely, National Park Service rangers Kent Cave and Ian Shanklin, and Elkmont friend and defender Lynn Faust.

Scholarly and personal insights that I gained from twelve years in New Mexico bear a disproportionate influence on this book about a locale that, on the surface at least, appears so markedly different. I am particularly indebted to a number of close friends whose personal examples complemented and enriched

Acknowledgments

Many influences opened my eyes to this vision of East Tennessee's history and have allowed me to present it in this fashion. I am most grateful to a generous Creator. But I hasten to add that I neither presume to understand the fullness of God's generous designs nor believe that any expression of gratitude for that benevolence is adequate. Like John F. Kennedy, I recognize that here on earth, the Almighty counts on ordinary folk to strive for His purposes. Hence I am grateful to the many mere mortals whose concrete, knowable contributions made this book possible. It is fitting that I begin a revisionist history of a region and people long identified by independence and individualism by emphasizing that scholarship is a collaborative venture. As such, it requires support and good will from a broad array of individuals and institutions. Without encouragement, sound advice, and patience from the University of Tennessee Press, I would simply not be writing these words. Financial support from the National Endowment of the Humanities, Webb School of Knoxville, and several private donors via the East Tennessee Foundation funded a sabbatical from my teaching duties during the 2005–06 school year that enabled me to complete research and compose the first two-thirds of this manuscript. Relatively unimpeded vacations the past three summers enabled me to complete the project. For this, I must again thank Webb School.

Thanks are also due to the generous and competent staffs of the following institutions for making my research productive and pleasant: the McClung Historical Collection of the Knox County Public Library and East Tennessee Historical Society, the John C. Hodges Library at the University of Tennessee, the Archives of Appalachia of East Tennessee State University, the Oak Ridge (Tennessee) Children's Museum, the Berea College (Kentucky) Archives, the Archives and Library of the Great Smoky Mountains National Park, and the Campbell County (Tennessee) Historical Society. At these locations, the following individuals proved particularly helpful to me in gathering the photos presented in this book: Vicky Bills, Ann Bridges, Shannon Wilson, Annette Hartigan, and Jerry Sharp.

Extending appreciation to all the individuals who contributed to an effort such as this can be a challenge. Finding a balance between exaggerating one's what I learned formally at the University of New Mexico about matters of cultural interaction, human identity, dignity, and resilience. These include former Menaul School student Maria Pino Benally of the Navajo nation, and *Hispanos* and former Menaul School colleagues Edmundo Vasquez, Jaime Quinones, and Maria Cordova Andrews. Former Menaul colleagues Sharon Rhutasel Jones, Jim and Cheryl Wormley, and Becky and Mike Davis, all "Anglos" in a land where there is no majority, taught me much about humility and how to respect other people and cultures. Dear friends and colleagues Pita Jacques Hopkins and Chris Hopkins deserve special mention. Their crosscultural marriage taught me much about cultural identity and interaction, and I will always treasure their special friendship.

Seeds sown in New Mexico sprouted and flourished in East Tennessee thanks in part to good friends and the intellectually fertile atmosphere at the Webb School of Knoxville. When former colleague Eve Falen informed me about Berea College's Appalachian workshop in the summer of 1988, she made a contribution to my intellectual journey that no one at the time imagined would lead to this book. When I returned to Webb that fall, Upper School Head Jim Snodgrass and Webb President William Pfeifer encouraged me to build upon the foundation laid at Berea. Steve Davis, head of the Upper School from 2000 to 2004, and fellow teachers Jit Koh and Sheila Jacobstein offered warm friendship and respectively shared with me African-American, Malaysian, and Jewish perspectives on the complex dynamics of cultural interaction. Sheila's husband, Knoxville businessman Dick Jacobstein, helped me better understand the challenges globalization poses for East Tennessee and (along with Sheila) provided me with a (truly needed) conservative conscience. Common sense and good humor from colleagues Elwood and Denise Pennington, natives of West Virginia, and fellow East Tennessean Clark Wormsley enhanced their fellow Appalachian's struggle to come to terms with his roots. Good friends Kirk and Kristan LaFon deserve special mention for their support and for encouraging Webb students to complete their service obligations in the Clearfork Valley and other regional locations.

As ideas in my head and lecture notes from my classes began to evolve into this manuscript, many people helped me rein in my wide-ranging mind and clarify thoughts that were often vague, general, and confused. At the front end of this process, I extend sincerest appreciation and good will to students at the Webb School of Knoxville and University of Tennessee Evening School who enrolled in the courses that gave rise to this book. When the magnitude of putting ideas into words overwhelmed me early in my sabbatical year, several of the persons mentioned earlier came to my aid. Among those who offered kind advice and stern criticism were Phil Obermiller, Chad Berry, Emily Satterwhite, Durwood Dunn, Kent Cave, Jack Neely, and Marie Cirillo. I am particularly grateful to several truly special friends who read one chapter after another as they emerged sporadically from my word processor These individuals include fellow teacher Scott Grunder, the Reverend Marc S. Sherrod, ThD, my brother Tim Banker, and my dear wife Kathy. After I completed a first draft of the whole, my good Clearfork Valley friend Carol Judy took time to read it. Historians Tyler Blethen and Paul Salstrom offered more formal critiques of an early draft of the entire manuscript.

The peculiar nature of this book made familial contributions essential to my effort. Late in their lives, both of my parents became interested in their family histories. Records they gathered provided the nucleus for the family histories that I share. Several relatives enriched that basic information. The late Aline Hardwick, my mother's first cousin, was the most serious genealogist of them all, and I appreciate information and photos that she, her husband, Joe, and son Doug have shared about our Thomas forebears. My father's sister Jo Pierce and cousins Sue Gibbs Paden and David Medema have addressed numerous questions and helped me pursue many queries about our Banker and Gibbs forebears. I am the fifth of six sons, and several of my brothers made essential contributions to my personal rediscovery. Collectively, all of them—Luke, Tom, John, Tim, and Joe—shared in the childhood on the farm by the river that proved so vital to their brother's musings and scholarly pursuits. This shared experience is the real prologue for this book.

As parent of an only child, I often reflect on my daughter Tollie's upbringing and compare it to my own in our family of six brothers. From our 1987 return to East Tennessee until she went off to college in 1998, Tollie made this farm her home and returned here for several years when she was in graduate school. Her youthful irreverence reminds me of my own earlier take on many of the issues raised in this book. Tollie now has two degrees in history and a third in information science and is a librarian at nearby Hiwassee College, and she sometimes even shares surprisingly mutual interests with her old Dad. Her quick and creative mind has challenged, enriched, and sometimes affirmed many ideas conveyed here. More practically, her skills as a professional librarian have often proved helpful to a father and scholar who is still relatively unfamiliar with the new and daunting world of information science.

Finally and most important, my wife Kathy's many contributions to this project deserve far more appreciation than words convey. In reading every line of every draft of every chapter, Kathy has been my most important editor and critic. She has uncovered comma and spelling errors and gently chided me about garbled prose and too-frequent lapses into self-absorption. Her good humor and forbearance have been essential for a project that has lasted far longer than we expected. Most important, when Dad died in 1987, Kathy first suggested that we might consider coming home, and for the next ten years she was the first among several superb caregivers who made mother's waning years as pleasant and dignified as possible. Each human relationship is unique, but Kathy's faith and graciousness mirror the love and creative spirit that my parents shared. Like their abiding influence, Kathy's very presence made this book both possible and necessary.

Prologue

....

East Tennessee Insights into Elusive Appalachia

Mere mention of the word Appalachia evokes images as complex as they are colorful: a landscape beautiful and bucolic, rustic and rugged, scarred and hardscrabble; a people noble and benighted, self-reliant and indolent, independent, ignorant, and impoverished. The inherent contradictions these labels convey lead me to suggest that another adjective—*elusive*—should be added to the list of Appalachian descriptors. Elusiveness is both cause and consequence of practically every Appalachian attribute, actual and imagined, spanning from admirable to disgraceful, and everything in between.

This elusiveness extends at least as far back as 1539, when Apalachee Indians greeted Spanish explorers at the coast of Florida's panhandle. The natives quickly rid themselves of Hernando de Soto and his meddlesome band. Tales of rich goldfields lured the ambitious and gullible *conquistadores* to mysterious mountains supposedly only several days' journey north—perhaps the first Appalachian whopper. The Spaniards' trek through the rugged uplands proved tragically disappointing—but not inconsequential. Within half a century, European mapmakers applied several derivations of the name Apalachee to the unforgiving mountains that produced little gold and even less glory for de Soto's band. The enduring designation "Appalachia" was, to be sure, a misnomer offering lasting proof of the natives' shrewdness. More important for purposes here, the sixteenth-century cartographers' "Appalachia" has proved as enduring, elastic, and elusive as it was inaccurate. Mapmakers nearly five centuries later still do not agree about the physical boundaries of the space called Appalachia.

Descriptions of the region's human inhabitants reflect a similar lack of precision. For more than a century and half, casual observers and commentators who should have known better have defined Appalachians as uniformly rural and "country," dismissing and diminishing the region's people with sweeping generalizations. Whether negative or positive, these perceptions more clearly reflect the eye of the beholder than they do any verifiable Appalachian realities.

Many reporters have addressed the origins and persistence of inaccurate, enfeebling assumptions about Appalachia's people and culture. I am writing this book because I believe those of us who reside here—and that is my definition of Appalachians—have accepted these images for too long. In this concern, I share the view of a fellow East Tennessee native who lamented several years ago that many Appalachians "firmly believe that Appalachia is someplace other than where they reside."[1] This book explores the causes and consequences of this self-denial within the history of the Appalachian subregion this observer and I share as our homeland.

Scholars and the Appalachian Awakening

In the turbulent years from around 1965 to 1980, as unprecedented domestic and global traumas accelerated a natural swing of historical revisionism that challenged long-popular understandings of the American past, early scholars in the fields of African American and women's history began offering insights and inspiration to many historically marginalized groups, including Native Americans,

1. Michael Montgomery, "Myths: How a Hunger for Roots Shapes Our Notions About Appalachian English," *Now and Then* 17 (Summer 2000): 8.

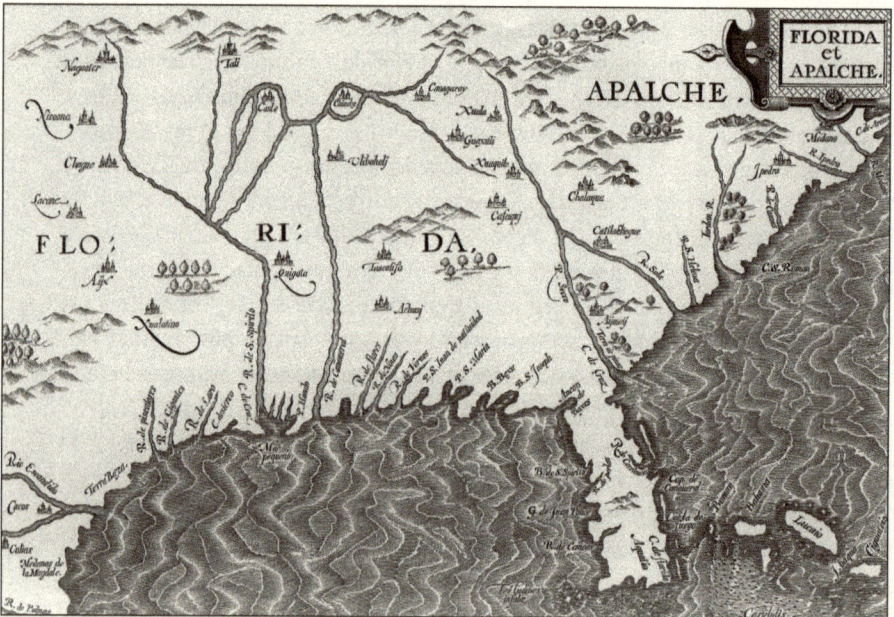

This 1597 map reveals the consequences of the Apalachee Indians' tall tale and the Spanish explorers' eagerness to find gold. The label *"Apalche"* overlays sites of Cherokee towns in the southern mountains that subsequent observers called the "Appalachians." (From Bureau of American Ethnology, *Fifth Annual Report*. Special Collections Library, University of Tennessee, Knoxville.)

Hispanos, and Appalachians. In an angry quest to address past wrongs, neglect, and misinformation, Appalachian studies pioneers addressed two essential tasks. One group explored the origins of the idea of Appalachia. Following the lead of cultural historian Henry J. Shapiro's *Appalachia on our Mind* (1979), this group persuasively argued that popular "Appalachian" images first appeared in the minds and literary offerings of late-nineteenth-century mainstream Americans, most notably local-color journalists and home missionaries. The needs of these outside commentators—and the anxieties of their audiences—Shapiro and his heirs suggest, influenced depictions of Appalachia more than did actual conditions in the mountains. Shapiro left to a second group of Appalachian studies pioneers the task of establishing the veracity of prevailing Appalachian stereotypes and, indeed, the idea of an "Appalachian reality" itself.

Ron Eller's seminal *Miners, Millhands, and Mountaineers* (1982) forcefully filled the void Shapiro had not addressed, exploring the dramatic effect extractive

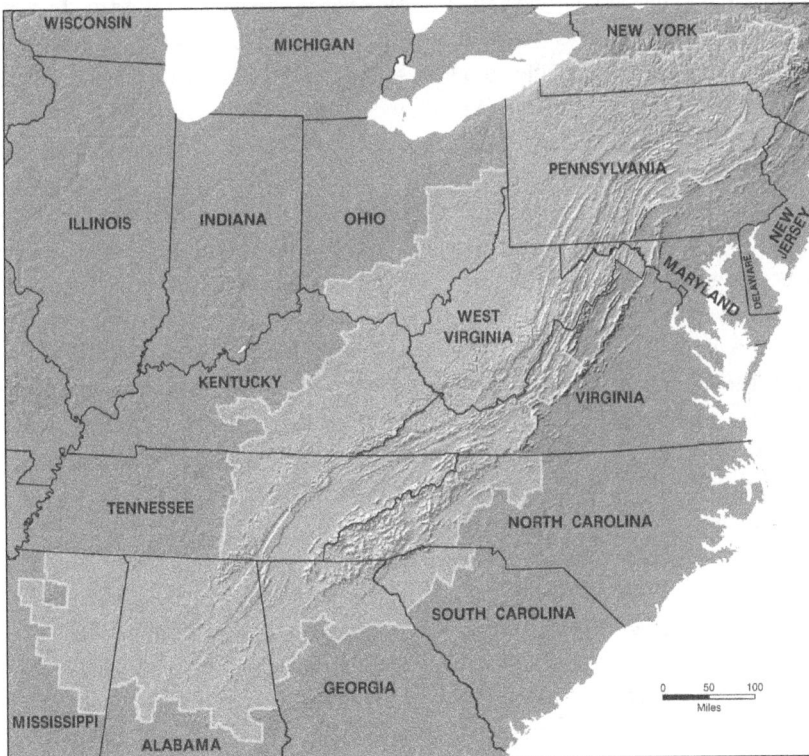

Cartographers have long disagreed about Appalachia's exact physical boundaries. This map from the *Encyclopedia of Appalachia* (University of Tennessee Press, 2006) reflects current consensus about the region's confines and is endorsed by the Appalachian Regional Commission.

East Tennessee Insights into Elusive Appalachia

industries had on the Appalachian region during the half-century between Reconstruction and the Great Depression. Eller also challenged conventional wisdom by attributing Appalachia's historic ills to contact with, rather than isolation from, mainstream America and its capitalist system. Yet just as Shapiro analyzed Appalachian images without addressing regional realities, Eller's analysis of those realities did not directly relate his provocative conclusions to ideas about Appalachia that Shapiro explored. For example, Eller did not link the actual hardscrabble conditions he described to the images of "Appalachian deficiency" the local colorists, home missionaries, and other commentators offered. Yet, their shortcomings aside, the pioneering works by Eller and Shapiro opened the floodgates for a wave of regional scholarship without which I could never have written this book.

By the time I returned to East Tennessee in the mid-1980s, revisionists clearly recognized that early Appalachian studies scholars had depicted the region in terms as uniform and static as the images they so angrily rejected. Indeed, their predecessors' portrayal of regional residents as "unfortunate and tragic victims of progress" unwittingly affirmed pernicious assumptions that Appalachians were mere objects of forces beyond their control, rather than genuine historical actors in their own right. By addressing this and other shortcomings, regional scholars have—over the past twenty years—given readers a more complex, complete, and credible Appalachia. For example, where Shapiro, Eller, and their immediate heirs focused almost exclusively on the industrial era (ca. 1870–1930), recent scholarship has shifted attention to the years immediately preceding and following that tumultuous epoch. Recent scholarship also offers persuasive evidence that geographical, demographic, economic, and cultural diversity have always existed within the Appalachian region. Recent studies explore the roles of immigrants, African Americans, and women, address aspects of the region's cultural history (including religion and the arts), and comment on environmental concerns. Collectively, this scholarship reveals that sweeping generalizations about a uniform, static Appalachia distort more than they illuminate.

For our purposes here, the most important shared trait of this revisionism is recognition that Appalachia's misfortunes cannot solely be attributed to opportunistic outsiders. Many scholars, for example, remind us that inherent geographical limitations (steep slopes, thin soils, a cooler climate, and distance from markets) must be considered in any discussion of the region's historic problems. Other recent studies suggest that a host of natives—land speculators, local entrepreneurs, uninformed masses, and shortsighted consumers—must share blame with outsiders for Appalachia's woes. These insights inform two recent, truly comprehensive regional historical surveys: Richard Drake's *A History of Appalachia* (2001) and John Alexander Williams's *Appalachia: A History* (2002).

Along with the March 2006 release of the long-anticipated *Encyclopedia of Appalachia,* with its more than 1,200 entries and 2,000 pages, these volumes offer salient evidence of the maturation and sophistication of Appalachian studies. Alas, this impressive scholarship and its provocative finding are still largely unknown beyond regional scholarly circles. And East Tennessee history is currently unfolding without the benefits that these new understandings of our past might provide.

At this important juncture in our understanding of our regional past, this book seeks both to advance and to broaden the "Appalachian conversation." I maintain we still have not adequately addressed the simple question Shapiro and Eller together left unanswered more than two decades ago: why Appalachia is so elusive to outsiders and, more important, to its own residents. By focusing on one of Appalachia's relatively neglected subregions, East Tennessee, I hope to test and qualify recent scholarly understanding of Appalachia as a whole. Because Appalachian studies' insights are so little known beyond academic circles, I hope to present my case in a way that will be accessible to non-scholars. Finally, I hope this admittedly quixotic quest might help diverse regional residents, particularly academics and "real people," to coalesce and address issues endemic to our history.[2]

Why East Tennessee?

Before highlighting several distinctive features and themes of this book, my decision to focus on East Tennessee demands further explanation. Honesty compels me to confess that my interests in my homeland were initially personal and practical. My East Tennessee roots go back to the earliest days of European settlement, and members of my family have resided here ever since. I spent the first eighteen years of my life on a farm at the confluence of the Tennessee and Clinch rivers. After eighteen years away, I returned to that farm in 1987, and I have made my home there ever since. As a youth, I rarely considered my East Tennessee identity, and I left for college in 1969, like many an Appalachian prodigal son, not planning to return. When my father's unexpected passing brought me home at age thirty-six—following eleven pleasant and fruitful years in New Mexico—I came reluctantly, having no idea how preoccupied I would soon become with my roots.

2. Consistent with my goal of reaching beyond an academic audience, I will not rely exclusively on traditional footnotes, as is customary in scholarly works. When I draw from specific concrete sources or when I make a verbatim quote, I will use footnotes to inform the reader of my source. More frequently throughout this book, I will draw general insights from an array of sources. To give proper credit, I have included a "notes on sources" section, as well as a bibliography, at the end of the book.

A second practical reason for my focus on East Tennessee is pedagogical. After an introduction to Appalachian studies at a three-week workshop at Kentucky's Berea College in the summer of 1988, I wondered how I might incorporate what I had learned when I returned to my second year as history teacher at Knoxville's leading college preparatory school. Students at Webb School of Knoxville are well informed and relatively affluent. Most reside in Knoxville's suburbs, and many of them continue their educations—as well as their careers—in places far removed from East Tennessee. They (and their teachers) are not, in their own minds, nor in the minds of many of their regional neighbors, "Appalachian." Although I could not bring myself to admit it for some time after returning from Berea, I too shared many of my Webb School colleagues' and students' misgivings and misperceptions about Appalachia, even as I began to seek ways to combat them. I became active in the field of Appalachian studies, but seven years passed before I offered, for the first time, the elective course "A History of East Tennessee and Southern Appalachia."

As I laid out plans for that course in the summer of 1996, I was still groping in the dark. The title and scope of the course came from a gut feeling that Webb students would be more likely to enroll in an elective focusing on East Tennessee than in a course on the region as a whole. A rehashing of familiar accounts of the State of Franklin, exploits of the likes of Sam Houston and Alvin York, the Civil War siege of Fort Sanders, TVA, Senator Howard Baker's key role in the Watergate saga, and the 1982 World's Fair, I reasoned, might give me cover to address potentially more controversial topics, such as strip-mining, uneven patterns of regional development, and perhaps even Knoxvillians' mixed feelings about their rural neighbors and their own regional identity.

Broader Contexts

Teaching that course gave birth to several emphases that pervade the following pages. Like the course from which it emerged, this book is a survey—of sorts. Rather than addressing every facet of the subregion's history over the past 250 years, I focus primarily on how East Tennesseans viewed themselves, beginning in the mid-1700s and concluding at the dawn of the twenty-first century. One's self-perception is, of course, very much shaped both by real experiences and by how one is perceived by others, a dynamic process that cannot occur in a vacuum. I have divided my narrative into three "parts," each of which represents a broad chronological era, reflecting my training as a historian and my commitment to restoring this story to broader historical contexts.

In part I (ca. 1750–1880), I reveal that early Americans did not use the label "Appalachia" in the modern sense(s) of the word with its contradictory mix of positive and negative metaphors and adjectives so often associated with the region. Neither residents of the region nor of the broader United States considered the region or its peoples to be in any way aberrant. To be sure, early settlers displayed "frontier" traits, but these were understandably temporary and, of course, not uniquely Appalachian. Moreover, these traits were an essential part of our greatest national myth, and thus deserved reverence rather than ridicule. During the early decades of the nineteenth century, when the Jeffersonian myth reigned supreme (at least in the minds of most Americans), East Tennessee yeomen—and their neighbors who optimistically held out hope that they, too, would eventually own their own land—were very much part of the nation's mainstream. But in the middle years of the nineteenth century, a combination of factors within and beyond the region dashed these hopes; as the title of an important recent anthology suggests, this was "Appalachia in the making."

The industrial era (ca. 1870–1930—part II of this book) is, as Eller and Shapiro recognized, essential for understanding both what actually happened in Appalachia and how Americans perceived that course of events. In this era, American industrialization and the accompanying ideal of progress took center stage. The former required Appalachian resources even as the latter spun off contradictory images of "Appalachia" that persist even now. A majority of Americans of this era, including many prominent East Tennesseans and many of my own forebears, viewed progress favorably. For this group, images of backward, benighted, aberrant "Appalachia" made the region's economic exploitation more palatable. Others—I call them antimodernists—embraced diametrically different, more positive views of rugged, independent yeomen. Sadly, like their "noble Red brothers," these "simple but pure" mountain folk faced the end of the trail. Like Shapiro and other commentators, I believe these powerful, persistent images—positive as well as negative—reflected more clearly the agendas and anxieties of those who held them than they did the reality of what was actually transpiring in Appalachia.

Part III of this book will examine an era (ca. 1920–2008) in which a profound ambivalence characterizes mutual attitudes of mainstream Americans and Appalachians. For the former, images of our region fluctuated. In the 1930s and 1960s, for example, Appalachia became an object of great attention and altruism. At other times, such as from around 1940 to 1960, Appalachia was for most mainstream Americans out of sight and out of mind. Throughout this same era, however, a few regional residents and sympathetic outsiders retained a more positive and hopeful take on their region and its relationship with the broader society. The third quarter of the twentieth century rewarded these optimists. An amalgam of academics and activists, insiders, and sympathetic outsiders forged the Appalachian studies movement, offering unprecedented regional resistance against outside exploitation and ridicule. However, the energy such efforts demand has neither been as uniform nor as enduring as a sympathetic observer might hope. Consequently, Appalachia and East Tennessee in our own times seesaw back and forth between bursts of activism and apathy, national attention and neglect.

Because events in East Tennessee also unfolded in broader geographical contexts, the lives of individual East Tennesseans and their communities can only be understood within broader state, regional, national, and global circles. But the opposite is equally true. New insights from East Tennessee and Appalachia can make our national story more complete and honest.

Appalachians All?

This book's most provocative and unorthodox assertion—that one should employ geographical, rather than cultural, considerations when defining Appalachia—originated from my discovery, years ago, that mapmakers uniformly place all of East Tennessee within Appalachian confines. Longstanding cultural criteria for who, where, and what constitute Appalachia, I believe, lie behind many self-perpetuating perceptions of the region that Shapiro and others have explored. Less obviously perhaps, assumptions that those conditions were uniform across the region enabled opportunists—but also Eller and many of the region's natives and defenders—to offer simple explanations (e.g., isolation, ignorance, outside exploitation) for complex regional conditions and ills.

Gradually, through teaching the course at Webb, I realized that using standard cultural determinants (e.g., levels of income and education and area of residence) alone to define a region and people suggests a static condition that simply has never existed in any human setting. Am I, for example, less Appalachian because I earned a PhD? Do the economic fortunes of my ancestors somehow make me less Appalachian? If one of my student's grandfathers migrated from Cocke or Campbell County to Knoxville or out-migrated to Texas or California a century ago, does that remove him (and his grandchild) from Appalachian status? Or, even more controversially, do we deny Appalachian identification to a "Yankee outlander" who came to Oak Ridge as a physicist for the Manhattan Project and later retired there? What about Latino émigrés, Appalachia's most recent newcomers? If none of them qualify as Appalachian, who does?

Three Representative East Tennessee Communities

This book's third essential emphasis suggests that East Tennessee, like the broader Appalachian region, is more diverse than many observers have previ-

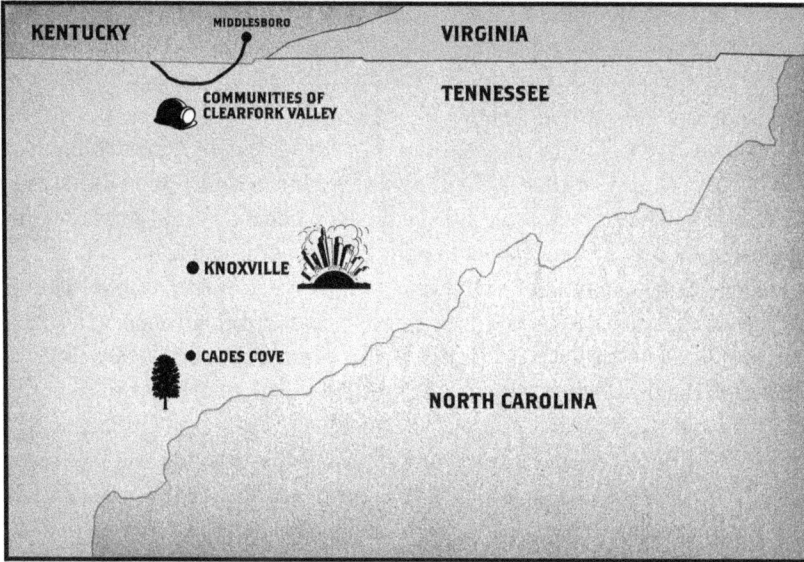

East Tennessee and this book's three representative communities all lie within the confines of what most observers concur is geographical Appalachia. Knoxville typifies valley/urban/modern Appalachia. For most observers, the two upland communities will seem "more Appalachian," with Cades Cove typifying "timber/tourism Appalachia" and the Clearfork Valley representing "coal Appalachia."

ously imagined. Beyond obvious racial and ethnic diversity, this variety results from two key factors: geography and individual predilections for change. By periodically focusing on three representative communities—Knoxville, Cades Cove, and the scattered settlements of the Clearfork Valley—I emphasize the influence and importance of East Tennessee's three geographic divisions: valley, mountain, and plateau. My selection of Cades Cove and the Clearfork Valley will surprise few readers. They largely fit the popular, contradictory Appalachian imagery described earlier and have been the focus of important works of Appalachian scholarship, as well as useful, popular accounts. On the other hand, the choice of Knoxville as my third representative community will undoubtedly raise some eyebrows. As my students often remind me, residents of East Tennessee's leading city have long viewed their rural neighbors with profound ambivalence. Knoxvillians have occasionally embraced positive regional images even as they more frequently denied and disassociated from more negative ones. Scholars often contributed to this tendency. For example, we Appalachianists, with our decidedly rural bias, long ignored urban centers, including Knoxville. Informed observers know quite well the stories of these three communities in isolation from each other. Recounting these stories collectively, however, and restoring

East Tennessee Insights into Elusive Appalachia

them to broader chronological and geographical contexts, better enables us to question the stereotypes and recognize their real and potentially pernicious effects. In other words, I hope to demonstrate that the whole of East Tennessee is greater than the sum of its parts.

Cades Cove will be familiar to most of my readers as a pioneer homestead and popular tourist destination in Great Smoky Mountains National Park. For my purposes Cades Cove represents the broader Smokies region straddling the Tennessee–North Carolina border. In parts 2 and 3 of this book, Cades Cove and its neighboring communities evolve into "timber-tourism Appalachia." The responses of Smokies residents to these enterprises and their impacts on their communities have varied considerably. As historian Durwood Dunn tells us so well, many leading Cades Cove residents initially viewed tourism with favor. Yet the creation of Great Smoky Mountains National Park ultimately brought about the death of the Cove as a living community, leaving only a nostalgic monument to an allegedly primitive bygone era. For the Cove's neighboring communities, such as Gatlinburg and Pigeon Forge, tourism brought very different but equally dramatic and controversial developments. The following pages will explore these developments in detail. For now it is sufficient to say the twentieth century wrought mixed effects on the broader Smokies region and forged an array of "Appalachian" conditions, including uneven (perhaps unsustainable) economic patterns, environmental havoc, clever (if potentially harmful) utilization of "hillbilly" imagery, and dependence on federal funding and assistance.

The Clearfork Valley is the setting for a string of hardscrabble communities lying just south of the Tennessee-Kentucky border.[3] Although they are less familiar than Cades Cove to most readers, the Clearfork communities have been the focus of important Appalachian scholarship and represent another part of East Tennessee and greater Appalachia. The Valley was only barely settled before the Civil War, and scholars have devoted little attention to its early history, making it a particularly valuable example for exploring myths related to pioneer Appalachia. In the latter two-thirds of the book, the Clearfork Valley will typify timber Appalachia, but more important, coal Appalachia and postindustrial Appalachia. The Valley's history illustrates both the benefits and burdens of reliance on extractive industries, in particular the effects of the coal industry. After World War II, the combined effects of unregulated strip-mining and massive out-migration ravaged Clearfork communities, creating the sort of conditions commonly reproduced in images from the 1960s' "war on poverty." In more recent days, Clearfork residents have struggled mightily to survive. Not

---

3. As there is no consensus on the proper spelling of Clearfork Valley, I have decided it would be consistent with the spirit of the book to defer to the locals and make "Clearfork" one word.

surprisingly, the Clearfork story shares many of the Appalachian traits present in the story of the Smokies region more generally. But in coal Appalachia, economic and environmental havoc are more pronounced, causing greater misery and even more dependence on outside assistance than in East Tennessee's other mountain region.

Recounting East Tennessee's story—and more specifically the stories of my first two representative communities—without including Knoxville is impossible. As one of the subregion's oldest communities, Knoxville has long been East Tennessee's economic, demographic, and cultural hub. Since its founding in the late eighteenth century, Knoxville has been both a market and distribution point for regional farm products. Beginning in the mid-nineteenth century, it served regional timber and coal industries in similar capacities, and when tourism burgeoned in the Smokies in the middle and late twentieth century, Knoxville again played a key role. The city's entrepreneurs, of course, promoted and reaped profits from both sides of these two-way enterprises, and the city as a whole benefited in countless ways from its status as regional economic hub. Affordable energy and construction materials from the hinterlands, for example, created jobs for working-class Knoxvillians, who in turn purchased more of the increasingly available consumer goods. More recently, Knoxvillians of all social stripes have found refuge in the natural havens and nostalgic enclaves of Great Smoky Mountains National Park, and frolic in tourist playgrounds lying just outside park confines. Tangible gains for the city as a whole and its individual citizens (in the form of increased personal incomes, access to material goods, etc.) contributed to a gap that, beginning in the middle third of the nineteenth century, clearly distanced the burgeoning city from its rural neighbors. Thus, Knoxville's role in the regional economy allowed it in many ways to become "less Appalachian" as the city's relative fortunes contributed to "Appalachian" conditions in the hinterlands.

Economic and demographic trends, of course, intertwine. In the periodic hard times that were hallmarks of the latter nineteenth-century American economy, frustrated East Tennessee farmers and unemployed loggers and miners flocked to Knoxville, where they found jobs in burgeoning industries and embraced new urban opportunities. Many of them made the city their permanent home. Consequently, at any given time in recent history, a large percentage of Knoxvillians have had rural, Appalachian roots. No less than immigrants elsewhere, Knoxville's in-migrants displayed varied, complex, often contradictory attitudes about their move. Like other residents of progress-revering nations, many of Knoxville's new arrivals found comfort and reassurance in images that affirmed the superiority of their new homes and confirmed negative notions about their old ones. At the same time, however, a lingering nostalgia caused some city residents to long for the good old days. If, as observers often suggest, Knoxvillians are confused about their past and their identity, this is hardly a recent phenomenon.

Knoxville's role as regional cultural hub also reflected these contradictory sentiments and influenced its relationships with the rest of East Tennessee. As home base for such powerful regional institutions as the University of Tennessee and the Tennessee Valley Authority—and as East Tennessee's media hub—Knoxville has long played a major role in shaping how outsiders view the region and how East Tennesseans see themselves. In this capacity, many Knoxvillians borrowed from and affirmed notions that the hinterlands were poor, backward, and strange. But that is only part of the story. By the end of the nineteenth century, the previously mentioned antimodernist impulse appeared in mainstream America and vied against (though it never seriously challenged) the more widely embraced cult of progress. Antimodernism eventually found its way to places such as Knoxville, where less successful inmigrants found strength in tradition, most notably religion and distinctive music and foodways. For very different reasons, at least a few disgruntled intellectuals echoed the nostalgia of these recent émigrés. These truly strange bedfellows helped nurture a very different set of Appalachian stereotypes, such as the "rugged yeoman," "stalwart pioneer," and ardent (if futile) defender of tradition. These contrasting images have tugged ever since at the hearts and minds of Knoxvillians, other East Tennesseans, and mainstream Americans. The emergence of Appalachian studies in the final third of the twentieth century is the most recent and important manifestation of this more positive, if occasionally overly romantic, take on Appalachia's elusive history.

New Insights into Old Realities

While my three representative communities reflect broad differences among mountain, valley, and plateau East Tennessee, each of the subdivisions has distinct demographic, geographic, and economic subparts (e.g., small towns and rural areas; wide coves, narrow hollows, and steep slopes; farms and extractive industries) that have long sparred with one another for economic advantage and political-cultural preeminence. Even more significantly, individual human occupants of these three divisions have always been more diverse than imagined. Observers often cite the allegedly regional trait of fierce individualism to account for a mind-boggling array of East Tennessee opinions on nearly everything. Without discounting this assertion, I contend that an even more subtle contribution to diversity in East Tennessee is that individuals tend to respond to change selectively. Some, but I believe few, of us totally embrace or totally reject new opportunities. Instead, most East Tennesseans (like most humans most of the time) engage in *selective acculturation*. To be sure, diverse predilections for change widened the gap that has divided East Tennesseans since the mid-nineteenth century. Allowing for some exceptions, we can generalize that many Knoxvillians and residents of the hinterland communities who identified favorably with the timber, coal, and tourist industries embraced progress *and* dissociated from allegedly "Appalachian" qualities. Conversely, residents of places such as Cades Cove and the Clearfork Valley, and less successful rural in-migrants to Knoxville, whom the new developments threatened or harmed, often opposed change. In the minds of many observers—and to some extent in their own minds—this group came to define traditional Appalachian traits.

This dichotomy of more and less assimilated Appalachians, however, only begins to reveal the extent of regional diversity. For many East Tennesseans, selective acculturation has meant just muddling through. But, contrary to long-held assumptions about assimilation, I learned in New Mexico that many people, particularly those from marginalized groups, embrace change creatively in order to retain—even enrich and preserve—essential vestiges of treasured bequests from their forebears, including religious practices and music and food traditions. Living in New Mexico also taught me that assimilated natives, particularly well-educated but disgruntled urbanites, often develop a disdain for progress and embrace modified forms of these cultural staples and more positive, romantic images of their mother culture. Often equally disgruntled outsiders affirm this outlook and become allies in what becomes an antimodernist crusade. All of this fosters kaleidoscopic cultural patterns that are cause and consequence of internal diversity and fragmentation. Prevailing misperceptions of Appalachia and existing accounts of East Tennessee's history have ignored and obscured these important developments.

When the human tendency to define oneself by drawing contrasts with one's neighbor is layered on top of these realities, we begin to see more clearly how East Tennesseans, despite their region's aforementioned diversity, came to epitomize uniformly contradictory Appalachian qualities (impoverished, isolated, ignorant, noble, simple, and so forth). Wise observers since at least biblical times have recognized that concentrating on the speck in another's eye is a convenient means of avoiding the beam in one's own. When this process is utilized to disassociate from a suspect or marginalized group, sociologists call it *intragroup distinction*. Most humans, of course, decide from time to time to disassociate from groups whose traits they do not share or which they reject, so it is unfair to suggest this practice is inherently malevolent. But one need only look at East Tennessee to see the pernicious effects when intragroup distinction occurs in a place defined by established, particularly judgmental criteria.

As proof, let's return to my earlier questions: are East Tennesseans who become formally educated, enjoy economic success, or move from the farm to the city or out-migrate beyond the region "Appalachian"? What about newcomers from the North or from Mexico who recently arrived here? Should they be included among Appalachians? If one assumes that Appalachia is static and uniformly aberrant (e.g., poor, ignorant, and rural) and culturally homogenous (e.g., "all WASP"), then the answer is, "No." And a self-perpetuating cycle of poor, ignorant, rural, and ethnically uniform Appalachians results. The simple fact that the Appalachians who remain after those who become educated and attain economic success withdraw from the region fit negative criteria that have long defined the region makes simplistic explanations for regional ills, such as isolation and ignorance, comfortably credible. Such insights, in turn, conveniently blind outsiders—and more "successful" insiders—to connections between their own good fortune and Appalachian woes. The process becomes even more pernicious when the more fortunate insider—in order to prove to others (and himself?) that he does not belong to the group in question—buys into the negative stereotype. The next step, joining in the denigration of his less fortunate neighbors, lends native credence that makes negative stereotypes more plausible to gullible, uninformed outsiders and—worse yet—to insecure insiders.

My experience suggests, however, that the fortunate insider, in the end, is not so fortunate after all. In the minds of most outside observers, the resulting stereotype typically becomes so inclusive and useful that it ensnares and dehumanizes even the fortunate native exceptions to it. (Just ask any of my Webb students who leave the region to attend college.) More seriously, if one assumes there are genuinely positive traits in our East Tennessee heritage (e.g., self-reliance, diligence, integrity) mindlessly discarding and denigrating that heritage deprives regional residents of positive cultural ballast that all twenty-first-century humans need to combat the stresses of our own chapter in human history. When the cumulative impact of these processes on East Tennessee is considered, it is obvious that all of its residents are ultimately weakened. Indeed, we become "Appalachians all"—in the most dehumanizing sense.

Personal Perspectives

I use the introductory section to each of the three parts to share stories from five generations of my East Tennessee forebears. In a similar way, I will begin chapters seven through nine and the epilogue with experiences from my own life, paying particular attention to my rediscovery of my own Appalachian roots after my 1987 return home. I do this for several reasons. First, I hope insights from my own admittedly ordinary ancestors will lend a human face to accounts of broader, more significant events in East Tennessee that too frequently become sterile in scholarly hands. Secondly, I hope this approach will help bridge the wide chasm that separates academically trained from amateur historians and particularly genealogists. Standing alone, much of my forebears' admittedly fragmentary genealogical information is little more than trivia. But combining this basic information with insights from more erudite and esoteric sources can enrich both sides of the academic-genealogical divide, producing a history that is both more accessible and more credible. Perhaps after reading my own only recently discovered stories, readers may dig more deeply and apply new scholarly insights to their own equally neglected and elusive pasts. Doing this, I believe, offers glimpses into that which is both unique and universal in each of our extended and collective lives. History offers the present few gifts more precious than this.

Because my own family stories are so central to my concern with Appalachian identity, readers may have questions, and some legitimate objections, to this aspect of the book. First, I confess that there is no evidence that any of my forebears ever shared more than casually my concern about the matter of Appalachian identity. Indeed, I draw from limited remaining records and personal and shared recollections to read between the lines in addressing their responses to this matter so essential to this book. In defense of this admittedly suspect practice, I only assert that reticence to comment on regional identity was common prior to the most recent generation—particularly among "successful" Appalachians.[4] In that respect, at least, my forebears were typical, and their general lack of attention to this matter is a key to the elusiveness I seek to explain. Astute readers may also wonder if the recent occurrences of my own Appalachian epiphany might lead to hyperbole and exaggeration. My answer is an unapologetic "yes." The light that illumines my take on Appalachia's elusive identity cannot help but obscure other perspectives on this complex subject. Finally, I must admit that I am an anomaly. Among my five brothers and twenty Banker and Thomas cousins, I am unusually preoccupied with the matter of our forebears' roots and identity, and this preoccupation cannot help but influence how I interpret these important matters. The careful reader should be mindful of these limitations—real and potential—for this book itself manifests the elusiveness it seeks to explain.

4. Although I use the term "successful Appalachians" at various points throughout this volume, I must confess that the subjective adjective leaves me uncomfortable. When I use it, I am most mindful of an insight from Carol Judy, my good friend from the Clearfork Valley. While acknowledging that she and her neighbors might be "money poor," she eschews sympathy from folk who may be "money rich" but poor in other ways.

Part 1

Before There Was an Appalachia, 1750–1880

Ancestors of my two grandmothers were among the earliest permanent European settlers in what is now East Tennessee. As pioneers in the late 1700s, my forebears were among the most celebrated and triumphant players in a powerful myth that Americans cherish. Yet, over the course of two generations, members from both family lines—along with countless other early East Tennesseans and Appalachians—experienced setbacks and tragedies that are missing in most conventional accounts of the American saga. When prominent, early-twentieth-century commentator William G. Frost described residents of our region collectively as "our contemporary ancestors," he evoked another powerful, enduring myth of my homeland and presumably about this latter group of my own ancestors, the diminished offspring of pioneers.

The word "myth" has many connotations. Here I use myth, as I do in my history classes, to convey ideals that hold deep cultural significance for those who embrace them and that are rooted in fact. Because they are constructed upon more than a germ of truth, pioneer and Appalachian myths are credible—even when they overlook or obscure evidence running contrary to their message. Myths are inherently neutral, but we humans often use them in constructive or destructive ways. Witness the long-term benefits of our nation's founding emphases on liberty and freedom; on the other hand, consider how those same ideals often resulted in tragedy for the native peoples of this land.

The admittedly limited information I have about my own ancestors' experiences in East Tennessee during the two generations between settlement and the industrial era contain all of these hallmarks of myths. But, these family stories offer a human face to little-known developments that from around 1790 to 1880 saw East Tennessee and greater Appalachia move from our nation's mainstream to its margins. My maternal grandmother, Nelle Bly (Brumit) Thomas (1895–1972), proudly traced her maternal lineage to Edward Morris, who in 1653 migrated from England to Virginia. In 1771, his grandson, Drury Morris, received a four-hundred-acre grant along the Watauga River. His status as a delegate in the Watauga Association suggests Drury attained some political as well as economic prominence. By the end of the American Revolution, several of his sons acquired vast tracts of land along the Holston River. I recall Nanny Thomas proudly proclaiming their prominent role in founding the settlement that became Morristown. Over the course of the next several generations, my grandmother's direct Morris descendants left the town bearing their name. Her great-grandfather relocated to more remote Carter County, where he became a barrel maker. According to the only record I have found, his son Thomas Jefferson Morris, my grandmother's grandfather, moved to the even more remote upland community of Valley Forge, where he worked as farmhand until his death in 1915.

Nanny Thomas's paternal (Brumit) lineage roughly paralleled that of her mother's. Genealogical records suggest they hailed from Yorkshire, England, although there is no indication of when they came to the American colonies, nor of where they first settled. Records reveal that in the early 1790s Samuel Brumit moved from Greenville, South Carolina, to Washington County, Tennessee, where he acquired a farm that his family held for three generations. My grandmother's father, David E. Brumit, was born in 1851. As an adult, he became a merchant in Elizabethton, most likely proof that the third Brumit generation had, indeed, lost their land. But David Brumit fared better than his father-in-law, Thomas Jefferson Morris. A listing in *Who's Who in Tennessee* in 1913 (the year of David's death) reveals that my great-grandfather had a "common school education," served in several political posts, and was active in church and community affairs.

This brief account of my Morris/Brumit forebears reveals some of the frustrations conventional historians have with genealogy. Fortunately several recent scholarly accounts of life in preindustrial Appalachia offer insights into the obviously declining fortunes of my ancestors. Short of the surfacing of a firsthand explanation, one may surmise that over the course of several generations my Morris/Brumit ancestors subdivided their property equally among all male heirs, much like many other antebellum Appalachian families. This practice, known as partible inheritance, caused no major problems for the first or second generations, when family landholdings were relatively large. However, by the third (and subsequent) generations, this practice—coupled with the traditional agrarian practice of having large families—sowed the seeds for crisis. East Tennessee's inherently hilly terrain and thin soils exacerbated the problem of shrinking farms, and along with some plain bad luck, accelerated a chain reaction of economic and social decline. Consequently, the devolution of my grandmother's forebears from prominent landholders to field hands and merchants over the course of three generations is understandable. Perhaps Thomas

Jefferson Morris was less ambitious than some of his contemporaries; my grandmother seemed to think so, but one cannot know for sure from existing records. However, neither lack of ambition nor any other single character trait alone adequately explains his—or his neighbors'—declining fortunes.

Knowledge about the paternal lineage of my other grandmother, May Olivia (Gibbs) Banker (1889–1970), offers more details into events that transformed East Tennessee between around 1790 and 1880. Family patriarch Nicholas Gibbs was born in Germany in 1733 and migrated to the American colonies as a young man. Like many émigrés to the trans-Appalachian frontier, Nicholas made brief stays in Pennsylvania and North Carolina before settling permanently, in 1792, just north of the emerging village that became Knoxville. Unlike many newcomers, he arrived in East Tennessee at the advanced age of fifty-nine with a large family in tow. Even though he acquired an estate of more than 1,300 acres, Gibbs's experiences in Germany and the colonies left him acutely aware that such an estate would dissipate quickly if divided equally among all his heirs. Consequently, between 1798 and 1810, he deeded his estate in roughly equal portions to his six male heirs. The largest single piece, a 280-acre tract that included the family's log home, was designated for youngest son Daniel, my great-great-great-grandfather. When Nicholas died in 1817, Daniel assumed responsibility for his mother, Mary, and the property officially transferred to Daniel when she died in 1833. Nicholas's 1810 will also provided for the liquidation of his portable property and equal distribution of the proceeds among his seven married daughters.

A generation later, when Daniel faced division of his 280-acre estate, he shared the same concerns as his father. Between 1808 and 1835, Daniel and wife Sally (Sharp) had eleven children, nine of whom lived to adulthood. While he followed the principles of his father, the significantly smaller size of Daniel's estate meant that Daniel's provisions for his heirs were less generous. Daniel divided the 280 acres between his two youngest sons and willed the family home site to Rufus, the youngest, who assumed responsibility for Sally (his mother) after Daniel's death in 1852. To enhance family cohesion, Daniel requested that the two younger sons pay one hundred dollars in cash to their older siblings. The eldest son was my great-great-grandfather, William Sharp Gibbs. William apparently purchased some land of his own before he married Malinda Clapp in 1834. Their youngest child, Washington Lafayette Gibbs (born in 1858), was my great-grandfather. A family history describes Lafayette as "a well educated man for his day [who completed] the classical course at the University [and] taught at Andersonville Academy." While I like to think my own penchant for books comes in part from this ancestor, lack of land doubtlessly shaped his life's course. Indeed, the fact that Lafayette Gibbs did not inherit a significant tract of land from his family's original East Tennessee estate gave him a common status with David Brumit, Thomas Jefferson Morris, and—new scholarship suggests—many other East Tennesseans who came of age in the mid- and latter nineteenth century. As the broader East Tennessee region experienced relative decline, so did many of its individual sons.

The circumstances individuals like my own forebears faced—and their responses to those challenges—did not alone bring misfortune to East Tennesseans in the middle third of the nineteenth century. Instead, a host of developments within the state of Tennessee, the American South, and the greater United States, combined to create the unpleasant "Appalachian" legacies that persist in East Tennessee into the present. Of these developments, none was more important than the sectional crisis between South and North and the resulting Civil War. The war disrupted every established East Tennessee routine, decimated the region's land and economy, caused tremendous loss in life and labor, and left the region demoralized and disdained by an array of outsiders. I know very little about the experiences of my East Tennessee forebears during these traumatic and tragic times. But I am fortunate to be the heir to interesting stories about the Civil War–era exploits of another forebear who moved to upper East Tennessee from Virginia shortly after the war ended. My mother's paternal great-grandfather, Philander Mitchell Thomas, served almost three years with the

Nicholas Gibbs Homeplace in 1910 with members of the John Gibbs family on the front porch. By the time this photo was taken, the dwelling had structurally evolved several times from its earliest days, and the author's direct forebears were no longer residing there. (Courtesy of Mark Groover and the Nicholas Gibbs Historical Society.)

Confederate Wythe County (Virginia) Volunteers and spent the last few months of the war in a Union prison camp. Several letters Mitch penned from the field, and colorful stories passed down for three generations, offer fleeting glimpses into his Civil War activities. In many ways, Mitch's experiences paralleled those of many East Tennesseans, who in the aftermath of Appomattox became his new neighbors.

Mitch's father, Wesley (born in 1803), and mother, Elizabeth (born in 1808), married in 1829. Either shortly before or soon after marrying, they built a modest single-pen cabin high atop Brierpatch Mountain in Grayson County, Virginia. From the now-dilapidated front porch, the vista stretches southward into North Carolina and southwestward into upper East Tennessee. The Thomas family must have prospered, for a second pen, and later a dogtrot, were added to the cabin before it was eventually covered with clapboards, a common practice intended to disguise a family's humble origins. Wesley's large family apparently made the customary contributions to their general well-being, clearing forests into pastures and constructing a network of stone fences that still stands in stretches today. Mitch, born in 1833, was the oldest of the children who lived to adulthood. The other six Thomas siblings—five sons and one daughter—lived long, apparently normal lives in an era that was far from normal.

When war broke out at Fort Sumter in 1861, Mitch was twenty-eight years old, married, and had a son nearly three years old. That he did not enlist with the Wythe County Volunteers until 1863 suggests that Mitch, like many other residents of remote Appalachian areas of several southern states, may have initially hoped the war would pass him by. Unionist sentiment was not uncommon in Grayson County, but the fact that at least three of his brothers also served the Confederate cause suggests his reasons were probably familial as well as cultural. In a letter to his wife, Mary, dated November 4, 1864, and sent from an encampment near Petersburg, Mitch reported that they "[heard] cannons day and night," but did not expect "the yanks will attact us hear." In conclusion, he wrote that "most of the men in camp think this war wil not last long." It is unclear whether Mitch Thomas might still have held out hope for Confederate victory at that late date in the war. Within a few weeks, he was captured and spent the last several months of the war in a Union prison camp near Bethesda, Maryland, where he apparently remained until well after the war ended. Family legend offers a blunt explanation for my forebear's extended stay in the camp. Having refused the Yankees' demand that he "swallow the yellow dog"—slang for the oath of allegiance ex-Confederates were expected to swear to the U.S. government—Mitch was not released until the prison was disbanded.

In the war's aftermath, Mitch left his ancestral home for reasons unexplained, purchasing a farm in upper East Tennessee. Perhaps, like many veterans, he carried unpleasant memories home from war. In many Appalachian communities, frictions between former Rebels and Unionists often flared, and this may have compounded Mitch's problems. Tensions may also have developed within the Thomas clan. Even before his enlistment, Mitch had moved his family to the west side of Brierpatch Mountain, a steep-sloped site poorly suited for large-scale farming, which locals still refer to as "the Mitch Place." By the early 1870s, Mitch had moved from Grayson County to Cook's Valley, Tennessee, located in the middle of the triangle of today's Tri-Cities (Bristol, Kingsport, and Johnson City). Remaining records reveal little about the specifics of Mitch's move—why he chose that locale, how he managed to acquire a farm there (the area had been occupied for nearly a century, and land prices would have been relatively high), or even what he hoped to achieve by leaving Grayson County. But one thing is certain: if Mitch Thomas came to East Tennessee hoping to escape the miseries and misfortunes wrought by Civil War, he must have been disappointed. In hindsight at least, it is painfully clear the war made East Tennessee's gradual, often-imperceptible slide from the nation's mainstream to its margins real and prolonged.

Mitch Thomas was not the only member of my family to come to East Tennessee after the Civil War. Around the time he moved to Cook's Valley, Luke and Henry Banker arrived in Knoxville. Their forebears had migrated from Germany to colonial New York in the mid-eighteenth century. In the 1780s, clan

Mitch Thomas constructed this dwelling some time after he relocated to upper East Tennessee's Cook's Valley in the aftermath of the Civil War. This 1926 gathering at the old Thomas home included the author's mother (the first girl to the left on the top step), grandparents (the younger couple at the center of the photo), and great-grandparents (the elderly seated couple). (Courtesy of Doug Hardwick.)

patriarch James Banker received a western New York land grant in return for service in the American Revolution. Thereafter his heirs drifted westward, residing briefly in Ontario before eventually settling in eastern Michigan. Little is known about the circumstances that brought father and son, Henry and Luke Banker, from Michigan to East Tennessee, but they apparently reached Knoxville with little more than the possessions they carried. Family legend suggests the locals considered them "carpetbaggers." By all accounts, their first days in Knoxville were filled with hardship, economic deprivation, and disappointment, another indication of the miserable state of affairs in East Tennessee as the final third of the nineteenth century began to unfold.

There is no evidence that any of the ancestors I have just described ever thought of themselves as "Appalachian." Yet, even as they and their East Tennessee neighbors were emerging from the Civil War, observers were applying that label to East Tennessee and the broader upland South. Then, as now, "Appalachia" had many, often contrasting mythical connotations. But before we can properly address them, we must first move beyond these personal accounts and explore in greater depth the array of circumstances and developments in early East Tennessee that made notions about the region's "Appalachian" traits so credible and enduring—and so inapt and demeaning for the likes of the next generation of my forebears.

Chapter One

East Tennessee Beginnings:
Cherokee and Pioneer Legacies and the Births
of Three Representative Communities

For countless millennia before my ancestors joined the great human migration into and beyond the Appalachians, today's East Tennessee was home to a diverse, ever-evolving array of humans. The first epoch in East Tennessee history began when prehistoric nomads arrived at an uncertain date in a misty past, and it ended with the tragic removal of most of their Cherokee heirs in 1838. For East Tennessee's native inhabitants, the appearance of Spanish explorers in the mid-sixteenth century, and the arrival of permanent British settlers two centuries later, produced dramatic, uneven, ultimately tragic consequences. Encounters between the "Overhill Cherokees" and the array of Europeans who invaded East Tennessee over the course of more than two hundred years were, however, far more complex than either mythical accounts from our great national saga or popular recollections of our region's pioneer past suggest. Although the Cherokees and their Caucasian competitors held radically different worldviews and understandings of land and nature, a similar intent to control East Tennessee's terrain became the focal point and ultimate prize of their cross-cultural collision. Insights from that encounter offer glimpses of patterns pervading much of East Tennessee's subsequent history.

Although details are debated, consensus suggests that nomadic hunters arrived in the Appalachian region 12–13,000 years ago. Over the course of several millennia, populations increased and levels of culture became increasingly sophisticated. This ascendant course peaked in the Mississippian era (ca. 900–1300 AD) when mound-builder cultures from the Mississippi Valley spread their influence into the Appalachian foothills. As their characteristic mounds reveal, these peoples developed a sophisticated worldview and a degree of social stratification that enabled them to construct impressive structures and urban centers. Surplus cultivation of corn and widespread trade networks (stretching as far as the high cultures of Meso-America) sustained Mississippian chiefdoms that peaked around the fourteenth century. But then, two centuries before Columbus's arrival, a mysterious array of interrelated economic, political, and environmental stresses initiated a slow decline of the Mississippian cultures. When the Spanish explorer Hernando de Soto trekked through what is now East Tennessee in 1539–40, he encountered the consequences of this cultural devolution.

Throughout the two and a half centuries after de Soto's visit, the "Overhill Cherokee" were the dominant (but never the sole) native presence in what became East Tennessee. In response to unprecedented challenges, the Cherokees displayed a remarkable capacity for cultural adaptation that demands we put away mythical understandings of Native American–white interaction. Neither longstanding images of bloodthirsty savages who deserved an unfortunate, inevitable fate, nor the more recently fashionable charges that greedy, aggressive whites unmercifully annihilated innocent Indian victims accurately capture what transpired. Despite disease-imposed demographic devastation, instinctive adaptive skills made the Cherokees surprisingly resilient. By developing sophisticated trade, diplomatic, and marital relationships with French and English intruders, the Cherokees forged a mutually beneficial "middle ground," which assured them a prominent role in East Tennessee's increasingly complex, intercultural politics, and introduced them to new cultural traditions. The ultimate collapse of the middle ground during the critical era leading up to the American Revolution has blinded some observers to its relative effectiveness. Until the final third of the eighteenth century, balancing old with new enabled the Cherokees to delay dependency on outsiders and minimize debilitating internal divisions. The Cherokees were only the first East Tennesseans to face such challenges.

The political key to the middle ground was a relative balance of power between the various groups occupying early East Tennessee. For two and a half centuries, Cherokee diplomats effectively played Spanish, French, and English interests—and those of their varied native neighbors—against one another to enhance Cherokee wellbeing. But the clear-cut British victory in the French and Indian War, and the subsequent flood of land-hungry settlers in today's upper East Tennessee—in defiance of Britain's ineffective Proclamation of 1763—upset that balance. For the first time, a large, permanent body of Caucasian neighbors lived among the Cherokees. When British-colonial relations ruptured in 1776, many Cherokees sided with the British. Ferocious native attacks on the burgeoning Watauga, Holston, and Carter's Valley settlements made the backcountry one of the bloodiest theaters of the Revolution. The attacks also affirmed both the settlers' allegiance to the patriot cause and their enduring enmity for the Cherokees. When the British sought peace with the American rebels and ceded Cherokee lands to the victors in the Treaty of Paris of 1783—without even consulting their Indian allies—the usually united Cherokees found themselves divided. One faction, led by Dragging Canoe, made the Tennessee frontier of the 1780s "a dark and bloody ground." Other Cherokees followed the lead of Dragging Canoe's aged father, Attakullakulla, and sought to reestablish a "middle ground" that would more shrewdly protect their interests. The greatest casualty of this schism was the long-standing Cherokee emphasis on intratribal harmony, and this internal fragmentation made the Cherokees even more vulnerable to land aggrandizing schemes of the young United States. Faced with a flood of white newcomers and a government unwilling to stop them, neither Dragging Canoe's militancy nor the more conciliatory approach of the accommodationists effectively protected Cherokee interests. But again, the ultimate Cherokee tragedy, this time their removal and the "Trail of Tears," has blinded many observers to the broader significance of events transpiring in Cherokee East Tennessee in the fifty years following the American Revolution. Even more than before, the twin challenges of economic dependency and internal fragmentation impeded native responses to their more numerous, land-hungry adversaries. Yet they again charted a complex course that enjoyed temporary success and foreshadowed subsequent, largely overlooked, patterns in East Tennessee's elusive history.

Middle Grounds in East Tennessee

Once Dragging Canoe and the militants recognized the futility of resistance in the early 1790s, most Cherokee leaders advocated a course of cultural accommodation that fortuitously complemented the "civilization program" of the new U.S. government. As a result, the Cherokees were seen as a notable exemplar of a policy that otherwise largely failed to achieve its goal of "civilizing Indians." But praise from government officials and Protestant missionaries for the "Cherokee renaissance" failed to account for the complexities of selective acculturation. No less than the middle ground of the colonial era, this acculturation process was more selective and less uniform than hopeful white observers wanted to believe. To be sure, interrelated Cherokee landholding, housing, economic, and gender patterns became by the early nineteenth century more like those of their Euro-American neighbors. Powerful mixed-blood Cherokee elites embraced plantation agriculture, acquired African slaves, constructed large, commodious homes, and enrolled their sons in distant boarding schools to learn English and "white ways." Polytheistic Cherokees of various social stripes embraced aspects of Christianity, and all but the most remote and traditional Cherokees adopted practical aspects of white material culture (including the Appalachian log cabin). In 1821, Sequoyah provided his people with a written alphabet, and within five years, thousands of Cherokees were literate, far surpassing the literacy rates of their white neighbors. Soon thereafter, the Cherokees and white missionaries published a newspaper (the *Cherokee Phoenix*), government documents, religious tracts, and the Christian Bible using Sequoyah's syllabary. Faced with unprecedented challenges, the Cherokee abandoned traditional, decentralized political institutions, and in 1827 they embraced a tribal charter modeled on the constitution of the U.S. government.

These achievements blinded many contemporaries (and indeed, most subsequent observers) to the complexities and contradictions of Cherokee accommodation. Selective acculturation may contribute to discernable group patterns, but even among a generally communal people, it is largely an individual process. For the Cherokees—no less than for subsequent generations of East Tennesseans—

This sketch of the eighteenth-century Cherokee warrior Cunne Shote graphically reflects Cherokee proclivities for selective acculturation. His attire and possessions combine traditional ways and those of European newcomers. (Courtesy of Hargrett Rare Book and Manuscript Library/University of Georgia Libraries.)

selective acculturation forged kaleidoscopic consequences that reveal the inadequacy of simplistic labels such as "progressive" and "conservative." For example, traditionalists who resisted acculturation and clung to native ways ironically became the most vulnerable to white demands for their lands. From the other side, the behavior of Cherokee progressives was so remarkable that few observers even today grasp or appreciate their role in the events surrounding removal. John Ross, primary author of the 1827 constitution, and first tribal chief under its authority, typified the progressives. Only one-eighth Cherokee, Ross bridged white and Cherokee cultures with ease; he was educated in white schools, had white business partners, and on numerous occasions supported U.S. government policies. But he became the most vocal opponent to relinquishing tribal lands and ultimately removal. Meanwhile, many Cherokee traditionalists accepted the white rationale that Indian culture could not survive in the midst of aggressive white neighbors, and voluntarily removed to lands west of the Mississippi in the aftermath of the War of 1812. Other traditionalists rejected Ross's leadership and supported the 1835 Treaty of New Echota, which approved removal to Oklahoma for personal, often petty reasons. While the details of that sad chapter are beyond the scope of this volume, two regional themes deserve mention. The wealth and success of the mixed-blood elites made them particularly aware of their people's tenuous hold on their traditional domain at a time when good land in East Tennessee and surrounding states was becoming increasingly scarce. Their success, in turn, earned resentment from both their land-hungry white neighbors and their less successful, typically more traditional Cherokee brethren. When the latter became strange bedfellows, the "Trail of Tears" became inevitable as the tables turned on the Cherokees' diplomatic prowess.

Old Myths, New Perspectives

The rest of this chapter utilizes insights from Appalachian studies to reconstruct important, often overlooked themes in East Tennessee's development during the settlement era and early national period. In recent decades, these insights led some regional scholars to question and qualify long-held assumptions about the settlers and about life in early East Tennessee. Their revisionism and irreverence was, of course, part of a broader questioning of our nation's enduring "pioneer myth." Buckskin-clad frontiersmen confronting fierce Indian foes and a vast wilderness are, of course, *the* heroes of our great natal saga. Tales of the inevitable triumph of the rugged pioneer—and his explorer, prospector, cowboy successors as our frontier shifted ever westward—have thrilled and inspired countless generations of Americans. In this saga, a diverse, largely rootless people found common identity and many distinctive, admirable traits: a fierce individualism and self-reliance, a practical egalitarianism, and "Yankee ingenuity" to name just a few.

Many familiar pioneer heroes appeared at least briefly in late-eighteenth-century East Tennessee. Daniel Boone crossed through our region en route to Kentucky, and Davy Crockett was born and raised here. Leading early East Tennesseans John Sevier, Isaac and Evan Shelby, and William Bean—and countless long-forgotten ancestors of many present regional residents—left distinct imprints on the region. They also personified pioneer traits as they crossed the rugged Appalachians and settled a temporarily isolated frontier, carved homes and farms from vast, dark forests, and fought the fierce Dragging Canoe and British Loyalist forces at King's Mountain. But there was more to East Tennessee's story than traditional accounts convey, and our region's pioneer past has, along with its many positives, a darker side. One need not abandon the former to acknowledge the latter. Indeed, coming to terms with these overlooked aspects of our regional saga is a first step toward grasping East Tennessee's elusive past and identity.

Considering my earlier emphases, it is appropriate that I begin by stressing that selective acculturation in early East Tennessee was a two-way process that left important Cherokee legacies still present in the region. This is most obvious in the name Tennessee, which most observers believe to be an approximation of *Tanasee*, the name of a Cherokee town. More significantly, early East Tennessee settlers learned fishing and hunting practices, the cultivation of corn, and embraced an array of uses for that and other valuable native plants from Cherokee neighbors. While most successful early settlers embraced aspects of Cherokee culture, a few also married Cherokee spouses. Perhaps most important, the settlers' encounters with the Cherokees reveal their own pragmatic penchant for selective acculturation.

That insight alone should cause observers to question long-held assumptions about the ethnic-cultural makeup of the trans-Appalachian frontier. In addressing notions that our forebears were "pure Elizabethan" or products of a "dominant Scotch-Irish imprint," we must again unravel seeds of truth from exaggeration. Many East Tennesseans, including my Morris and Brumit forebears, were English, and (as one might expect in what was then colonial North Carolina) most basic governmental and cultural institutions originated in the mother country. But my German Gibbs forebears represented just one of many competing groups—including French, Scots, Irish, African, and Cherokee—who added distinctive traits, foodstuffs, and musical and linguistic traditions to East Tennessee's early cultural mix. The Scots-Irish imprint on frontier Appalachian culture was powerful—a tradition of mixed farming and herding well suited to the region's hilly terrain, a pious Presbyterianism that fueled the region's abiding religiosity, and a tradition of distilling corn and other grains into whiskey and other beverages are only a few distinct examples of the Scots-Irish legacy. But the Scots who came to colonial America via Ireland were themselves mostly poor seminomads who practiced selective acculturation out of necessity. Moreover, the diverse mix of settlers converging on Cherokee lands in the late eighteenth century were typically on the second, sometimes third, leg of a New World migratory path. The blending of cultural traditions over the course of this long sojourn is most evident in the distinctly Appalachian log cabin that resulted from pragmatic modifications of a distinct Finnish architectural tradition that Swedes introduced in the Delaware Valley in the late 1600s. Talk of pure Appalachian culture has long been pervasive, but that assertion reveals far more about those who expound it than realities in locales like frontier East Tennessee.

"Isolated" and "independent" are two other often-used descriptors of pioneer Appalachia. While some recent scholars jettison these terms completely, most informed observers now add the qualifier *relative* when they discuss these two alleged Appalachian hallmarks. To be sure, almost anyone who showed up in East Tennessee prior to 1800 was an independent soul. And there truly were some individuals, such as the proverbial Daniel Boone, who when seeing smoke from a neighbor's chimney lit out for less crowded terrain. But after Boone and the long hunters first penetrated the region in the 1760s, most settlers came with families, and they quickly organized communities. Soon thereafter, they established limited political institutions, such as the Watauga Association, and gradually more permanent governmental entities evolved. Clergymen typically despaired the devil's presence in the Tennessee backcountry, causing early settlers to knit together quickly in churches. Thereafter, periodic waves of revivalism revealed a penchant for socialization that made organized religion a central feature of East Tennessee life. Like their twenty-first-century heirs, early East Tennesseans often chafed against distant rule and oppressive institutions, but this resistance and the rhetoric of individualism accompanying it was selective, often self-serving, and had practical limits.

Notions about East Tennessee–Appalachian isolation have been particularly persistent. Of course, rugged terrain on the region's borders east and west and the long unnavigable Tennessee River give credence to such assertions. But exaggerations of that insularity influence the region's history more than the isolation itself. As already demonstrated, East Tennessee was not isolated when Cherokees reigned supreme here in the sixteenth and seventeenth centuries, and with each passing generation, notions of isolated East Tennessee have become less true. From around 1780 to 1840, East Tennessee was relatively isolated, but so were most rural areas of the antebellum United States. Commerce provided important links to the outside world. From the end of the American Revolution to the middle third of the nineteenth century, regional drovers herded livestock along the routes of ancient Indian trails to Charleston, Baltimore, Philadelphia, and locales in between. Each year, flatboats loaded in Knoxville slowly made their way to New Orleans, and their navigators returned to East Tennessee via the Natchez Trace with the latest news and trade goods from the greater world. By early in the nineteenth century, East Tennessee ginseng made its ways to markets in China, and early archaeological digs from sites in Knoxville offer evidence of rich and valuable Oriental pottery that came back to East Tennessee in return.

These insights raise questions about another assumption—that antebellum Appalachian East Tennessee was a land of independent yeomen. To be sure, small-scale farmers were predominant in early East Tennessee, and these husbandmen and their families typically produced much of what they consumed. But a unique regional economic orientation was less responsible for these patterns than were temporary conditions typical throughout the American backcountry. Moreover, pre–Civil War East Tennessee had its own array of ambitious entrepreneurs who engaged (with varying degrees of success) in diverse commercial and industrial pursuits. This diversity and unappreciated integration into broader economic and cultural networks will become even more apparent in the pages ahead. First, however, one must consider an even more basic matter that was *the* priority of most frontier/antebellum East Tennesseans, and which became a source of considerable confusion and misinformation for their heirs and those of us attempting to make sense of their experiences. This subject, of course, is land.

For seventeenth-century Englishmen and Europeans, colonial North America represented a place where the familiar reality of too little land and too many people—which had long undergirded feudal society—was turned on its head. By the era of the American Revolution, when conditions in the new nation's long-settled regions began to approximate European circumstances, backcountry areas where land was still open and abundant captured people's attention. Therein lies a major reason for the American fascination and preoccupation with "the West"—which during the time frame of this chapter included East Tennessee.

Early systematic attempts to analyze "Appalachian" distinctions emphasized the region's yeoman roots. But in recent years, as regional scholarship matured, assumptions about early Appalachia have undergone intense scrutiny. New scholarship, for example, presents John Sevier, James Robertson, William Blount, and many early East Tennessee heroes in an unfamiliar fashion. Far from disinterested public servants determined to create a yeoman utopia in the East Tennessee wilderness, they were first and foremost speculators whose rapacious desire for land and windfall profits fueled hostility for Cherokees and the British. After the Revolution, complicated consequences of North Carolina's appropriately named "Land Grab Act" spurred these men to ambitious political efforts: the spontaneous founding of the short-lived "State of Franklin," creation of a more legitimate, interim government called the "Southwest Territory," and ultimately establishment of the state of Tennessee. Other evidence hints that in the uncertain days when the young U.S. government seemed unable to address frontier needs, Sevier, Blount, and others temporarily flirted with Spain, possibly as a more reliable "mother" authority. Of the opportunistic Blount, who had a hand in all of these schemes and faced impeachment from his U.S. Senate seat in 1798 because of his shady role in the Spanish intrigue, one scholar observed. "there was no such thing as a conflict of interest." To be sure, these early Tennesseans were men of their times. New scholarship simply challenges popular notions about those times and offers less pleasant, but more honest, insights into East Tennessee's early years. Indeed, the aggrandizing schemes of these and other land speculators were so successful that as early as statehood in 1796 Tennessee was well on its way to becoming a land of haves and have-nots. Statistics for the era 1790 to 1810 reveal that more than 55 percent of all Tennesseans were landless, and that in East Tennessee approximately one-sixth of the residents held more than one-half of the land. The pattern is even more skewed when one considers that absentee speculators owned much of East Tennessee during this early era.[1]

From White's Fort to Knoxville

The Patriot victory in the American Revolution opened the floodgates for settlement beyond the Appalachians. Even while war still raged, upper East Tennessee settlers and speculators asserted the Cherokees had forfeited rights to their lands by allying with the British; when hostilities waned, they looked longingly south and west. The new national government's feeble condition and preoccupation with more pressing matters, along with general confusion in North Carolina

---

1. Quoted in John R. Finger, *Tennessee Frontiers: Three Regions in Transition* (Bloomington: Indiana Univ. Press, 2001), 100. Statistics revealing skewed landholding patterns in antebellum East Tennessee are offered by Wilma A. Dunaway, "Speculators and Settler Capitalists: Unthinking the Mythology of Appalachian Landholding, 1790–1860," in *Appalachia in the Making: The Mountain South in the Nineteenth Century*, ed. Mary Beth Pudup et al., 50–75 (Chapel Hill: Univ. of North Carolina Press, 1995). Dunaway expands on this theme and its broader Appalachian contexts in *The First American Frontier: Transition to Capitalism in Southern Appalachia, 1700–1860* (Chapel Hill: Univ. of North Carolina Press, 1996). Lee Soltow, "Land Inequality on the Frontier: The Distribution of Land in East Tennessee at the Beginning of the 19th Century," *Social Science History* 5 (Summer 1981): 275–91, offered a similar perspective long before Dunaway.

about its western lands, allowed early Tennesseans simultaneously to use legal and extralegal means to advance their interests. The political sagas of the State of Franklin, of the "Territory South and West of the River Ohio," and of Tennessee statehood are told elsewhere; suffice to say here that land speculators—John Sevier, William Blount, James White—played prominent roles in these maneuverings and in the founding of Knoxville. The least ambitious of the three was White, a Scots-Irish, Revolutionary War veteran from Iredell County, North Carolina. Despite his more modest drive, White's decision to move his family to land just below the junction of the Holston and French Broad Rivers, and his acquisition of a tract of more than a thousand acres a few miles downstream (on what later became known as the Tennessee River) in 1785, earned him the title of Knoxville's "founder." The following year, White constructed a fort and a cluster of fortified cabins on the downstream site, and he made plans to sell lots to (what he hoped would be) eager buyers.

"White's Fort," situated on a hill between two creeks that emptied into the north bank of the Tennessee River, might have been just another soon-bypassed frontier outpost had it not been for William Blount. This most ambitious of early Tennessee speculators hailed from a wealthy North Carolina family, served in that state's legislature and the Continental Congress, and pushed a reluctant North Carolina to ratify the new federal constitution in 1788. Blount and his brothers were among the most influential instigators and beneficiaries of North Carolina's "Land Grab Act," and when efforts to advance those interests by supporting the State of Franklin evaporated, Blount parlayed a casual acquaintance with President Washington and his pragmatic Federalist leanings into an appointment as governor of the Southwest Territory. Blount's priorities, negotiating a treaty with the Cherokees and securing a territorial capital, reflected lofty personal ambitions, but they also revealed a practical inclination to temporarily settle for less when his grand schemes exceeded his grasp. Blount's concerns and compromises conveniently benefited White's nascent settlement. There, in 1791, Blount and forty-one Cherokee chiefs negotiated for seven days, displaying a pomp and shrewdness that reflected mutual preferences of the governor and the native diplomats. Blount had hoped to convince the chiefs to give up lands (he already claimed) as far south as the great bend of the Tennessee River and as far west as the Cherokees might concede. Instead, the resulting Treaty of Holston gave the Cherokees approval to existing settlements in and around White's Fort and south of the French Broad, and gained federal protection for settlers there.

Blount's decision to make White's Fort the territorial capital reflected a similar inclination to compromise. A year earlier, he had suggested to his brother that a desirable location might be the "mouth of the Clinch [near] my land on Emory's River." At the time, that was the site of Fort Southwest Point, and a Blount claim of more than five thousand acres was nearby. When the Cherokees refused to relinquish more land in that vicinity, Blount settled for White's Fort. Despite allegations to the contrary, Blount and White were not business partners, and Blount did not own land in the vicinity of White's Fort at the time he named it territorial capital. But the governor wasted little time in taking advantage of his decision. In 1791, he and White jointly acquired more than two hundred acres adjacent to White's original tract. Within weeks, White's son-in-law, the surveyor Charles McClung, laid out a grid of streets and sixty-four half-acre lots. A lottery that distributed those lots on October 3, 1791, marked Knoxville's official birth. The name change to Knoxville, and other developments from the 1790s, offered harbingers of patterns that would persist long after the settlement's days as a struggling frontier outpost.

Naming the new capital after Blount's immediate political superior, Secretary of War Henry Knox, was a calculated move that did not achieve its anticipated benefits. Knox never visited his namesake city, and there is no evidence that Blount's attempted flattery earned the settlement special favors. But that was only the most apparent of several outward ways Blount, White, and the community's other early leaders sought to enhance their project. Like surveyors of many other urban centers on the trans-Appalachian frontier, McClung laid out the new town along the lines of Philadelphia, the new nation's most preeminent city. Even McClung's selection of street names (e.g., Market, Locust, Walnut, Broad) revealed a penchant for imitation as well as a personal familiarity with the Quaker city. A rectangular grid and straight lines were considered a clear distinction between organized town life and the more relaxed, lethargic patterns of the country. This urge to distinguish itself from its rural neighbors became a major theme in Knoxville's history. Aspirations of urban sophistication were also evident in at least some of the settlement's early structures. Blount had the first frame building west of the Appalachians constructed to serve as his home and official office. Intrigued by the building's windows, the Cherokees called it "the house with many glass eyes." In 1794, a Blount acquaintance reported, "here are frame houses and brick chimnies."[2] Knoxville's ten stores and seven taverns made the city larger and more impressive, the acquaintance exclaimed, than the governor's own hometown, Washington, North Carolina. White displayed a public spirit uncharacteristic of frontier-city officials, setting aside two lots for a church and selling four more at a reduced rate for an educational institution. On Blount's invitation, printer George Roulstone left North Carolina

2. Finger, *Tennessee Frontiers*, 141. The glowing appraisal of early Knoxville's assets came from visitor Abishai C. Thomas and is recorded by William J. MacArthur, *Knoxville's History: An Interpretation* (Knoxville: East Tennessee Historical Society, 1978), 11–12.

The blockhouse and barracks at White's Fort in 1792 as depicted in a 1901 painting by Lloyd Branson. This illustration clearly conveys an image of Knoxville as a frontier community. (Courtesy of Calvin M. McClung Historical Collection.)

and began publication of the *Knoxville Gazette* in 1793. Such signs of civilization made Knoxville *the* choice to become state capital when Tennessee entered the union as the sixteenth state in 1796.

Discussion of early Knoxville's pretensions would not be complete without at least brief mention of a joint scheme that emerged from the minds of Blount and Dr. Nicholas Romayne, an eccentric New York physician and occasional Columbia College professor. At Columbia, Dr. Romayne was remembered as "a 300-pound phenomenon . . . erudite but emotional, calculating but rash, enormous but indefatigable." For Governor Blount, the plan to lay out the two-mile-square settlement adjacent to Knoxville was simply a "scheme that may afford profits . . . without the possibility of a loss."[3] The vision evaporated in 1795, apparently when Blount shifted attention to Tennessee statehood. But this would not be the last time Knoxville would become preoccupied with lofty (some would say impractical) aspirations, nor the only time more immediate concerns would undermine such ambitions.

A closer look at the real Knoxville of the 1790s suggests less rosy prospects. Many of the new town's native neighbors were less than satisfied with the

3. See Jack Neely, "Knoxvilles That Never Were," in *Secret History II: Stories About Knoxville, Tennessee* (Knoxville, TN: Scruffy City Publishing, 1998), 167–68.

East Tennessee Beginnings

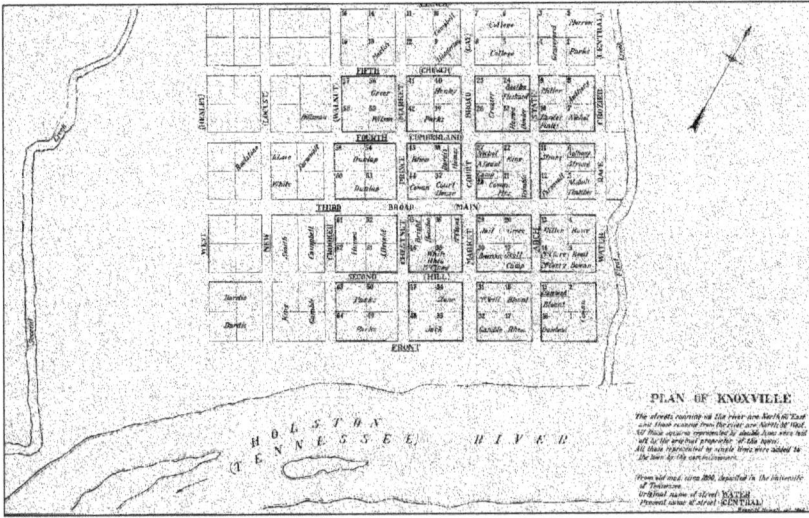

Original layout of Knoxville from 1792 sketch by surveyor Charles McClung. McClung brought street names from Philadelphia, where he had recently resided, to the new settlement on the Tennessee frontier. Along with Governor Blount's "mansion," which was constructed shortly thereafter, McClung's street grid reflected a penchant for imitation and a distancing from frontier roots early in Knoxville's history. (Courtesy of Calvin M. McClung Historical Collection.)

Holston Treaty. In September 1793, a force of more than one thousand Cherokees and Creeks attacked and killed thirteen settlers at Cavet's Station, eight miles east of Knoxville. Had they attacked Knoxville, they might have had even greater success, for at that moment fewer than forty men protected the settlement. Only discord among the warriors and fear of possible retaliation from forces under John Sevier saved the vulnerable outpost. On another front, many of the anticipated cultural advancements proved illusory. Log cabins remained the city's most common architectural form well into the nineteenth century. Not until 1816 did Presbyterians establish a permanent congregation on the site that White reserved, and the pretentiously named "Blount College" barely survived past infancy. In short, the aforementioned facades failed to hide the more crude aspects of Knoxville's frontier beginnings.

Other visitors offered images of early Knoxville that contrasted with the accolades of Blount and his friends. For example, Prince Louis Phillipe and an entourage of Frenchmen, who spent several days in the city in 1797, described the countryside as "nasty and inhospitable," disparaged the shiftlessness of Knoxville residents, and found the city's food and buildings lacking. When the prince complained about the absence of chamber pots in a local inn, the innkeeper suggested he relieve himself through a broken window. The Frenchmen reported a pleasant swim in the Tennessee River—to escape unmerciful heat and

East Tennessee Beginnings

bedbugs from the same establishment. The prince's brother kindly suggested Knoxville "would be quite picturesque . . . if not for the wearying regularity of streets and houses in American towns." If nothing else, this dubious compliment is evidence that Knoxville's alleged ills were not unique, nor as subsequent critics would charge, "distinctly Appalachian."

The observation of another Frenchmen five years later revealed a more serious and enduring challenge for East Tennessee and its leading city. "Of all parts in the US now inhabited," botanist André Michaux soberly wrote in 1802, "[East Tennessee] was the most unfavorably situated—being on every side circumscribed by considerable tracts of country that produce the same provisions and which are either more fertile or nearer to the sea."[4] In reality, East Tennessee's relative geographical disadvantages had mixed effects for Knoxville. On the one hand, they assured the city economic preeminence within East Tennessee. Nearby valley farmers produced bumper crops of corn, wheat, and vegetables, as well as hogs, cattle, horses, mules, and poultry. As subsequent generations pushed away from the valley and onto less fertile soils and steeper terrain, valley producers, Knoxville consumers, and Knoxville-based businesses that processed agricultural products (such as flourmills, tanneries, and distilleries) enjoyed decided advantages. By 1800, the city was home for an array of craftsmen— blacksmiths, carpenters, coopers, wheelwrights, and silversmiths—who served the broader region. Knoxville's first private bank opened in 1811, funneled capital to its cash-starved East Tennessee neighbors, and reaped profits in return. Thanks to wise leadership from Hugh Lawson White (son of the city's founder) the bank was far more stable and effective than most frontier financial institutions. Well before the Civil War, Knoxvillians served as crucial middlemen for small-scale extractive industries—iron, timber, coal—typically associated with the postwar industrial era. But the same geographical conditions and relative isolation that made these businesses possible also meant that most of them were small-scale and served limited local markets. More seriously, they left East Tennessee as a whole, and Knoxville as its commercial center, at a disadvantage when new lands opened up in Middle and West Tennessee and beyond. East Tennessee's relatively cool climate, thin, rocky, and infertile soils, and steep terrain made it less attractive than these other lands. Further, mountain barriers on East Tennessee's eastern and western flanks left Knoxville—as the subregion's wholesaling and bulking center—at a great disadvantage in competing for trade beyond the region. Similarly, East Tennessee's only transportation asset, the

4. François André Michaux, *Travels to the Westward of the Allegheny Mountains* (1802), reprinted in vol. 3 of *Early Western Travels, 1748–1846*, trans. and ed. Reuben Gold Thwaites (New York: AMS Press, 1966), 282.

Tennessee River, initially proved an illusory advantage. Muscle Shoals at the river's "great bend," and numerous eddies and "sucks" on the upper Tennessee left the river navigable only several months of the year, and then only to downstream, mostly flatboat traffic. Even when the latter survived the treacherous course through Muscle Shoals, the Tennessee's circuitous path to the Ohio and Mississippi made river trade originating in Knoxville and ending in New Orleans relatively expensive.

Consequently, much of East Tennessee's early commerce was over land up and down Indian trails, and after 1800, on crude roads to Philadelphia, Baltimore, Charleston, and lesser trade centers. Bulky corn, wheat, and other regional products were not worth enough to ship overland, but whiskey and some produce flowed out of Knoxville in slow-moving, mule-drawn wagons. Knoxville was also the center for a flourishing droving business. Cowboys drove vast herds of cattle, swine, horses, mules, sheep, goats, and even turkey and geese from Knoxville feed lots to the aforementioned coastal cities, and after cotton began to surge in the early 1800s, to markets in the lower South. Drovers had the advantage of a product that carried itself to distant markets, and their business generated demand for feedstuffs and fodder and many related business opportunities in Knoxville. But, like the celebrated cattle trade of the post–Civil War West, East Tennessee's droving business was more colorful than profitable. In sum, East Tennessee's relative isolation did provide Knoxville with some temporary benefits: these conditions assured sufficient economic success to allow pretentious antebellum Knoxvillians to feel superior to folks in the surrounding hinterland. But by the middle third of the nineteenth century, changes in the broader national economy and the natural limits within East Tennessee's relatively self-contained economy weakened Knoxville economically and politically. In turn, these misfortunes strained Knoxville's relations with those same rural neighbors.

Knoxville's political fortunes paralleled its economic interests. During the founding era of the 1790s, Knoxville enjoyed prestige and considerable economic importance as capital of the Southwest Territory, and later as Tennessee's first state capital. Moreover, the presence of U.S. troops in these early years not only saved Knoxville from devastating Indian attacks but also enhanced many local businesses, setting a pattern of dependency on federal funding (an often begrudged East Tennessee hallmark). Likewise, Blount's initial identification with the Federalists who dominated national politics in the 1790s gave the city a sense of mainstream status that continued after 1800, when Knoxville and greater East Tennessee—like much of the rest of the nation—shifted political support to the Jeffersonians. But these advantages proved illusory and short-lived.

By the first decade of the nineteenth century, Indians no longer threatened either East or Middle Tennesseans, a change that allowed the latter to fully

East Tennessee Beginnings

benefit from their subregion's physical advantages. One early observer reported that the Cumberland Basin was to East Tennessee as "the fertile plains of Flanders [were] to the barren deserts of Africa."[5] This natural advantage allowed Middle Tennessee permanently to surpass its eastern neighbor in population, prosperity, and relative importance within the state. After 1810, Tennessee had a nomadic state capital, as Knoxville lost and regained that political plum to Middle Tennessee rivals several times, before Nashville garnered that distinction permanently in 1826. Moreover, American successes in the war that broke out with Great Britain and its Indian allies in 1812 opened to settlement Indian lands in West Tennessee and in the lower South and Midwest, spurring the nation's transition toward a commercial economy, developments that further set back the interests of Knoxvillians and East Tennesseans. Ironically, the latter were among the war's most enthusiastic supporters. In the ensuing years, the limitations of Knoxville–East Tennessee became increasingly apparent, and farsighted observers advocated economic reforms including, most prominently, a transportation remedy for Knoxville's relative geographical isolation. The much-ballyhooed 1828 arrival of the steamboat *Atlas* in Knoxville ultimately proved disappointing, and steam transport between Knoxville and the Mississippi system did not become regular until the 1840s. Meanwhile railroad promotion and attempts to modernize East Tennessee agriculture and other aspects of its intraregional economy enjoyed minimal success. Less apparent at the time were seeds of discord between Knoxville and its rural neighbors sown by these developments, but these seeds germinated in the prewar era to become yet another defining East Tennessee characteristic. Periodic outbreaks of yellow fever and cholera further set back Knoxville's fortunes and morale. All of this contributed to the city's laggard population growth. In 1795, Knox County had 11,573 residents; thirty-five years later, its population had grown to only 14,498. Meanwhile, Nashville and surrounding Middle Tennessee were flourishing.[6]

Despite these setbacks, Knoxvillians in 1842 celebrated the fiftieth anniversary of the city's founding with unusual gusto. Reportedly almost all of the city's two thousand residents participated, and riverboats and stagecoaches brought in countless out-of-town visitors, who joined the all-day festivities. Prolific and lengthy speeches, elaborate banquets, and much drinking highlighted the day's events. Perhaps the hoopla in 1842 was Knoxville's way of deflecting attention from its many misfortunes. But such hindsight obscures an important reality:

5. Quoted in Finger, *Tennessee Frontiers*, 77.

6. Stanley J. Folmsbee, "Growth of Knox County to 1861," in *The French Broad–Holston Country: A History of Knox County, Tennessee*, ed. Mary Utopia Rothrock, 38 (Knoxville: East Tennessee Historical Society, 1946).

even as their world was rapidly moving into a new market economy, many antebellum Americans still envisioned their nation as an agrarian republic and clung to Jeffersonian ideals. By this standard, many Knoxvillians and East Tennesseans still thought of themselves as "mainstream." The optimism they displayed in the 1842 festivities reflected that assumption.

Cades Cove: An Atypical Representative Mountain Community

Even as countless migrants passed through Knoxville, and many East Tennesseans left the region for greener pastures after the War of 1812, the Appalachian subregion still had land available in the smaller valleys, coves, and hollows branching from the greater Tennessee Valley. In these hinterlands, many little settlements emerged in the middle years of the nineteenth century, offering land and hope to potential yeomen. Included among these new communities were Cades Cove, nestled in the folds of the Great Smokes, and a string of hardscrabble settlements in the Clearfork Valley.

For tourists and casual observers, scenic Cades Cove has long typified frontier Appalachia. Its primitive log cabins and pristine setting conjure nostalgic, romantic images—notions historian Durwood Dunn sought to dispel. While it is true that this wide and fertile mountain cove was far more attractive and advantageous for settlers than many settings "just over the next ridge," Cades Cove can serve as an important example of life in the lands surrounding the Great Smokies and other East Tennessee locales, where farming was a vital means of livelihood throughout most of the nineteenth century. Dunn's portrayal of antebellum Cove life is the most thorough correction yet completed of popular notions associated with "pioneer Appalachia."

Cades Cove is located in easternmost Blount County, near its boundary with Sevier County. As their names suggest, both counties were organized in East Tennessee's founding era. White Americans visited this locale at the foot of the Smokies in the mid-1780s, around the time James White established his outpost on the Tennessee River. By 1800, with the Indian threat diminishing and the best lands in the greater Tennessee Valley already claimed, settlers migrated to the southeast, making permanent homes in these rolling foothills. Cherokees had long inhabited this domain, naming the large, U-shaped valley we know as Cades Cove "Tsiyahi," the otter place. Some natives remained in 1818, when the Cove's first, permanent European settlers, John and Lucretia Oliver, arrived. The Olivers' story followed a pattern familiar in the annals of the American frontier. John was raised in Carter County (the upper East Tennessee domain of my own maternal ancestors). Even at this early juncture, good land there had become scarce, and John as a young man worked as a collier. Wartime disruptions created an opportunity for Oliver, as they would for many future young East Tennesseans. In 1814, he returned home from serving under Andrew Jackson in the East Tennessee militia at the Battle of Horseshoe Bend. Oliver's swagger and confidence reflected broader regional and national sentiments in the unlikely aftermath of what is best described as "the second war for American independence." Eager for land of his own, John in the fall of 1818 responded to an overture from Carter County neighbor and land speculator William Tipton, who claimed the large, scenic cove surrounded by the Smokies, even though it was still technically Cherokee land.

John, Lucretia, and an infant daughter spent their first night in the Cove in an abandoned Indian hut. Constructing a crude log cabin was their first task. That first year, when they were the only Caucasians in the Cove, aid from sympathetic Cherokee neighbors saved the Olivers from starvation. To be sure, isolation and independence characterized this pioneer phase in the Cove's history, but the Olivers' experiences were hardly romantic, and frontier conditions quickly passed. When John cleared fields the following spring, he learned he had chosen his new home well: this was a fertile, well-watered valley. The surrounding forests provided fuel and timber for shelter and abundant game to supplement John's farming. By the early 1820s, numerous Carter County relatives and friends joined the Olivers, and Cades Cove became a flourishing, dynamic mountain community. From the beginning, the fertile valley soil assured relative prosperity, attracting a diverse array of settlers. Collectively, Cove residents shared values—a sense of egalitarianism, love of land, commitment to community, and openness to change—that improved their chances for survival and enhanced their wellbeing. As Dunn reminds us, most antebellum Americans shared this "system of values."

Indeed, Dunn's thorough analysis of Cove life in the pre–Civil War years dispels practically every assumption about frontier Appalachia. Yes, the Cove was initially remote, but its isolation was never absolute, and it diminished quickly as ambitious farmers and entrepreneurs transformed a web of Indian trails into roads suitable for wagon traffic. Natural avenues directed Cove residents away from nearby western North Carolina and toward the Tennessee valley, connecting them in turn to distant markets in Pennsylvania, New York, and the lower South. By 1860, five roads passed through the Cove; the two used most regularly carried travelers, news, and commerce to and from nearby Maryville and more distant Knoxville. Nature itself provided Cove residents with some of their most valuable trade items and sources of cash income, including chestnuts, ginseng, grains, vegetables, and especially apples, which made their way to Knoxville and beyond, as did Cove-produced eggs, butter, honey, and molasses. Natural balds in the surrounding mountains became attractive to valley cattlemen from as far away as Knoxville, and a seasonal herding-grazing enterprise quickly developed, bringing profits and regular outside contacts to Cove residents. Harbingers of developments associated with other locales and a later era also appeared in these early years. Prominent Cove entrepreneur Daniel Foute was instrumental in establishing both a flourishing iron smelting enterprise and a "resort hotel and spa" in nearby Montvale Springs. Foreshadowing future trends, occasional tourists praised the Cove's scenic beauty, touting it as a potential escape from frenzied routines elsewhere. Settlers of varied backgrounds and outlooks came and went from the Cove. This diversity and the Cove's relative prosperity assured those who stayed access to new farming technologies and miscellaneous household goods. By 1850, frame houses were replacing log cabins as the preferred form of residence.

Collectively, prosperity fostered among Cades Cove residents a relatively progressive worldview, influenced in large part by an essentially Calvinist Baptist faith. Although a decided preference for the self-defined "primitive" wing of this

This twentieth-century photograph of the Elijah Oliver Home in Cades Cove clearly reflects Appalachian proclivities for selective acculturation. The original home was constructed around 1830, but the kitchen at the back of the structure and front porch were added later. In the early twentieth century, when many Cove families supplemented their incomes by catering to a burgeoning tourist trade, the far side of the front porch was enclosed to provide accommodations for guests. (Great Smoky Mountains National Park Photo Library and Archives.)

loose-knit congregational persuasion might appear to suggest otherwise, Cove Baptists in the pre–Civil War years were aware of and debated issues widespread in the broader church and antebellum society. The Primitive Baptist insistence on local autonomy and limited clerical authority placed them in the main current of the robust religiosity that the Second Great Awakening fueled throughout the broader United States. Most important, that religiosity fostered a community spirit that ran counter to popular notions about "Appalachian individualism." As the Cove's "invisible government," the church "had more power over the community than either civil authorities, political parties, or prominent entrepreneurs."[7] Indeed, the resulting Cove social order approximated the Jeffersonian ideals of limited government and of a self-disciplining, egalitarian society more nearly than did other antebellum communities, where dimly understood commercial development rendered those ideals fragile.

In sum, life in Cades Cove at mid-century was generally comfortable and positive, although certainly not idyllic. Much like the Cherokee they pushed from this rich setting, Cove residents knew that both benefits and costs accompany change. But, like many Cherokees and most antebellum Americans, Cove residents approached this universal opportunity (and dilemma) with a pragmatism that sought to both preserve the best of the old and reap benefits from the new. And they realized far more clearly than many subsequent observers that selective embracement of the latter could enhance the former. Hindsight suggests that residents of Cades Cove in the middle years of the nineteenth century were better equipped to approximate inherited American ideals than were many of their East Tennessee neighbors.

Early Settlement in the Clearfork Valley

Later in this book, I will periodically highlight notable similarities in the histories of Cades Cove and my third representative East Tennessee community—a string of settlements in the Clearfork Valley roughly paralleling the Tennessee-Kentucky border. Yet a number of contrasts are more immediately obvious. Whereas the Clearfork Valley was the focus of one of the first and most provocative scholarly analyses of Appalachia's industrial era (ca. 1870–1930, and part II of this book), its antebellum history still awaits a chronicler comparable to Durwood Dunn. In the absence of an in-depth scholarly analysis (and, to be fair, of the types of primary resources that make such possible), serious and dedicated popular scholars perpetuate images of the frontier phase in the Clearfork

7. Durwood Dunn, *Cades Cove: The Life and Death of a Southern Appalachian Community, 1818–1937* (Knoxville: Univ. of Tennessee Press, 1988), 99, 111.

that Dunn refutes for Cades Cove. As just one example, the best popular study presently available of the Clearfork, tells us:

> The early people in the Clearfork Valley were extremely isolated . . . [and] made their livings from tending the fields and preserving their foods. They had plenty of timber for their cabins and crude furniture . . . trees furnished heat for warmth, animals from the mountains and fish from the river supplemented the food supply . . . They [the settlers] remained in the Valley, intermarried with neighboring families, and expected little more than a living . . . Life went on in the Clearfork—if it was not always perfect, it was simple.[8]

This is undoubtedly an accurate snapshot of the region in its frontier phase, but that phase was temporary (as it was in Cades Cove and the greater United States), and the Clearfork's early history was likely more complex than imagined. In the absence of more analytical studies of the Clearfork communities, knowledge about East Tennessee's broader history, and studies of similar locales in other parts of the greater Appalachian region, offers glimpses of a more dynamic and ultimately less romantic past.

Permanent settlement did not come to Clearfork until relatively late in East Tennessee's history, but early long hunters (including Daniel Boone) were acquainted with the area before settlement in even upper East Tennessee. But, after Boone discovered a route to the Kentucky bluegrass through the Cumberland Gap (near the headwaters of the Clearfork River), prospective settlers bypassed the Clearfork until more attractive lands in the Tennessee Valley, Kentucky, and even Middle Tennessee, began to fill up. Today, Tennessee's portion of the Clearfork Valley stretches east to west across Claiborne and Campbell counties. The latter counties were established in the early 1800s by settlers who found more fertile valley lands around Knoxville no longer available or affordable. As was the case with Cades Cove and the Smokies' foothills to the southeast of the Great Valley, the wider hollows and bottomlands of this more rugged land to the northwest attracted settlers first. More remote settlements, like those in the Clearfork, typified what early Appalachian scholar Cratis Williams called "branchwater communities." They drew few permanent settlers until well after the War of 1812.

Risking environmental determinism, one must assert that a hardscrabble geography above all else shaped early history in the Clearfork. In contrast to fertile, U-shaped Cades Cove, the Clearfork is a V-shaped valley that cuts a jagged path through the Cumberland Plateau. The Clearfork's thin soils, cooler temperatures, and steep terrain challenged the heartiest farmer to attain even a

8. Bonnie Page, *Clearfork and More* (Lake City, TN: B. M. Page, 1986), 8.

semi-subsistence existence. The Clearfork belongs to what economic historian Paul Salstrom insightfully distinguishes as "newer Appalachia," a region still in the preindustrial stage of development when ravages from the Civil War disrupted East Tennessee. The Clearfork was never completely isolated from the outside, and existing evidence reveals some commercial contact with Knoxville and beyond. But its geographical limitations forced most early farmers to scramble to provide for their families. By the time of the Civil War, the second generation's equitable division of farmlands among typically large numbers of heirs, and the overuse of inherently limited soils, foreshadowed a crisis in the making. After the war, when Clearfork residents sold timber and coal rights to eager entrepreneurs and then sold their labor for extraction of those resources, the crisis became full blown. Salstrom calls this set of circumstances "the roots of Appalachian dependency."

It is important to acknowledge that only hindsight illumines these distinct patterns. Until thorough scholarship reveals otherwise, it appears that Clearfork residents in around 1840 thought of themselves as "typical." To be sure, they had to work harder to sustain themselves than did many folks in Knoxville, farmers in the Great Valley, or even Cades Cove's yeomen. But many of them either owned land or held out expectations that they would inherit land or gain it through some other means. For those who saw these dreams as illusory, there was always land in "the West." And for those who were not to be farmers, employment prospects beckoned in Knoxville or other more burgeoning urban centers. For antebellum Americans as a whole, such optimism masked a narrowing spectrum of economic opportunities that would have frightened a less sanguine people. For many East Tennesseans, these prospects eventually became painful realities. Early obliviousness to these future travails made residents of the Clearfork, most East Tennesseans, and many other residents of the southern mountains, representative of their time and nation. Assertions that they were "aberrant Appalachians" would have made no sense to them.

Appalachia in the Making

This chapter began with East Tennessee's Native Americans and considered how the "coming of civilization" fostered significant changes in Cherokee life. Responses to those challenges and opportunities fostered division and discord among the Cherokee. By around 1840, most of the Cherokees, whether they embraced or rejected the white man's ways, had been forced to abandon ancestral lands, including a small corner of southeast Tennessee. Ironically, East Tennessee land speculators and yeoman who agitated for removal found themselves, even before the Trail of Tears, facing a host of strikingly similar dilemmas. Chapter two will examine those struggles and suggest that, while avoiding removal, many white East Tennesseans suffered results that their earlier Cherokee neighbors and adversaries would have found familiar.

Scholars considering these developments a century and a half later have engaged in similarly divisive debates. Revisionist scholarship has become so persuasive that many Appalachianists and scholars in general have abandoned the long-influential "yeoman thesis," which argued that small-scale, independent subsistence farmers were the primary actors in this historical story. Even my Berea College mentor and good friend Richard Drake, the yeoman thesis's most vocal and persistent exponent among Appalachianists, has qualified his argument. Land-ownership statistics reveal that by the middle of the nineteenth century, yeoman-like conditions were in decline in East Tennessee. But an even closer look at East Tennessee in the context of broader U.S. patterns cautions against totally jettisoning the yeoman thesis. Indeed, evidence suggests that as long as the possibility of graduating from poverty to a yeoman competency continued, as it did for some whites at least until the aftermath of Cherokee removal, the ideal remained powerful. Paradoxically, as that possibility became less of a reality, many East Tennesseans, along with other Americans, embraced it with even greater intensity. One may attribute this apparent contradiction to a linkage between nostalgia and cynicism (even hypocrisy), but ideals so powerful and admirable that they still endure into our very different twenty-first century doubtlessly also contributed to this outlook. Most likely both factors led antebellum East Tennesseans to cling to—and consider themselves exemplars of—the yeoman ideal. This affirmation served several useful purposes, first deflecting attention from growing wealth gaps within the region and between East Tennessee and other parts of the antebellum United States, and then, in turn, reassuring regional residents that they were part of the national mainstream. Herein lies an important clue for understanding East Tennessee's elusive past and the elusive identity of the greater Appalachian region: when East Tennesseans left behind their pioneer era in the middle third of the nineteenth century, these convenient rationales became increasingly questionable.

Chapter Two

Mid-Nineteenth-Century Crises:
From Mainstream to Margin in East Tennessee

East Tennesseans experienced extraordinary devastation and miseries from the traumatic events that wracked the United States in the middle decades of the nineteenth century. Sectional tensions, secession, and the call to arms in 1861 fragmented an already divided people. The strategic importance of the Tennessee Valley for both Union and Confederacy led to countless skirmishes and several extended battle campaigns that bloodied East Tennessee soil. Feeding two ravenous armies devastated thriving Valley farms, and when the conflict stalemated, violence penetrated even remote hollows in the Smokies and branch-water communities of the Clearfork Valley. Wartime anger and atrocities fueled a cycle of vengeance that ensnared even the most innocent East Tennesseans. Miseries continued after hostilities officially ceased when an unlikely sequence of events brought East Tennessean Andrew Johnson to the White House. But the accidental president proved ill-prepared for challenges that had severely tested the martyred Lincoln. Following impeachment and near-removal from office, Johnson returned to East Tennessee in 1869, only to learn that his homeland's misfortunes mirrored his own.

Because devastation, discord, and distrust lingered in postwar East Tennessee, "the war" became *the* explanation for grinding poverty, feuding, suspicion of others, and a host of other alleged "Appalachian" ills. Yet thirty years of Appalachian studies scholarship suggest that the war was only the last in a series of setbacks that in the middle years of the nineteenth century began to push the greater Appalachian region from the nation's mainstream to its margins. Making sense of these mounting misfortunes requires acknowledgment of "the law of unintended consequences," recognition that developments within and beyond the region intertwined, and, most important, rejection of convenient diagnoses that exclusively blame villainous outsiders or deficient natives for all that went wrong. Two of history's most powerful, unforgiving, and relentless forces—geography and timing—were particularly unkind to East Tennessee well before war forged even more apparent miseries.

Large Families and Harsh Realities

Evidence that some regional miseries took root in traditions that most frontier-era East Tennesseans and Americans deemed essential reveals just how unkind fate can be. In the Tennessee backcountry, large families provided needed labor and a form of social security. Anecdotal evidence of this demographic hallmark of frontier East Tennessee abounds. Regional patriarch John Sevier, for example, fathered ten children with a first wife and eight more with a second. Nicholas and Mary Gibbs (my four-times great-grandparents) brought thirteen children when they began farming north of Knoxville in 1792. Their youngest son, Daniel, and his wife Sallie (née Sharp, the next in line of my direct Gibbs forebears), birthed twelve children between 1808 and 1835. Of those twelve, ten reached adulthood and married, and in turn, produced families averaging just under seven children per household.

Large families were, of course, typical for the broader American society of the day. Indeed, abandoning the Old World tradition of primogeniture and distributing one's assets in a roughly equal fashion among all male heirs became a defining hallmark of the young American republic. However, as previous discussions have shown, after two or three generations, the practice of partible inheritance produced a chain reaction: shrinking farms, ever more intensive use of those dwindling acres, declining productivity, and ultimately, poverty and despair. This pattern became particularly pronounced in less geographically blessed locales, such as East Tennessee and the broader Appalachian region, where hardscrabble farming, privation, and other distinctive "Appalachian" traits began to appear well before the mid-nineteenth century.

The admittedly limited scholarship on antebellum East Tennessee informing this study confirms this assertion in general, even as it suggests the effects of partible inheritance varied from place to place and over time. Mark Groover's exhaustive examination of three generations of my Gibbs forebears reveals they possessed valuable material goods (e.g., pewter ware and fine china), raised impressive livestock herds, and produced abundant crops. The Gibbs's good fortune, however, does not necessarily negate the negative effects of partible inheritance in antebellum East Tennessee. As I explored in more detail in the introduction to this section, from the days of clan patriarch Nicholas Gibbs to the era of the Civil War, the Gibbs estate dwindled, through subdivision of property, from 1,300 acres to less than 200. Still, my Gibbs forebears fared better than many of their nineteenth-century East Tennessee neighbors.

Another angle for assessing the impact of large families on the overall well-being of antebellum East Tennesseans is to consider partible inheritance's effects in this book's "three representative communities." For an urban community such as Knoxville, the issue might appear relatively unimportant, but there can be little doubt that this broader demographic concern indirectly affected the region's economic hub in complex, often contradictory ways. Hard times in hinterland areas by the 1840s led some rural folk to seek employment and other opportunities in Knoxville, where manufacturing was beginning to flourish. Although this influx of rural émigrés assuredly brought benefits to Knoxville, some city residents displayed characteristic disdain for the newcomers. The editor of the *Knoxville Gazette*, for example, reported in 1846 that poor, ragged men were "seen everyday lounging on [Knoxville's] street corners."[1] This situation resulted (at least partly) from misfortunes in other East Tennessee locales.

Large families were, to be sure, customary in antebellum Cades Cove. But Durwood Dunn persuasively argues that the years between settlement in 1819 and the Civil War were the Cove's "golden age." Rich soils earned cash income that, along with a fluid population, encouraged outside influences and produced a relatively progressive society that in many ways typified antebellum America. Cove residents often joined other Americans in migrating westward, and new arrivals often invigorated the Cove's population and culture. In the 1850s, decreases in population led to increased farm sizes and unprecedented prosperity. In short, before the Civil War, Cades Cove offered few signs of the overcrowding, cultural inbreeding, and abuse of farmlands that recent general histories of Appalachia attribute to partible inheritance. Here, however, one is wise to recall Dunn's warning about drawing broader generalizations from Cades Cove's history. Indeed, a look at other antebellum East Tennessee hinterlands during this era suggests that Cades Cove's good fortunes, like those of my Gibbs forebears, were as aberrant as they were temporary.

Although we still await systematic scholarly analysis of the communities of the Clearfork Valley for the antebellum years, Paul Salstrom's general hypothesis about "newer Appalachia" offers plausible insights into what might have transpired along the Clearfork in the years leading to the Civil War. Salstrom's "newer Appalachia" is the region of the Cumberland-Allegheny Plateau where "Appalachian" geographic disadvantages—steep terrain, poor soils, and isolation from markets—are most pronounced. The cycle of partible inheritance was also particularly devastating there. But Salstrom's most important assertion is that historical timing cemented newer Appalachia's woes. As his label suggests, areas such as the Clearfork Valley were not settled until more attractive lands in the Tennessee Valley—and more advantaged hinterland locations such as Cades Cove—had filled up. Moreover, unlike the latter, the Clearfork was settled after 1830, when lands elsewhere in East Tennessee, and in the nation as a whole,

1. Quoted in Dunaway, *First American Frontier*, 189.

were becoming more scarce and expensive. With opportunities to migrate else-where diminishing, settlers pushed ever farther up creek beds and V-shaped hollows. In these locales, even the most hardworking farm families experienced disappointing results. After a few productive years when their land was newly settled, between around 1840 and 1860 newer Appalachia's farmers experienced decreased crop yields and livestock production. Meanwhile, population in newer Appalachia grew 62 percent in the 1840s and 49 percent in the 1850s.[2] These harsh realities, Salstrom asserts, sowed seeds for discord and ill will within East Tennessee, exacerbated longstanding tensions that divided East from Middle and West Tennessee, and widened the gap between the Appalachian South and the rest of the burgeoning antebellum United States. This was "Appalachia in the making," but the blur of historical events and the fact that not all East Tennesseans shared in these misfortunes temporarily blinded both regional residents and outsiders to that unpleasant fate.

Manifest Destinies

Large families and the tradition of partible inheritance were hardly the only preferred features of life in early East Tennessee that went awry. The very arrival of settlers in the Tennessee Valley in the late 1700s reflected another such trait, mobility, which was hardly unique to East Tennessee. Throughout the first half of the nineteenth century, East Tennesseans not only cleared new lands of their own, but also supported, with their votes and their lives, policies assuring access to more land beyond the region. This, East Tennesseans and antebellum Americans instinctively knew, was essential to the Jeffersonian ideals most of them embraced. The aggressive Indian policy culminating in removal, for example, opened up Cades Cove, the Clearfork Valley, other remote parts of East Tennessee, and of course, more distant lands. Contributions from East Tennessee "war hawks" in Congress and volunteers on battlefields were vital to American successes in the War of 1812, which opened Indian lands in West Tennessee, the lower South, and the Midwest for settlement. By the 1820s, those lands became stepping-stones across the Mississippi to Missouri, Louisiana, and Mexican-held Texas. Tennesseans, of course, played prominent roles in Texas independence in 1836, and when President James K. Polk went after more Mexican land a decade later, Tennesseans flocked to the front in numbers that made "the Volunteer" their state's enduring symbol.

2. Paul Salstrom, *Appalachia's Path to Dependency: Rethinking a Region's Economic History, 1730–1940* (Lexington: Univ. Press of Kentucky, 1994), 13–19. Salstrom explains these developments in greater detail in that book's chapters 1 and 2.

Appalachian scholars typically use the term "out-migration" to refer to the movement of large numbers of regional residents to urban centers of the North and Midwest from the early days of World War II to around 1970, and emphasize the negative effects of this demographic shift. Yet Appalachianists to date have devoted little attention to the even more prolonged movement of humans within, through, and beyond the mountain South in the first half of the nineteenth century, and have rarely questioned conventional wisdom emphasizing the positive effects of this development. Both anecdotal accounts and census figures reveal the magnitude of this demographic upheaval. Sam Houston and Davy Crockett were only the best known of many East Tennesseans identified with the popular acronym of the day: "GTT"—gone to Texas. Countless other East Tennesseans went west: gold fever enticed the affluent, quixotic Knoxvillian Hugh Heiskell to California in 1849. Heiskell's diary recounts a remarkably pleasant journey across the plains and Sierra Nevadas, but ends abruptly when he succumbed to fever in a Sacramento Valley mining camp. Joseph Reddeford Walker has received more historical attention than Heiskell. Born in Roane County in 1798, Walker, like many young East Tennesseans of the day, became a young adult in Missouri, and by the early 1820s was engaged in the Santa Fe trade. Over the next half-century, Walker was a mountain man, fur trapper, and trailblazer extraordinaire. Perhaps the first white American to see Yosemite Valley, he helped blaze the trail that Heiskell and countless other pioneers followed to California. Walker prospected for gold in California and Arizona and then returned to California, where he ranched until his death in 1876. The exploits of Walker's brothers further reveal East Tennesseans' significant roles in "the winning of the West": one brother died defending the Alamo and the other two followed Joseph to Arizona and California.

The Walker family may have been exceptional, but many present-day East Tennesseans can point to ancestors lured away by the West who never returned to East Tennessee. A genealogist from Campbell County (at the western end of the Clearfork Valley) recently chronicled her forebears' sequential journeys from Tennessee to Missouri in the 1820s, to California in the 1850s, and Oregon in the 1870s. A perusal of the genealogical record of my own direct line of the Gibbs family reveals a similar penchant for mobility. In the years on either side of the Civil War, children and grandchildren of Daniel Gibbs ended up in Kansas, Oregon, Missouri, and Iowa, as well as various locations in Tennessee.

Because almost no attention has been given to how Manifest Destiny and out-migration affected antebellum East Tennessee, we are left with the popular assumption that it was beneficial. That conclusion reflects more about the power of the frontier myth than about East Tennessee realities. Of course, there is evidence—for example in Dunn's assertions regarding 1850s' Cades Cove—that

Like the more famous Sam Houston, Roane County native Joseph Walker was one of many native East Tennesseans who caught "Manifest Destiny fever" and abandoned the land of his birth for Missouri and subsequently more western locales in the middle years of the nineteenth century. Artist Alfred Jacob Miller included this and several other portrayals of Walker in a collection of fur-trade-era paintings. (Courtesy of Joslyn Art Museum of Omaha, Nebraska.)

out-migration temporarily stemmed tensions created by the cycle of partible inheritance. Similarly, Salstrom's suggestion that Appalachian areas settled prior to around 1830 experienced fewer problems than newer Appalachia—because their surplus populations could more readily migrate elsewhere—seemingly confirms historian Frederick Jackson Turner's "safety valve" thesis. But evidence of a brain drain in third world regions in our own times should cause us to question the long-range validity of such assertions. The career of Tyler Heiskell, who accompanied his cousin, Hugh Heiskell, the Knoxville forty-niner, to California, offers anecdotal affirmation for this premise. After Hugh's death, Tyler wrote home in 1850, "I would rather see a Knoxville paper than find an ounce of gold." Yet the homesick Tennessean never made East Tennessee his home again. He was elected to the California legislature in 1856 and spent the remaining forty years of his life in the Golden State. The same was true of the talented Joseph Walker, described as "a man of limited education [but] one of the most intelligent men to explore the West."[3] In both cases, California's gains came at East

3. Gordon B. Dodds, "Joseph Reddeford Walker," in *The Reader's Encyclopedia of the American West*, ed. Howard Lamar, 1233 (New York: Thomas Y. Crowell and Company, 1977).

Tennessee's expense. Texas similarly benefited from native East Tennessean Sam Houston; by the turbulent 1850s, his home region sorely needed the Texas statesman's wisdom and patience.

Modernity and Its Costs

Historical timing compounded the effects of partible inheritance and out-migration. Less romantic but more powerful and enduring developments, which simultaneously challenged antebellum Americans (albeit in more subtle ways), included economic modernization and a new, more democratic approach to politics and governance. Together these powerful forces exacerbated deep-rooted sectional divisions and fueled crises of epic proportions. We should not be surprised that in East Tennessee, which had lost many of its most talented native sons—and faced internal woes of its own—events mirrored and sometimes magnified these national struggles.

Economic modernization is such a pervasive and dimly understood force that historians still struggle to explain its origins and grasp its effects. Moreover, modernity's cultural twin, the ideal of progress, holds a powerful sway on the American imagination. Like the mythical "West," modernity and progress defy informed explanations and color popular recollections of our past in ways that both elevate and deceive. In the current context, "modernization" refers specifically to the "market revolution" that swept across the United States after around 1815. Of course some Americans, such as planters of the Tidewater South, produced for distant markets even in colonial times. But until the War of 1812, the American commercial economy remained largely an appendage to Europe. The fortuitous and temporary convergence of an array of forces during and after that war, including increased national pride and cohesion, more favorable federal fiscal policies, availability of new sources of capital and new lands, and a transportation revolution, forged the surge in production for domestic markets that is our present concern.

These developments occurred simultaneously with the maturation of settlement in much of East Tennessee and southern Appalachia. Not surprisingly, the triumphal and traumatic events transpiring during this era of change have long been overlooked, and regional scholars have only begun to consider them. The traditional, still widely accepted view is that until the Civil War the region was the domain of small-scale subsistence producers who were isolated and lacked access to outside markets. Recent scholarship, however, reveals that isolation in East Tennessee and broader Appalachia was relative and never absolute, that many antebellum farmers and businesspeople produced for markets and traded outside the region, and that cities—including Knoxville—emerged to expedite commerce with distant markets. Relatively rich soils and natural (though inadequate) transportation avenues made the East Tennessee Valley better suited for the market revolution than the mountain and plateau regions on its east and west. Hence valley farmers, such as my own Gibbs forebears, enjoyed relative prosperity, and even more remote, agriculturally blessed locales, such as Cades Cove, initially flourished in the new market economy.

Ironically, the same forces that accelerated the market revolution in the broader United States following the War of 1812 fostered ominous consequences for East Tennessee's agrarian capitalists. By the 1820s, former Indian lands in the Midwest became flourishing farms producing corn, wheat, swine, horses, mules and cattle, all staples of the early East Tennessee economy. Steeper terrain, thinner soils, and the effects in many locations of at least a generation of cultivation left East Tennessee farmers at a competitive disadvantage. Moreover, navigable rivers and newly constructed canals and railroads gave midwestern farmers closer proximity and more affordable access to domestic urban markets. East Tennessee farmers compensated for these new realities by shifting the focus of their trade away from traditional markets in Philadelphia and Baltimore to the lower South, where former Indian lands, also opened up by the War of 1812, became "the Cotton Kingdom." Thus, by around 1840, much of East Tennessee's grains, pork, beef, horses, and mules fed slaves and enhanced the fortunes of the South's powerful planter elite. This economic shift eventually had ominous consequences for East Tennessee.

Even though the instinctive economic pursuit of early East Tennesseans was farming, early observers recognized potential for manufacturing and development of other regional raw materials. Spurred by changes in the broader national economy and the struggles of regional farmers, farsighted East Tennesseans envisioned development of regional resources, including timber, iron, copper, and coal. To be sure, inadequate local capital and markets impeded these prospects, but by around 1850, East Tennessee had far more small-scale industry than popular notions about the region suggest. Mountain barriers to the region's east and west and the limitations of the Tennessee River as a year-round outlet for hauling heavy freight most seriously limited further development of the region's natural endowments. Hence, when completion of a long-awaited Chattanooga-to-Bristol railroad increased access to the outside world in 1858, entrepreneurs who were already tapping East Tennessee raw materials for local markets believed they were on the cusp of even greater success and prosperity. But then came the Civil War.

Before I address the war itself, a closer look into the mindset of East Tennessee railroad promoters will offer glimpses into why outsiders, and some insiders, began by the middle years of the nineteenth century to think of Appalachia as aberrant. The railroad crusade was only the most vocal of several efforts to alleviate regional ills that brought attention to the region after 1830. As East Tennessee's fortunes declined, both altruistic and entrepreneurial impulses drove antebellum East Tennesseans to advocate an array of reforms and adjustments. This is hardly surprising; both capitalist innovation and reform were hallmarks of the broader antebellum society. Moreover, historians have long noted diverse, sometimes contradictory, motives among those who sought to correct the nation's shortcomings. In addition, reform rhetoric sometimes fostered unintended—and occasionally harmful—consequences for the intended beneficiaries.

Like many reformers (and many subsequent altruists who would strive to uplift Appalachia), David Deaderick walked a fine line between raising alarm about regional ills and proving that East Tennessee was capable of improvement. An entry in his diary in 1825 reported, for example, that public violence, drunkenness, and other "uncivilized" behavior had diminished in the region since the frontier era. Moreover, even when he acknowledged the region's relative disadvantages in comparison to Middle and West Tennessee and to the Midwest, Deaderick asserted that East Tennesseans were more moral and less smitten with the "wealth fever" that he believed produced undesirable traits in many antebellum Americans. If East Tennesseans could overcome their own shortcomings, Deaderick optimistically concluded, the region could become the stable, sustainable society a republic demanded.[4]

Deaderick agreed with many other regional reformers that agricultural improvement was a key first step in uplifting East Tennessee. Few regional farmers, he lamented, rotated crops or made use of manure as a natural fertilizer, and he described plowing as "generally badly done." The *Tennessee Farmer*, published in Jonesborough through much of the 1830s, echoed Deaderick's concerns. One column addressed out-migration from East Tennessee, suggesting that destructive farming methods made distant pastures greener. In both 1840 and 1850, regional farms were producing about three hundred bushels of soil-exhausting corn for every ton of hay. By contrast, farmers in the more prosperous Valley of Virginia in the same years planted a greater variety of crops and produced only thirty-six bushels of corn for every ton of hay. The two regions offered similarly contrasting patterns in livestock production. The ratio of swine (voracious corn consumers) to cattle in East Tennessee was 4.2 to 1, compared to 1.6 to 1 in the Valley of Virginia. In 1854, a former governor of Tennessee bluntly observed that fifty years of shortsighted farming practices in East Tennessee left "the best meadowlands

4. Samuel C. Williams, ed., "Journal of Events (1825–1873) of David A. Deaderick," *East Tennessee Historical Society Publications* 8 (1936): 126–30.

unreclaimed."[5] Sadly, however well intentioned they were, the reformers' depictions of traditional regional farmers helped to sow the seeds for what ultimately became sweeping, generalized images of "ignorant, short-sighted Appalachian farmers" and a "backward, needy, but deserving Appalachia."[6]

Entrepreneurially inclined reformers emphasized that an improved transportation system able to overcome longstanding geographical barriers and link East Tennessee to larger markets was *the* panacea for the subregion's longstanding ills. Of course, improved roads, enhanced navigation on the Tennessee River, and ultimately, a regional railroad system, were all expensive undertakings, requiring both private support within the region and action from political bodies in distant Nashville and Washington. Like the agrarian reformers, promoters of improved transportation emphasized both East Tennessee's "neediness" and its "potential." But rhetoric driven by economic interests was even more hostile to tradition-minded East Tennesseans than that of the altruists.

From as far back as James White's establishment of his fort on the bluff above the Tennessee River, East Tennesseans—and particularly Knoxvillians—saw the Tennessee as their connection to broader markets and influences. But that link proved as elusive as it was enticing. After meandering south from Knoxville to Muscle Shoals in present-day Alabama, the Tennessee turns abruptly north across West Tennessee, feeding into the Ohio for a short stretch before finally merging into the Mississippi near today's Paducah, Kentucky. In the flatboat era, the downstream journey to New Orleans proved more a respite for bored East Tennessee boaters than a source of financial profit for farmers and manufacturers. Natural impediments—sucks, shoals, and eddies—became more dangerous in the dry season, when the river was low; they were even more ominous on the tributaries feeding into the upper Tennessee: the Holston, French Broad, Clinch, and lesser channels with headwaters in locales such as the Clearfork Valley and the Smokies.

Ever-optimistic East Tennesseans saw steamboats, which began regular navigation on the Mississippi and its larger tributaries in the 1820s, as the remedy for the isolation that held their region back. But even after the *Atlas* successfully navigated Muscle Shoals to make its celebrated 1828 arrival in Knoxville, steamboat traffic on the upper Tennessee was seasonal and erratic. The so-called golden age for Tennessee River steamboats (ca. 1840–1860) spurred Knoxville's emergence as a wholesaling center and temporarily benefited strategically located river communities. Perhaps most important, steamboat traffic complemented the reorientation of East Tennessee commerce to the orbit of the Deep South in the decades leading up to the Civil War. Yet even on the day the *Atlas* arrived in

5. Rothrock, *The French Broad–Holston Country*, 76–77.

6. Williams, "Journal of Events (1825–1873) of David A. Deaderick," 138.

Knoxville, farsighted Knoxvillian Dr. J. G. M. Ramsey urged his fellow East Tennesseans to set their sights on a more promising, exciting, and expensive transportation alternative: the railroad. The energy and effort East Tennesseans devoted to that cause over the next twenty years reveals the power of Ramsey and the railroad's appeal.

Historians often emphasize that the railroad—with its powerful steam engines, extensive utilization of iron and coal, corporate capital–raising structure, and unprecedented profits—is the perfect symbol for the mid- and late-nineteenth-century surge of American industry. If so, East Tennesseans' difficulties in bringing the iron horse to their region was also a harbinger of less sanguine things to come. Those delays, however, did not result from lack of effort. In the 1830s, leading East Tennesseans joined voices and forces with railroad promoters in South Carolina. Conventions in Knoxville in 1831 and 1836 promoted tracks that would have linked Charleston to Cincinnati and the Ohio River via the French Broad valley and Cumberland Gap. The envisioned road would have cemented East Tennessee's emerging economic ties with the lower South and reduced costs for importing goods into the region. At the time, East Tennesseans paid $13,750 to transport $70,000 worth of goods overland from traditional Mid-Atlantic trade partners, a burden the proposed rails promised to reduce. Completion of such a road would make Knoxville "the great commercial center between Charleston and Cincinnati."[7]

By 1833, tracks were laid from Charleston to Augusta, but East Tennessee's persistent nemeses, geographical obstacles and bad timing, halted construction. Engineering through mountainous terrain, rivalries with other cities that challenged Knoxville's presumed preeminence, and the devastating Panic of 1837 all set back the ambitious project. Promotional efforts continued through the 1840s, but Manifest Destiny, war with Mexico, and more aggressive railroad campaigns in other, more favored locales deflected attention from East Tennessee's needs. By the 1850s, when conditions within and beyond the region were more favorable, the South Carolina to Ohio River route was abandoned. Instead, railroad promoters turned to the relatively level and more affordable avenue provided by the Tennessee Valley, which had been the region's primary transportation corridor since Cherokee times. Two initially separate efforts eventually converged in 1858, when the East Tennessee Virginia and Georgia Railroad linked Chattanooga to Bristol via Knoxville. Finally East Tennesseans had affordable transportation both to the Deep South and, it appeared, to its traditional Mid-Atlantic markets. The new railroad, claimed the *Knoxville Register*, "bound together North and South with a bond indisolvable."[8]

7. MacArthur, *Knoxville's History*, 19.

8. Quoted in David C. Hsiung, *Two Worlds in the Tennessee Mountains: Exploring the Origins of Appalachian Stereotypes* (Lexington: Univ. Press of Kentucky, 1997), 158.

The Civil War, of course, quickly severed this bond. But a longer-range view reveals that East Tennessee's successful railroad campaign sowed the seeds for other, less obvious divisions. By the time the ETV&G was completed in 1858, Middle and West Tennessee and their hub cities (Nashville and Memphis) had their own railroad connections to the south Atlantic, Gulf of Mexico, and upper Midwest. But no railway linked Tennessee's three largest cities, and "modern technology reinforced the state's regional distinctiveness."[9]

Historian David Hsiung's suggestion that negative depictions of backcountry Tennesseans had existed since the time of the American Revolution, but that threats from Indian, Spanish, and British enemies temporarily discouraged development of internal divisions and distinctions that might have highlighted those alleged deficiencies, is particularly relevant to this discussion. However, when those common threats diminished after the War of 1812, divisions within East Tennessee deepened. For Hsiung, reform efforts within East Tennessee, particularly increasingly frantic appeals from railroad promoters, gave rise to what became negative regional stereotypes. Regional residents who in the same era moved to more remote locales (such as the Clearfork Valley and hollows in the Smokies beyond well-endowed Cades Cove) where they struggled against the effects of partible inheritance, responded either ambivalently to the railroad cause or opposed it as an expense primarily benefiting residents of the Valley and regional elites. As East Tennessee's status became more precarious, debates over the railroad became rancorous, and regional elites increased verbal denigration of their less-advantaged neighbors. For example, the 1831 *Railroad Advocate* pronounced railroads East Tennessee's "only hope." "Without them," the treatise concluded, "[East Tennessee] will continue to be a depressed, languishing region—too unpromising to invite much capital or enterprise from abroad or to retain that which may grow up in her own bosom." As Hsiung concludes, regional elites and railroad promoters increasingly "saw themselves as an island in a sea of ignorance."[10]

Jacksonian Democracy and East Tennessee's Declining Political Fortunes

East Tennessee's political leaders, from William Blount to Andrew Johnson, were acutely aware of national trends and regularly sought to identify with shifting political persuasions dominating the broader United States. Under the guidance of the ever-pragmatic Blount, East Tennessee leaned Federalist, but after 1800,

9. Finger, *Tennessee Frontiers*, 201.
10. Hsiung, *Two Worlds in the Tennessee Mountains*, 159–61.

East Tennessee's allegiance shifted to the Jeffersonians. When Andrew Jackson emerged from the War of 1812 as a great national hero and as a figurehead of what became the dominant faction of the old Jeffersonian coalition, East Tennesseans saw him as one of their own and embraced Jacksonian Democracy. But by the time an electoral landslide swept Jackson to the presidency in 1828, some East Tennessee Democrats began having second thoughts about the "Old Hero," and more specifically, the regional implication of his brand of politics. Their discontent emerged from petty personal differences (most notably Jackson's feud with regional patriarch John Sevier) and longstanding rivalries between their once-dominant subregion and up-and-coming Middle and West Tennessee.

After the War of 1812, the dominant planter-slavery economies of East Tennessee's rivals emerged arm-in-arm to control state politics. Jackson's strong base in Middle Tennessee at best ignored East Tennessee interests and often advocated policies and divided funds that shortchanged East Tennessee. Moreover, President Jackson's adamant opposition to federally funded internal improvements (e.g., roads, canals, railroads) further angered East Tennesseans, who by the 1830s hungered for funding from any and all sources for railway construction. Consequently, by Jackson's second term, East Tennessee became a Whig stronghold. When Jackson insisted on promoting his loyal ally, Martin Van Buren, to the presidency in 1836, East Tennesseans completely broke ranks, endorsing native son Hugh Lawson White (son of Knoxville's founder) as a Whig candidate. Timing again dealt East Tennessee a weakening blow. Van Buren's electoral victory, soon followed by the Panic of 1837, left East Tennessee not only politically isolated but unable to raise monies for its much-coveted railroad. Indeed, with Middle and West Tennessee Democrats dominating the state government in Nashville, East Tennessee did not receive even its fair share for two of the primary uses of state monies at that time: road construction and education. The former was particularly harmful because building roads in hilly East Tennessee costs more per mile than in rolling, relatively flat Middle and West Tennessee. When it came to funding public education, Tennessee before the Civil War was far from generous, but typical short-funding for out-voted East Tennessee caused it to lag behind even the other two regions. When East Tennessee's economy shifted to a Deep South orbit after around 1840, the subregion's representatives in the state legislature further compounded its problems by allying with the pro-planter agenda Middle and West Tennesseans advocated, to the detriment of the actual needs of their East Tennessee constituents. For all of these reasons, charges that East Tennessee even before the Civil War suffered from isolation and ignorance were not completely unfounded. These, of course, are two distinct "Appalachian" hallmarks.

Slavery, Sectionalism, and More Setbacks for East Tennessee

East Tennessee's struggles with slaveowner-dominated Middle and West Tennessee were, of course, mere skirmishes in the nation's ever-deepening sectional crisis. As the nineteenth century unfolded, East Tennesseans found themselves in between two diverging, increasingly jealous regions. That East Tennessee shared some traits with the cotton-slave Deep South, and others with the North, where manufacturing and urbanization were becoming increasingly important, won it little respect from either and disdain from both. Like two massive millstones, North and South threatened to grind into grist all that lay between them; this reality accelerated East Tennessee's shift to the nation's margins.

Slavery's role in these escalating tensions has always been controversial. For our purposes, myths about the "peculiar institution" merge with Appalachian myths to distort East Tennessee's role in the drama of American sectionalism. My definition of myth, of course, assumes that seeds of truth lend credence to powerful ideas, and this was certainly true in both of these cases.

Perhaps the most common misconception about Appalachian slavery is that it simply did not exist. In truth, slavery was less common in the mountains than in the rest of the South, but it did exist. In the case of East Tennessee, the best estimate is that at the time of the Civil War approximately 10 percent of the regional population were African slaves, compared to 25 percent in Tennessee as a whole, and more than 50 percent in states such as Mississippi and South Carolina. Among East Tennessee's white households, approximately 10 percent owned slaves in 1860—a considerably smaller percentage than in Tennessee as a whole and in the flatland South. Perhaps the most distinctive feature of Appalachian slavery was the relatively small size of slave units. In East Tennessee, only 3 percent of masters owned more than twenty slaves, and only one owned more than two hundred. Within East Tennessee, slaves could be found most commonly on large valley farms, but many East Tennessee slave owners lived in urban areas, most notably Knoxville. There slaves were often skilled laborers (e.g., carpenters, blacksmiths, etc.), and owners garnered income by leasing their valuable human property to others.[11] Beyond East Tennessee's urban areas and central valley, slavery was less common, but still present. Cades Cove entrepreneur Daniel Foute owned large numbers of slaves. But he apparently maintained them at other Blount County locations, because both the 1850 and 1860 censuses for the Cove community report no slaves. Considering the terrain and nature of settlement in the Clearfork Valley, slavery was understand-

---

11. John Cimprich, "Slavery's End in Tennessee," in *Appalachians and Race: The Mountain South from Slavery to Segregation*, ed. John C. Inscoe, 189 (Lexington: Univ. Press of Kentucky, 2001).

ably rare. However, evidence suggests there was some limited slavery in the fertile Powell Valley and in the nearby town of Jacksboro. Moreover, we know that slavery was a common source of labor in extractive industries, such as timbering and coalmining, which in the 1850s began to appear on a small scale in areas of "newer Appalachia," such as the Clearfork.

When discussion moves beyond numbers and where slaves might have been found, many long-held notions about Appalachian slavery come under scrutiny. For example, anecdotal accounts led some observers to believe slavery in the region was more benign and racism less prevalent in the mountains than in the flatland South. We still do not have adequate studies to assess the accuracy of these assumptions for East Tennessee, but these notions draw largely from accounts of residential slaves and those who worked in regional resorts, and ignore the fact that many regional slaves worked long hours in dangerous extractive industries. Regarding racism in the region, revisionists simply acknowledge that bigotry was widespread across all of the antebellum United States (including the North) and that latter-day quibbling among scholars and others over whether Appalachian racism was milder is a yet another debate that reflects more about those who engage in it than mountain realities.

Scholars have long recognized that antislavery sentiment prior to around 1830 was stronger in the upper South than in any other part of the nation. For example, Jonesborough (in upper East Tennessee) and Maryville (near Knoxville, and county seat of Blount County, where Cades Cove is located) were centers of antislavery agitation. Quakers—such as the Jonesborough-based journalist Elihu Embree, and "New Light" Presbyterians at Maryville College—spearheaded these efforts. Compared to the more strident Garrisonians, who emerged after 1831 in New England, these East Tennesseans were moderates advocating gradual emancipation. Indeed, the popular "Colonization Movement"— temporarily based in Jonesborough—advocated returning freed slaves to Africa, and thus appealed to pervasive white fears of a biracial society. This solution was particularly attractive to East Tennesseans who were more "anti–slave owner" than antislavery. Touting East Tennessee's antislavery leadership also ignores that many of those who expressed even moderate moral qualms about slavery (e.g., the Quakers and "New Lights") left East Tennessee for the North and Midwest when the issue became more rancorous, after 1830.

By utilizing long-overlooked records and restoring the issue of slavery to broader historical contexts, we may conclude that environmental and economic circumstances contributed more than other influences to both the relative absence and peculiarities of regional slavery. The terrain of East Tennessee (and other parts of the mountain South) was simply not conducive to plantation production of cotton and other crops that made slavery profitable. As a form of labor in a chronically worker-short economy, and in a society so racist it felt no need even for such a word, Negro slavery was for most people simply a fact of life. Indeed, the vast majority of East Tennesseans who did not own slaves did not instinctively oppose human bondage. Powerful American forces that were hardly unique to Appalachia—a self-elevating sense of white superiority; reverence for property rights; deep-seated preference for local control; and the hope of even the poorest white of someday attaining slave-owner status—combined to make most antebellum East Tennesseans content with the "peculiar institution."

All of these considerations very much influenced East Tennessee's important contributions to broader debates over slavery as a political issue. Even when war broke out in 1861, most Americans at best dimly glimpsed the moral ramifications of American sectionalism, which have distorted understandings of the war ever since. Indeed, from colonial times through the antebellum era, political rather than moral considerations had made slavery the most obvious and divisive issue between North and South. The federal constitution allowed for "slave states" (those with state constitutions recognizing slavery as a form of property) and "free states" (those that did not allow slavery). From 1789—when the constitution was adopted—to the 1850s, slave and free states remained roughly equal in number and in influence, and vied over any array of other issues—including tariffs, a national bank, and federally funded internal improvements—more vociferously than the matter of slavery itself. Repeated additions of new western territories time and again raised the question of whether slavery should be allowed to expand. And each time Americans revisited this conundrum, the widening North-South gap made compromise even more difficult. After 1831, strident minorities on both sides of the Mason-Dixon line increasingly recast the debate in moral terms that further undermined national harmony.

For its part, Tennessee entered the Union in 1796 as a slave state, a stance that East Tennesseans rarely questioned. But as the antebellum years advanced, they were closer to the founding fathers and the national mainstream than regional extremists who drove a reluctant nation toward war. East Tennessee representatives in Congress consistently favored compromise, whether in 1820—when debates flared over Missouri statehood—or throughout the 1850s, as the nation debated the far more controversial issues unleashed by the triumph of Manifest Destiny. For East Tennesseans, loyalties to Whig and Democratic parties, and other concrete issues—most important, their frantic efforts to secure funds for a regional railway—gained far more attention than slavery. East Tennesseans instinctively rejected arguments from sectional extremists. In an intellectual world that was increasingly romantic, rhetoric from Southern "fire eaters" and Northern abolitionists rejected reason, which the founders considered the bedrock of a republic. Pragmatic demands in the backcountry, an instinctive Calvinist distrust of certainty, and their own precarious status in between the two regions inclined East Tennesseans toward "good common sense," a simple but genuine version of the Fathers' rational creed. That outlook—along with America's political mainstream—however, were the biggest losers from the unfortunate events of the 1850s. Ironically, clinging to mainstream standards and virtues pushed East Tennesseans even more toward the nation's margins.

The colorful lives and political careers of East Tennessee's Andrew Johnson and William G. (Parson) Brownlow represented the complexities and contradictions both of their region and of their era. Both men shared the virulent racist views of the age. Both defended slavery (indeed, Johnson owned a few slaves). Yet, both men vocally opposed extreme sectional sentiments and became ardent Unionists. In joining forces, they overcame deep personal and political differences. Johnson, self-educated orphan and apprentice tailor, became a Democrat who more truly championed Tennessee's "common man" than did Andrew Jackson. In the 1850s, Johnson's two terms as governor regained for East Tennessee a temporary preeminence in state politics, while simultaneously winning disdain and the promise of revenge from its rivals in the state's middle and western sections. Brownlow, the fiery Methodist parson, became a firebrand journalist and one of East Tennessee's leading Whigs. He was among Johnson's staunchest foes in the decade leading to the Civil War. After battling each other "on every political stump in Tennessee" for twenty-five years, Johnson and Brownlow found common cause in the events that fell between the election of Abraham Lincoln in November 1860 and the outbreak of war five months later. Their roles in these developments, and in the subsequent sagas of war and reconstruction, differ so much from popular, mythical accounts—northern, southern, *and* American—that Johnson and Brownlow are either largely forgotten or relegated to the roles of failures and villains. As casualties of the sectional crisis and of American mythmaking, they are perfect symbols for their native East Tennessee and Appalachia.

Secession, Civil War, and Tragedy for East Tennessee

The interim between Lincoln's election and the Confederate attack on Fort Sumter was the most perilous period in United States history, and within the state of Tennessee and its eastern third, forces eerily mirrored the nation's fragmentation. East Tennessee was, indeed, a microcosm containing representatives of most of the nation's disparate parts, as returns from the four-sided presidential election of 1860 revealed. Republican Lincoln was not even on the Tennessee ballot, and native son John Bell, whose party's "Constitutional Union" name evoked its simple platform, garnered 48 percent of the state's vote. Of the divided Democrats, "southern" candidate John Breckinridge received 45 percent of Tennessee's vote, and "northern" nominee Stephen Douglas managed just 8 percent. The former Whig stronghold of East Tennessee gave a clear majority to compromise candidate Bell, and the splintered Democrats fared more poorly in East Tennessee than in the state as a whole. This pattern persisted after South Carolina seceded from the Union a month later, and continued still when six other Deep South states joined South Carolina in forming the Confederate States of America in February 1861. Indeed, in a statewide referendum just five days after the birth of the Confederacy, Tennesseans rejected, by 55 percent to 45 percent, a call for a special state convention "to take into consideration our federal relations." A closer look at the state's three divisions suggests a more complex story: three-quarters of West Tennesseans favored the convention; Middle Tennesseans were divided almost evenly; and over 80 percent of East Tennesseans rejected what they saw as a secessionist ploy.[12]

Four months later, after Confederates attacked Fort Sumter and President Lincoln responded with a call to arms, Tennesseans reversed course in yet another referendum. Middle Tennesseans joined West Tennesseans in the vote of June 9, 1861, which gave an overwhelming 69-percent endorsement for secession. In East Tennessee, 69 percent rejected secession.[13] In hindsight, the lack of stronger East Tennessee support for the eventually victorious Northern, Republican, and pro-Lincoln forces appears an obvious portent of the tragedies that followed. But two other matters were more immediately and concretely important. First, East Tennessee—perhaps more than any other locale in the nation—contained elements from every side of this family feud. Secondly, both Union and Confederate strategists deemed East Tennessee too important to respect the wishes of the perhaps more than one-third of the region's residents who hoped the war might pass them by. After being pushed toward the nation's margins for several generations, East Tennessee returned to center stage—ironically assuring its marginal status would continue for years to come.

Like most Americans, East Tennesseans have long been fascinated with their forebears' roles in our nation's greatest conflict. We now know that more affluent East Tennesseans, particularly wealthy Knoxvillians, tended to support the Confederacy, probably due to economic and familial ties with the Deep South. Conversely, the region's poorer residents, particularly those from the hin-

12. Paul H. Bergeron, et al., *Tennesseans and Their History* (Knoxville: Univ. of Tennessee Press), 134; Eric Russell Lacy, *Vanquished Volunteers: East Tennessee Sectionalism, from Statehood to Secession* (Johnson City, TN: East Tennessee State Univ. Press, 1965), 174.

13. Lacy, *Vanquished Volunteers*, 180.

terlands, were more likely to remain loyal to the Union. Many of them, of course, equivocated on the issue until northern victory was imminent.

From the war's beginning, both sides sought to control Cumberland Gap at the east end of the Clearfork Valley. Since the days of Daniel Boone, the Gap was the preferred pathway into Kentucky for East Tennessee Loyalists joining the Union cause and for Union troops seeking to penetrate the Tennessee Valley on their way to more southern destinations. Countless skirmishes occurred in the surrounding area as both sides gained and lost (several times) control of the strategic Gap. The sharp ravines and V-shaped hollows that made the Clearfork unrewarding for farmers made it the perfect setting for Union and Confederate guerilla bands and for opportunistic outlaws, who became some of the most ferocious and feared of the war's protagonists.

The greater Tennessee Valley, with its newly completed rail line and relatively prosperous farms, held even more strategic and economic importance for the warring sides. Immediately after the June 1861 vote cemented Tennessee's ties to the Confederacy, upper East Tennessee Unionists met in Greeneville,

This sketch from *Harper's Weekly* depicts unidentified troops moving through the rugged terrain of Cumberland Gap in 1862. Cumberland Gap was strategically important for both the Union and the Confederacy and changed hands four times over the course of the Civil War. (Courtesy of Calvin M. McClung Historical Collection.)

Mid-Nineteenth-Century Crises

Thomas Smiley's 1859 photograph, one of the earliest-known photos of Knoxville, looks east from the photographer's residence toward downtown, where the cupola of the Knox County Courthouse can be seen in the upper right. The juxtaposition of frame structures and back-yard gardens suggests that even as Knoxville was gaining prosperity and prominence on the eve of the Civil War, it had not completely abandoned its rural origins. (Calvin M. McClung Historical Collection.)

intent on imitating western Virginia's secession from its own Confederate state. When Jefferson Davis and Tennessee state officials blocked this effort, some loyalists set out to destroy key bridges along the ETV&G Railroad's route from Chattanooga to Bristol. To teach the "bridge burners" a lesson, Confederate officials abandoned their initial policy of "forbearance and conciliation." Harsh retaliation only heightened tensions, encouraging many East Tennessee "unde-cideds" to head north through Cumberland Gap to enlist in the Union army.

The war particularly devastated the Tennessee Valley economy. During the war's first two years, occupying Confederate forces "impressed" livestock, food, and firewood from local farmers, particularly known Unionist sympathizers. Rebel officers rarely offered compensation for confiscated goods, but when they did, they typically made payment in depreciated Confederate currency. After near simultaneous Union victories at Vicksburg and Gettysburg in July 1863, a major adjustment in Northern strategy brought General Ambrose Burnside's army to the Tennessee Valley; in September, when Confederate forces were pre-occupied elsewhere, Burnside took over the city of Knoxville. East Tennesseans, including many professed Unionists, quickly learned that troops in blue were as voracious and ungenerous as those in gray. Leading Unionist T. A. R. Nelson reported the Union army was "more destructive" than the Confederates—they burned fences, stole horses, and carried away foodstuffs of all kinds. "If nothing is done," he concluded, "starvation and ruin are before us."[14] When both armies set up camp in the Valley during the winter of 1863–64, matters only became worse for East Tennesseans. In October, Knoxville became the focal point of a prolonged siege. With Burnside's troops occupying the high ground around Fort Sanders, Longstreet's troops eventually made a frantic, futile assault. After the failed siege, one Confederate officer observed, "East Tennessee is bleeding at every pore . . . [and] is literally eaten up."[15] Knoxville, which had begun to distance itself economically from its neighbors in the 1850s, was devastated. The long-sought railroad was in ruins, recently established factories were in rubble, and Knoxville's ascendancy as regional economic and cultural center was temporarily sidetracked. By spring 1864, Longstreet's army moved north into Virginia, and much of the Union force joined Sherman on his march through Georgia. But in the absence of any legitimate force, chaos reigned in East Tennessee, as lawless bands—often loyal mainly to themselves—plundered and terrorized local residents.

In general, guerilla activities were most common and savage in remote locales. By the late years of the war, an absence of able-bodied men made many of these communities particularly vulnerable. Local legends abound in the Clearfork Valley about residents who suffered dehumanizing depredations. The war also ravaged Cades Cove's once prosperous economy and stable community. From the beginning of the conflict, a variety of influences inclined Cove residents toward the Union. Slavery had barely made inroads there; Cove patriarch John Oliver never deviated from the national and egalitarian sentiments he had learned as a member of Jackson's army in the War of 1812. Perhaps most important, religious influences—Quaker, New Light Presbyterian, and particularly Primitive Baptist—made Cove residents suspicious of the values and demands of the secessionists. On the other hand, two of the Cove's leading—and wealthiest—citizens, and several younger residents, supported the Confederacy. A few families split over the matter, with brothers and even fathers and sons finding themselves on opposing sides. Twenty-one Cove residents enlisted in the Union army, twelve joined Confederate forces, "but the majority of Cove men . . . hid out in the mountains . . . [where some] joined small bands to fight the Rebels."[16]

14. Quoted in Robert Tracy McKenzie, "'Oh! Ours is a Deplorable Condition': The Economic Impact of the Civil War in Upper East Tennessee," in *The Civil War in Appalachia: Collected Essays*, ed. Kenneth W. Noe and Shannon H. Wilson, 204 (Knoxville: Univ. of Tennessee Press, 2001).

15. Ibid., 205.

16. Dunn, *Cades Cove*, 129.

By 1863, a combination of the Cove's rich farm lands, an increasingly war-pinched economy, and an absence of able-bodied men, made Cades Cove vulnerable not just to units of both armies but to opportunists thriving on wartime chaos. A band of North Carolina–based, pro-Confederate bushwhackers, which included several sons of the Cove in their ranks, made Cove farmers and Unionists a regular target. As in countless other small communities, the old men, women, and children of Cades Cove devised creative schemes to foil the bushwhackers. Cove patriarch Russell Gregory had refused to take sides when his son Charles enlisted with the Confederates in 1861, but by 1863 murder, mayhem, and imminent starvation convinced him to assume tacit leadership of the Cove's Home Guard. After successfully intercepting one assault by the bushwhackers (who by then included his son Charles in their ranks), Gregory was brutally murdered during the raiders' return. By war's end, once-progressive Cades Cove had changed dramatically, with uncharacteristically "provincial and introspective" new leaders. Bitterness, fear, and distrust lingered. "Intolerance of any innovation or change, suspicion and fear of strangers, and excessive reliance on the extended family proved difficult or impossible to discard."[17] Thanks to its rich soils, the Cove more readily overcame economic devastation than it overcame the war's emotional traumas.

Postwar Blues

The end of the Civil War temporarily brought East Tennessee a degree of homogeneity that did not exist in the prewar era and that diminished further in subsequent times. Ravages of war devastated the mountain, valley, and plateau zones epitomized by my three representative communities. Knoxville, which before the war had advanced beyond its hinterland neighbors economically and culturally, was momentarily set back by military occupation and economic havoc. Simultaneously, Cades Cove fell into economic and social patterns more similar to those in the hardscrabble Clearfork communities than to those John Oliver and the Cove's other proud and progressive patriarchs might have imagined possible. Moreover, these patterns persisted—as they did in the Clearfork—due primarily to the inevitable legacies of partible inheritance and limitations of nature. Politically, a few defiant Rebels kept the Democratic Party alive, but most East Tennesseans at war's end declared loyalty to the Union and embraced the victorious Republicans.

The disappointing and humiliating events of Reconstruction did little to alter patterns forged by war. Southerners have long derided Reconstruction as

17. Ibid., 140.

"a fool's errand," an appraisal that—while self-serving—was not totally unfair. The pragmatism and principle motivating emancipation simply could not erase a long-embedded culture of racism, and while military defeat assured survival of the Union, southern independence and defiance persisted long after Appomattox. Had he not been assassinated, one wonders how these challenges and setbacks might have tarnished the reputation even of Abraham Lincoln. When presidential responsibilities passed to East Tennessean Andrew Johnson, who had neither Lincoln's savvy and skill nor his political capital, disaster was inevitable. Johnson returned to East Tennessee in disgrace in 1869 and found his homeland devastated, divided, distrustful, and particularly disappointed. Thanks in part to the catalyst of war, the North that many East Tennesseans had supported was on its way to a manufacturing frenzy that assured it unprecedented wealth and hegemony. The South, on the other hand, was headed in the opposite direction—toward a century as the nation's most impoverished region. Within the South, the Appalachian region—and within Tennessee, the state's eastern division—experienced despair and derision only surpassed by the misery of the freed slaves.

If the Civil War alone had caused East Tennessee's misfortunes, they might have been more readily overcome. But the war only exacerbated the preexisting problems examined in this chapter. After soldiers returned home, the even less forgiving forces of geography and timing resumed their debilitating effects. By around 1880, East Tennessee and the broader Appalachian region were firmly entrenched on the nation's margins, and new power brokers emerged in both North and South to replace the forces that had dominated the nation from the Revolution to the Civil War. For the nation as a whole, newly powerful forces and supposed "norms" appeared in the industrial Northeast and Midwest, and to a lesser extent, in urban centers throughout the country. "Progress" was the watchword of this new America. A similar, but still distinct, pecking order emerged in the vision of a "New South." This ambitious phoenix was most apparent in cities like Atlanta and Nashville, but it also appeared in more limited ways in Knoxville. New South apostles embraced selective aspects of "progress" even as they romanticized and clung to both admirable and despicable attributes of the Old South. For the emerging mainstreams of the North and the "New South," the Appalachian region served important roles as resource provider and setting for powerful myths. In the minds of most observers, this Appalachia was isolated and homogenous. But, no less than in the years before the Civil War, East Tennessee's and Appalachia's marginal status was intertwined with larger forces and was more complex than imagined. Exploitation of the region's resources, and perpetuation of the myths that justified that exploitation, required dehumanization of regional residents. But to bring "progress" to the mountains and extract profits from them, outsiders and native allies found common cause. Over the next half-century, both partners in this alliance strove to create an Appalachia that simultaneously yielded profits and appreciated the fruits of progress. That twin agenda, and the powerful paradox it engendered, still affects the lives of present-day Appalachians and East Tennesseans.

Part II

Appalachia Discovered:
Insights from East Tennessee, 1870–1930

Since the seminal works of Ron Eller and Henry Shapiro, regional scholars have devoted particular attention to the exploitation of regional resources and the array of stereotypes and images popularly associated with Appalachia. Over the years, increasingly sophisticated analyses have refined our understandings of both of these essential concerns. Yet, as my focus shifts to the era when my own East Tennessee grandparents came of age, I find even the finest revisionist accounts of our region's past incomplete. As best as I can determine, no feudists, moonshiners, or other stereotypical "Appalachians" lurk in my family tree. None of my direct forebears were coal miners or loggers, nor did any of them gain fortunes from those extractive industries. Of my four grandparents born in East Tennessee between 1887 and 1895, only my maternal grandfather was raised on a working farm, and he left home soon after reaching young adulthood. Three of my four grandparents completed high school, and two of them graduated from college. When my grandparents married, both newlywed couples settled in emerging urban centers, where they emulated many mainstream ways. The homes where they raised my parents more nearly resembled suburban residences from a Sinclair Lewis novel than the exotic, primitive log cabins local colorists of the era so vividly and frequently described. In short, my grandparents were not *culturally* "Appalachian," but they lived in the heart of *geographical* Appalachia. And, most important, their lives intertwined inextricably with the Appalachian images and realities that emerged in the half-century following the end of the Civil War.

All of this might be of little concern if my grandparents' experiences were unique, but they were not. Around the turn of the century, rural folk flooded into urban-suburban centers within and on the outskirts of the Appalachian region. There they joined descendants of earlier residents and other newcomers, primarily blacks from the lowland South, and a few foreign immigrants, to foster a dramatic—yet still dimly understood—demographic transformation. Between 1900 and 1920, the rural population of the Tennessee Valley grew by slightly less than 15 percent. Population growth in East Tennessee's more remote hinterlands was much slower; for example, the population of mountainous Sevier County grew by only 1.4 percent between 1900 and 1910, and slowed to 0.4 percent the decade thereafter. Meanwhile, the urban population of the Tennessee Valley exploded. From 1900 to 1920, valley residents classified as urban increased by more than 243 percent. By 1930, nearly half of the valley population resided in cities with 10,000 or more residents. Most of these émigrés came to Knoxville, Chattanooga, upper East Tennessee's Tri-Cities, and lesser towns seeking economic improvement and the benefits of modernity.[1]

Some of these new city dwellers found the move disappointing, but anecdotal evidence suggests that by the 1920s many of them achieved at least marginal middle class status in the emerging towns and cites. This was clearly the case for my Banker and Thomas grandparents, who respectively resided in Knoxville and Bristol. Success, however, had its costs: urban, "successful" Appalachians became invisible. This transformation freed the likes of my grandparents from the burdens of a history that Appalachians even today find unpleasant and demeaning. But it also threatened to deprive them of a sense of identity during a time of rapid change and cultural trauma. Some regional commentators, including the late poet Jim Wayne Miller, believe the effects of this Faustian transaction have been real, pernicious, and enduring. No matter how one assesses the actions of the likes of my grandparents, there can be little doubt that their "invisibility" is one clue that must be addressed if we East Tennesseans are to understand—and come to terms with—our past. We should not be surprised that the likes of my forebears are absent from accounts of that past. As I have already revealed, their relatively modest, uneventful lives did not fit prevailing images and assumptions about their region. More significantly, as part II will make more clear, they and most of their fellow invisible Appalachians rarely commented directly on the matter of their regional identity. Yet that very reticence—and the profound ambivalence it fails to disguise—offers valuable glimpses into the elusive history and identity that our forebears bequeathed to modern East Tennesseans.

1. C. E. Allred, et al. *Economic and Social Study of Tennessee: Part IIA, Comparative Study of the Counties,* University of Tennessee Extension Series, vol. 1, no. 5 (Knoxville: Univ. of Tennessee Extension Service, 1924), 27; Tennessee Valley Authority, Department of Regional Planning Studies, *The Population of the Tennessee Valley* (Knoxville: Tennessee Valley Authority, 1937) 40, 43. These statistics are also discussed in Bruce Wheeler and Michael McDonald, "The Communities of East Tennessee, 1850–1940: An Interpretive Overview," *The East Tennessee Historical Society Publications* (1986): 27.

Part II

The introduction to part I recounted the circumstances that brought the families of my four grandparents to East Tennessee. On my mother's side, I concluded with the story of the Civil War exploits of Virginian Mitch Thomas and his decision to relocate to a farm in Cook's Valley, Tennessee, shortly after the war. Mitch's grandson, my grandfather George Tollie Thomas, was born on that farm in 1887. By the time he came of age, the twin specters of partible inheritance and modernization revisited his family. When Tollie (as he preferred to be called) enrolled at Milligan College in nearby Elizabethton in 1910, most of the farm was left to his older brother, Will. Thus, Tollie Thomas became the first member from his family to leave full-time farming and an "Appalachian" existence behind. Among the many influences leading Granddaddy to that decision, the most obvious was my maternal grandmother, whom he met at Milligan College in 1912. My grandmother's Morris and Brumit forebears also knew intimately the twin effects of partible inheritance and modernization. Her maternal grandfather, the descendant of affluent land barons who founded Morristown, had become a farm hand in the hardscrabble mountain community of Valley Forge by the Civil War. Around the same time, my grandmother's father, David Brumit, became a merchant in Elizabethton. Almost certainly, the sharply reduced size of the Brumit's once large estate contributed to that decision. After his first wife died, David Brumit married the considerably younger Caroline Morris in 1894. The following year, my grandmother was born. She was named Nelle Bly Brumit, after Nellie Bly, a journalist who gained fame when she traveled around the world in "less than 80 days." That name leaves little doubt that David and Carrie Brumit had lofty expectations for their only daughter. Their decision to send Nelle to Milligan College, truly an exceptional opportunity for any young woman at that time, affirms that assumption. Soon after Nelle's graduation in 1916, my grandparents married and moved to Bristol, which was then emerging as the transportation, economic, and cultural hub for upper East Tennessee and Southwestern Virginia. My grandfather had studied to become a minister, but pastoral salaries were not large, and by all accounts, my grandmother's ambition to reestablish the more advantaged status of her forebears was a major influence on Granddaddy's decision to become a bookkeeper with one of Bristol's emerging businesses. Thus, for my Thomas grandparents, education and a rural-to-urban migration became a means of escape from "Appalachian" status and an entry card to modernity and middle-class standing. When my mother was born, in March 1919, her family was comfortably distant from their Appalachian roots—or so it must have seemed. Perhaps that explains why both of my grandparents' disapproved when Bristol temporarily became a center for commercial country music in the 1920s.

My Thomas grandparents were not the first of my forebears to pursue the advantages of higher education, nor the first to relocate to a city. When Nicholas

Gibbs's once-large estate north of Knoxville shrank to the point that it could support only a few of his heirs, his great grandson, Washington Lafayette Gibbs, took the "classical course" at the University of Tennessee and became an educator. After teaching music for a number of years in Andersonville, a community thirty miles north of Knoxville, where his wife's extended Longmire family lived, Lafayette moved his family to the burgeoning Knoxville suburb of Park City. Among the advantages of this move were better schools for his three children, including my grandmother, May Olivia Gibbs, who was born in 1889. To her father's great dismay, my grandmother fell hopelessly in love with the ill-educated son of a "Michigan carpetbagger" during her final year at Park City High School (1910–11).

Luke Banker faced many difficulties after his arrival in post–Civil War Knoxville. After the death of his first wife in 1870, he married native East Tennessean Josephine Mitchell. That marriage produced two sons who died in infancy, before my grandfather, Luke Henry Banker, was born in 1888. Pop (as we grandchildren knew him) was an avid reader who reportedly enjoyed learning, but he dropped out of school and pursued the first of many ambitious business ventures to help his mother make ends meet after his father died in 1902. Several years later, when Luke met May Gibbs, Lafayette Gibbs understandably believed his daughter could do better. When efforts to sway his infatuated daughter from her suitor failed, Grandpa Gibbs took May to live for more than a year with relatives in Eugene, Oregon. A truly beautiful cache of letters (mostly written from Luke to May—in flowing prose that belied his fifth-grade education) reveals the futility of Mr. Gibbs's intervention. When he and May returned to Knoxville on the train in August 1912, Luke Banker met them at the station. A month later my grandparents were married, and a year thereafter my father was born. According to family legend, Dad's middle name—Eugene— was a tribute to the year my grandmother spent in the Pacific Northwest.

After taking a position with the U.S. Post Office in 1915, my grandfather initially delivered mail in a horse-drawn wagon. But in the 1920s he embraced the automobile as the way of the future and continued his federal duties in a tin lizzie. For more than two decades, Pop dabbled during his after-work hours in an array of businesses. His most successful venture was a mail-order chicken hatchery. Unfortunately, fire struck the hatchery in 1924, bringing my grandparents to involuntary bankruptcy. When Lafayette Gibbs died in 1931, he reportedly still held misgivings about his son-in-law. Ironically, by that time Pop's business instincts converged with fortunate historical timing to put him on the road to financial stability and success. When the new McGhee-Tyson Airport opened twenty miles southeast of Knoxville in the mid-1930s, my grandfather secured a contract to rent eleven Ford cars and trucks to the Knoxville Post Office to carry freight and mail between the city and the airport. The coming of TVA, and later the Manhattan Project—which overnight gave birth to the city of Oak Ridge, twenty miles to Knoxville's other side—greatly expanded business at the airport and for my grandfather. He quickly recognized a need to transport passengers and added a fleet of limousines to his service. By World War II, the success of Banker's Knoxville Airport Transit Service was evidence that Luke H. Banker had achieved the financial success he had long pursued. This attainment further removed his family from an "Appalachian" lifestyle.

Although the term "Appalachia" was beginning to assume many of its modern connotations in the era when my grandparents came of age, I have no doubt my interest in the matter of "Appalachian identity" would puzzle all four of them. Still, I expect Tollie and Nelle Thomas and Luke and May Banker might have indulged me. All of them were relatively well read and informed. As regular churchgoers, they may have been familiar with such works as Samuel Tyndale Wilson's *The Southern Mountaineers* and Edward Guerrant's *The Galax Gatherers*, two widely read promotional pieces for the Appalachian Home Missions cause that Henry Shapiro suggests greatly shaped notions of a "strange, peculiar, and needy Appalachia." Perhaps one or more of them read the widely popular local-color literature that initially appeared as short stories and in serial fashion in popular new magazines of the era. Charles E. Craddock's *In the Tennessee Mountains* and one or more of the novels of John Fox Jr. (two authors Shapiro cites extensively in *Appalachia on our Mind*) may have been on their bookshelves. By the 1920s, I expect they may also have been familiar with Horace Kephart's *Our Southern Highlanders*. I believe my grandparents were at least acquainted with notions about "Appalachia" that were being bantered about in their own era. And I have no doubt they did not identify with those accounts.

If quizzed about her Appalachian identity, a young May Banker would likely report that she gave the matter little thought. She was, of course, descended from one of East Tennessee's early settlers and large landowners, and she, her father, and brothers were all formally educated and resided in urban-suburban settings. Nanny Thomas and Pop Banker would, I expect, even more bluntly reject association with the surrounding region. I recall Nanny accompanying our family on occasional trips to Granddaddy's Cook's Valley farm, and I have particularly distinct memories of a visit in the mid-1950s to the old Thomas home high atop Brierpatch Mountain in Virginia. Nanny was by nature a worrier, and it was obvious to my brothers and me even as children that she worried whenever she left her comfortable, modern home in Bristol for the country. I also gather that Nanny became quite embarrassed when her widowed mother married a man who tended a boarding house in a southwest Virginia coal town. Nanny's Appalachia had little room for grimy coal miners or hardscrabble farmhands

May Gibbs's 1911 graduation photo from Knoxville's Park City High School. The photo of Nelle Brumit was probably taken at the time of her 1912 high school graduation in Elizabethton, TN, or later that fall when she enrolled at nearby Milligan College. (Author's personal photograph collection.)

This photo of G. Tollie Thomas with sheep in arms was taken on the Cook's Valley farm where he was raised. The photo dates from around the time (1910) he left the farm to enroll at Milligan College. At about that same time Luke H. Banker took a job with the U.S. Postal Service in Knoxville. (Author's personal photograph collection.)

and was best confined to a few heirlooms and the quaint crafts that by the 1930s were marketed by the likes of the Southern Highland Craft Guild, which she eventually collected.

Pop Banker shared Nanny Thomas's disregard for their rural neighbors, but for reasons that were quite different. Pop's attitudes toward his fellow East Tennesseans stemmed primarily from his full embracement of the American success myth. Pop was a wonderful grandfather and a jovial teaser, but he was also, by all accounts, an aggressive, hardnosed businessman. The fact of his being the son of an outsider ostracized by insiders—someone who knew intimately the disgraceful poverty and hardships associated with Appalachia—must have made distancing himself from that category even more imperative.

This brings me back to Tollie Thomas. Perhaps because I carry his name as my middle name and share his penchant for books, I have always felt a special affinity for my maternal grandfather, even though he died prematurely, and my memories of him are hazy. He reportedly enjoyed returning to the farm in Cook's Valley and to his ancestral home in Virginia, but his love for my grandmother apparently kept him in Bristol and distant (literally and metaphorically) from his roots. Granddaddy's basement woodshop was his one refuge, maybe even a link to his past. The beautiful furniture and clever toys he crafted are living testimony to his handiwork. But a collection of cartoons found in his woodshop after his death in 1954 interest me more. For many years, Granddaddy's employer, Mitchell-Powers Hardware, distributed calendars adorned with humorous cartoons of "The Mountain Boys." Although their creator, Paul Webb (of *Esquire* magazine), privately conceded he had almost no firsthand knowledge of Appalachian culture, his cartoons conveyed practically every Appalachian-rural stereotype ever imagined. Webb's Tolliver brothers and their hillbilly neighbors were poor, isolated, lazy, ignorant, bearded, dirty, gun toting, inebriated, and sexually unrefined. Why, I wonder, did Granddaddy save these cartoons? He knew firsthand that these images were at best caricatures. A pensive man, he may have even considered the pernicious effects of those inaccuracies. What do Paul Webb's "mountain boys" reveal about this onetime farm boy who had become learned and moved to the city? What can they tell us about his take on his Appalachian identity?

Insights from the experiences of "successful" immigrants, blacks, Native Americans, and others suggest several tantalizing approaches to these queries, which spin off, in turn, even more questions. Was Tollie Thomas laughing at his ancestors? Or at the rural folk who came regularly to Bristol to shop and sell their farm products? Was he laughing at himself? Did such graphic portrayals of rural ways affirm his move to the city? Or was he laughing at Paul Webb and the foolish outsiders who did not know the richness of mountain culture? Did the

"Shecks, Ah wish Maw would stop
makin' her soap in Paw's still."

PIPE COUPLING
MANUFACTURERS, Inc.

Telephone 1400

P. O. Box 488

MARTINS FERRY ★ ★ OHIO

BLACK AND **HOT DIP** GALVANIZED COUPLINGS

In the 1930s and '40s, Paul Webb's "Mountain Boys" appeared regularly in *Esquire* magazine, of-
fering mainstream readers a steady stream of "Appalachian" images. The author's grandfather,
Tollie Thomas, who had been raised on a rural East Tennessee farm, collected reprints of these
cartoons, which were used as advertisements for companies doing business with his Bristol,
Tennessee employer. (Originally reprinted in 1949 by Pipe Coupling Manufacturers Inc. of
Martin's Ferry, Ohio.

ignorance and insecurities of those who poked fun at his culture amuse Tollie
Thomas?

In the half-century that part II of this book addresses, many assimilated
Appalachians, much like my ancestors, distanced themselves from inherited traditions and the cultural ballast those traditions provided. At the same time, other
East Tennesseans lived lives that offered seeds of truth to emerging Appalachian
stereotypes. As we will see, the lives of these two groups of turn-of-the-century

East Tennesseans intertwined more than they knew. Contrary to popular notions about assimilation, traditions associated with Appalachia never completely disappeared, and some of them grew stronger and more entrenched. Our region's elusive past and identity are products of that dissociation and that cultural resilience. That we of succeeding generations have not acknowledged the profound personal and regional effects of our forebears' identity struggles assures that Appalachia remains elusive down to our own times.

Chapter Three

Queen City of the Mountains:
Knoxville and the Vision of a New South

I can only wonder why my great-great- and great-grandfathers, Henry and Luke Banker, moved from Michigan to war-ravaged Knoxville in the late 1860s. Perhaps the multiple misfortunes they experienced in their new home in the years thereafter explain why they left no explanation for a move they may have considered dubious. A report from the *Richmond Whig* that a Knoxville paper re-printed in the fall of 1868 may shed light on what my forebears left unexplained. "Knoxville" the column declared, "is perhaps the widest awake and livelist [*sic*] town of its population, not only in Tennessee, but in the southern states." The reporter's contention that Knoxville's ten thousand residents had "all the conveniences of a city—gas, water works, paved streets, &c, &c," exaggerated both the city's size and its services. But the reporter's prediction that Knoxville was on the verge of a wholesaling-induced economic boom proved prescient. Perhaps that expectation, combined with the report's claim that many "beautiful, cultivated, and intelligent ladies, both married and single" made their homes in Knoxville, lured my forebears to East Tennessee.[1]

The reporter's glowing appraisal serves two useful purposes here. First, it manifests a self-reassuring bravado that Knoxville has exhibited from the days of William Blount to the 1982 World's Fair. During the half-century after the Civil War, this heady boosterism was, for better and worse, an essential Knoxville trait. Secondly, historians have too long overlooked the broader significance of this characteristic swagger from the heart of Appalachian East Tennessee. A closer look at Gilded Age Knoxville reveals important glimpses into the regional elusiveness that is this book's greater concern.

Anyone who had been in Knoxville just five years earlier would cer-tainly have been surprised at the optimistic tone of the 1868 report from the

---

1. Reprinted in *Knoxville Daily Herald*, Oct. 31, 1868.

Richmond reporter. When Union and Confederate armies departed the city in early December 1863, Knoxville was devastated and demoralized. Days earlier, General Longstreet's futile assault on Fort Sanders ended the Confederates' nearly three-week siege of Knoxville. Union and Confederate units had set up camps astride the city's recently completed suburbs and railroad tracks—products and symbols of a new Knoxville that, after years of uncertainty, had emerged in the 1850s as the economic hub for productive farms of the Tennessee Valley. New Knoxville's suburbs and railroad facilities were the most notable casualties of the Confederate siege. Smoldering ruins of once "fine residences," twisted rails of the ETV&G, and the furious, bloody assault on Fort Sanders brought war's horrors to Knoxville. Those miseries did not end when the two armies left town.

Union victory brought Parson Brownlow and other loyalists back to Knoxville, and their hostility toward Confederate sympathizers unleashed a cycle of violence, assassinations, lynching, and general mistrust that continued beyond the final fifteen months of the war. While Reconstruction for East Tennessee was less harsh than for other, more defiant parts of the old Confederacy, the difference was only a matter of degree. Moreover, postwar Knoxville's miseries and misfortunes were not all manmade. Periodic epidemics swept through the city; an 1866 smallpox outbreak was particularly devastating. A flood the following year saw the Tennessee River crest thirty-three feet above its normal level and sweep away bridges, several manufacturing establishments, and livestock; perhaps as many as two hundred Knoxvillians, mostly poor folk living along the river and the First and Second Creeks, lost their homes. In March 1869, lightning during a violent thunderstorm started a fire that left much of the city's Gay Street business district in ashes.

Yet Knoxvillians rebounded from these setbacks with surprising resiliency and energy. Union control during the war's final months probably saved the city from the unpleasant fate Atlanta and other, more defiant Confederate cities experienced. Many Knoxville Confederates and Unionists had been friends and business allies before Fort Sumter; after Appomattox, pragmatists from both camps sought reconciliation. More than one hundred Unionists, for example, pledged to refrain from violence against ex-Rebels. Even firebrand Parson Brownlow, appointed governor of Tennessee when the war ended, was unusually forgiving. When fifty Knox County Confederates sought his pardon between 1865 and 1867, the governor approved all but eight (and President Andrew Johnson, another East Tennessee Unionist, pardoned six of the latter). Former enemies cooperated against the raging waters of the 1867 flood. Perhaps most important, with Brownlow directing affairs in Nashville, East Tennessee and Knoxville enjoyed a rare privileged relationship with the state government, thereby securing the funding that facilitated the rapid rebuilding of East Tennessee railroads. By 1871, words from another Richmond journalist echoed and exceeded the optimistic appraisal of 1868: "No city of the South except Atlanta," he observed with less hyperbole and more accuracy, had "improved more rapidly since the war than had Knoxville, Tennessee."[2] By that time, Henry and Luke Banker were in town, and within a few years another of my Banker ancestors, Washington Lafayette Gibbs, would move into Knoxville from his family's ancestral home, twenty miles to the north. Escaping limited opportunities as a farmer, Grandpa Gibbs enrolled in the state university.

Knoxville's resurgence as East Tennessee's economic and cultural hub was truly proof the Civil War era was a temporary setback, rather than a true historical watershed, for the city and region. Indeed, economic trends and patterns that began in the 1850s reappeared in the postwar years to inaugurate the city's "golden years." Trends in Knoxville and greater East Tennessee from around 1870 to around 1930 mirrored to a great extent national developments, dispelling notions that the region was isolated. A nationwide panic in the mid-1870s slowed economic growth, but from around 1875 to 1893 an unprecedented surge of industrialization fueled phenomenal economic expansion in the nation and in Knoxville. Hard times reappeared in the mid-1890s and cooled this economic surge, but growth returned during the decade and a half leading up to World War I, and surged again during the war years. In hindsight, it is obvious that the foundation for the post-1900 prosperity for the nation at large, and East Tennessee in particular, was shaky. But, even as inherent regional limits began once again to undermine East Tennessee's general prosperity, most contemporary regional observers were oblivious to those defects. Indeed, throughout the entire half-century examined in part II of this book, Knoxville's boosters viewed East Tennessee's potential as unlimited.

City promoters proudly proclaimed Knoxville the "Queen City of the Mountains." The title may have been little more than mindless hype, but it succinctly captured the most distinctive feature of Knoxville's newfound prosperity and status. Knoxville's wealth and the many accomplishments accompanying it were due in large part to the city's role as regional hub for greater East Tennessee and much of the southern Appalachian region. Considering the importance of the region's hinterlands for Knoxville's successes, it is surprising that commentators on the city's history have rarely addressed the broader contexts for Knoxville's development, or related the city's decline as the Great Depression approached to flaws in the broader regional economy. For Gilded Age East Tennessee and Knoxville, this oversight is particularly ironic and misleading.

2. Quoted in Bruce Wheeler, *Knoxville, Tennessee: Continuity and Change in an Appalachian City* (Knoxville: Univ. of Tennessee Press, 1983), 17.

This 1906 pamphlet from the Knoxville Board of Trade promoted Knoxville as a wholesaling center and "Queen City of the Mountains." (Special Collections Library, University of Tennessee, Knoxville.)

Cartographically, Knoxville lies clearly within Appalachian confines; the surrounding region accounted for much of its burgeoning wealth, and many of its newest residents, like W. Lafayette Gibbs, had only recently arrived from the region's farms and rural areas.

Throughout American history, powerful myths have impeded attempts to grapple with rural-urban differences. Jeffersonian agrarianism once gave rural dwellers the upper hand in debates about the preferred nature of our society, but after the Civil War, the myth of progress—closely identified with American urbanization—gained ascendancy. As the experiences of my grandmother Thomas and great-grandfather Gibbs so clearly demonstrate, the ideal of progress shaped the formal educations and evolving worldviews of many rural-to-urban East Tennessee émigrés at the dawn of the twentieth century. Less powerful, but equally enduring, has been the counter-myth of antimodernism. American antimodernism is rooted in antebellum romanticism, but since the Gilded Age, disgruntled urbanites have predictably idealized premodern, rural cultures. For more than a century, these powerful ideas have so successfully sparred with one another that few of us escape their paralyzing effects.

"Urban and rural landscapes," William Cronon writes in *Nature's Metropolis*, "are not two places but one. They created each other . . . and they now depend on each other for their very survival." "To see them separately," he concludes, "is to misunderstand where they came from and where they might go in the future."[3] Cronon's views have particular implications for the "three representative

3. William Cronon, *Nature's Metropolis: Chicago and the Great West*, New York: W. W. Norton, 1991), 384, 19.

communities" I have chosen as a focus for this work. His insights point to new approaches to Knoxville's boom years (the focus of this chapter), and to the developments in "timber and coal Appalachia" explored in chapter four.

Alan Batteau's *The Invention of Appalachia*—his insightful follow-up to Henry Shapiro's *Appalachia on Our Mind*—opens with a line with important implications for urban Knoxville's relations and attitudes toward her rural neighbors: "Appalachia is a creature of the urban imagination." The many, varied, and often contradictory images of "Appalachia," Batteau continues, emerged from the "economic opportunism, political creativity, or passing fancy of urban elites."[4] Yet, in this chapter, and in chapter five, I will suggest that both of these perceptive observers overlook an essential point. Shapiro's assertion that the "discovery of Appalachia" was pronounced "more often in New York and Boston and Philadelphia than in Asheville and Knoxville," stands in sharp contrast with my contention that residents of Knoxville were, at least, codiscoverers. To be sure Knoxvillians may not have been the first to create notions of a "strange and peculiar Appalachia," but I have no doubt that many residents of East Tennessee's leading city found those images just as useful, perhaps even more so, than urban Northerners. As we will see in chapter five, proving this contention is problematical, but certainly anecdotal accounts of the experiences of the likes of my grandparents clearly point in that direction.

Three impediments blur our ability to glimpse these realities. The first is our difficulty in coming to terms intellectually with urbanization within the Appalachian region. Second are notions of a static Appalachian culture, which allow no place for "invisible" regional residents who move to urban locales and attain at least limited economic success. Thirdly, we must not overlook the power of intragroup distinction. That the human penchant for ignoring one's own faults by focusing on the faults of others has left its ugly mark on our own history and self-perception should be cause for neither surprise nor embarrassment.

This book's unorthodox approach to the era of around 1870 to 1930 offers an opportunity to see East Tennessee and greater Appalachia with new, perhaps even more honest and understanding eyes. Convenience alone caused me to present the histories of Knoxville and its hinterland neighbors during this economically important era in separate chapters. Hopefully each chapter will demonstrate clearly that (to borrow and modify one more line from William Cronon) "erasing the false boundary" between Knoxville and East Tennessee's hinterlands can help us "begin to recover their common pasts."[5] Similarly I ask readers' indulgence with my decision to relate the experiences and perceptions of turn-of-the-century East Tennesseans to the broader mainstream discovery

4. Allen W. Batteau, *The Invention of Appalachia* (Tucson: Univ. of Arizona Press, 1991), 1.

5. Cronon, *Nature's Metropolis*, 19.

of Appalachia in yet another separate chapter. As I explore East Tennessee's turn-of-the-century realities in chapters three and four, I will provide markers indicating my intention to return to perceptions of those realities in chapter five. Ideally those markers will help readers keep track of the threads running between Appalachia's realities and perceptions of "Appalachia."

For readers more comfortable with concrete evidence, demographic and economic statistics leave no doubt that the period from around 1870 to 1930 was overall an era of tremendous growth for East Tennessee's leading city. These numbers reveal trends within the era that largely mirror broader national patterns; closer scrutiny, however, hints at some distinctly regional developments that observers of Knoxville's economic history have largely overlooked. Statistics for Knoxville's population reflect actual increases in numbers *and* the fact that the city between 1890 and 1920 annexed significant portions of surrounding Knox County—both of which offer evidence of burgeoning optimism in the city. The 1870 census reported Knoxville's population at 8,682 persons; by 1900 it had increased to 32,637, and in 1930 it reached 105,802. Percentage-wise, the city's population surged more than 133 percent in the bustling 1880s. In the subsequent two decades, that rate slowed to 45 percent and 11 percent.[6]

Economic growth pushed and paralleled Knoxville's population expansion. Knoxville had always been East Tennessee's wholesaling center, but providing the needs of first Confederate and then later Union armies during the Civil War spurred wholesale businesses. After the war, newly rebuilt railroads, the availability of new consumer goods from surging factories in the North, and growing markets as residents of the surrounding rural hinterlands discovered consumerism, combined further to expand Knoxville wholesaling. By 1882, the city was home for forty-four wholesalers, half of whom began operation after the Civil War. In 1885, the Tennessee Agricultural Commission proclaimed Knoxville the South's fourth-leading wholesale center (behind New Orleans, Nashville, and Atlanta) and reported an annual volume of trade passing through Knoxville in the $15–20 million range. Eleven years later, the Traveler's Protective Association moved Knoxville up to the South's number-three wholesale center, estimating annual trade through the city at $50 million. In turn, entrepreneurs reinvested the surging profits from Knoxville's wholesale trade into other manufacturing pursuits. Extractive industries, primarily timber and coal from more remote East Tennessee locales, were popular among Knoxville investors. Investors also established a number of new manufacturing establishments in the city itself in the 1880s, including Knoxville Woolen Mills in 1884 and Brookside Cotton Mills

6. Statistics are drawn from the U.S. Census of: 1880, 1890, 1900, 1910, 1920, as presented in Jennifer Brooks, "'One Grand United Hymn': Boosterism in Knoxville, Tennessee at the Turn of the Century" (master's thesis, Univ. of Tennessee, 1991), 98–102.

in 1887. The Traveler's Protective Association in 1896 proclaimed the former "the largest producing woolen mill in the world" and the latter one of the South's largest cotton mills. Statistics from the 1887 *Merchant's Guide and Industries of Knoxville* displays graphically Knoxville's manufacturing success during the first seven years of the fabulous 1880s. Most important, these statistics were a harbinger to even more economic growth.

Not surprisingly, in the 1890s, when the U.S. economy faced its greatest challenges up to that time, all of these trends—the increase of new industrial establishments, the increase in numbers of wage earners, and the percentage value of city products—plummeted. Statistics for the first two decades of the twentieth century are not exactly comparable, but the general picture suggests Knoxville rebounded economically. Growth, however, was slow until World War I spurred an unusual economic spurt.[7] These general trends between 1900 and 1915 clearly reflected regional realities, offering a rude reminder that, for all of the region's progress after the Civil War, East Tennessee's inherent economic disadvantages had not disappeared. The years 1900–1915 offered harbingers of hard times for the region and its leading city, when "normalcy" returned in the 1920s. This chapter will take a closer look at the post-1900 years, but first we must examine more closely other aspects of Knoxville's golden years, which, as is often the case with "golden years," were aberrant. My one unshakable conclusion echoes Cronon and Batteau: the fortunes, misfortunes, and the identities of Knoxville and its hinterland neighbors were inextricably intertwined. Hopefully in this and the following two chapters, that insight will begin to erase the false boundaries that have long blinded East Tennesseans to how we came to our present juncture.

The New South Comes to Knoxville

As the title of this chapter reveals, I share the historical inclination to label Knoxville a "new South city." Still the Knoxville that emerged from the Civil War was actually a second incarnation of the "new" Knoxville that had appeared in the 1850s. More than most southern cities of the postwar era, Knoxville had all of the ingredients that new South visionary, Atlanta journalist Henry Grady, deemed essential for the creation of a mixed economy in the South that would mirror the best aspects of the victorious North's manufacturing-urban society. Four key factors intertwined to forge Knoxville's post–Civil War economic explosion and the complex cultural and social consequences unleashed by that boom: the city's location, which made it a regional transportation hub, a rich

7. Johnson, "'The City of Tomorrow with the Spirit of the Past,': Bankrolling the Industrial Development of Knoxville, Tennessee, 1875–1907" (master's thesis, Univ. of Tennessee, 1994), 42–46. My assessment of the post-1900 period is drawn from the Censuses for Manufacturing for 1900, 1910, and 1920 presented in Brooks, "One Grand United Hymn," 99–100.

treasure trove of regional resources, a talented group of businesspeople, and an abundant pool of affordable, hardworking laborers.

Knoxville from its founding benefited from its central locale within the greater Tennessee Valley. Surrounding mountains and the only occasionally navigable Tennessee River initially assured Knoxville a preeminent role in the relatively self-contained and isolated region, but completion of railroad connections to outside markets in the 1850s marked Knoxville's emergence as modern East Tennessee's economic hub. The rebuilding and consolidation of the ETV&G Railroad and construction of a host of smaller lines in the years after the war cemented that status. By the 1890s, a number of complex deals and efforts at consolidation resulted in the emergence of the Southern Railway system, with Knoxville as one of its hub cities. The Louisville and Nashville (L&N) emerged shortly after the turn of the century as a second important rail network connecting Knoxville to cities and markets beyond the region. Two rail lines became particularly important: the Knoxville and Ohio connected Knoxville to the coalfields to the city's north, including the Clearfork Valley; the Knoxville, Sevierville, and Eastern (KS&E—better known among locals as the "Knoxville, Slow, and Easy") linked Knoxville to the timber fields and eventually to the tourist Mecca of the Great Smokies, which opened in the first decade of the twentieth century. Early rail promoters emphasized region-wide benefits of railroads. For example, the *Knoxville Daily Sentinel* reported in August 1887 that "Knoxville will share the benefits from the new roads. The prosperity of the country goes hand in hand with the growth and greatness of the city." Years later, William MacArthur, one of the most astute commentators on this era in Knoxville's history, noted, "The new wealth created by the railroads [poured into] the pockets of Knoxvillians, especially the great merchants, mill and mine owners."[8]

The railroads were directly related to the second key for Knoxville's post–Civil War economic boom: the region's vast and largely untapped natural resources. Though never as productive as the farms of Middle and West Tennessee or the Midwest, Tennessee Valley farmers produced corn, wheat, and other grains, vegetables and fruits, and an array of livestock that sold in Knoxville and passed through it en route to markets beyond the region. Farmers in the more remote hinterlands produced many of these same products, but with less successful results. But livestock that could be herded to nearby railheads, and specialized products—such as apples and chestnuts—continued to earn cash for more remote locales, including Cades Cove. East Tennessee agricultural products fed Knoxville's burgeoning population and many of the city's emerging industries: flour mills, meat-packing plants, tanneries, distilleries, and an array of textile mills. But East Tennessee's greatest resources at the end of the Civil

8. MacArthur, *Knoxville's History*, 30.

War were its vast hardwood forests and deposits of iron, coal, copper, marble, lead, and other minerals. A few ambitious entrepreneurs had begun to tap these resources before the Civil War, but limited markets—and inadequate means to get these bulky products to market—constricted those antebellum economic pursuits. After the war, rebuilt and expanded railroads took regional products to new markets that the explosion of industrialization created in the Northeast and Midwest. This combination initiated East Tennessee's great era of extractive industries and fueled Knoxville's 1880s economic surge. Chapter four will provide more in-depth treatment of the regional timber and coal industries from a hinterlands (as opposed to Knoxville) perspective.

Human resources—a cadre of talented entrepreneurs and a host of hardworking, affordable laborers—were also essential for Gilded Age Knoxville's economic surge. The most distinctive and important entrepreneurial asset of Knoxville's mid- to late-nineteenth-century business leadership was a broad span of backgrounds that complemented a commonality in their values and worldviews. Charles McClung McGhee, pre–Civil War East Tennessee's wealthiest planter and a descendant of Knoxville founder James White, was clearly the most prominent of this group. Shrewd Civil War–era investments increased McGhee's inherited wealth, and in the year the war ended McGhee founded the People's Bank of Knoxville and opened a banking and commission business in New York City. Those actions laid a foundation for McGhee's most important business enterprise: the rebuilding, consolidation, and expansion of East Tennessee's railway network. To oversee this rail empire, McGhee spent much of his time until his retirement in the 1890s in New York, where he advanced his personal interests and those of his hometown. McGhee also invested heavily in many of latter-nineteenth-century East Tennessee's leading businesses, including his son-in-law's wholesaling firm, C. M. McClung and Company; Knoxville Iron Company; Roane Iron Company; Coal Creek Mining and Manufacturing; White Lily Flour Mills; and Knoxville Woolen Mills. McGhee also became one of Knoxville's most prominent philanthropists.

Perez Dickinson, another of Knoxville's Gilded Age entrepreneurs, had come to East Tennessee from his native Massachusetts in 1829. Four years later, he joined forces in the mercantile business with his brother-in-law, James Hervey Cowan, heir to one of Knoxville's first prominent families. Cowan, Dickinson and Company sold groceries, dry goods, and shoes, setting the mold for Knoxville wholesaling. An avowed Unionist (and tacit abolitionist), Dickinson left Knoxville from 1861–1863, but he returned at the end of the war to become president of the newly established First National Bank. In 1869, Dickinson founded and became the first president of the Knoxville Industrial Association (forerunner of the city's Chamber of Commerce), and in that and other capacities he was one of Knoxville's most vocal promoters until his death in 1901.

Shortly after Dickinson's 1864 return to Knoxville, a host of other talented outsiders (some dubbed them "carpetbaggers") arrived to invest their resources and considerable business talent in the city's emerging economy. Edward Jackson Sanford initially came to Knoxville in 1853 as a carpenter, but after serving as an officer in the Union army, he returned to the city in 1864 and established a pharmaceutical firm. Two other former Union officers and Ohio natives, Andrew Jackson Albers and William P. Chamberlain, joined forces with Sanford in 1872 to establish a firm that invested in railroads, iron manufacturing, coal mining, and textile mills. As president of the Mechanics' National Bank and vice president of East Tennessee National Bank, Sanford joined Charles McClung McGhee as a leading financier for the variety of enterprises that exploded in Knoxville between around 1875 and the mid-1890s. Yet another prominent "carpetbagger" was William Chamberlain's brother, Hiram, who came to Knoxville as Burnsides's chief quartermaster and stayed after the cessation of hostilities. Using borrowed capital and the expertise of experienced Welsh ironmasters, Chamberlain established Knoxville Iron Company in 1867, which paved the way for many other heavy industries and railroad shops. To secure fuel for its iron foundries, Knoxville Iron established mines in the rich coalfields north of the city. William MacArthur reports that "at times [Knoxville Iron] seemed to be more in the coal than iron business" and sold coal to the public "by ton or basket."[9]

Finally, several of Knoxville's Gilded Age entrepreneurs came from abroad. Perhaps the most prominent of this group was Peter Kern. After migrating to the United States from Germany in 1853, Kern settled in Georgia, where he enlisted in the Confederate army in 1861. After being wounded, he furloughed in Knoxville, and when Burnsides's Union forces occupied the city, Kern decided to forego further fighting. Soon he and another German businessman established a company producing ice cream, cakes, and candies. Kern's ice cream parlor, on Gay Street, became a popular center for Knoxville social life, and Kern's Bakery became one of the city's (and region's) flourishing businesses. Kern became involved in many civic projects, served many years as a director of East Tennessee National Bank, and was Knoxville's mayor from 1890 to 1892.

For all of their variety, Knoxville's Gilded Age business elite shared a worldview mirroring in many respects the outlooks of leading tycoons of the era, such as John D. Rockefeller and Andrew Carnegie. This group fueled and reflected the optimism of Knoxville's boosters, seeing themselves as instrumental players in the unprecedented economic expansion transforming the region and nation. In 1875, the *Knoxville Daily Chronicle* reported: "Our merchant princes are increasing in number, and fortunes that a few years back would have been considered

9. Ibid., 32–33.

10. Quoted in Wheeler, *Knoxville, Tennessee,* 17.

fabulous are now undoubted facts."[10] Advocates of "unrestrained capitalism and unfettered urban growth," they were confident they deserved the wealth they accrued, and that the changes their efforts wrought were, or at least would be, beneficial to all East Tennesseans. Hindsight, however, suggests this view might be misleading. One historical observer's extensive analyses of Knoxville's Mechanics' National Bank suggests the city's business leadership was innately conservative and preferred safe investments, most notably wholesaling firms and extractive industries. As we have seen, those pursuits achieved great returns during the booming years of the 1880s, but in the years following the Panic of 1893, such cautious investments proved less profitable and less sustainable.

Historical observers have largely overlooked the other, numerically much greater "human resource" that was essential for Knoxville's post–Civil War economic surge—a large pool of workers. A surge in the city's population was, of course, an important key to the appearance of a hard-working, relatively inexpensive workforce in the city. Many factors, including natural increase and annexation, which widened the city limits, contributed to this growth, but most observers agree that in-migration was the critical contributor to Knoxville's demographic boom. A few newcomers came from abroad, and others, such as my Banker forebears, moved from states other than Tennessee. But far more émigrés, including African Americans and rural whites, came from East Tennessee and other nearby locales. At the time of the Civil War, blacks made up slightly more than 20 percent of Knoxville's 3,700 citizens, but when Union forces occupied Knoxville in late 1863, former slaves poured into the city. New jobs created by the postwar economic surge lured in the newly freed, and by 1880, blacks made up almost a third of the city's population. White émigrés from East Tennessee's outlying areas contributed even more to Knoxville's exploding population. Even though this group is vitally important to this study, tracking their presence is frustratingly problematical. Census takers did not distinguish between mountain and lowland birthplaces within the same state, nor were they able to account for the high level of geographical mobility within a state between one decennial census and the next. Moreover, this group's penchant for selective acculturation, and the consequences of social mobility, make them far more difficult to follow than representatives of racial or ethnic minorities. Nonetheless, anecdotal accounts suggest this "invisible" group made up a major portion of the workforce and contributed to the emerging middle class, typified by my great-grandfather, Washington Lafayette Gibbs.

Until more detailed research is completed, we can surmise that the motives and behavior of these newly urban Appalachians were diverse and complex. Clearly, both push and pull factors led rural East Tennesseans, like Grandpa Gibbs, to move to the city. To understand the former, we must recall the economic, environmental, and emotional effects of partible inheritance for traditional farming communities in East Tennessee's hinterlands. A crisis in the making when the Civil War began, the effects of partible inheritance became full blown by around 1880, particularly in hardscrabble areas such as the Clearfork Valley and the foothills, coves, and hollows of the Smokies. Many rural farmers found economic alternatives in the coal mines, timber camps, and other extractive industries emerging in hinterland areas, but hardships and instabilities in those pursuits convinced some rural residents to seek opportunity and employment in Knoxville's railroad shops, iron foundries, textile mills, and other manufacturing and retail establishments. At the same time, city conveniences, new technologies, better educational opportunities for their children, and many other attractions pulled hinterland residents into Knoxville in the years before, but particularly after, 1900. In the first two decades of the twentieth century, the rural population of the Tennessee Valley increased by slightly less than 15 percent, while the Valley's urban population surged by more than 243 percent. Between 1900 and 1930, the fraction of Tennessee Valley residents living in cities of more than ten thousand increased from slightly more than one-third to just under one-half.[11] We will explore the experiences and behaviors of this group later, but for now it is important to emphasize that many of them—along with African Americans and other immigrants—made up a workforce accustomed to hard physical labor, long hours, and low wages. As such, they were yet another key to Knoxville's turn-of-the-century economic surge.

Perceptive observers of the day were very much aware of the symbiotic nature of Knoxville's burgeoning economic enterprises. City-based railways, wholesale firms, extractive industries, and other manufacturing pursuits intertwined in a complex web of supply and demand, producers and consumers, and employers and employees. The city's leading businessmen—Charles McGhee, Perez Dickinson, Edward J. Sanford, and others—diversified their investments and energies to benefit all of these business endeavors and encouraged lesser investors to do likewise. City boosters echoed those sentiments, particularly emphasizing the benefits of these enterprises for Knoxville. Writing in his own *Knoxville Daily Chronicle* in the heady year 1886, Knoxville editor William Rule observed, "Every ton of [East Tennessee] coal contributes to the prosperity of Knoxville . . . . Every block of marble contributes something to Knoxville's growth . . . every pound of spelter [zinc] puts money in Knoxville's pockets."[12]

11. Secondary resources that address Knoxville's demographics and, in particular, rural in-migration to the city include: Mary Utopia Rothrock, *The French Broad-Holston Country: A History of Knox County, Tennessee.* Knoxville: East Tennessee Historical Society, 1946., 221; Wheeler, *Knoxville, Tennessee,* 22–27; and Wheeler and McDonald, "The Communities of East Tennessee," 27–29.

12. Undated clipping from William Rule vertical file in McClung Collection.

While hindsight makes these patterns and the optimistic expectations they fueled more apparent, the same is true of the symbiotic ties they created between Knoxville and East Tennessee's hinterlands. The railroads and wholesale businesses that initially spurred Knoxville's economic surge in the 1870s could not have existed without each other, but also not without East Tennessee's more remote locales. To be sure, the railroad on its own was a powerful entity, which directly and indirectly employed thousands of Knoxvillians and spurred economic growth, creating tens of thousands of additional jobs. But the railroad's raison d'etre was to link Knoxville to outside providers and markets and to do the same for locales within the region. Within a few years of the rebuilding of rail lines after the Civil War, the volume of trade between city wholesalers and rural East Tennesseans surged. Individual "drummers" continued to pay regular visits to isolated farms and crossroads country stores, but railroads made delivering products to remote markets more affordable. Even more important, the railroad whetted the appetites of rural dwellers for new products. The railroad also carried hinterland products and residents back to Knoxville and beyond, winning for rural dwellers cash necessary for entry into the new consumer economy. Even more important for East Tennessee's hinterlands, railroads directly and indirectly stimulated demand for key regional resources even as they provided a means to transport those same products, which in earlier eras could not be effectively marketed. East Tennessee timber became ties and trestles essential for construction and ongoing railway maintenance. And, of course, in that age of steam, East Tennessee coal fueled locomotives. The railway also hauled these same products to Knoxville and from that hub to distant locales and urban centers. In East Tennessee's emerging new city and beyond, modernization's appetite for construction materials and energy was insatiable.

Fabulous profits from railroads and wholesaling spurred a second, even more energetic economic surge in Knoxville in the 1880s. Shrewd business people reinvested those profits even as they encouraged investments from outside the region to expand and make more efficient the hinterlands' extractive industries. By 1890, Knox County alone had twenty-eight marble quarries and six lumber companies with capital investments over $100,000, and more than fifteen coal companies had established their headquarters in Knoxville. Railroad and wholesale profits also financed the array of foundries, textile mills, paper mills, and lesser enterprises appearing in 1880s Knoxville. The miracle of economic growth gave birth, in turn, to an array of retail establishments and service industries to meet the needs of the city's surging populace. So long as prosperity continued, the interests of the various Knoxville-based enterprises, and of East Tennessee's representative parts, meshed together, giving credence to the capitalist ideal that growth benefits all.

By the 1890s, outside developments called that notion into question, as the nation and region faced its worst economic crisis to that time. After 1900, renewed economic growth, combined with the persuasiveness of the growth ideal, blinded Knoxvillians and East Tennesseans to more serious flaws in the regional economy. Among many influences, Knoxville's economic dependence on East Tennessee's rural hinterlands, which in the boom years was one of its most notable assets, gradually became one of its greatest liabilities. But before exploring those developments, we must first examine another set of crises that growth brought to Knoxville.

Beneath the Gilding

Historians have long recognized that the twin forces of industrialization and urbanization fostered for Gilded Age Americans both exhilarating achievements and bewildering challenges. Hence, it should come as no surprise that Knoxville's economic surge in the final third of the nineteenth century brought in its wake not only wealth and new opportunities but also a host of new problems. For all of the hype and optimism of Knoxville's boosters and New South visionaries, the city in the boom years of the 1870s and '80s was not a pleasant place. In the upheavals following the Civil War, crime was rampant, and that legacy combined with stresses from rapid growth to make homicides and violence a common feature of city life. Knoxville saloons also had plenty of customers. In 1879, one observer estimated that the city's twenty-five drinking establishments served more than five thousand drinks daily, at an expense of $550 per day (or $200,750 per year). Prostitution, cockfighting, gambling, and other vices flourished in "the Bowery," a rough-and-tumble district where the rail lines and First Creek converged.[13] At the same time, provisions for sanitation were inadequate, livestock roamed city streets, and disease and early death were common. In the 1870s and 1880s, cholera and yellow fever epidemics swept through the upper South. Knoxville lost many residents, and only its relatively higher elevation saved it from the health disasters that beset Nashville, Memphis, and other regional cities. The city's streets were paved poorly, if at all. Dust and the soot from the coal furnaces that heated homes and fueled industrial establishments left the city's air sooty and grimy.

13. Knoxville's urban woes are graphically described in MacArthur, *Knoxville's History*, 35–38; Alfred Grey and Susan Adams, "Government," in *Heart of the Valley*, ed. Lucile Deaderick (Knoxville: East Tennessee Historical Society, 1976), 91–93; and Wheeler, *Knoxville, Tennessee*, 29–30.

In response to these urban woes, Knoxville followed the lead of larger urban centers, adapting old cultural institutions and adopting new ones. The city gradually (often reluctantly) assumed greater responsibility for police and fire protection, public health and sanitation, and education. But private organizations continued to be the city's first line of defense against many of the other challenges accompanying modernity. A private company, for example, provided the city's water service until 1907, even though observers more than twenty years earlier had considered that arrangement completely inadequate. Yet another example of adaptation to new circumstances in Knoxville was St. John's Episcopal Church's establishment of an orphanage in 1873. That same year, female representatives from the city's leading congregations came together to form the Knoxville Benevolent Association, intending to provide a helping hand for the city's "worthy poor." The YMCA, which had been established before the Civil War, was revitalized and expanded to help address the city's new challenges.

In a myriad of other, less spontaneous ways, late-nineteenth-century Knoxville marched toward modernity. The public outlook mirrored the optimism of the city's leading businesspeople, and thanks in part to the general prosperity of the era, Knoxville imitated—and occasionally even led the way—in embracing trends historians associate with progressivism. Mainstream Protestant churches (Presbyterian, Methodist, Baptist, Episcopalian) remained the city's most vital social institutions. In the booming years of the latter nineteenth century, many of the city's leading congregations built impressive new sanctuaries and followed increasingly formal trends in preparing and selecting clergy. Most of the downtown churches followed other national trends, supporting increasingly bureaucratic denominational structures, which oversaw global, national, and local missions, and embraced the "social gospel," with its emphasis on addressing human needs "in this world," while also offering a broad array of programs and services to address the spiritual and social needs of their parishioners. Roman Catholics had established a Knoxville parish even before the Civil War. With greater Catholic migration, their presence expanded, and they opened St. Mary's parochial school shortly after the Civil War. In 1928 they established St. Mary's Hospital. Between the Civil War and 1900, Reformed and Orthodox Jewish congregations were established in the city. Although denominational preferences were strong, Knoxvillians displayed a healthy ecumenical attitude. This attitude was most obvious in the establishment of the previously mentioned Knoxville Benevolent Association in 1873, and its successor institution, the Associated Charities of Knoxville, founded fifteen years later. Yet there were many other notable examples of interfaith cooperation. In 1872, the city's First Presbyterians, for example, invited members of the newly established Temple Beth-El congregation to use their sanctuary until they could construct a synagogue.

Prior to the Civil War, education in Knoxville had largely been a private concern, but in the postwar years the city (and Knox County) again followed national trends in establishing a system of tax-supported public schools, including separate schools for the children of the city's burgeoning African American population. Tennessee lagged behind other states in its support for public education, but compared to Middle and West Tennessee, East Tennessee placed greater emphasis on education. Within East Tennessee, Knoxville's commitment to education was impressive. In 1869, 72 percent of the city's white children and 76 percent of its black children were enrolled in school. The presence of East Tennessee University undoubtedly contributed to Knoxvillians' emphasis on education. The university had been small and had emphasized a classical curriculum in the prewar era, and its first graduating class after the war (1871) numbered only four. But the name change to the University of Tennessee in 1879 revealed greater state interest in the institution and (again mirroring broader national trends) led to dramatically increased enrollments and a number of progressive curricular changes. By the turn of the century, the university emerged as the center for educational reform in Tennessee. With financial support from the (Rockefeller-funded) General Education Board and leadership from Professor Philander C. Claxton, the university from 1902 through the World War I era sponsored the innovative "Summer School of the South," a crusading effort to advance teacher education and improve rural schools. Nationally prominent instructors taught students from every southern state, and enrollments reached over 2,500—a significant number for a campus that served 350 students when the program began in 1902. Knoxville and Knox County provided financial and moral support for the endeavor and took great pride in its successes. The city also became the location of a Presbyterian-related school for freed slaves in 1875. By the end of the century, Knoxville College was a beloved institution among the city's nascent black middle class, and its alumni staffed segregated black schools throughout East Tennessee.

The same ferment and prosperity that assured the above advances also brought Knoxville many other accoutrements of civilization. In 1885, financier-philanthropist Charles McClung McGhee established the Lawson McGhee library on Gay Street as a memorial to his daughter. By 1917, that greatly expanded Knoxville library moved to a new location a block away, as a city-supported institution free to the public. In 1872, Swiss immigrant, tailor, and businessmen Peter Staub constructed a three-story "opera house" and theater on Gay Street. Over the years, "the Staub" hosted nationally prominent operas, dramatic productions, entertainers, and lecturers. Several subsequent renovations increased seating capacity to almost two thousand. With the advent of commercial silent films by World War I, the Staub added movies to its repertoire. By 1920, at least four movie houses were open in Knoxville.

An Appalachian City and Its Identity

Residents of "the Queen City of the Mountains" looked upon these and many other advances with great pride. Indeed, by the time a nationwide panic ended the city's remarkable period of growth in the mid-1890s, Knoxville had in many ways become "a city"—and Knoxvillians were confident their march toward modernity would resume in the century ahead. These developments and assumptions are particularly important for this study, for mainstream America's discovery of Appalachia took root and flourished in the very urban institutions and values that Knoxvillians eagerly embraced in the closing decades of the nineteenth century. No one could doubt that the hinterlands, which surrounded the city and were so vital to its economic and demographic livelihood, were part of this amorphous and alarmingly aberrant region, but what about Knoxville itself?

The judgment that Appalachia's culture and people were "strange and peculiar" reflects a cognitive preference for strict dichotomies: urban vs. rural, modern vs. traditional, complex vs. simple, cosmopolitan vs. provincial, educated vs. ignorant, and so on. In reality, neither the nation's cities nor its remaining rural areas ever fit as neatly into these categories as observers imagined. Yet this sort of clarity held particular appeal for turn-of-the-century Americans, whose commitment to progress and to an idealized, homogenous national culture simultaneously fostered pride and anxiety. If, as Alan Batteau reminds us, "Appalachia [was a] creature of the urban imagination," then prevailing notions about the region truly created a conundrum for turn-of-the-century Knoxvillians.

Almost 85 percent of Knox County's population in 1900 was Caucasian. But only a minority of Knoxvillians were descendants of early city residents, while a far larger number were more recent émigrés from the hinterlands, or were the offspring of émigrés. That demographic reality, and the tremendous importance of hinterland resources for the city's recent economic surge, raises many questions historians of the city have overlooked for too long. How did Knoxvillians, old and new, view broader East Tennessee and southern Appalachia? More specifically, how did they respond and contribute to the broader mainstream discovery of Appalachia? How did that development, in turn, influence Knoxvillians? These questions will be a focal point of chapter five. But we must briefly address these issues here because they bore important implications for Knoxville's post-1900 development.

Knoxvillians' views of the region were both diverse and dynamic. Of the many influences contributing to this diversity and dynamism, one must consider the varied backgrounds of Knoxville's "native" population and the fact that those individuals responded selectively to urbanization's challenges and opportunities. Within those broader contours, one must also consider several interrelated variables, most notably demographic and economic conditions within the region, as well as outside influences. These variables, of course, were never static, further complicating an already complex picture.

We can begin to clarify this opaque scenario if we focus first on the time-frame from around 1870 to the mid-1890s, the era that to this point has been the primary focus for this chapter. Considerable evidence is available about the views of descendants of the city's original founders. The opinions of this affluent, well-educated group are widely captured in archives, libraries, and other repositories. Indeed, three prominent Gilded Age Knoxvillians wrote and published histories of the local population, highlighting in particular the contributions of East Tennessee loyalists to Union victory in the Civil War. Journalist William Rule's *The Loyalists of Tennessee in the Late War* was published in 1887. The following year, Thomas Hume, an Episcopal clergyman and president of the University of Tennessee, completed *The Loyal Mountaineers of Tennessee.* Nine years later, *The Covenanter, the Cavalier, and the Puritan,* by prominent Knoxville attorney Oliver P. Temple, was released. This trio's primary motivation was less to refute the increasingly popular and influential accounts of local colorists and home missionaries, which scholars now consider the sources for stereotypical "Appalachian" imagery, than it was to increase awareness of East Tennesseans' often overlooked contributions to history. Still, their views challenged many notions about the region that were becoming widespread. Much like Berea College president W. G. Frost, whose appeal on behalf of "our contemporary ancestors" became the most widely known depiction of turn-of-the-century Appalachians, Rule, Humes, and Temple emphasized the primitive nature of mountain culture to prove their direct ties to the nation's founding fathers. For outside readers, this insight helped explain the region's alleged ignorance and penchant for violence. That the three Knoxvillians to at least some extent accepted those characterizations gave them further credence.

The mid-1890s represents a significant turning point in Knoxville's history, as the effects of the nation's worst economic crisis to date found its way to East Tennessee. Between 1893 and 1897, railroads went into receivership, factories laid off workers, unemployment surged, and the ranks of the poor and needy mushroomed. On January 19, 1893, the *Knoxville Sentinel* reported that Charity Relief Headquarters served 2,000 persons on Saturday, 1,500 on the following Monday, more than 600 on Tuesday, and more than 700 on Wednesday; on Thursday it ran out of food and suspended service. Such calamities undoubtedly shook the city's optimism. In this unpleasant context, Knoxvillians' attitudes toward rural folk in their midst and in the hinterlands became more harsh and less forgiving. From this ferment, a yearning for antimodern alternatives emerged. In time, as we will see in chapter five, antimodernist impulses profoundly influenced the attitudes of many Americans toward Appalachia.

Into a New Century

Renewed prosperity, however, restored characteristic optimism for most Americans and Knoxvillians. This was peculiarly evident in the city's responses to a fire that devastated a large part of its Gay Street business district in 1897. Local observers immediately dubbed it "the million dollar fire" as a means of making everyone aware of just how much the economy of this once sleepy town had grown. And the city's quick response in rebuilding the destroyed district offered concrete proof that their optimism was real. The following decade and a half, the heyday of the so-called Progressive Era in the nation at large—and seemingly in Knoxville—was an era of calm, prosperity, and innocence. Still, hindsight reveals concerns that caused worry among the city's more prescient leadership. To be sure, Knoxville's population grew, but the 11.3-percent increase from 1900–1910 contrasted alarmingly with the 45-percent increase during the panic-ridden 1890s and the 133-percent increase during the surging 1880s. Economic statistics for the era are less than complete, but the overall picture belied the city's outward optimism. The number of industrial establishments declined by 27 percent. Part, but certainly not all, of that decline can be attributed to consolidation of existing businesses. Compared to the previous two decades, the rates of increase for total capital invested, and for the wage-earning population, also declined.[14]

Many factors contributed to the slowing of Knoxville's economic growth. Recent observers have emphasized, in particular, the passing of the dynamic business leaders who oversaw the city's tremendous post–Civil War expansion. Rather than adjust to changing times, the less ambitious and more conservative new generation of businesspeople allowed once-dynamic businesses, such as Knoxville Woolens, to close down. The city's new elite, according to some scholars, emphasized short-range dividends over wise long-term investments. When African American and rural émigré laborers moved into nearby neighborhoods, the elites fled to new, prestigious suburbs on the city's west side. But at least two important qualifications belong here. First, one historian suggests that, even in the earlier age, Knoxville's leading businesspeople were inclined to avoid innovation, and invested in only cautious endeavors. Secondly, one cannot help but acknowledge a continued outward optimism among many city residents during the first decade and a half of the twentieth century.

The responses of some city officials and boosters to the less-than-encouraging demographic and economic trends of the era from around 1900 to 1915 is perhaps the most notable indicator of an outlook that was persistently upbeat. For our purposes, those responses are even more important, for they reveal

14. Wheeler, *Knoxville, Tennessee*, 29–33

much about the city's evolving attitudes toward its hinterlands and toward the greater Appalachian region. To stir its economy, the city in the late 1890s began annual fall street fairs and carnivals to draw customers from surrounding rural areas to the city and its businesses. A visit from "the Prophet of the Smokies," a legendary Rip Van Winkle–like figure (with great white whiskers and two horns atop his head) officially opened each fall carnival. The prophet's home, wrote a reporter in 1897, was "far up the steeps amid the everlasting peaks . . . above the thunder and storm." Upon receiving a key to the city from Knoxville's mayor, the prophet extended hearty greetings "to the children of this splendid metropolis . . . my peculiar pride and joy."[15] Each year, the prophet celebrated Knoxville's expansion and predicted an even grander future, revealed in projected growth indicators common to that era: miles of paved roads and highways, increased smoke from the stacks of city factories, and the city's huge appetite for annexing nearby communities. Did this mixture of bravado and (attempted) humor reflect adolescent-like awkwardness with Knoxville's rapid rise? To assert that the Prophet's annual visits reveal qualms among some Knoxvillians about their roots and an uneasiness with their relatively privileged status in the greater East Tennessee community is plausible— but perhaps lends too great an influence to hindsight.

By 1910, Knoxville's fall carnivals evolved into something more elaborate and serious. The city that fall hosted the first of two "Appalachian Expositions," and in 1913 was the site for a National Conservation Exposition. City boosters had occasionally used the label "Appalachia" in promotional efforts, but the Expos of 1910 and 1911 represented Knoxvillians' most intentional identification with the region. The two fairs revealed Knoxville's continued quest for "New South" status and, in particular, targeted several impediments to that vision, including the city's allegedly conservative and apathetic elite and its growing population of in-migrant highlanders. The fair's progressive promoters saw these two groups as strange bedfellows and pointed to their shared resistance to taxation and government regulation as a major cause for the city's laggard growth since the Panic of 1893. Outspoken Expo backer, and recently arrived Knoxville businessman, William J. Oliver, believed that overcoming this lethargy and myopia was essential to the shared destiny of the city and greater East Tennessee.

The fair's first two official goals are particularly relevant for our purposes: "First: To stress the vital importance of conserving the forests and streams of

15. Jack Neely, "The Prophet," *Metro Pulse,* Oct. 4, 2001; Fred Brown, "Prophet of Smokies," *Knoxville News-Sentinel,* July 19, 1992; Robert Williams, "Judge Bob Recalls . . ." *Knoxville News-Sentinel,* Mar. 30, 1947.

16. Facing page: Robert Lukens, "The New South on Display," *Journal of East Tennessee History* 69 (1997): 8.

From the late 1890s through World War I, the Prophet of the Smokies visited Knoxville annually, promoting the city's economy and future. He highlighted, in particular, the city's important economic ties with East Tennessee's hinterlands. This photo appeared in the *Knoxville News* in 1916. (Courtesy of Calvin M. McClung Historical Collection, with special thanks to Vicky Bills.)

the Appalachian region; Second: To exploit the resources and potentialities of this wonderful mountain empire."[16] For twenty-first-century eyes, this juxtaposition of "conserve" and "exploit" appears peculiar, but most Americans of a century ago saw no contradiction. Knoxvillians, in particular, became excited with the prospect of this celebration, and in the months leading up to the 1910 expo, offered poems, songs, even a special new beverage ("Appalachianade") to show their support. National figures (most notably Theodore Roosevelt), a midway, fireworks, aeroplanes, and dirigible balloons attracted large audiences and much attention. Visitors to the "Minerals and Forestry Building" encountered a more serious two-fold message. Displays sought to increase awareness of the economic potential of East Tennessee's mineral and timber resources and demonstrated new, more efficient methods for their exploitation. For Progressive-Era Americans, "conservation" and "responsible exploitation" were synonymous. At another 1910 exhibit, a log dwelling, replete with "old-fashioned flowers, newspapers as wall decorations, [and] unwholesome odors" depicted "the primitive side of Appalachian culture."[17] Next door, a teacher from a nearby mountain settlement school hosted a commodious two-room cabin displaying handicrafts from the school's industrial department. That mountain home symbolized the "New South future" of East Tennessee's unfortunately still isolated and ignorant—but clearly salvageable—highlanders.

The expos' overall messages were not unlike those of William Rule and other earlier regional spokesmen: rural East Tennesseans had potential to become like their Knoxville neighbors. And the bountiful resources in their

17. Ibid., 22.

midst were essential to the inextricably linked wellbeing of city and hinterland; this, of course, was the inevitable triumph of progress. If anyone doubted that message, yet another visit from "the Prophet of the Great Smokies" in 1916 (five years after the second exposition) reminded East Tennesseans and residents of the region's leading city of their destiny. Knoxville, the Prophet pronounced, would soon become "the Golconda of the earth [and] center of culture, progress, and prosperity."[18] Strangely enough, that was the Prophet's last reported visit to the city he claimed to be his "peculiar pride and joy." Perhaps he came to realize that the very extractive industries essential to Knoxville's "successes" brought "Appalachian" miseries to East Tennessee's hinterlands.

Troubled Knoxvillians and the Contradictory 1920s

As the Prophet waxed eloquent in Knoxville's Chilhowee Park in 1916, war in Europe was transforming the world and the United States. Knoxville and East Tennessee felt the impact of these distant rumblings. Historians have devoted scant attention to the impact of World War I on Knoxville, but hindsight suggests the war years were even more of a watershed for the city than the 1890s, for they brought profound changes to Knoxville's ties to greater East Tennessee and to its view of Appalachia. Temporary wartime demands stirred important demographic and economic changes: in-migration to Knoxville increased as many more former rural residents left their ancestral homes; wartime enlistments and employment increased many East Tennesseans' exposure to the bigger world and consumerism; wartime demands for coal, timber, and agricultural products artificially spurred hinterland industries, bringing a burst of temporary wealth to those areas and to Knoxville. A new euphoria, mixed with new anxieties, spread across the land as the nation ventured for the first time onto the global political stage. Rural East Tennessee and greater Appalachia felt these developments in peculiar ways.

Neither the nation nor residents of East Tennessee were content with the normalcy they so eagerly sought in the war's aftermath. In the nation at large, 1919–20 saw economic recession and labor unrest; a Red Scare and the ugly reappearance of nativism; resurgent racism and the revival of the Ku Klux Klan; and a hasty retreat from both the progressives' domestic idealism and the lofty global visions of Woodrow Wilson. Knoxville was hardly immune to these painful national trends. In 1919, streetcar workers went on strike. A race riot broke out on Gay Street, shattering illusions that Knoxville was somehow different from other southern cities. Tensions from the riot simmered into the 1920s, as

18. Neely, "The Prophet."

The Main Entrance and Mountain Cabin from the 1911 Appalachian Exposition offered visitors contrasting images of East Tennessee and the greater Appalachian region (Main Entrance image from Elena I. Zimmerman's *Knoxville: A Postcard Memoir, 1900–1930* [East Tennessee Historical Society, 1991]; Mountain Cabin image courtesy of Calvin M. McClung Historical Collection.)

many blacks departed the city and a local KKK klavern emerged as a powerful force. A hostile, reactionary mood arose in response to assorted local and national developments, and many of the disenchanted were relatively recent working-class émigrés from East Tennessee's rural regions.

Historians have moved far beyond popular "jazz age" notions of the 1920s and emphasized that economic trends underlay and exacerbated the era's social and cultural tensions. After the brief postwar recession of 1919–20, a "new" economy rose up around the automobile, petroleum, new construction, and new manmade fibers. Meanwhile, "old" industries based on railroad, coal, agriculture, and traditional textiles fell ever further behind. East Tennessee's hinterlands fell into the latter camp. Hardscrabble farmers and laid-off coal miners and loggers saw rural East Tennessee lapse into prolonged recession long before the stock market crash of 1929. And Knoxville, even as many of its residents sought to emulate aspects of the "new" 1920s culture, sat astride an economy that depended almost entirely on the "sick" industries of the 1920s: railroads, coal, textiles, and agriculture. At first, the city fared better than the hinterlands, but when the full national crisis struck in 1929–30, Knoxville also faced hardships of "Appalachian" proportions. When that occurred, the hinterland folk finally had an advantage—because they were accustomed to harsh realities.

Historical observers of 1920s Knoxville have related the city's misfortunes to the slowing of the city's economic growth during the years between around 1900 and World War I. In explaining the slowed growth of the city's economy, William MacArthur observes, "A prosperity built on railroads and wholesale merchandizing, on limited mineral resources, and textile manufacturing began to fade." Contemporaries, including Knoxville native James Agee, were the first of many observers to blame the shortsighted conservatism of the city's elite for an outward ugliness and provincialism that would still define Knoxville long after the advent of a second global conflict ended the depression. MacArthur is not so sure about this assessment. Displaying a cautiousness that mimicked the outlook of those he described, MacArthur suggests that Knoxville's earlier boosters may have simply "oversold themselves on the city's fabled advantages."[19] This was neither the first, nor the last time, Knoxville would experience this misfortune.

Like Oliver, Agee, and other disgruntled Knoxville progressives of the 1920s, recent scholarly commentators on this era in the city's history ignore MacArthur's insightful assessment. Instead they focus on how several attempts to seriously address the city's ills dismally failed. In 1912, reformers pushed through changes in the city charter to provide for a commission form of mu-

19. MacArthur, *Knoxville's History*, 49.

nicipal government. Nine years later, when that system proved ineffective, and with corruption rampant, Knoxvillians adopted the even more progressive city manager model for city governance. When the city expended $15,000 to lure Louis Brownlow, Petersburg, Virginia's nationally known city manager, to fill the same post in Knoxville, city progressives were certain better days were ahead. Instead, Brownlow's penchant for "scientific government" and his call for increased taxes to pay for long-neglected services were met with intense hostility. In 1926, when public support withered and allies on the city council disappeared, Brownlow suffered a nervous breakdown and resigned.

Brownlow, his supporters, and recent scholars blame an "unholy alliance" for these misfortunes. Knoxville's much-criticized elite, according to this camp, was part of the problem. Their crime was standing idly by and allowing more despicable foes to effectively strangle Knoxville's most promising reform effort. The latter, more active villains were reactionary recent arrivals from East Tennessee's rural hinterlands led by their own populist demagogue: South Knoxville city councilman Lee Monday. Brownlow spared few words in denigrating his powerful foe: "He was a hillbilly and gloried in it . . . an orator in the good old mountain fashion." Brownlow concluded his long tirade with the charge that Monday was "representative of his district and his clan, the East Tennesseans."[20] Brownlow's venom stands in stark contrast to the admittedly paternalistic, but generally cordial, words earlier elite observers, such as William Rule and the expo promoters, offered to describe East Tennessee's rural folk, both those who came into the city as well as those who stayed behind in the hills.

Brownlow's assessment of Knoxville and the surrounding region has proven remarkably resilient. The most scholarly history of Knoxville to date describes the city's rural-to-urban émigrés with hyperbole almost equal to Brownlow's: "Few had left behind their Appalachian mores, their suspicion of government . . . their rough and tumble democratic politics, their belief in the superfluity of education, their fundamentalist religions, or their hatred for those who possessed more than they did." As proof of these allegations, the author quotes extensively from an 1885 city newspaper article blaming rural newcomers for an array of vices that characterized "the Bowery," Knoxville's most violent and crime-ridden district. Those vices included "pool halls, gambling dens, saloons, cocaine schools, and houses of prostitution."[21] Whatever one makes of the charges, there can be no doubt they represented common perceptions of rural East Tennessee. When regional natives who did not conform to those stereotypes rushed to

20. Louis Brownlow, *The Autobiography of Louis Brownlow: A Passion for Anonymity* (Chicago: Univ. of Chicago Press, 1958, 190.

21. Wheeler, *Knoxville, Tennessee,* 27.

disassociate from the likes of Monday, they of course, gave native credence to those sweeping denigrations. Monday and his followers were left to represent the region.

Was there any truth to Brownlow's charges? Surely there was. East Tennessee has always had its share of rural reactionaries who opportunistically use what Brownlow called "redneck demagoguery" to exploit a prejudiced, uninformed public. But from a broader historical perspective, the return to normalcy and repudiation of progressivism were hardly regional developments.

Chapter Four

New South Realities: East Tennessee's Hinterlands as Resource Producer for Industrial America

Cades Cove, as much as any single place, epitomizes the contradictions that make Appalachia so elusive. It is pristine and primitive, extinct yet enduring, remote yet teeming with humanity. As the most visited site in our nation's most visited national park, Cades Cove is truly one of East Tennessee's most beloved, yet endangered, settings. Surrounding peaks reach to the heavens, but the Cove itself is a very earthly place. Abandoned cabins ringed by split-rail fences evoke a quaint, pastoral charm that lures tens of thousands of visitors annually. They come from nearby East Tennessee and from around the world, mostly in private, single-family automobiles that on a typical summer or fall day leave the Cove's Loop Road as congested as the countless cities from which many of the visitors seek escape. Indeed, the very contradictions of modernity that gave rise to the idea of "Appalachia" a century and a half ago are still alive and well in Cades Cove.

Contrary to popular notions, Cades Cove prior to Great Smoky Mountains National Park was neither homogenous, isolated, and inbred, nor quaint, changeless, and idyllic. From its settlement in 1819 to the Civil War, Cades Cove was vibrant, dynamic, diverse, and surprisingly progressive. It is true that Civil War–era traumas temporarily turned some Cove residents inward and that for much of the remainder of the nineteenth century, suspicions of change and outsiders and excessive dependence on extended families and entrenched community traditions vied against instincts that were more open and progressive. At the very time local colorists, home missionaries, and other commentators portrayed Cades Cove in the most blatantly stereotypical and aberrant terms, progressive elements gradually reclaimed leadership in the Cove community. Like Henry Shapiro, Durwood Dunn persuasively argues that the views of these outsiders revealed more about their own anxieties than they did about realities in the Cove. For them, and for countless visitors ever since, Cades Cove and greater Appalachia provide an alternative to puzzling contradictions. It is hardly surprising that a place modern arrogance could ridicule and nostalgic sentimentalism could romanticize and revere all at the same time became invaluable and enduring as well as elusive.

Two other Dunn assertions make the ironies surrounding popular fascination with Cades Cove more glaring and important for this chapter. Social and political life in the Cove of the latter nineteenth century, Dunn maintains, was "largely indistinguishable" from that of other rural Tennessee communities, and "were only exaggerations of existing currents in the broader mainstream of American society." But Dunn also warns readers against concluding that life in Cades Cove was typical of the greater Appalachian region. This disclaimer should not lead readers to believe that a "typical Appalachia" existed somewhere else. Dunn makes clear that we must abandon the notion of a uniform Appalachia and begin thinking of the region in more nuanced, realistic, and honest terms.[1]

"Cove families differed from other Southern Appalachian families," Dunn asserts, "in their ability to raise large surplus crops and in the availability of a regional market some forty miles away in Knoxville."[2] Those fortuitous realities assured early Cades Cove's relative prosperity and cultural vibrancy. The Cove did not rebound as readily as Knoxville from the economic and emotional effects from the Civil War, but those effects were clearly not as permanent as many have imagined. By around 1900, Dunn reports, a distinctly progressive spirit emulating broader, national trends and sentiments reappeared in the Cove. The same attributes—rich soils and access to markets—that had assured the Cove's antebellum fortunes continued to minimize the effects of partible inheritance in the latter nineteenth century. Nearby, less-blessed hollows of the Smokies, and remote, rugged locales such as the Clearfork Valley, were less fortunate. In these hinterland settings, Civil War–era traumas exacerbated economic, environmental, and demographic crises that were in the making even before the war commenced. In the war's aftermath, as the greater United States rushed toward urban modernity and an industrial-consumer economy, the crises in these hardscrabble locales became ever more apparent to local residents and outsiders. As we explore how the former adjusted to these new circumstances and how the latter came to represent a distinct "Appalachia," I must reiterate the assertion from the prologue that Appalachian images (positive and negative) were not mere fabrications but instead drew from regional realities. Secondly, as we focus on the development of extractive industries in East Tennessee's hinterlands and the symbiotic relationship that developed between those areas and Knoxville, we should not forget William Cronon's wise assertion that "city and country share a common past and fundamentally reshape each other."[3]

1. Dunn, *Cades Cove*, 10, 147, 163.

2. Ibid., 183.

3. Cronon, *Nature's Metropolis*, 7.

Hard Times in the Hinterlands

In the difficult decades of the latter nineteenth century, East Tennessee's hinterland residents faced inevitable change. Contrary to notions that "Appalachia" was aberrantly homogenous, static, and isolated, "Appalachian" East Tennesseans responded to their new realities in a variety of ways that, by both design and default, brought them into closer contact with other Americans and outside forces. For simplicity's sake, we may place those adjustments into two broad categories. Like earlier East Tennesseans swept up in the forces of Manifest Destiny, many rural folk moved from the region to greener pastures in the West and, by the turn of the century, to burgeoning urban centers of the Midwest and Northeast. There, as Jeff Biggers provocatively argues, regional expatriates contributed a distinct, albeit long-overlooked, Appalachian influence to the broader American story. A more common, though even more overlooked, destination for rural out-migrants was Knoxville and other regional cities. The latter's relative proximity made them a logical destination for "shuttle migrants." But moves that were initially temporary often became permanent. Either way, pressure (from without and within) led many rural East Tennesseans who relocated to regional locales like Knoxville and beyond the region to distance themselves from their roots. More significantly, out-migration deprived the hinterlands of the energy and talent of many creative individuals.

For hard-pressed rural East Tennesseans who stayed home, continued attempts to scratch out livings on the region's ever-shrinking, ever-more-exhausted, hillside farms offered an understandable but unattractive path. By the eve of the Great Depression, repeated subdivision of farms passed the saturation point, even as a blight mysteriously decimated long-essential chestnut forests, cementing many hinterlanders' doom. As on the dustbowl-ravaged Great Plains, misfortune and ever-diminishing prospects spurred further out-migration, until miseries in cities like Knoxville drove some new arrivals to retreat to farms that could not sustain them. In-depth studies of eastern Kentucky and West Virginia offer insights particularly appropriate for settings such as the Clearfork Valley and less-blessed locales in the Smokies—locales that shared much in common, geographically and demographically, with those other hardscrabble Appalachian settings.

Hinterland residents who did not leave their ancestral homes had no choice but to discover and develop new means of economic livelihood either to supplement or replace traditional agrarian pursuits. Although the alternatives pursued were diverse, they were almost all extractive industries of one form or another. These economic pursuits tied East Tennesseans to distant, erratic, and puzzling forces that offered, in turn, stark, mutually harmful options. For example, in the 1890s, Walland—a Blount County community near Cades Cove—became the site for the Schlosser Tannery, which imported cowhides from as far away as Chicago and Argentina. The tannery used bark from surrounding forests to make tannin to process leather for export to distant markets. Around the same time, Polk County in southeast Tennessee became the center of a thriving copper industry. These Faustian arrangements produced mixed effects; regular paychecks assured tannery and copper workers access to the emerging consumer economy, but both industries' environmental and long-range economic effects proved disappointing. The tannery badly polluted the Little River, and when manmade products became substitutes for leather by around 1930, the tannery abandoned Walland. Polk County's copper mills endured until 1987, but smelting left that corner of East Tennessee denuded, and as late as my childhood, the "Copper Basin" looked like a moonscape. These patterns typified most extractive enterprises, particularly the timber and coal industries, which became rural East Tennessee's most important and profitable economic pursuits during the half-century leading into the Great Depression.

East Tennessee's hinterlands provided only two of five key factors essential to both the Appalachian timber and coal industries. Chapter three touched upon the first key factor: the presence in post–Civil War East Tennessee of vast, largely untapped coal deposits and some of the world's richest forests. The second factor was labor. In the words of one observer, the "mountain people . . . were hardworking, inventive, reliable, and, as a matter of honor, expected to give a full day's work for a full day's pay."[4] Initially, many East Tennessee miners and loggers worked seasonally. Even later, when they pursued those endeavors full time, they (or other family members) continued to till crops, tend livestock, hunt, distill liquor, and supplement their incomes in diverse other ways. As a general rule, part-time and former farmers preferred work in the forests and mines to the more regimented, indoor routine of urban textile mills.

Conventional accounts have long suggested that the other three key factors for East Tennessee coal mining and timbering came from outside sources. But Knoxville, in fact, served as intermediary in each of these three areas. Take, for example, capital. East Tennessee's relative economic disadvantages, coupled with the technological demands of extractive industries, made large amounts of outside capital necessary. Knoxville businesspeople, such as Charles McClung McGhee and Edward J. Sanford, invested heavily in local railroads, mines, and timbering, but their ability to persuade outside entrepreneurs to invest in these

---

4. Gene Aiken, "Mountain Ways: Little River Lumber Company & Railroad Have Colorful History," *The Star*, Mar. 10, 1989. I found this clipping in the Cades Cove folder of the vertical files collection, Great Smoky Mountains National Park Library. Indications are that this newspaper was based in Gatlinburg and is no longer being published.

pursuits proved even more important. They helped entice capital from the North and from abroad, particularly from the British Isles.

Markets for regional coal and timber and railroads to carry these bulky products to those markets were two additional keys to East Tennessee's Gilded Age economy. Again, conventional and more recent accounts overlook the role of urban centers within and on the outskirts of the region as important immediate markets and rail hubs for regional products. Knoxville, for example, increased coal consumption from zero tons in 1868 to 120,000 tons in 1892. Similarly, the city experienced a housing boom from 1895 to 1904, which resulted in the construction of more than five thousand new (mostly wooden frame) homes.[5] Still, the primary destination for East Tennessee timber and coal were even more distant markets in the North and Midwest. Indeed, without industrialization's insatiable demands, these local industries would never have developed. By around 1900, a profound and abiding dependency on Knoxville—and on outside investors and markets—became an important shared hallmark of East Tennessee's timber and coal industries.

In addition to their common dependency, the Appalachian timber and coal industries shared a number of other distinctive similarities. Both were, of course, rural industries that had to create accommodations to house and meet other provisions for their laborers. This alone made them outwardly different from more customary forms of American industry. Over the half-century that is the focus of this chapter, an array of company towns housed East Tennessee's miners and loggers. The spectrum spanned from temporary, crudely constructed early coal and timber camps to "model towns" that several of the more successful mining companies established by World War I. From the laborer's perspective, these options shared several, potentially less desirable, traits. By providing housing for workers and their families, companies assured themselves a ready return from wages in the form of rental payments. This income, along with elevated prices at company stores, sometimes earned profits for employers at times when their businesses were otherwise struggling. More seriously, maintaining the right to deny housing to workers who displayed interest in unions, or who proved disruptive in any other fashion, gave employers considerable leverage over employee behavior.

The practices and worldviews of the owners of East Tennessee's timber and coal industries were also strikingly similar. Indeed, in more than a few cases, the same individuals engaged in both enterprises. Perhaps the most notable example was the Scottish entrepreneur Alexander Arthur, who spearheaded

5. "Our Coals: An Exhaustive Paper Before the Chamber of Commerce," *Knoxville Daily Tribune*, Apr. 17, 1892. Knoxville's housing boom is discussed in Smoky Mountain Historical Society, *The Gentle Winds of Change* (Sevierville, TN: Smoky Mountain Historical Society, 1986), 112.

New South Realities

timbering efforts on the Pigeon River along the Tennessee–North Carolina border in the early 1880s. Later in the decade, Arthur became the primary face of the American Association (a British company), which pursued an ambitious, ill-fated scheme to develop coal around Cumberland Gap at the east end of the Clearfork Valley. In coal-bearing regions, dual pursuits of timber and coal were natural, since removal of the former was a first step in digging for the latter. Michigan lumberman Justus S. Stearns, for example, came to the area along the Tennessee-Kentucky border in the 1890s intent on continuing his timber interests. Over time, however, Stearns and his heirs made most of their extensive profits from coal.

The region's timber and coal barons were simultaneously "captains of industry" and "robber barons." Mostly nonnative to the region, these investors instinctively evoked American ideals of individualism, social Darwinism, and the New South mindset. Many of them also displayed ungenerous, if often paternalistic, attitudes toward the region and its people. Their ambitious, aggressive business practices and social views emulated John D. Rockefeller and Andrew Carnegie. Like the latter, many East Tennessee entrepreneurs were deeply religious. The fabulous successes and profits they achieved left little doubt in their minds that the Almighty smiled on their efforts. The same considerations blinded many of them—and most of their contemporaries—to harmful human, economic, and environmental practices so apparent to subsequent observers. As closer investigations of the two industries will reveal, these were complex men whose lives intertwined with the controversies of their times, and they and their enterprises brought both benefits and costs to East Tennessee. By 1930, many of these businesspeople, like the owners of the Walland Tannery, had abandoned East Tennessee with large fortunes and left economic, environmental, and human havoc in their wake. "Appalachian" conditions in much of our region are an undeniable legacy of these realities.

While outwardly quite different, the work experiences and daily lives of East Tennessee loggers and coal miners were also similar. Hours were long, the work was physical, dirty, and dangerous, and compensation was meager. But latter-day observers too often allow hindsight to distort this story. From the perspective of the Gilded Age, and of people accustomed to barely eking out a living from unforgiving hillside farms, "public work" offered entry into the cash economy, the chance to acquire modern "stuff," hope for a better future for their children, and pride in their accomplishments.

Still, timbering and mining were dangerous. Accidents—falling trees and coal mine roofs, out-of-control machinery, and myriad other acts of God and man—often maimed and sometimes killed individual workers. Such events generally garnered only local attention, but that in no way lessened their importance for individual workers and their families. On the other hand, mining explosions on several occasions in the early twentieth century took the lives of scores of miners, earning East Tennessee brief attention in the national media. There were also more subtle and long-term effects of East Tennessee's extractive industries. For many individuals, this included permanent disabilities from on-the-job accidents, afflictions such as "black lung," and a sense of personal defeat and dehumanization that the scholar John Gaventa calls "quiescence." For the region as a whole, we cannot overlook the (already-mentioned) decision to abandon badly eroded forests and mined-out tunnels that honeycombed the rugged Cumberlands; these practices left environmental legacies that later generations would rue.

As we consider East Tennessee's timber and coal industries side by side, we should also remember that the two industries shared roughly similar chronologies. From the late-eighteenth-century arrival of Euro-Americans, regional residents utilized timber for construction, fuel, and other purposes; even before the Civil War, a few residents utilized coal as a supplemental source of fuel. After Civil War–era visitors recognized a greater potential value for these regional resources, the first significant phase of regional resource extraction began. During this first phase (which lasted about two decades), the extractive processes were relatively modest. Local elites often put up capital for early timber and coal companies, local farmers worked seasonally in these pursuits, and the overall social and environmental effects of these small-scale enterprises were only mildly disruptive. Hard times of the 1890s coincided with subtler, but no less dramatic, changes to usher in a second phase for both industries, which lasted until the eve of the Great Depression. Growing demands for regional resources called for greater supply, and these realities awakened the interest of the nation's ever-expanding big businesses in Appalachian coal and timber. Outside investors carried with them a greater sense of business efficiency and introduced new technologies that dramatically increased both production and environmental harm. As the effects of partible inheritance became more painful, regular paychecks and company-supplied housing lured younger regional residents away from hardscrabble farming. Over time, more and more locals took up mining and timbering as full-time pursuits. Hence the social effects of extractive industry's second phase were far more disruptive and posed greater threats to traditional values and institutions. Finally, by the mid-1920s, regional miners and loggers learned several painful economic lessons. In that transitional and traumatic decade, market demands and integration into the national economy proved capricious. Ironically the poverty, paranoia, and social and environmental degradation that extraregional economic integration left in their wake were labeled "Appalachian." "Modern" might be a more apt adjective.

Commercial Timbering Comes to the Smokies

With the exception of Knoxville and several other larger valley communities that had removed most of their timber resources before the Civil War, practically all of East Tennessee was still heavily forested when the postwar era began. Cades Cove's earliest residents had, of course, cleared forests to make way for farming and provide housing, fuel, and other basic needs. After the Civil War, many Cove farmers supplemented their incomes by cutting trees such as cherry, walnut, yellow poplar, and white pine, which were hauled by wagon to Maryville and Knoxville or sold to their neighbors for home construction, fabrication of tools and furniture, and other purposes. But the large-scale, commercial timbering of the industry's second phase never made its way into the Cove, although timber companies often employed Cove residents in forests just beyond its confines. The Cove's fertile soils, which kept farming relatively profitable, and the fact that the railroad spurs that penetrated even more remote mountain settings never entered the Cove, explain its relative good fortune in avoiding the loggers' crosscut saws and skidders prior to creation of the national park.

A string of small settlements along the Little River, just across Rich Mountain, and the series of ridges making up the Cove's northern boundary, offer more representative examples of East Tennessee timbering, particularly its second phase. Changes wrought by loggers were first evident in the names they gave to mountain communities. The Cherokee name Tuckaleechee had long applied to the broader area, but the newcomers quickly dropped that. Lesser locales previously known only by the family names of their residents also attained new, official titles. Tang became Townsend, in honor of Colonel Wilson B. Townsend, who in 1900 made that community home for his Little River Lumber Company. As Townsend's company extended its reach ever deeper into the mountains, timber camps appeared. Someone important was apparently fond of the suffix "mont," because several of the bustling camps took on the names Smokemont, Tremont, and Elkmont.

W. B. Townsend and Little River Lumber Company and Railroad

Prior to the 1890s, timbering along the Little River was selective and concentrated on trees that were readily accessible, and which brought top dollar in regional cities and distant markets. Cherry, poplar, and ash were often cut from locations near the river, and water and animal power were the primary means of carrying them to market. "Splash dams," which provided sufficient water flow to carry logs out of the mountains, were a seasonal, inefficient, often dangerous expedient. The labor source, mostly local farmers and their sons, seeking to supplement meager incomes, was also seasonal. We will probably never know how much lumber was removed from the Little River watershed before around 1900, but there seems to have been no serious depletion.

In response to an array of forces, inside and outside the region, some locals after 1890 became more willing to sell their time, labor, and timber acreage to investors. Forests in Michigan and Wisconsin that had been more accessible to burgeoning cities and industries of the Northeast and Midwest had become depleted, and new lumber supplies were wanted. And Knoxville-based "drummers" enticed rural East Tennesseans with the lure of consumerism. Colonel Townsend's 1898 visit to Tuckaleechee Cove was the proverbial turning point in the history of Smokies lumbering. A veteran Pennsylvania lumberman, Townsend came to East Tennessee at the request of John W. Fisher, another Pennsylvanian, and operator of the Schlosser Tannery in Walland. Fisher's enterprise required tree bark to fabricate tannins necessary for processing leather. Townsend and associates, shrewd businesspeople who had already invested in timber and coal operations in Eastern Kentucky, wasted no time in taking advantage of the opportunity. In 1900, they established Little River Lumber Company and Little River Railroad, and the community that became headquarters for both was transformed overnight into Townsend. Big business and progress had come to the Smokies, and rapacious exploitation of the Little River basin began.

W. B. Townsend's startup investment of $150,000 in the Little River Railroad was only his initial contribution to the transformation of lumbering in the Great Smokies. His acumen as a businessman, and the trust it won, brought the enterprise vastly larger investments, which allowed for the purchase of an initial forty thousand acres of mountain timber and the construction of the mill and rail center bearing Townsend's name. Over the next three decades, the company acquired an additional thirty to forty thousand acres of timber. As Little River loggers pushed beyond the already-thinned forests in areas along the river and up the steep terrain toward the North Carolina line, Townsend's skills as a businessman and engineer were put to the test. At the "staggering" cost of $360,000, the railroad was extended eighteen miles along the narrow, circuitous gorge of the river's east prong to the timber camp that became known as Elkmont. Innovative gear-driven locomotives and specialized narrow-gauge tracks were developed and utilized for the project. When especially steep grades required expensive and precarious switchbacks, the company installed incline rail equipment, which used large winches to pull cars up the grade and let them back down by controlled gravity. Little River's most incredible innovation was an incline track laid on a suspension bridge, which traversed the Meigs Creek waterfall at one of the east prong's highest points. By World War I, the high point of logging in the Smokies, more than two hundred miles of rails penetrated some of the most remote mountain terrain. Derailments were frequent, and an occasional tragic accident briefly captured attention from as far away as Knoxville. The crash that killed the engineer Gordon A. "Daddy" Bryson at Elkmont in 1909 produced a well-known ballad memorializing Bryson as an "Appalachian Casey Jones."

Townsend was also an innovator in utilizing steam-powered equipment that could move logs more efficiently to his railroad. Ground skidders were initially used, but in 1912 the company, in conjunction with the Clyde Iron Works of Minnesota, developed a system that saved time and reduced costs by moving logs from distances as great as 3,500 feet on cables suspended high in the air. Machine logging was as destructive as it was efficient. An overhead skidder cut a swath of destruction. Sparks from steam-powered equipment found combustible tinder in the debris loggers left behind, and tremendous fires resulted. Denuded slopes eroded and left deep ravines and polluted streams in their wake. Fish and fauna virtually disappeared from what only a generation before had been a mountain habitat teeming with wildlife.

Both "official" and firsthand accounts suggest the loggers and mountain people liked and respected Colonel Townsend. Like their employer, most locals were accustomed to and appreciated hard work. They were also, by most accounts, reserved and respectful of authority and probably would not have made

Overhead skidder utilized by Little River Lumber Company in the Smokies (ca. 1920s). Advancements in technology accelerated cutting of the forest and devastation of the mountain habitat. (Great Smoky Mountains National Park Library and Archives.)

New South Realities

public any disparaging comments about Townsend even if they held them. For his part, Townsend displayed a genuine, if paternalistic, interest in the local population, a disposition markedly different from the stereotypical northern speculator often associated with Appalachian extractive industries. Several memoirs, and the efforts of local historians and journalists, offer valuable, if incomplete, native perspectives on the Smokies timber industry. Loggers typically worked ten hours a day, six days a week, and received twenty to thirty cents per hour. Low wages most likely explain why, even in the machine era, the task of felling trees was still largely a manual process. Equipped with double-bit axes, wedges and heavy hammers, and long, sharp-toothed, crosscut saws, three-person teams felled trees as large as eight to ten feet in diameter. Occasionally four-person crews used twelve-foot saws to take down larger trees. Production, according to one firsthand account, "varied with time, place, and condition." The same observer indicated that a Little River crew in 1913 "was expected to cut 10,000 board feet per day." That, on average, meant "cutting and bucking 10–12 trees, 24–30 inches in diameter" each workday. Another former sawyer recounted: "If you had a sharp saw and a good buddy at the other end of it, that was about as much fun as playing a fiddle." But, he added, "if you had a bad working buddy, one who didn't know what he was doing, he could get you killed in a minute."[6] In the early days, workers with teams of draft animals snaked logs to streams where they were "floated to market." The coming of the railroads and advent of skidders reduced the need for this arduous effort, but never completely eliminated it, since logs still had to be moved from where they were cut to the skidders. In locations where they moved large numbers of logs, crews sometimes constructed V-shaped slides. In the early days, many loggers were jacks-of-all-trades, but with increased mechanization, some workers specialized as skidder operators, mechanics, and locomotive engineers and brakeman; others worked in the permanent saw mill in Townsend and smaller sawing operations in Tremont and Elmont.

Life for loggers varied greatly depending on where one worked. Little River provided two basic types of housing for its employees. Operation centers like Townsend, Tremont, and Elkmont offered an array of permanent housing that varied in quality with one's work status. For typical native employees, accommodations were simple and Spartan. The company provided loggers in the forests portable housing that could be moved on railroad flatcars as operations moved from depleted forests to new areas ever farther into the mountains. The typical dwelling was known as a "set off house," a ten-by-twelve-foot room with a large eye bolt in its roof. A log loader used the latter to load the cubicle

6. Vic Weals, "Mostly Downhill from Fish Camp: Lumberjack Recalls Life's Satisfactions," *Knoxville Journal*, Aug. 18, 1983.

New South Realities

on a flatcar whenever a move occurred. Rows of "set off houses" along railroad tracks were generically known as "stringtowns." Townsend abhorred the reputations of boomtowns and encouraged women to accompany their husbands. To counter their seminomadic status, loggers' wives planted gardens and tended chickens, "prettied up" their modest abodes, and raised children in the timber camps. Townsend, a devout Methodist, also recognized religion's stabilizing effect. While he always promoted his own preferred denomination, he recognized and accepted the Baptist and nondenominational preferences of his workers.

In each of their main camps Little River had company stores providing groceries, tobacco, clothing and other basic necessities. Employees could make purchases with cash, but they more typically used company-supplied scrip, known as "doogaloo." In the words of one logger, most workers "hardly ever drawed any money," but instead "took it all up in groceries and overalls."[7] Churches, schools, and recreational facilities were located in Townsend and Tremont and sometimes in the larger, more substantial, temporary camps. Despite what latter-day observers see as a harsh and difficult existence, contemporary accounts and subsequent recollections suggest most Little River loggers were content with their lot. Although the company's heyday coincided with the spread of organized labor in the United States, and an era that saw many clashes between unions and management, those patterns were notably absent from Little River's logging towns and camps.

Townsend's business skill and good luck not only enabled Little River Lumber to avoid many negative boomtown traits but also assured it relative success throughout the 1920s, a decade when most Appalachian extractive industries began to experience significant misfortunes. World War I had spurred a tremendous increase in demand for lumber, boosting both employment and profits; the emerging aviation industry, for example, created an unprecedented demand for spruce. Similarly, home construction was one of the growth industries of the outwardly prosperous 1920s, and housing booms in nearby Knoxville and more distant urban centers meant a steady demand for Smokies lumber. But by around 1925, these aberrantly advantageous circumstances began to wane. Of nearly twenty lumber companies that operated in the Smokies during this era, Little River was the most successful and longest lived. Best estimates suggest that from 1901 to 1939, the company removed from the Smokies "over 1,500,000,000 board feet of lumber and many more thousands of cords of pulp and acid wood and other wood products."[8] The same observer reports that the company's financial records "are fragmentary at best . . . [but that] the operation was essentially a

7. Smoky Mountain Historical Society, *Gentle Winds of Change*, 125

8. Lambert, "Logging in the Great Smokies, 1880–1930," *Tennessee Historical Quarterly* 21 (Dec. 1961): 362.

profitable one" for both its investors and the economy of the area. Gradually, as timber thinned, companies abandoned the mountains, and in 1930 Little River alone was still there.

Townsend, Elkmont, and Mountain Tourism

One might assume that a combination of developments in the following decade—the nationwide Depression, Townsend's death in 1936, and the environmental havoc mechanized logging brought to the Smokies—explains the demise of Little River Lumber Company. Indeed, the company's fortunes gradually dwindled for more than a decade, before it ceased operations in 1939, but practices and policies Townsend implemented almost simultaneously with the beginning of logging operations were the primary reasons. Chapter five will explore these developments in greater detail than we will here and relate them, in particular, to East Tennesseans' and outsiders' evolving understandings of Appalachia. First, however, to bring our discussion of lumber extraction during this earlier era to a close, we must briefly address these events and their immediate and tragic effects for residents of East Tennessee's hinterlands.

Ever the farsighted entrepreneur, Colonel Townsend knew that extractive industries eventually cannibalize the very resources that make them possible. Hence, from the time he set up Little River Lumber Company in 1900, Townsend sought to devise means to dispose of (at a profit if possible) cutover timberlands.

Even before the Civil War, Knoxvillians saw the mountains as havens from their own city. Montvale Springs, a popular Blount County resort established in 1832, became known as the "Saratoga of the South." By the late 1890s, wealthy men from the city trekked regularly to the Smokies to hunt, fish, and camp—activities that reacquainted them the nation's endangered pioneer legacies. Knoxville's Elks Lodge, for example, held annual summer jamborees on a remote mountain above the Little River.

When Townsend began operation of his rail line in 1908, he added a special passenger car dubbed the "Elkmont Special," which he ran one day a week. The service proved so popular that the next summer it operated on a daily basis. Soon wives and families began to invade what had been a male-only domain. In 1910, Townsend sold more than fifty acres of cutover land between Little River and Jake's Creek to a group of affluent Knoxvillians, who organized the "Appalachian Club." Collectively they constructed a members-only lodge, and individuals built a string of rustic cottages that soon became known as "millionaire's row." The former timber camps of Elkmont quickly evolved into a "posh, social club." When this group shunned other, slightly less affluent,

Knoxvillians, Townsend in 1912 displayed a pragmatic egalitarianism. Three Knoxville brothers purchased one hundred acres of cutover land nearby and established the Wonderland Park Company. Quick construction of the sprawling, white clapboard-covered Wonderland Hotel, and chicanery surrounding the subdivision of the property into twenty-six-foot by fifty-two-foot lots for cottages, suggests the brothers sought a quick return on their investment. Another group of Knoxvillians purchased the dubious enterprise in 1915, and their Wonderland Park Company devised strategies similar to those of their neighbors for developing sites for cottages and an array of recreational purposes. While tensions between the competing organizations continued for years, they shared two notable similarities. First, they represent a significant step toward the tourist-based enterprises that largely replaced timber as the driving force behind the economy of the greater Smokies region. Secondly, by the 1920s, members from both clubs, for a variety of reasons, embraced "conservation," an equally influential impulse in the transformation of the Smokies economy.

Conservation emerged as a popular force during the first two decades of the twentieth century. Locally it was a central theme of Knoxville's Appalachian Expos in 1910 and 1911, and *the* focal point for the city's 1913 National Exposition. On the national stage, President Theodore Roosevelt and his close friend, Gifford Pinchot (whom Roosevelt had appointed the nation's first "Chief Forester"), addressed natural resource–related issues with attention and zeal never before

As the Smokies became a popular tourist destination in the early twentieth century, Knoxvillians and mountain residents increasingly interacted. In this photo (ca. 1915), a group of mountain locals roast a hog for visiting tourists. (Courtesy of Calvin M. McClung Historical Collection.)

New South Realities

seen in Washington. Yet for those early-twentieth-century pioneers, "conservation," as the promoters of Knoxville's 1910 Expo boasted, meant primarily "more efficient exploitation" of natural resources. Little River Lumber Company's "scientific forestry" typified that efficiency. Broader progressive impulses called for increased government regulation of resource development, an impulse that at once challenged, but also created, new opportunities for the likes of W. B. Townsend. If handled properly, the promise of federal stewardship offered an even more attractive opportunity than wealthy tourists for disposing of Little River's cutover lands. Throughout much of the 1920s, two groups sparred over the future of the Great Smokies, advocates of a national forest (the true "conservationists" by the contemporary definition) and "preservationists," who favored a national park. Chapter five will explore that debate in detail. For now, it is sufficient to say the preservationists prevailed, and that Little River Lumber was among the biggest winners. In July 1926, Townsend signed an agreement transferring to the state of Tennessee 76,507 acres for $273,557 ($3.57 per acre), with the provision that his company could continue harvesting timber along the Little River's Middle Prong for fifteen additional years.[9]

This deal, which led to the creation of Great Smoky Mountains National Park, was conceived by truly opportunistic bedfellows. In Townsend's defense, he probably initiated contacts with Knoxville's business community and government officials with the assumption that yoking tourism and conservation would complement, not replace, Little River's logging efforts. Perhaps, however, Townsend saw bailing out to the federal government as a viable means of addressing the environmental mess his mechanized logging had created. Receiving compensation for disposing of cutover lands was for Little River a win-win situation. Tragically, the paternalistic Townsend displayed less interest in the immediate consequences of this deal for his employees and the region's native peoples. Dorie Cope, who with her husband spent most of her young adult life in Little River timber camps, but had to relocate to Knoxville when the national park gained control of their ancestral lands, put it best: "The lumber companies had opened the door to the outside world. We became aware of 'things'—things that money could buy, things that made life easier (or harder), things to see, things to do . . . They had opened a door—a door we were forced to use as an exit from our ancestral homes."[10]

9. Daniel S. Pierce, *The Great Smokies: From Natural Habitat to National Park* (Knoxville: Univ. of Tennessee Press, 2000), 114; Virgil F. Carmichael, "The Acquisition of Land in the Creation of the Great Smoky Mountains National Park," *Smoky Mountain Historical Society Journal and Newsletter* 25 (Spring 1999): 2–10.

10. Florence Cope Bush, *Dorie: Woman of the Mountains* (Knoxville: Univ. of Tennessee Press, 1992), 220–21.

New South Realities

When Smokies natives later discovered their neighbors in Elkmont had made arrangements allowing them to retain their summer homes, some became bitter, and the fruits of that bitterness persist even today. From a present-day perspective, the long-range benefits of Great Smoky Mountains National Park for subsequent generations of East Tennesseans and Americans, including the descendants of people like Dorie Cope, are obvious and indisputable. That in itself blinds most of us to the immediate costs and tragic human consequences of these developments. Yet observers at the time had yet another excuse for overlooking the tragedy unfolding in their midst. As the nation plunged into the Great Depression, residents of the Smokies were not the only, nor even the most, afflicted of East Tennessee's Appalachian residents. To become acquainted with the group that held that dubious distinction, we must shift our attention to East Tennessee's other key extractive industry: coal.

King Coal Comes to East Tennessee

Coal is—as it long has been—both a burden and a blessing for southern Appalachia. Currently, in response to ever-increasing petroleum prices, many observers are once again touting the benefits of Appalachian coal. "The U.S.," Senator Lamar Alexander of Tennessee recently observed, "is the Saudi Arabia of coal." But other observers also remind us that heavy costs accompany exploitation of this valuable resource: increased mining accidents, fatalities, and injuries; environmental damage; and climate change. We will now explore these controversial aspects of the coal industry.

Coal has never been as important for East Tennessee as it is for West Virginia or Eastern Kentucky, but for a string of counties on the eastern flank of the Cumberland Plateau, stretching diagonally northeast to southwest across Tennessee's narrow girth from Kentucky to Alabama, coal has been very important. The Clearfork Valley, at the northern end of this swath, typifies "coal Appalachia" as much as West Virginia does. Conventional accounts of East Tennessee have overlooked this hardscrabble region, yet both the general benefits and the human and environmental costs of exploiting Clearfork coal cry out for attention. One cannot understand Clearfork history without addressing coal, but neither can one begin to comprehend the history of greater East Tennessee, the development of notions about Appalachia, or even fully assess the achievements of American industrialization, without coming to terms with this controversial industry and its legacies.

The chronology and broad contours of East Tennessee's coal industry during the era from around 1880 to 1930 mirror those of the timber industry. Coal was mined in Roane County as early as 1814, and antebellum East Tennesseans used coal as a supplemental energy source and for specialized endeavors, such as blacksmithing and the region's nascent iron industry. On the eve of the Civil War, Tennessee had six coal producers, who in total employed nearly four hundred miners and an estimated output valued in excess of $423,000.[11] In tune with the New South vision, local entrepreneurs and outside businesspeople bought up mineral lands in the 1870s, and in the following decade Tennessee coal production increased fivefold. Growing markets and railroads to reach them were essential for the emerging enterprise. The first significant field was Coal Creek, about thirty miles north of Knoxville, which became important when the Knoxville and Ohio railroad pushed north in the 1870s. In 1883, the railway was completed to the Kentucky border, and connections were made with the L&N, linking East Tennessee to the Ohio River. With access to burgeoning northern markets, East Tennessee coal production exploded. The Jellico field, which lay at the western end of the Clearfork Valley, and straddled both the rail line and the Tennessee-Kentucky border, proved particularly rich.

Most early mines were small-scale endeavors. From around 1870 to 1890, East Tennessee Coal was so accessible that relatively little start-up capital was required, and many ambitious natives initially vied with outside investors to open mines and impromptu coal camps. Many mines employed only a few miners (often local farmers seeking to supplement meager incomes), and some early mines operated only several months each year. The mouths of these "drift mines" opened where coal seams broke the earth's surface, and miners with picks, shovels, augers, and dynamite gradually worked their way ever deeper into the earth. Teams of mules (sometimes ponies) typically carried the coal to the surface, where it was ultimately transferred via a tipple to railroad gondolas. These early enterprises did not significantly disrupt traditional social patterns and had minimal environmental impact. But these arrangements proved inefficient, and excessive competition and overproduction plagued the industry. By 1890, growing markets and increased emphasis on efficiency and economies of scale in the greater American business community transformed East Tennessee's coal industry. One consequence was increased rancor between miners and the coal companies.

The Coal Creek Rebellion

The intriguing and complex story of the 1891 Coal Creek Rebellion, the first great showdown in the East Tennessee coalfields, is told elsewhere and will be only

11. James Fickle, "Mining," in *The Tennessee Encyclopedia of History and Culture*, ed. Carroll Van West (Nashville: Rutledge Hill Press/Tennessee Historical Society, 1998), 627–28.

briefly recounted here. The drama unfolded in the context of post–Civil War Tennessee's decision to adopt a convict labor system. The specific grievances of miners were secondary to that broader concern. Faced with pressing budget demands, the need to replace a state penitentiary the recent war had demolished, and with a burgeoning inmate population of freed slaves (a product of postwar bitterness and racial anxieties), Tennessee in 1866 followed the lead of several other states in leasing convicts to private companies. The latter paid a set fee per inmate and assumed responsibility for feeding and housing the convicts. This arrangement proved equally lucrative to the state and its business partners. In 1884, Tennessee Coal, Iron, and Railway Company (better known as TCI) became the state's primary lease associate. Between 1870 and 1890, Tennessee netted a profit of $771,000 from the system, and participating employers benefited from lower labor costs. More significantly, the system became "an effective club to hold over the heads of free laborers," as TCI vice president and convict-leasing advocate A. S. Colyar bluntly phrased it.[12]

In 1891, these realities precipitated upheaval at Coal Creek, where the miners belied many popular notions about the Appalachian coal industry. First, many of them lived on their own property rather than in company towns. Secondly, the local farmers and the large contingent of experienced Welsh miners composing the work force shared traditional values toward private property, individualism, and hard work. They had several times responded coolly to union efforts, but were solidly unified in the face of conditions they considered "unfair" and "un-American." The flush times the coal companies experienced in the booming 1880s made the miners' low wages and lack of leverage painfully apparent. Specific grievances included: the payment of wages in scrip, which made miners susceptible to price gouging in company stores; a demand for an independent checkweighman (to weigh their coal as it came from the mine); and objection to company demands that they sign an ironclad agreement, which waived almost all of the miners' rights, including the right to bargain collectively. When miners at the Tennessee Coal Mining Company's Briceville mine refused to sign the ironclad oath in April 1891, the company responded with a lockout and announced it would reopen its mine on July 4 with convicts leased from TCI.

From the miner's perspective, the convicts were strikebreakers, and on July 14, three hundred armed miners surrounded the Briceville stockade housing the convict laborers. With minimal confusion, no violence, and much popular support, they loaded convicts and company guards on a train bound for

12. See Perry C. Cotham, *Toil, Turmoil, and Triumph: A Portrait of the Tennessee Labor Movement* (Nashville: Providence House Publishers, 1996), 56–79. Colyar's "effective club" remark is quoted by James B. Jones Jr., "Convict Lease Wars," in West, *The Tennessee Encyclopedia of History and Culture*, 204.

Knoxville. They also petitioned Governor John Buchanan to intervene in their cause, which they likened to earlier American struggles for liberty and against slavery. In response, the cautious governor expressed sympathy for the miners but warned against redressing unjust laws unjustly. Several weeks later, after no concrete action was taken, a second insurrection occurred. More than two thousand miners forced company guards and one hundred state militiamen to release convicts from two mines. Again insurgents shipped the convicts and guards by rail to Knoxville, and no blood was shed. The governor again met with representatives of the miners, but his subsequent meeting with coal company officials made clear they would not abandon the lucrative convict labor scheme. The governor then returned convicts to Coal Creek accompanied by the entire state militia; he also called a special meeting of the Tennessee General Assembly to address the matter. When the legislature failed to resolve the issue, 1,500 miners stormed and burned the Briceville stockade on Halloween. Over the next several days, the rebels set free 480 convicts from several nearby mines and destroyed some coal company property. At that point, several operators agreed to abandon convict labor and began rehiring free miners. But, as public sympathy for the miners waned and pressure from several larger mines persisted, the governor again returned convict laborers to Coal Creek mines. Meanwhile many free miners who had been active in the insurrections were blacklisted, and with convict laborers again available, companies reduced hours for many free miners. Over the next several months, resentful miners and green, inexperienced state guardsmen often clashed, and a confrontation initially notable for nonviolence occasionally became bloody and destructive. Although still convinced of the justness of their cause, most miners saw the futility of their actions and sought political and legal remedies for their grievances. The convict lease arrangement became *the* issue of the 1892 Tennessee gubernatorial campaign, and incumbent Buchanan and two other candidates pledged to end the system. After defeat at the polls, Buchanan called the General Assembly into another special session and appointed a commission to investigate the state's penal system. The following spring, the state's new governor signed into law provisions for a new state penitentiary, located on nine thousand acres of Morgan County coal land. The convict lease system was abandoned, but prisoners mined coal for the state of Tennessee at Brushy Mountain State Prison until after World War II.

For our purposes, two aspects of the Coal Creek Rebellion are significant. First, at a time when Americans were avidly reading about the Hatfields and McCoys and other outbreaks of mountain feuding in the national press, news from the Tennessee coalfields offered further evidence of an "innately violent Appalachia." Secondly, just as the Little River Basin was representative of the second phase of Appalachian lumbering in the Smokies, extensive mining in the

Clearfork Valley, which began after the Coal Creek Rebellion, became representative of East Tennessee coal mining's second phase. In both settings, greater capital investments, which typically came from outside the region, distinguished the second from the earlier phase. In the case of Clearfork mining, the major initial player was the American Association, Ltd. In the booming mid-1880s, Scotsman Alexander Arthur convinced British investors that the area around Cumberland Gap (which at the time had fewer than sixty families engaged in small-scale farming) could become the future location for a great iron and steel industry. Shortly after the company organized in 1887, Arthur, who was hired to manage its property, acquired more than 100,000 acres straddling the Tennessee-Kentucky border. Just north of the border, he acquired 5,500 acres in the Yellow Creek Valley, and laid out plans for the city of Middlesborough. By 1889, the city had a population of five thousand people, along with seven churches, many hotels, six banks, a library, an opera house, a golf course, many drinking establishments, and several residential areas. Arthur built his own palatial home across the state line in Harrogate, Tennessee, where he also oversaw construction of a sanatorium and the seven-hundred-room Four Seasons Hotel. Meanwhile he continued to acquire land for the American Association on all sides of Middlesborough, including more than 80 percent of Claiborne County at the east end of the Clearfork Valley. Rather than mine coal and cut timber itself, the American Association served as a land agent. Arthur and company officials took advantage of the locals' goodwill and ignorance of the value of their property (and of the minerals beneath its surface) to acquire the land at minimal cost; when they faced occasional resistance, they resorted to deceit, legal chicanery, and occasionally violence. In the words of Ron Eller, "Scores of coal and timber companies leased tracts of land from the Association, and company towns shot up on almost every creek to house the thousands of miners who poured into the district."[13]

Boom times, however, never last. By 1890, British investors lost confidence in Arthur and Middlesborough, and when panic struck the United States in 1893, the scheme collapsed. American Association, Ltd., declared bankruptcy and was replaced by American Association, Inc., and Middlesborough became Middlesboro. But for locals, the name changes were merely cosmetic. Arthur's idyllic visions may have evaporated, but by the time prosperity returned in the late 1890s, outsiders controlled most of the area's acreage, and extraction of timber and coal replaced hardscrabble farming as the driving forces in the regional economy. When a new railroad linking Jellico to Middlesboro was completed in 1905, coal became king in the Clearfork Valley, and for the first two and a half decades of the twentieth century, the region prospered—at least outwardly.

13. Ronald D Eller, *Miners, Millhands, and Mountaineers: Industrialization of the Appalachian South, 1880–1930.* Knoxville: Univ. of Tennessee Press, 1982, 84.

The Clearfork Valley and Coal's Golden Age

Completion of the Clearfork spur line of the Southern Railroad in 1905, and general prosperity in the United States for most of the next two decades, was critical for the Clearfork coal boom. For most of the twentieth century's first three decades, Campbell and Claiborne Counties (through which the Clearfork River flows) were Tennessee's leading coal producers. World War I spurred even greater demand for coal and a sharp increase in coal prices and profits, fostering a prosperity that persisted until the mid-1920s. Investors, mostly from the North and Midwest, avoided the excesses of the Middlesboro debacle, establishing smaller, more stable company towns on the slopes above the Clearfork River and the adjacent railroad. From Pruden in Kentucky to Morley in Tennessee, mines and coal camps mushroomed at Fork Creek, Eagan, Clairfield, Rock Creek, Rose's Creek, Buffalo, Anthras, Tackett Creek, and many other sites. Today some of these communities are wide spots along Tennessee's winding Route 90; others have largely disappeared under lush vegetation. Most of the coal camps were initially quite rustic, but with greater profits and a desire to attract dependable and loyal miners and fend off union appeals, some of the larger companies by around World War I engaged in what Crandall Shifflett appropriately calls "contentment sociology." Housing and sanitation were upgraded and an array of changes were implemented to make company towns more attractive. The camp at Eagan, for example, had a YMCA offering a variety of recreational activities to miners and their families. Each camp had its own baseball team, and competition between company teams became an integral aspect of coal camp life. Most companies also provided space for public schools for the children of miners, and established churches (often of the company's favored denomination) on their grounds. When they realized that miners preferred independent Baptist and Holiness traditions, some companies provided space for small church houses of those persuasions. Looking back at this earlier era, many former miners and their (now-grown) children express pride in their accomplishments and a nostalgic longing for what they fondly remember as close-knit, caring communities.

Although the Clearfork mines attracted some blacks from the lowland South and some Italians, most of the miners were locals who found mining more economically rewarding than farming the Valley's steep slopes. The railroad and important coal camp structures took up the little bottomland existing along the Clearfork, and well before 1900 partible inheritance had shrunk farms to the point they could not support families. Under such circumstances, many natives gladly accepted offers from outside investors to purchase their meager acreage and turned to "public work" in the mines. Like lumbering in the Smokies, coal mining in the Cumberlands remained largely a manual pursuit throughout the boom years of the early twentieth century. New laborsaving technologies were available (and widely used in mines in Britain, continental Europe, and in the midwestern and northern states of the United States); their relative absence in the mines of the South was largely due to the relatively low cost for labor there. When business was booming, miners before the turn of the century worked as many as sixty hours per week. By World War I, this dropped to forty-eight hours, and by the eve of the Depression hours were reduced on the average to forty. Miners were paid by the amount of coal they produced, and the typical Appalachian miner in 1900 averaged $2.00 income per day, although an exceptionally diligent miner might make as much as $3.00.[14]

Clearfork mines utilized the "room and pillar system," which when done properly, allowed up to 95 percent of the coal in a seam to be removed. Typically, pairs of miners worked together in small rooms off from a main entry tunnel, using short-handled picks, shovels, chest augurs, and dynamite to loosen and remove "rooms" of coal. As loosened coal was removed in cars typically pulled by mules or ponies, a "pillar" was left in place to support the roof. Coal car tracks were then extended into the newly opened rooms. Pillar drawing, the final step in finishing up a mine section, was dangerous. If not done properly, it resulted in either decreased production or in roof falls and cave-ins. Miners were responsible for setting timbers to minimize roof falls, an arduous process requiring much of the miner's valuable time. Taking too much time for this pursuit reduced the amount of coal he could produce, and hence his income; taking too little might cost him his life.

Coal mining throughout this era was one of the nation's most dangerous professions. The Clearfork mines avoided sensational disasters, but greater East Tennessee did not. The Fraterville mine, located along Coal Creek (about halfway between Knoxville and Jellico), was widely known for its safety record and benevolent treatment of its workers. But on May 19, 1902, a gas pocket exploded in the mine. Fatality counts varied from 184 to 216; either way it ranks among the costliest mine disasters in U.S. history. Perhaps most telling, after the explosion only three adult males were left in Fraterville. The disaster made news around the world, helping spur the establishment of the U.S. Bureau of Mines in 1910. A year later, at nearby Briceville, an explosion in the Cross Mountain Mine killed eighty-four members from a crew of eighty-nine miners; rescuers from the new federal agency saved the five survivors. Several victims from both of these explosions, helplessly blocked from escape by massive roof falls, wrote notes to family members and friends as they gradually expired from lack of oxygen. Publication of those deeply personal and wrenching notes in the national press put a human face to the plight of miners, helping bring about further legislative efforts to ad-

14. Ibid., 178.

Eagan coal camp (ca. 1925) was atypical of Clearfork Valley company towns during the years of the coal boom. (Courtesy of Clearfork Community Institute.)

dress mining hazards. While Clearfork miners avoided disasters of this magnitude, knowledge of them must have taken an emotional toll. And the number of Clearfork miners who died or were maimed in roof falls and other accidents, and who lived out their days with black lung and other debilitating afflictions and injuries, has never been counted. The number was undoubtedly large.

An Industry and Valley in Distress

By the mid-1920s, more systemic economic problems beset coal mines all over southern Appalachia. World War I had temporarily reduced tensions between several major West Virginia companies and the United Mine Workers, but in the dark days immediately after the war, hostilities reappeared. Violence from both sides culminated in the 1921 Battle of Blair Mountain, the largest labor showdown in U.S. history. Only direct intervention by federal troops (including an attempt to bomb miners from airplanes) put an end to the conflict. Blair Mountain served as a major setback for the UMW, and efforts to unionize the Appalachian coalfields were stymied until the New Deal. Tensions ran high at mines in the Clearfork and in greater East Tennessee, but violence did not occur until neighboring Harlan County in Kentucky earned its reputation as "Bloody Harlan" in the early 1930s. Closer by in Wilder, Tennessee, west of Jellico, coal operators resorted to violence to successfully subvert unionization efforts.

Of greater significance for the Clearfork mines were major changes in the American economy in the aftermath of World War I. During the war, coal companies began to utilize labor-saving machinery to meet temporarily increased demands and to compensate for a shortage of miners, caused by military enlistments. After the war, demand declined just as soldiers returned home expecting to resume their old jobs. An even more serious problem was the transition to autos and trucks as the nation's primary means of transportation and hauling freight. For many miners, as for many of their neighbors, who still tried to eke out an existence from the depleted soil of hillside farms, depression came well before the crash of 1929. Since then, the coal industry has been fickle. Occasional booms during national crises (e.g., World War II and the 1970s energy crises) have contrasted markedly with more typical downswings.

For the communities of the Clearfork Valley and the Little River basin, the short-term benefits from the coal and timber booms of the years 1900–1925 must be weighed against long-range economic, environmental, and emotional scars. Both the benefits and costs of progress were New South realities that fostered an array of "Appalachian" images. An inclination of both outsiders and insiders to accept these images without question or qualification is a major cause of the Appalachian elusiveness that is this book's primary concern. Chapter five will explore how developments in turn-of-the-twentieth-century East Tennessee's three representative communities contributed to the discovery of "Appalachia."

Chapter Five

Appalachia on Their Minds: East Tennesseans and the
Discovery of an American Region, 1875–1925

In the final decades of the nineteenth century, an array of forces—modernization, industrialization, and urbanization—converged and intertwined to transform the United States and how Americans understood themselves. Longstanding notions of Appalachian isolation to the contrary, these powerful, exciting, and bewildering forces profoundly influenced East Tennesseans and the primary concerns of this book. Modernity intensified interdependency between East Tennessee's diverse subregions even as it deepened Appalachia's ties to broader national economic and cultural forces. The excitement and bewilderment that accompanied these developments foreshadowed what we twenty-first-century folks have recently discovered as "globalization."

As the title suggests, this chapter's exploration of developments in the Appalachian subregion of East Tennessee during the half-century that straddles the year 1900 borrows heavily from historian Henry J. Shapiro's seminal study *Appalachia on Our Mind.* Focusing on East Tennessee allows for fuller consideration of the contention that we regional scholars have collectively failed to connect the dots between the images of "Appalachia" that Shapiro first analyzed and the regional realities that Ron Eller, his heirs, and this book's chapter four examine. In this pursuit, I benefit from insights from the little-known second wave of Appalachian studies scholarship, particularly historian David Hsiung's 1997 examination of upper East Tennessee during the years that spanned from the American Revolution to the Civil War. Hsiung argues persuasively that Shapiro's middle-class local colorists and home missionaries, whose aspirations and anxieties informed—and often distorted—Gilded Age understandings of "Appalachia" did not "invent" the notions they offered. Instead, economically successful, mid-nineteenth-century upper East Tennesseans provided outsiders with stereotypically degrading images of their hinterland neighbors primarily because they believed those less affluent folk did not share their truly American faith in progress and modernity. This chapter applies Hsiung's contention to all of East Tennessee and carries it into the half-century when modernity came to America *and* Appalachia. New insights into the experiences of other historically marginal groups affirm this emphasis. Studies of interaction between other American minorities and mainstream culture spurred a similar evolution of Appalachian studies and influenced both the questions regional scholars have pursued and their responses to those questions. Without ignoring notable differences among America's many "others," we can acknowledge that selective acculturation and cultural persistence are two critical themes in twentieth-century American cultural politics; their relevance for Appalachian–East Tennessee encounters with the mainstream and modernity demands examination. Finally, new insights into human identity from other disciplines, cross-disciplinary studies, and literary efforts further affirm this effort. The assertion that identity (for individuals and groups) is a *"constructed source of meaning and experience"* that can only be understood by restoring it to broader cultural and chronological milieus, illuminates the glimpses into intra–East Tennessee cultural interaction and the "discovery" of Appalachia that are this chapter's primary concerns.

"Seeds" for "Appalachian" Images in Antebellum East Tennessee

Although images of a distinct "Appalachia" did not fully emerge until the latter nineteenth century, earlier seeds for those images deserve brief attention here. East Tennessee served as a setting for several prominent examples of what literary scholars call the "Old Southwestern Humor Tradition." This literary genre was notable for exaggerated use of dialect, crude, often bawdy humor, and trickster "country" protagonists who rely on wit to humiliate and overcome more sophisticated (typically urban) adversaries. The array of semifictional accounts about the life of East Tennessee native (and national hero) David Crockett, which were wildly popular in the antebellum years, were a prime example of this genre. Another example was Knoxville resident George Washington Harris's *Sut Lovingood: Yarns Spun by a "Nat'ral Born Durn'd Fool,"* published in 1867. Both set patterns that subsequent authors embraced, American readers found entertaining and useful, and that eventually became identified specifically with the Appalachian region.

Civil War–era commentators made both formal and informal contributions to emerging popular notions about Appalachia. Many of the soldiers, journalists, and others who passed through East Tennessee during the war years and commented on the subregion's rich timber and mineral resources also described its people. From their commentaries, seeds for two starkly contrasting images appeared. Sympathetic writers emphasized East Tennessee loyalty to the Union;

from their reports emerged notions of a "worthy Appalachia" that deserved a helping hand from home missionaries and other altruists. Other commentators highlighted the cycle of violence unleashed during the war, which continued well after Appomattox in some East Tennessee locales. These writers provided substance for those who saw inborn brutality as a distinctive "Appalachian" trait. As different as these grossly stereotypical images were, they shared the misconception that East Tennessee and greater Appalachia were culturally homogenous regions.

The full-blown "Appalachian" images that persist today took hold during the so-called Gilded Age. This was an era of tremendous growth and outward prosperity that disguised (however thinly) a host of new and old problems. Everyday Americans responded to these countervailing, bewildering forces with a spirit of bravado and denial. Audacity, awkwardness, altruism, and anxiety mixed mysteriously as mainstreamers responded to an array of "others," including recently freed African Americans, newly defeated Indians, scores of new arrivals from abroad, and "strange and peculiar" folk that American industrialists, journalists, and home missionaries encountered in the southern Appalachians. The account in chapter three of Gilded Age Knoxville reveals that East Tennessee's "successful" residents were not immune to these influences.

By the early 1890s, economic miseries unmasked the accumulated effects of denial and introduced controversial adjustments to modernity, which often manifested themselves in rediscoveries of nature, fascination with what one historian calls the "cult of the primitive," anxieties about racial and cultural heterogeneity, and the growing rural-urban dichotomy. I place this collection of impulses under the broad umbrella of antimodernism. Beginning in the traumatic 1890s, these emergent and formative forces profoundly influenced American views of both the physical space of the Appalachian region and its human inhabitants.

Local Colorists

The southern mountains along with the West, New England, the plantation South, and Cajun Louisiana were "picturesque little corners of the nation" that attracted local colorists. Local color, Henry Shapiro tells us, emerged to entertain middle-class readers of new mass-circulation monthlies. Two prominent examples were *Harper's New Monthly Magazine* and *Atlantic Monthly*, both of which were widely popular despite a "paucity of aesthetic merit." Shapiro asserts that comparison was "at the heart of local-color writing," and that the genre was constructed around "confrontations between the *we* readers and the *them* read about." According to Shapiro, more than 90 sketches and over 125 short stories published between 1870 and 1890 collectively "established Appalachia in the public consciousness as a distinct region, in but not of America." Thereafter, Shapiro maintains, mainstream Americans "tended to approach the southern mountains . . . with the assumption that [this] really was a strange land inhabited by a peculiar people and responded in . . . appropriate ways." Shapiro points to Tennessean Mary Noailles Murfree as the trailblazer of Appalachian local color.[1]

To many an unwitting reader, Murfree's identification as "Tennessean" lent credibility to her reputation as a regional expert. But that assumption reflected a misperception about the Volunteer State common among outsiders. Mary Noailles Murfree hailed from Middle Tennessee and had only limited contact with the state's eastern end. With guidance from an affluent, respected, bookish father, Mary and her siblings were well educated and read widely in both classical and popular antebellum American literature. Her primary contact with "Appalachia" came from extended stays for fifteen consecutive summers at Beersheba Springs, a resort on the edge of the Cumberlands catering to wealthy patrons from Nashville and Chattanooga. There Murfree as a youth heard exotic stories about folk from nearby hills and hollows; occasionally she even encountered some of these people when they brought produce or did odd jobs at the resort. Like many other local colorists, she wrote short stories the new monthly magazines published in serial form. Writing under the penname "Charles Egbert Craddock," Murfree became a popular contributor to *Atlantic Monthly* in the 1870s. Over a long career, she wrote forty-five short stories and eighteen novels. Of these, the vast majority were set in the Appalachian South. *In the Tennessee Mountains*, a compilation of eight of her *Atlantic Monthly* stories, was published in 1884; a year later *The Prophet of the Great Smokies* appeared. Together these two volumes established Murfree's reputation as both author "and authentic voice" of southern Appalachia.

Murfree's credentials for that accolade are dubious. Some observers suggest she spent no time at all in Tennessee's eastern end until 1885—after publication of *In the Tennessee Mountains*. Other accounts suggest that as a young woman she once or twice visited Montvale Springs, a popular resort in the Smokies' foothills. Durwood Dunn concedes that in the 1880s Murfree stayed for "extended periods in Cades Cove with the family of 'the Old Squire,'" and that the Cove was the setting for many of her most popular stories. But the Cove historian found much to criticize in Murfree's writings. In Dunn's words, Murfree's mountaineers are "static, unrealistic, doll-like manikins who bear no likeness to the

---

1. Henry D. Shapiro, *Appalachia on Our Mind: The Southern Mountains and Mountaineers in the American Consciousness, 1870–1920.* Chapel Hill: Univ. of North Carolina Press, 1978, 8, 11, 14, 18, 19.

Cove people." He is particularly critical of her use of dialect and "her complete blindness [and] insensibility to the [Cove] folk culture." Feuds, moonshining, "winsome mountain youths and their haggard elders," and unrequited romances between naïve mountain natives and sophisticated yet disgruntled outsiders provided the characters and plots for Murfree's stories. Dunn concludes that she "deserves credit only for perpetuating numerous stereotypes and misconceptions." In her defense, Murfree appeared genuinely concerned about the mountaineer's fateful collision with modernity. But, like contemporaries who waxed melodramatically over the Indians' "end of the trail," she could not grasp the complexity of cultural interaction as it unfolded in the mountains. More seriously, she was blind to the ways her own needs (and those of her readers) shaped her pathos. Finally, she failed to see how her work became useful for those with less altruistic agendas. Murfree's success in transplanting themes and motifs she learned as a youth in the Cumberlands to the more majestic Smokies led readers to assume this amalgam truly reflected life in the Tennessee mountains. But hindsight leaves no doubt that her reputation for "fidelity in the rendering of [all] mountain life" was a sham.[2]

Murfree's successor as Appalachia's leading local colorist was John Fox Jr. A native of the Kentucky bluegrass, Harvard graduate, and failed coal operator, Fox found success as a writer around 1900. His popularity came after the Gilded Age had ended, but that same popularity suggests that many characteristics and needs of that era lingered well after. Fox's first book, *A Mountain Europa*, was actually set in the Jellico area at the west end of the Clearfork Valley, where the Fox brothers established coal operations in the late 1890s. From Jellico, Fox wrote: "I am drinking in like a sponge the peculiar life and peculiar ideas of this mountain race and their beautiful natural environment."[3] Soon thereafter, Fox's business interests took him to Big Stone Gap, Virginia. His most famous works, *The Trail of the Lonesome Pine* and *The Little Shepherd of Kingdom Come*, are set in eastern Kentucky and southwestern Virginia.

A common theme in the collective works of Fox and Murfree is anxiety. The curiosity they and their readers displayed about mountain feuding, moonshining, and crude social behavior; their need to single out "others" by distorting dialect and attributing customs peculiar to a few to a larger, allegedly homogenous group; and their genuine but patronizing concern for the harm wrought by progress clearly did not capture an Appalachia that was diverse and dynamic.

2. Dunn, *Cades Cove*, 161–63.

3. "John Fox, Jr.—Famed Author Wrote of Life and Times in Campbell County," in Miller McDonald, *Campbell County, TN USA*, vol. 1 (LaFollette, TN: County Services Syndicate, 1993–1994), 175–76.

Home Missionaries Come to East Tennessee

As it was for local colorists, Appalachia was only one among many battlegrounds for churches sending missionaries to the region in the final decades of the nineteenth century. Indeed, scholars of American religion consider the half-century between the American Civil War and the 1920s the "great era of Protestant missions." Mainstream denominations from the British Isles, Western Europe, and particularly the emerging United States expended tremendous energy and money in carrying the Christian gospel and "civilization" around the world. Leading Protestant churches borrowed structures, strategies, and rhetoric from the emerging world of big businesses to conduct this crusade. Lest they fall behind, Roman Catholics quickly followed suit. Within the United States, this work was generically called "home missions," and ambitious mission entrepreneurs quickly discovered an array of "exceptional populations" as much in need of the "twin blessings of Christianity and progress" as any "foreign heathens." In the words of one Presbyterian mission promoter, "exceptional populations were people who are with us but not of us."[4] The group initially included southern freed slaves and an assortment of people "out West," including an array of Indians, *Hispanos,* and Mormons. Over time, foreign immigrants in the nation's burgeoning cities, native Alaskans, and (after the Spanish-American War) natives of the Caribbean region were added to the mix. Missionary rhetoric utilized an array of pejorative adjectives—"degraded," "benighted," "superstitious," and "ignorant"—to justify mission endeavors, but always balanced gloomy assessments with evidence that these "unfortunate others" were "redeemable" and "deserving."

In the mid-1880s, writings by Mary Noailles Murfree and others led the nation's leading churches to discover another "exceptional" people much closer to home. The fact that these "strange and peculiar" people resided in the very midst of the celebrated Anglo-Protestant denominations, were in fact nominally "Christian," and of basically the same ethnic stock as mainstream Americans, made them the most perplexing, yet promising, of the exceptional populations. As Appalachian studies pioneer Loyal Jones often observes, "never have so many Christian missionaries been sent to save so many Christians as has been the case in this region."[5] That this apparent paradox did not deter mainstream church leaders reveals more about their needs than those of the mountaineers who

---

4. Quoted from an undated, anonymous handwritten statement entitled "Suggestions for Workers—From Woman's Executive Committee for Home Missions," Presbyterian Historical Society archives, Philadelphia, RG 105, Box 2, folder 6.

5. Loyal Jones, "Old-Time Baptists and Mainline Christianity," in *An Appalachian Symposium: Essays Written in Honor of Cratis D. Williams,* ed. J. W. Williamson, 120 (Boone, NC: Appalachian State University Press), 1977.

were the target of their effort. Mainstream missionaries of a century ago offered a simple two-fold diagnosis of Appalachian ills: "isolation and ignorance." As unfortunate as the situation may have appeared, these conditions could be overcome, and Protestants, of course, had a panacea that would bring that result: "Christian education." Consequently, in the years that are the focus of this chapter, mainstream denominations established scores of mission schools across the Appalachian south, where the absence of public education was glaring. East Tennessee was home to a number of denominational schools, ranging from elementary day schools to academies, boarding schools, and several colleges.

In competition with countless other home and foreign enterprises for funding and support, missionaries of the Appalachian field had one great advantage: the people they sought to uplift were, in the famous words of Berea College President William G. Frost, "our contemporary ancestors," making them uniquely deserving and "capable of civilization." Missionary rhetoric also implied that regaining these "lost sheep" could counter a growing heterogeneity that frightened many "main stock" Americans at the end of the nineteenth century. Thus, mission promoters effectively played upon both altruistic and ungenerous human impulses, including racism and xenophobia. Like the local colorists and writers within the nascent field of advertising, missionaries exaggerated selective evidence to convince supporters among mainstream Americans that the peoples of the southern mountains were, indeed, "strange and peculiar." Commentators devoted particular attention to the deficiencies of mountain religion, particularly the "ignorant dogmatism and demagoguery" of mountain preachers. But reports from the field in the 1880s and '90s found fault in practically every facet of Appalachian life, and offered a variety of explanations for those ills. Practically every observer pointed to the absence of public schools. Other common themes were the mountaineers' laziness and lack of ambition and public responsibility. A few observers pointed to thin mountain soils, the mountain farmer's distance from markets, and his poor methods of cultivation. Few personal defects went unnoticed. One report attributed regional ills to "the disgusting snuff-dipping practices of the mountain women."[6]

Local colorist and early missionary views of "mountain culture" were so similar that, in the early 1880s, church officials recommended that parishioners read Murfree's fictional accounts to become familiar with the mountaineers' culture and "needs." By the end of that decade, most denominations had monthly mission publications, but even then they sometimes used the secular press to

6. These missionary depictions of "Appalachia" are drawn from issues of the Presbyterian *Home Mission Monthly* from the 1880s and '90s. They are cited in Mark T. Banker and Reuben A. Holden, *Toward Frontiers Yet Unknown: A 90th Anniversary History of Warren Wilson College, 1894–1984* (Swannanoa, NC: Warren Wilson College, 1984), 3.

Appalachia on Their Minds

present their cause. Frost's famous "Contemporary Ancestors" address, for example, appeared in 1899, in the same *Atlantic Monthly* that regularly carried stories by Murfree and Fox. A notable difference in the two groups' depictions of mountain culture was an inclination in missionary accounts to recognize variety in the regional population. Reports on the "more civilized" folk of the region's emerging urban centers and more fertile valley regions gave missionaries proof of the "redeemability" of mountain culture, a trait that was more critical for their cause than that of the local colorists, whose most ostensible objective was selling their articles and books.

East Tennesseans Respond

How did residents of East Tennessee respond to the local colorists' and early home missionaries' depictions of "Appalachia," which became increasingly widespread in the prosperous 1880s and hard-pressed in 1890s? And how did their responses, and behavior in general, relate to assumptions that our region was "strange and peculiar?" As we learned in chapter three, at least some among Knoxville's leading citizens initially objected to what they saw as stereotypically degrading portrayals of their region. Indeed, three members of the city's elite penned book-length histories of East Tennessee seeking to refute those accounts. A closer look at the writings of William Rule, a Republican journalist and one of Gilded Age Knoxville's most outspoken boosters, offers particular insight into this response. Even though he was an urbanite and a Knoxville promoter, Rule championed the virtues of rural life and often chastised young rural folk for migrating to the city. In the booming 1880s, Rule time and again emphasized in his columns how important East Tennessee's "boundless natural resources" were for the city of Knoxville. "COAL is King in East Tennessee," he wrote in 1889, "and always will be." Although Rule was not blind to problems within the region, he was quick to refute popular explanations for those ills. In response to sensational newspaper coverage of feuding and violence along the Kentucky–West Virginia border, Rule wrote in 1887, "The press of the country abounds in misrepresentation of these mountain people." To be sure, he added, Appalachian residents were "generally illiterate, uneducated, [and] uncultured," but he attributed those ills to the South's "inefficient public school system," rather than to inherent defects. While conceding that there were rural "localities . . . where the people are immoral," he concluded that this was no different than the cities and other locales.[7] Rule's commitment to creating positive images of his native East Tennessee was undoubtedly genuine, yet his responses to negative notions about Appalachia ironically gave credence to those same images.

7. Quoted in Robert Taylor Jr., "The New South Mind of a Mountain Editor: William Rule, 1877–1898," *East Tennessee Historical Society Publications* 47 (1975): 111–12, 116–17.

Fewer records exist to shed light on the responses of Knoxville's more average folks to the discovery of Appalachia by representatives of latter-nineteenth-century American society. But in that absence, I turn to the anecdotal accounts about my grandparents and great-grandparents that I shared earlier. To be sure, my grandparents were children during this era, and their middle-class families were perhaps not typical. But I believe my forebears' mixed and varied responses to the world around them were representative of many others. They were, as people of that era, intent on improving their lot and convinced that progress was the ticket to that end. They were also skilled practitioners of selective acculturation. And there is abundant evidence that they and many other of East Tennessee's rural-to-urban migrants retained aspects of their inherited culture even as they jettisoned others. Foodways, music traditions, and religious practices are among the most common cultural customs that survive, indeed even thrive, amid the mysterious forces of acculturation. In the case of Knoxville, we know, for example, that as early as the 1880s rural visitors to the city's Market Square often joined together on Saturday nights to "make music" after selling their produce; those early "jam sessions" may have been an initial step in the commercialization of country music. In regard to religion, a striking fact of Knoxville church history in the post–Civil War era was the mushrooming of Holiness and Church of God congregations; historian Deborah Vansau McCaulley asserts that these were distinctly "Appalachian" traditions. As "successful" Appalachians, my grandparents did not embrace these religious offerings, but their Methodist and Baptist faiths reflected the deep and abiding religiosity that is an Appalachian hallmark. Finally, fond personal memories of my grandmother Banker's chicken and dumplings and a lifetime of enjoying fried chicken and deviled eggs at potluck dinners offer evidence of the rich resilience of distinctive regional foodways even among those who did not think themselves "Appalachian."

How did residents of East Tennessee's hinterlands respond to portrayals by outside journalists and home missionaries during the 1870s and '80s? Clearly, some more affluent hinterland residents (particularly those who were among the earliest investors in extractive industries) often depicted their neighbors in less than generous terms. When outside commentators embellished those native accounts, some among the local elite found convenient, reassuring rationales for activities subsequent observers see as exploitative and shortsighted. As allies with outsiders in the "march of progress," hinterland elites believed themselves deserving of acclaim, not criticism. Hence, many of them affirmed pejorative depictions of neighbors who found the fruits of progress less satisfying.

Did small-scale farmers, loggers, and coal miners respond to accounts from local colorists and home missionaries who presented their culture in a negative light? Our answer can only be speculative and qualified. Even less than Knoxville's new arrivals and less-affluent citizens, the average hinterland resident rarely kept the type of records that provide answers for latter-day researchers. Moreover, other pressing concerns preoccupied these working-class Appalachians, leaving them precious little time to be acquainted with, much less formally respond to, "foolish outsiders." Finally and most important, during the prosperous 1880s, promises of the American dream seemed achievable to many of these individuals. This fortuitous combination of circumstances may have softened sensitivities about negative portrayals of their culture and assuaged pragmatic hinterlanders' inclinations to selectively embrace mainstream ways and values. But even more than their cousins who moved to the city, many hinterland residents retained vestiges of distinctive foodways and musical and religious traditions. In other words, members of both of these regional groups often engaged in selective acculturation and intragroup distinction. Even if unintentional and subconscious, these complex cultural processes enabled East Tennesseans—no matter where they resided or what their social and economic status—to construct a distinct sense of identity that survived modernity and its mysterious codependencies.

Images of Violent Appalachia

As we have seen, the end of prosperity in the mid-1890s precipitated a wave of crises in the entire United States that reverberated in East Tennessee. These crises proved fertile for more negative views of Appalachia. Few observers, however, have considered how "new realities" within our region and particularly its hinterlands gave seeds of truth to these new understandings. Consequently, we have rarely considered how these ideas served the needs of both outsiders and at least some residents of our region during this turbulent era.

When Americans, including East Tennesseans, learned about the Coal Creek Rebellion (see chapter four) in the early 1890s, many of them initially sympathized with the miners' nonviolent struggle against their employer's use of convict laborers as strikebreakers. Over time, however, as news sources began to report on violence (however limited) in the Tennessee coalfields, sympathy waned. Soon, there were reports of feuding in eastern Kentucky and West Virginia, and of even more serious labor unrest elsewhere in the nation. For those contemporaries, and for many observers ever since, the events at Coal Creek seemed proof of the innately violent nature of Appalachians. It apparently mattered little that bloodshed at Coal Creek was minimal, or that violence erupted after only calmer, more rational attempts failed to curtail the grievances. Few commentators acknowledged that the coal companies and state government were equally (if not more) responsible than the miners for the violence that did occur, or that violence at Coal Creek paled in comparison with labor-management showdowns at

Homestead, Pullman, and countless other locations across the nation in the turbulent, traumatic 1890s.

Observers who presumed that rural East Tennesseans were "innately violent" found further confirmation in their newspapers in the winter of 1892–93. Just when conditions deteriorated at Coal Creek and full-scale economic panic took hold of the broader United States, Sevier County in the foothills of the Smokies saw an outbreak of vigilante activity. Ironically, a perceived violation to community propriety fueled this outburst. (Even more ironically, the source of that concern was a group of prostitutes recently arrived from Knoxville.) In response, self-styled "White Caps" sought to restore order by threatening those who deviated from "traditional community mores." When threats proved inadequate, the White Caps engaged in extralegal raids and violence. Some locals quickly recognized the group itself violated community traditions and served the interests of an embittered, paranoid segment of the county elite. Soon, community elements bearing longstanding differences with the White Caps organized their own vigilante group, "the Blue Bills," to "restore order." Through much of the 1890s, the two groups sparred with each other, and violence escalated as each side sought revenge against the other. Eventually, pressure from Knoxville and the Tennessee government subdued the two groups, but exaggerated media coverage of those efforts did as much to confirm notions about "violent mountaineers" as the violent activities themselves. Such tales entertained and offered mainstream readers escape from their own pressing ills and anxieties. But East Tennesseans, as part of that broader society, were not immune to those needs. Indeed, the most thorough study of the drama emphasizes that tensions between emerging Knoxville and traditional rural areas such as Sevier County created the atmosphere that gave rise to the White Caps, and that the embarrassing events led Knoxvillians to distance themselves even further from their "Appalachian" neighbors. Ironically, by joining in the criticism of what was truly uncivilized behavior by a handful of their more despicable neighbors, regional natives affirmed blatant stereotypes that damned their region as a whole.

That contemporaries attributed the behavior of the White Caps to alleged traits of the larger region is understandable. But over the past thirty years, scholars have offered compelling evidence that such outbreaks were not unique either to East Tennessee or to southern Appalachia. Indeed, extralegal violence (e.g., vigilante justice and lynching) occurred in many rural and urban settings across the nation during the trying 1890s. In-depth analyses suggest "Appalachian feuding" and similar activities elsewhere were primarily rooted in social tensions related to broader processes of economic modernization. In other words, contact with, rather than isolation from, the cultural mainstream produced many real and imagined regional ills. Perhaps because such explanations are less colorful, and because opportunists (both inside and outside the region) have found such notions so useful, this accentuation of what was truly an aberrant pattern within Appalachian East Tennessee has persisted long after the violent activities subsided. Images of gun-toting, revenge-seeking hillbillies are standard fare in an array of depictions from the seemingly harmless Paul Webb cartoons my grandfather saved in the 1930s and '40s, to the 1950s musical rendition of Al Capp's Li'l Abner, to a far more serious dramatic production that won a Pulitzer Prize in 1992, one hundred years after the White Caps first emerged in Sevier County.

Outsider-Insiders Come to Appalachia

By the late 1890s, a return to prosperity ushered in the Progressive Era. Like other periods of relative consensus and cohesion in the United States, the years from around 1900 through the First World War were notable for a general prosperity and outward calm. A complex web of confident and cautious forces intertwined to forge progressivism, nothing less than the nation's first serious attempt to adjust to new realities wrought by modernization. Events in East Tennessee largely paralleled these national patterns, although progressivism in governments was never as important here as in the Midwest and several western locales. Progressive emphases on order and faith in rationality, science, and the American way (i.e., "progress") peaked with the American decision to enter the war in Europe in 1917. For East Tennessee's hinterlands and Knoxville, wartime demands for foodstuffs, coal, and timber temporarily spurred a prosperity that masked more systemic ills. By 1919, the fever pitch of wartime anxieties and a host of unkind realities at home and abroad rudely confronted progressive optimism and naiveté. In greater East Tennessee, the war accelerated unsettling demographic, economic, and social trends that were already underway. Consequently, the years 1919–21 ushered in tensions that mirrored traumatic trends in the nation at large and echoed sentiments from the similarly trying 1890s.

Progressivism's pervasive imprint influenced American understandings of nearly every facet of their culture, including life in the southern Appalachians. With the subsidence of panic-induced anxieties, the brief era of local color ran its course. Accounts of Appalachia shifted from exotic entertainment that typically ignored evidence that "got in the way of a good story," to more thorough, systematic analyses reflecting progressivism's serious, "scientific" bent. A few writers in the new century, to be sure, continued to approach the region with a literary flair. Among them, Emma Bell Miles is particularly important for our purposes.

Emma Bell Miles was the first true "outsider-insider" to comment on Appalachian culture. When she was ten years old, Emma's schoolteacher parents moved from Kentucky to the then hardscrabble environs of Walden's Ridge,

Tennessee. A recent commentator describes Emma as "a visionary teacher, artist . . . self-taught folklorist [and] avid devotee of traditional crafts," and "one of the first authentic voices within the [Appalachian] region."[8] Contemporaries beyond her immediate community hardly knew her at all. Emma's formal education was sporadic yet effective, but her informal training in the woods, and amongst Walden Ridge's mountain folk, was more powerful and enduring. Indeed, she fell in love not only with the place, but also with one of its sons, Frank Miles. That romantic attachment in itself violated a principle proscribed by Murfree, Fox, and other commentators whose ties to the region were less intimate but deemed more appropriate by most observers. Yet even as Miles taught mountain children in a one-room log school and lived with her complex and crude (and sometimes cruel) mountain husband up on the ridge, Miles intermingled regularly with wealthy elites from Chattanooga. The latter were patrons for Miles's artistic and literary pursuits, which assured her family's economic survival. Miles's parents and wealthy patrons never approved of her romance with either the mountains or Frank Miles. Indeed, her patrons subsidized a year of artistic training in St. Louis in 1900 and expressed dismay when she returned to the mountains the following year to marry the man she loved.

As one insightful commentator observes, "it was Emma Bell Miles' fate (and good fortune) to live between two cultures." Her often painful ambivalence for those two worlds and "profound biculturalism," this writer suggests, were the dominant themes of her most important and enduring work.[9] *The Spirit of the Mountains* reflected positive notions about cultural diversity and concerns about modernity, which emerged in the minds of at least a few American intellectuals from the trauma of the 1890s. Although the vast majority of Americans never embraced cultural pluralism or antimodernism, these two impulses have sparred with a more comforting and powerful view of progress ever since. Miles's combination memoir and love song offered readers an Appalachia that was credibly complex. Perhaps for that reason, the work was hardly noticed when it was published in 1905, and remained largely unknown until the advent of Appalachian studies seven decades later.

As a child of outsiders who came to a hardscrabble East Tennessee community to teach, but who stayed and embraced the region, Emma Miles was representative of a number of individuals who made important, largely overlooked, contributions to emerging "Appalachian" imagery. Encounters between these

8. Richard Blaustein, "East Tennessee Public Folklore," in *Encyclopedia of Appalachia*, ed. Rudy Abramson and Jean Haskell, 859 (Knoxville: Univ. of Tennessee Press, 2006).

9. David Whisnant, "Introduction to New Edition," in *The Spirit of the Mountains*, by Emma Bell Miles, xvi (Knoxville: Univ. of Tennessee Press, 1975).

Emma Bell Miles from the frontispiece of *The Spirit of the Mountains* (1905). Miles's forthright but generous embrace of her rural neighbors just outside of Chattanooga presaged more realistic perceptions of Appalachia appearing off and on throughout the twentieth century, before finally taking a more systematic form with the advent of Appalachian studies in the 1970s. (The Jean Miles Catino Collection, Lupton Library Special Collections, University of Tennessee at Chattanooga.)

outsider-insiders and the regional folk reveal that selective acculturation is a two-way process. Some outsider-insiders came to the region with the home mission effort. Indeed, many who did remained affiliated well beyond the Progressive Era with institutions that emerged from that ferment. Among the latter were schools that evolved into today's Berea, Berry, Alice Lloyd, and Warren Wilson Colleges. After 1900, a number of secular uplift agencies appeared and responded to the region's people and culture in ways very similar to more overtly religious, denominationally affiliated "mountain workers." Eastern Kentucky's Hindman Settlement School is a prominent example of these secular uplift agencies. For an array of understandable reasons, official histories of these institutions (as well as scholarly observers) until recently failed to see the cultural interaction that occurred in both church-affiliated and secular uplift agencies in the early decades of the twentieth century.

Several distinctive aspects of that interaction gave rise to images of "Appalachia" that differed significantly from those offered by earlier local colorists and the first wave of home missionaries. First, outsiders became insiders in part as a result of long tenures of service in the mountain region. Like Emma Bell Miles, some of them were second generation, but many others came as young adults in the late 1800s and spent entire careers in the mountains. For example, Elizabeth Williams was involved in the founding of Presbyterian-related Asheville Farm School in 1894, where she remained until that mission school evolved into Warren Wilson Junior College in 1942. That an inordinately large number of these long-term altruists were women was neither unique nor insignificant. Numerous accounts of the far-flung missionary enterprise and feminist studies offer compelling evidence that women missionaries of this era tended toward greater cultural flexibility than their male counterparts. Locals may have referred to them as "quare women" and "fotched on," but there can be little doubt that many "lady missionaries" shared Emma Miles's genuine love of the mountain people, and that locals reciprocated that affection. A second, long-overlooked dimension of the interaction was the surprising cultural resilience resulting from the mountaineer's effective selective acculturation. For example, relatively few of the young men and women attending the network of Presbyterian mission schools clustered around Asheville converted to Presbyterianism, but many of them took back to their homes (and mostly Baptist churches) new farming methods, ideas about health and sanitation, and communication and business skills that enriched their own lives and their communities. Those who charge that exposure to missionaries made such individuals "cultural Uncle Toms" fail to appreciate the dynamics of selective acculturation, mountaineers' agility in navigating that process, and the cultural resilience it ensured.

Shifting our focus back to the other side of the two-way, crosscultural processes that unfolded in countless mountain settings, the length of the outsiders' tenures, and sheer volume of their descriptive accounts, leaves no doubt that their embrace of the region was genuine and enduring. To be sure, those accounts tended—by subsequent standards—to be patronizing. But (compared to their predecessors and to many more recent altruists), some members of this group were willing to examine systematically actual conditions in the mountains, and make appropriate adjustments in their strategies. Those adjustments typically reflected the "social gospel" impulse that called Christians to address human needs "in this world," and not merely in the "life beyond." To be sure, ethnocentrism did not disappear. But cultural benchmarks rooted in insights from the emerging field of cultural anthropology gave rise to far more benevolent understandings of cultural differences, and of "Appalachian" culture in particular, than the assimilationist agenda of the first wave of outsiders who came to the Appalachians. We still have much to learn about the complex dynamics of cultural interaction, but we can with certainty conclude that outsiders who came to Appalachia from the late 1890s to around 1930 found many niches on the continuum between the melting pot and multiculturalism. Many who spent extended careers in the mountains no doubt ended up at the latter end of that spectrum, and some paid dearly for challenging powerful and enduring impulses of the greater American outlook. The experiences of two individuals with ties to East Tennessee reveal the validity of these assertions.

The more than thirty-year career of Samuel Tyndale Wilson at East Tennessee's Maryville College reveals that the missionary enterprise was more dynamic, and that missionary encounters with regional residents were more complex, than often assumed. Wilson, whose parents were missionaries, was a Maryville alumnus. His alma mater had been founded in 1819, as a Presbyterian response to disturbing conditions on the Tennessee frontier. Although Maryville was not one of the Gilded Age–era mission schools for "exceptional populations," that ferment was very evident on the campus when Wilson returned there to teach, and during his tenure as president, which spanned the first third of the twentieth century. When Presbyterians decided to publish a broad overview and rationale for their mountain work shortly after the turn of the century, they turned to Wilson, who penned *The Southern Mountaineers* in 1906. Over the next nine years, the book went through five editions and was widely recognized as "the most comprehensive work on the southern mountains published to that date." Assessments of that book by subsequent readers reveal much about their own inclinations and agendas. Church leaders and college officials traditionally tended to accept without question more hagiographic aspects of *The Southern Mountaineers*. Scholars from the 1960s and since, on the other hand, criticize Wilson's portrayal of "mountain ignorance and isolation" and his emphasis on the ameliorative effects of economic modernization (including nearby exploitation of the Smokies by the likes of the Little River Timber Company). Neither stance is lacking in merit, but both largely overlook evidence of evolving perceptions of "Appalachia" in the book's several editions. Wilson used terms such as "the Appalachian Problem" and "the Appalachian Promise" and never abandoned the idea that the region must change. But even in the first edition, Wilson chided readers for thinking of Appalachia in starkly uniform terms, describing three distinct classes of regional residents. The "submerged mountaineers" who were the target of Presbyterian home mission efforts, he emphasized, were only the third and relatively smallest of these groups. Moreover, each new edition of *The Southern Mountaineers* incorporated insights from John C. Campbell's increasingly systematic and scientific studies of actual mission conditions. Campbell, even more than Wilson, was a product and promoter of progressivism. For reasons presumably related to Wilson's more pressing duties as a college president, the East Tennessean never fully addressed the implications of Campbell's "surveys"—particularly as they related to the missionary enterprise. That was a paradox John C. Campbell could not, or at least chose not, to evade.

A native of Indiana, John C. Campbell prepared for the ministry and for a career in education at Andover Seminary, and began teaching in north Georgia after his 1895 graduation. By 1908, Campbell had become acquainted with several other regional workers who shared his progressive assumption that a thorough, "scientific" survey of mountain conditions and uplift efforts was essential. For four years, the Russell Sage Foundation funded Campbell's pursuit of that goal, and in 1913 the agency appointed Campbell to direct its Southern Highland Division, headquartered in Asheville. Until his death in 1919, Campbell and the Southern Highland Division "were one and the same." Even as he continued his extensive and seemingly endless survey, Campbell also promoted, among progressive-minded benevolent workers, a new vision of "mountain work" and of "Appalachia." This he conveyed in his posthumously published book, *The Southern Highlander and His Homeland.* In the words of Henry Shapiro, that vision abandoned earlier emphases on "Americanization [and] looked to creation of a viable mountain culture . . . as an alternative version of, rather than as the opposite of America."[10] In other words, John C. Campbell (like Emma Bell Miles) was a cultural pluralist.

Campbell's provocative vision stirred conflict with more traditional-minded regional workers. His many different duties also often brought him to mission and uplift stations scattered throughout East Tennessee. One of Campbell's most significant innovations was the annual "Conference of Southern Mountain Workers," which provided opportunity for those engaged in Appalachian uplift to share personal and professional experiences. The conference also encouraged interagency cooperation, which Campbell and many other progressives believed was sorely needed for the work to become more effective. Beginning in 1914, Knoxville was the site for that annual meeting, and each spring more than one hundred "mountain workers" converged on East Tennessee's leading city to learn from each other and from a host of recognized experts on regional conditions and the dynamics of cultural interaction. Campbell cautiously sought to introduce more conservative participants to his own expanded vision of "Appalachia." Twice, for example, he invited U.S. Commissioner of Education Philander C. Claxton to address the conference. Formerly a professor at the University of Tennessee and chief promoter of the university's "Summer School of the South," Claxton chided his audience for contributing to negative and misleading regional stereotypes. On another occasion he emphasized how extractive industries had impoverished the region.[11]

10. Shapiro, *Appalachia on Our Mind*, 264.

11. "Many Mountain Workers Arrive . . . Claxton Speaks," *Knoxville Sentinel*, Apr. 10, 1917; "New Germany Claxton View," *Knoxville Sentinel*, n.d., probably Apr. 10, 1917. See comment at end of chapter.

A youthful John C. Campbell. Campbell served as a missionary educator in several Appalachian locations from 1896 to 1907, and as head of the Russell Sage Foundation's Southern Highland Division, he promoted the Council of Southern Mountain Workers. The interdenominational agency sought to make the missionary effort in Appalachia more responsive to actual regional conditions. The council's annual conference met in Knoxville from 1914 to 1921 and periodically thereafter. (Courtesy of John C. Campbell Collection, University of North Carolina Library.)

Few records from the conferences remain in city repositories. However, conference records (housed at Berea College) do contain clippings from Knoxville newspapers, and those clippings reveal Knoxville's characteristic ambivalence about Appalachia. For example, a Knoxville reporter expressed amazement with Professor Claxton's positive descriptions of mountain peoples at the 1917 annual meeting.[12]

That early-twentieth-century Americans—including many East Tennesseans and Knoxvillians in particular—were not ready for either Emma Miles's *The Spirit of the Mountains* or John C. Campbell's *The Southern Highlander,* and indeed, did not want their provocative, iconoclastic views of "Appalachia"—reveals much about the primary concerns of this book. Readers should not, however, assume that public apathy for these two volumes revealed waning interest in the Appalachian region. The popularity of another regional study offered by yet another outsider-insider belies such a notion. Horace Kephart's *Our Southern Highlanders* was originally published in 1913, almost exactly in between the appearance of Miles and Campbell's works. But as the book's subtitle, *A Narrative of Adventure in the Southern Appalachians* suggests, Kephart's Appalachia was, in many respects, more like that of the local colorists. His personal life and

12. "Many Mountain Workers Arrive . . . Claxton Speaks."

writings epitomized powerful antimodernist forces, which appeared briefly in the 1890s, bore a distinct (often overlooked) influence on views of the region during the Progressive years, and appealed in diverse (and contradictory) ways to the schizophrenic American mind of the 1920s and years thereafter. In the eight years after its 1913 first printing by the relatively obscure Outing Press, *Our Southern Highlanders* sold ten thousand copies. Outsiders and, reportedly, Appalachian natives alike praised its authenticity. Recognizing the book's popularity, Macmillan Company purchased rights to it in 1921 and published an expanded edition in 1922. From then until 1967, *Our Southern Highlanders* went through eight printings, and when the University of Tennessee Press reprinted it in 1976, the book's cover claimed it to be "the standard by which all other books on the southern mountain region are judged," and that it was the "most widely known and cited" volume on southern Appalachia.

Like Campbell, Kephart deserves more attention from scholars than he has received. And just as Campbell's personal and intellectual journeys offer clues to the lack of public interest in his portrayal of Appalachia, the soap opera that was Kephart's personal life helps explain public enthusiasm for his version of "Appalachia." Kephart's pilgrimage from Yale librarian to scholar of the

Horace Kephart (ca. 1930), from the frontispiece of *Our Southern Highlanders* (University of Tennessee Press, 1976). Kephart's colorful accounts from western North Carolina's "back of beyond" echoed early local colorists' accounts, proving more popular among mainstream readers than the more nuanced and accurate depictions of Appalachia offered by his contemporaries, Emma Bell Miles and John C. Campbell.

Appalachia on Their Minds

American frontier to outdoorsmen to renowned "Appalachian expert" would be incredible if one attempted to capture it in a novel, yet those varied and outwardly contradictory personas and adventures reflected and touched powerful chords in the American psyche. Kephart's personal traumas in the turbulent 1890s mirrored those of the greater society. The acclaimed scholar abandoned professional success and a loving wife and family, was fired from a prestigious job, sought escape in alcohol and seclusion in the great outdoors, and pursued nostalgic, primitive yearnings he only dimly understood. Kephart's quest for the genuine frontier experience he could not adequately record as a historian carried him shortly after 1900 to "a back of beyond" in remote western North Carolina. There Kephart the seeker found what he sought. The rugged mountaineers of the Smokies were the "contemporary ancestors" Kephart yearned to emulate, and they became the lead actors for *Our Southern Highlanders.* Kephart wove colorful phrases from the distinctive mountain dialect into tales of moonshining, bear hunts, and feuding, which echoed Murfree and Fox. Most Americans, then and since, found Kephart's journalistic flair more alluring, and his "Appalachia" more appealing and more credible, than Campbell's statistics-laden assertions or Miles's poetic, personal memoirs. Appalachia's complexity preoccupied Miles and bewildered Campbell. But Kephart's powerful, personal epiphanies exorcized the uncertainties that were his demons. After visits to the greater Appalachian region, including East Tennessee, he "found the southern mountaineers everywhere one people." In the expanded 1922 version of *Our Southern Highlanders,* Kephart wrote:

> To make sure that I was not generalizing too hastily . . . I studied in detail the mountain counties of the South . . . and here I found beyond question my conclusion that the typical southern highlanders were not the [region's] relatively few townsmen and prosperous valley farmers . . . but the great multitude of little farmers living up the branches and on the steep hillsides . . . These, the real mountaineers, were what interested me; and so I wrote them up.[13]

Kephart's "authentic" book barely mentioned the burgeoning and devastating timber industry just over the ridge from its author's idyllic haven. It similarly overlooked traumas exploding in regional coalfields, the imminent demographic disaster resulting from generations of partible inheritance, and challenges that bewildered scores of Appalachian in-migrants to urban settings such as post–World War I Knoxville.

13. Horace Kephart, "Horace Kephart *By* Himself," *North Carolina Library Bulletin* 5 (June 1922): 52.

Nostalgia and Normality

As the popularity of Kephart's book suggests, the more subdued and nuanced depictions that Miles, Wilson, and Campbell offered in the twentieth century's opening decades never managed to dislodge popular notions of a "different, deficient Appalachia." Limited available evidence suggests these images were equally persistent among the region's diverse residents. Leading Knoxvillians of the Progressive Era often echoed journalist William Rule from the similarly prosperous 1880s. They, too, acknowledged their city's dependence on the resources and peoples of East Tennessee's hinterlands. A unifying theme of the visits from the "Prophet of the Smokies" and the expos of 1910, 1911, and 1913 was the need to strengthen ties between the East Tennessee hub city and its hinterlands. Moreover, the Prophet's pronouncements and the "Appalachian cabin" at the 1910 expo clearly revealed that early-twentieth-century Knoxvillians, hinterland elites, and undoubtedly many hinterlanders retained faith in "progress." Programs such as the University of Tennessee's acclaimed "Summer School of the South" and Campbell's "Conferences of the Southern Mountain Workers" revealed continued belief that modernity offered benefits for less-fortunate East Tennesseans. Generally positive recollections of regional natives about life in the coal and timber camps, and their willing embrace of selected aspects of mainstream ways, suggests many everyday East Tennesseans during this era shared that conviction. But neither Progressive Era altruists nor the targets of their efforts should be seen in a vacuum. Compared to commentators on the region from the decades on either side of their epoch, Miles, Wilson, Campbell, and other regional writers of the Progressive Era displayed a genuine respect and empathy for rural Appalachians. And compared to the experiences of their forebears from the 1890s and heirs from the 1920s, rural East Tennesseans had reason to reciprocate that respect and good will.

Complex, sometimes contradictory antimodern inclinations complicate attempts to understand East Tennesseans' take on their regional identity. These impulses emerged from the turbulent 1890s, persisted throughout the Progressive Era (among at least some regional observers and residents), and regained strength in the turbulent '20s. Yet the cultural pluralism Miles and Campbell envisioned never gained more than a minimal following. The popularity of Horace Kephart's *Our Southern Highlanders,* however, reveals the allure and power of another, starkly different antimodernist impulse that had tremendous influence on events unfolding in East Tennessee in the first third of the twentieth century. Like Kephart and many other turn-of-the-century Americans, many urban East Tennesseans of this era were for the first time discovering the great outdoors. This was most evident among Knoxvillians, who by the late

1890s flocked to the Smokies to hike, camp, fish, and hunt. Havens such as Elkmont offered opportunities simultaneously to reconnect with nearly extinct frontier practices and to escape from the monotony and miseries of the urban society. It was not coincidental that the same group of farsighted businessmen who promoted Knoxville's 1910 and 1911 "Appalachian" expos similarly dubbed their private, exclusive Elkmont enclave the "Appalachian" club. Like contemporaries who escaped to locales as distinct as the New York's Adirondacks and Santa Fe and Taos in New Mexico, these decidedly non-Appalachian East Tennesseans embraced what historian Roderick Nash calls "the cult of the primitive." Kephart and earlier local colorists' portrayal of idealized mountaineers appealed to their nostalgia. This was most concretely evident in the simple, rustic cabins they initially constructed in Elkmont and in the satisfaction they gained from "roughing it." Subsequent generations succumbed to impulses to modernize these facilities, but their heirs' tenacious fight to retain a presence in the Smokies throughout the twentieth century reveals the genuine power of this antimodernist impulse and the nostalgia it engenders.

One topic of contention in ongoing debates over Elkmont is how did "mountain natives" (i.e., the families that farmed in the Little River basin before the arrival of Townsend's timber company and the tourists from Knoxville) respond to these developments? My answer, that they responded in a variety of ways, should not surprise readers who have followed the central premises of this book. That answer also covers, I suggest, the responses of most everyday East Tennesseans to other early twentieth-century developments. Like farmers in coal country who gladly took jobs in mines—and whose families embraced outward fruits of progress in company towns—and like Smokies neighbors who responded similarly to opportunities offered by lumber companies, natives of the Little River area responded to the newcomers with a characteristic Appalachian pragmatism. The tourists who flocked to the Smokies offered cash-strapped mountaineers an opportunity to garner income and embrace the benefits of progress. Perhaps the fact that many of these "outlanders" displayed an interest in the mountaineers' hardscrabble lifestyle encouraged Little River folk in this ultimately painful bargain. Some natives sold their ancestral lands. Many others sold their labor. Subsequent observers have questioned the wisdom of their choices and lamented that the mountaineers were innocent victims of forces they did not comprehend. But, as Durwood Dunn's recent analysis of the tragic last days of Cades Cove reveals, the situation was not that simple.

Cades Cove in the 1890s had largely regained its pre–Civil War prosperity and did not experience directly the White Cap activities that broke out just over the mountains in nearby Sevier County. But, like many rural American communities in that turbulent decade, Cades Cove did not escape modernity's mys-

John C. Oliver carrying the mail in the late 1920s. The Cove patriarch promoted many progressive causes, including (to his later regret) plans for what became Great Smoky Mountains National Park. (Courtesy of Durwood Dunn.)

terious demands and dependencies. Indeed, by the turn of the century, Cove residents embraced most of the distinctly progressive—dare we say "liberal"—inclinations characterizing American life of that forgotten era. No single individual within Cades Cove more completely epitomized that trend than John W. Oliver, great-grandson of the Cove's pioneer settler. After completing training to become a teacher at nearby Maryville College and receiving business training in Louisville, Kentucky, Oliver returned to the Cove in 1904 and began a thirty-two year career as a rural mail carrier, a position that put him in contact with every Cove family. Meanwhile, his success as a farmer and his status as a preacher in the Primitive Baptist Church—the Cove's preeminent social institution—made him the community's foremost patriarch. In the words of Durwood Dunn, Oliver was "the Zeitgeist of American progressivism in all of its manifestations."[14] Oliver's life was a perfect illustration of the complex dynamics of selective acculturation. Over the first three decades of the new century, Oliver promoted by personal example almost every progressive cause: scientific farming, better hygiene and healthcare, conservation, public education (serving young women as well as men), and prohibition.

Oliver's commitment to conservation made him a friend and ally to Elkmont's seasonal residents, who by the 1920s called for transforming his beloved mountains into a national park. In 1924, he began renting tourist cabins and

14. Dunn, *Cades Cove*, 22.

personally escorted affluent Knoxvillians and other park promoters on hikes to such spots as Gregory's Bald, Spence Field, and Thunderhead.

Oliver only too late realized that park planners included Cades Cove and his own beloved 337-acre farm in plans for their proposed national park—a plan that made removal of Oliver and his neighbors necessary. In a fashion uncharacteristic of a stereotypical Appalachian, Oliver fought in the courts to retain the property he dearly loved. As it was for the Cherokees, Oliver's litigation proved unsuccessful. In what can only be described as paradox layered upon paradox, Knoxville civic leader David Chapman ("the father of Great Smoky Mountain National Park") and other park promoters resorted to popular, degrading hillbilly images to win their case against Oliver. Their success in creating Great Smoky Mountains National Park bestowed inestimable benefits to all of East Tennessee, but honest recognition of how this development transpired should give us a moment of pause.

East Tennesseans, Appalachia, and the Turbulent '20s

The Cades Cove tragedy unfolded in the midst of more general misfortune and misery. Far from the fun-loving "roaring '20s" of popular recollection, the 1920s were an era of wrenching adjustments and many outward contradictions. Issues that had divided Americans in the 1890s—rapid and bewildering change, rural-urban differences, the increasing diversity of the nation's population and culture, and doubts about progress itself—resurfaced. Pervasive nostalgia and an outwardly conservative political leadership temporarily contained deep economic and cultural cleavages. But, as the Depression made cruelly apparent, that vision of society and government was no match for the volatile forces modernity unleashed. Consequently, the mid- to late 1920s were truly one of the most unsettling eras in American history. East Tennessee was not immune to that ugliness.

Reading preferences of East Tennesseans such as my grandparents during the 1920s most likely mirrored those of the national reading audience. While one cannot prove this assertion with absolute certainty, I have little doubt many regional forebears readily embraced Horace Kephart. And I fully expect many of them, like the nation's general readership, paid little attention to Emma Bell Miles and John C. Campbell. The obvious explanation for this expected preference was the profound mood shift accompanying the "return to normalcy" and the abrupt end to progressivism. But I maintain that among East Tennesseans the new realities explored in chapters three and four magnified national misfortunes. A race riot on Knoxville's Gay Street in 1919, and the subsequent emergence of the second Ku Klux Klan as a major force in city politics, dashed the

Many of these tourists at "John Oliver's Lodge" in August 1930 were Knoxvillians who championed a national park in the Smokies. They were often unsympathetic with individuals who, like the hospitable John Oliver, challenged the National Park Service's assertion of eminent domain in its acquisition of their ancestral homes. (Great Smoky Mountain National Park Library and Archives.)

city's longstanding claims of racial tolerance and spurred many blacks to leave the city. Unprecedented labor unrest in West Virginia's coalfields threatened to spread to East Tennessee, and by the end of the decade management hostility toward attempts to unionize mines in Wilder, west of the Clearfork Valley, resulted in murder and mayhem. In the grand showdown between new and old Americas, the Scopes Trial in Dayton—midway between Knoxville and Chattanooga—became center stage in 1925, and East Tennessee became the target of those relishing ridicule of "fundamentalist rednecks." Knoxville itself divided over this culture war. The city's conservative elite either supported the state of Tennessee's official stance opposing the teaching of evolution in public schools or refrained from the debate. But at least one outspoken native, thirty-one-year-old journalist Joseph Wood Krutch (whom *The Nation* sent to Dayton), offered a very different perspective. Uninformed northern journalists who offered unkind, sweeping denigration of his home region infuriated Krutch, but he became even angrier with old friends in Knoxville and at the University of Tennessee.

> If Tennessee has become the laughing stock of the world, it is not because she has her villages which are a half century behind the centers of world thought, but rather because among her sons who know better there is scarcely one who has the courage to stand up for what he thinks . . . The legislator is afraid of some fundamentalist hid in the mountains; . . . the [university]

president is afraid of the legislature; the faculty is afraid of the president; and the newspaper editor is afraid of someone who is afraid of someone else . . . In Tennessee bigotry is militant and sincere; intelligence is timid and hypocritical . . . [15]

Ironically, Krutch's scathing appraisal of his home region's educated urban elite provided grist for those who found pleasure in denigrating uniformly deficient Appalachians. Such unintended consequences from the words of a "successful Appalachian" was not unprecedented in 1925. They would happen all too often in the years thereafter.

But the hoopla in Dayton that summer was not the only source for such images. As events in Dayton attained fever pitch, the long-simmering feud between Knoxville's city manager, Louis Brownlow, and the "redneck reactionary," Lee Monday, described in chapter three, boiled over. When Brownlow succumbed to a nervous breakdown, Knoxville progressivism went into long-term hibernation. Brownlow's unguarded rhetoric about "hillbillies," "good old mountain ways," and disparaging insinuations about "Monday's clan—"the East Tennesseans" doubtlessly drew from seeds of truth. But the narrow-mindedness of Monday's recent rural-to-urban émigré followers was hardly unique to 1920s East Tennesseans. This was, of course, the America of Warren G. Harding's "normalcy." Brownlow's charges echoed the assault that leading Knoxvillians leveled against John Oliver for standing in the way of their national park. Collectively, East Tennesseans affirmed conclusions about themselves that many drew recklessly from the Scopes Trial and the broader discovery of "Appalachia."

As historical observers, we have the luxury of moving above this emotional fray and assessing it in broader contexts. The uncertainties and shifting perspective of East Tennessee's more fortunate residents on their region's "Appalachian identity" is one theme from the era around 1875 to 1925 that historians of Knoxville and Appalachian scholars have overlooked for too long. In the culturally calm, economically prosperous 1880s, and again in the Progressive Era, the likes of William Rule and the promoters of Knoxville's Appalachian Expos recognized the city's symbiotic dependence on the region's hinterlands and developed relatively cordial ties with their hinterland neighbors. A few perceptive observers, such as Emma Bell Miles and John C. Campbell, recognized regional pluralism. But this generosity and enlightened self-interest disappeared in the traumatic 1890s and again in the troubled 1920s. Antirural rhetoric from the likes of Louis Brownlow and David Chapman, and understandable disassociation by the likes of my own grandparents from distorted perceptions of their region, left scars still apparent in today's East Tennessee.

15. Jack Neely, "Bigotry, Militant, and Sincere," *Metro Pulse*, July 2, 1993.

One reason these scars are so enduring is that we East Tennesseans know only snippets about these and other colorful events from the half-century culminating in the Brownlow-Monday feud and the forced removal of Oliver and his neighbors from their beloved Cades Cove. We do not adequately know either the broader national or regional contexts in which those showdowns occurred.

By 1930, circumstances converged again to bring hardship, poverty, and hopelessness—stereotypically "Appalachian" traits—to practically all of East Tennessee. Indeed, the region as a whole in 1925 was much like it was in 1875—temporarily uniform in its "Appalachian" miseries. We will begin part III by addressing how East Tennesseans dealt with and emerged from the Great Depression. But much like the Civil War (in part II) the Depression was more interlude than watershed for this latest era in East Tennessee–Appalachian history. Our ongoing struggle to come to terms with the mysterious dependencies that make that past and identity so elusive is the most salient and enduring theme in East Tennessee's recent history and its unfolding present.

Part III

Appalachia, East Tennessee, and
Modern America, 1920–2006

By the time my parents were born in the twentieth century's second decade, the term "southern Appalachia" had two distinct meanings. The map accompanying John C. Campbell's *The Southern Highlander* in 1921 offered what became the widely accepted physical definition of the region. Spanning southward from West Virginia to Alabama's northeast corner, "geographical Appalachia" includes all of East Tennessee. Indeed, Knoxville and Bristol, the two burgeoning urban centers where my father and mother were raised, are near the center of what Campbell called the "Southern Highland Region." Perhaps Campbell chose that label because he deemed recently popular, more familiar depictions of "Appalachia" hopelessly misleading. That other "Appalachia" was a uniform, static place, peopled by "strange and peculiar" folk whose lives contrasted starkly with modern standards in the rapidly changing United States. My forebears, and many of their East Tennessee neighbors, often distanced themselves from popular understandings of "Appalachia." This dissociation was understandable, but its consequences for the likes of my forebears, their heirs, and our region have been mixed.

Thirty years of Appalachian studies scholarship has deepened our understanding of the importance of both geographical and cultural Appalachia in the twentieth century. Regional coal, timber, and other raw materials contributed significantly to the nation's great surge of industrialization and modernization. Meanwhile, images from cultural "Appalachia" served as a useful foil for Americans who were at once proud and bewildered by those same developments. Turn-of-the-twentieth-century Americans found escape from their anxieties and reassurance for their aspirations in nostalgic recollections of noble pioneers, frightening tales of feuding highlanders, and raucous accounts of hillbilly buffoons. Although actual conditions in geographical Appalachia differed greatly from popular perceptions of cultural "Appalachia," the two were more intertwined than regional observers have recognized. Disentangling the two Appalachias lures one into an intellectually bewildering maze.

The experiences of Appalachians on the greater American stage in the twentieth century were hardly unique. Like most peoples—particularly those we deem "minorities"—regional residents had more than one identity, and they shifted their primary allegiance from one to another as needed. During World War II, for example, Navajo "code talkers" and black "Tuskegee Airmen" placed loyalty to our nation above identification with their more immediate group, and temporarily set aside concerns about racism and injustice. Once the war was over, however, members of these groups returned home keenly aware of our national hypocrisy, and some of them became actively engaged in movements to gain civil rights for their respective peoples. The Appalachian experience was similar yet different. Compared to racial minorities (or even religious minorities, such as Jews), we Appalachians can more readily cross the line "into mainstream status," and if we choose, can return to our roots (or some portion thereof) with less attention and controversy. As a wise African American colleague helped me realize, this unique status works two ways. It was an asset for the likes of my grandparents, because it enabled them to achieve many physical benefits and comforts (and pass them down to heirs including myself). But this was also a liability. Embracing progress and its powerful accompanying myths led regional residents of a century ago to sell their resources, labor, and identity perhaps too readily.

However one views this transaction, it was only the beginning of a cycle that shaped our region in the twentieth century. Feeding outside needs for coal, timber, and other resources set a stage in the middle years of the last century (when my parents came of age) for an unsustainable economy and environmental havoc. And these two distinctive "Appalachian" hallmarks became proof of our region's innate deficiencies, both imagined and real. The costs were most immediate for East Tennessee's hinterland areas, but valley urban communities such as those where my parents were raised did not completely escape the effects of these developments and the images they fostered. Part III explores how twentieth-century East Tennesseans responded to the challenges of our times— not the least of which was dealing with elusive views of our past and ourselves that we inherited.

A cursory glance at the era from around 1920 to 1960 (the timeframe for chapter six) reveals that many familiar patterns from the recent past continued. The two hinterland regions continued largely to serve outside needs at considerable cost and dubious benefit to many natives. Knoxville, of course, played its customary leading role. City residents, many of whom had deep roots in rural East Tennessee, continued to display a profound ambivalence toward "things Appalachian." Some city residents held tightly to regional ways; others did so selectively. But overall, the pattern of intragroup distinction that earlier "invisible

Appalachians" such as my forebears practiced was a common feature of Knoxville life midway through the twentieth century. As a result, the self-perpetuating cycle I have previously described continued, as many of East Tennessee's own people joined with outsiders in considering East Tennessee a backwater.

A less visible development during this period, which produced results many observers—including many East Tennesseans—still do not recognize, was the "Appalachian awakening." Appalachia's awakening began in the early twentieth century, with the efforts of people such as Emma Bell Miles and John C. Campbell. But Americans were not ready for Campbell's call for a diverse, "viable mountain culture [within a] pluralistic United States," and the movement went dormant.[1] In the iconoclastic 1930s, native intellectuals for the first time joined sympathetic insider-outsiders in an attempt to reawaken interest in Appalachia.

My parents, like most people, were the products of a complex commingling of forces, including the very interesting times and places where their lives began. Dad was born in Knoxville in 1913; my mother in Bristol six years later. The peaking and waning of progressivism in this era profoundly influenced my parents and left important, albeit overlooked, effects on East Tennessee.

I know very little about either of my parents' childhoods and nothing at all that would suggest they were anything but normal. My father's youth was clearly marked by his parents' financial woes. Those difficult circumstances, along with effects of the subsequent Depression, left him with a deep commitment to making do. Even now, twenty years after his death, his barn is filled with "things we might need someday." Overall, both of my parents and their families were quite fortunate during the hard times of the Great Depression. Pop Banker's involuntary bankruptcy preceded the stock market crash by several months and was apparently the family's lowest point in that difficult era. His entrepreneurial success in the 1930s and '40s assured his family a relatively advantaged economic standing. My father was also personally fortunate in the darkest days of the Depression, when the newly created TVA hired workers for the Norris Dam project. Dad, who was twenty at the time, started his TVA career there, pushing a wheelbarrow and operating a jackhammer. With jobs scarce, the federal agency was glad to allow him to divide his time between work on the dam and attendance at the University of Tennessee.

Similar good fortune blessed Mother's family during the Depression years. Scarcely a month before the crash of October 1929 led to the closing of most of Bristol's banks, my Thomas grandparents withdrew nearly fifteen years worth

1. Henry J. Shapiro, introduction to *The Southern Highlander*, by John C. Campbell, xxii–xxiii (Lexington: Univ. of Kentucky Press, 1969). Also see Shapiro's references to Campbell in *Appalachia on Our Mind*.

of savings to build a two-story brick home in a respectable Bristol neighborhood a few blocks south of the Tennessee-Virginia line. The impressive Dutch colonial residence proved a stable investment, satisfied my grandmother's yearning for at least modest prominence, and stands today as a proud reminder of my grand-father's craftsmanship and good luck.

The matter of my parents' sense of identity is, of course, vital to this book, and here evidence from their childhood years is thin. As dutiful children, nei-ther of them overtly challenged their parents' tendency to distance themselves from their own regional roots. But bits of evidence, pieced together and restored to broader contexts, hint that both Mom and Dad may have been more kindly disposed toward "Appalachia" than their parents. Mother enjoyed regular visits with her grandparents at the farm in Cook's Valley and less regular, but more extended, trips to the home of her more distant Thomas ancestors and cousins atop Brierpatch Mountain in southwest Virginia. As a boy, Dad often sold po-tatoes on Knoxville's Market Square, where like many other Knoxvillians, he was fascinated by many of the colorful "mountain folk" who came to the square on Saturdays to sell their wares. Dad also contributed nickels and dimes to the campaign to establish Great Smoky Mountains National Park, as did many other Knoxville school children of the 1920s. As a teen, he hiked and fished in the new park's confines.

Mom and Dad in their younger years may have been fascinated with "things Appalachian," but there is no evidence they were aware of John C. Campbell or

Katherine and Tollie Thomas (the author's mother and grandfather) visit with Uncle Jake Thomas on the front porch of the old Thomas homeplace on Brierpatch Mountain in Grayson County, Virginia, in 1922. Occa-sional visits there, and more regular trips to the Cook's Valley, Tennessee farm, where Tollie Thomas was raised, kept the author's grandfather and mother in touch with their regional roots. (Author's personal photo collection.)

Vendors at Market Square in 1928. Rural East Tennesseans and Knoxvillians, including the author's youthful father, interacted regularly at Market Square from the latter nineteenth century until the 1950s. (Courtesy of McClung Historical Collection.)

the subdued phase of the "Appalachian Awakening" underway around the time they enrolled at the University of Tennessee in the 1930s. That is hardly surprising considering their family backgrounds, the serious circumstances of that era, and that the university itself was slow to awaken to this regional effort. Depression-era realities, ongoing global conflicts, and reminders of his parents' not-too-distant financial hardships undoubtedly influenced Dad's decision to pursue practical subjects, such as business and law. TVA's offer of a solid administrative labor-relations position when he completed his studies at the university rewarded that decision. Mother's circumstances were more comfortable. She was one of a handful of classics majors at the university in the mid-1930s. Preoccupied with Greek, Latin, Shakespeare, and Eugene Banker, she had little time for anything else. After a chance meeting in the university library, my parents' romance blossomed. They often went to the Smokies on dates, and Dad's success in convincing his bookish, rather sedentary sweetheart to wade out and fish in cold mountain trout streams is a testimony to his charm, the power of the mountain ambiance, and just plain love. They were married in December 1940.

Pressing challenges in the early 1940s clearly affected my parents' life as newlyweds. Global crises abruptly ended the Depression, but thrust the world into even greater peril. In 1942, officials of the top-secret Manhattan Project informed TVA that they needed Dad's skills in personnel management, and soon thereafter my parents and my oldest brother moved to Oak Ridge, where Dad was on the hiring end of one of the most mysterious and exciting endeavors in U.S. history. Mom, Dad, and their growing family experienced the ups and downs of life in the "city behind a fence." By appearances at least, they were by 1950 solidly middle class, suburban, and comfortably established in what many now consider an idyllic "happy days" lifestyle. But appearances can be misleading.

As early as the late 1940s, my parents occasionally trekked through the surrounding East Tennessee countryside in search of a farm. In the fall of 1950, that quest led them to property just south of the confluence of the Tennessee and Clinch Rivers, a few miles from the sleepy little town of Kingston. On Thanksgiving weekend 1950, my parents moved with four little boys (and me on the way) into a rundown farmhouse on seventy hardscrabble acres. By all accounts, my four grandparents were collectively alarmed. Were Gene and Katy Banker abandoning the gains their forebears' hard work and good fortune had

Katherine Thomas and Eugene Banker (ca. 1940). After meeting at the University of Tennessee in the mid-1930s, the author's parents often dated, hiked, and fished for trout in the newly established Great Smoky Mountains National Park. A love for the Smokies was one gift they passed down to their six sons. (Author's personal photo collection.)

achieved? The move was, of course, atypical at the time. Yet it was a portent of a significant change in outlook that became more pronounced throughout the Appalachian region in the final decades of the twentieth century. My parents in 1950, to be sure, were only dimly aware of all of this. They were far too preoccupied with more pressing concerns to reflect on the history they were making.

For a couple raised in urban settings, my parents embraced rural life with unusual relish. With help from their sons and new neighbors, they raised huge gardens, milked cows, raised beef cattle, hogs, and chicken for meat (and eggs). Mother churned butter and preserved produce from their gardens as well as blackberries, apples, and other gifts from nature. With help from a local carpenter, they refurbished the old farmhouse and built several fine barns. The folks originally considered their improvements on the old house temporary, and for at least a few years planned to build a "big house" on an adjacent hill overlooking the Tennessee River. But my parents took pride in the sprawling farmhouse that never quite escaped rustic status. Years later when he reflected back on his life on the farm, Dad commented that it was "a good place to raise boys and dogs." By then, the "back to the land" movement had swept through our part of the world, and many from the '60s counterculture and others of that ilk embraced "simple lifestyles." As far as I know, Mom and Dad never considered that they might have been pioneers in this cultural upheaval, which proved so favorable to the Appalachian awakening and cultural survival that concerns us here.

My parents' relations with their new country neighbors and their responses to the revival of interest in "Appalachia" in the 1960s are more difficult to track, but I believe the word "ambivalent" best describes their experiences and attitudes. First, relations with our neighbors on James Ferry Road were at once cordial, yet somewhat distant. Faced with many more farm duties than he could possibly handle, Dad often hired neighbors to rebuild fences, put up hay, and help with such uniquely skilled projects as butchering hogs. In his position as a personnel officer at Oak Ridge National Labs, Dad helped several new acquaintances secure good, cash-paying positions. He was also genuinely interested in their lives. One of my earliest memories was attending a tent revival conducted by a neighboring itinerant preacher. On the other hand, neighbors did not always appreciate Dad's penchant for sharing advice about "scientific farming." When he attempted to explain the advantages of contour plowing to an elderly farmer, the old fellow bluntly told Dad that his head was "full of [bovine excrement]." Yet Dad relished having a foot in two very different worlds: the cosmopolitan, urbane routine at Oak Ridge National Laboratory, and his life in the country. I sense that Mother had less success in closing the gap between her urban sophistication and the more basic lives of women neighbors.

In November 1950, Gene and Katy Banker purchased a farm near Kingston, Tennessee. To the great dismay of both of their families, they and their four young sons moved into what had once been a tenant house on the farm. Three months later, the author was born. (Author's personal photo collection.)

At the time my parents moved to the farm, the word "Appalachia" would have evoked almost no response from them or from most of their contemporaries. In those pretelevision days, a small yellow radio sat on the mantle in our kitchen. After sending her older sons off to school, Mom often listened to the radio as she pursued a variety of chores and tried to keep an eye on we younger boys. Sometimes we listened to the "Lone Ranger" or the "Arthur Godfrey Show," but my clearest memory was Mom's disdain for country music—standard fare on the few local stations we could pick up. Mother made clear that "we didn't listen to hillbilly music," yet her stance was not absolute. Tennessee Ernie Ford was mother's high school classmate, and she showed unusual tolerance for the occasional cornball humor in his radio appearances. His recordings bridged several popular musical genres, but had a distinct country flavor. Nonetheless, when we heard them on the radio, Mom was justly proud. After she acquired a record of Ford's most popular hits, my brothers and I nearly wore it out. Still, when I left home for college in 1969, I shunned country tunes as "not our kind of music."

With the advent of the 1960s, and particularly President Lyndon Johnson's "war on poverty," images of "Appalachia" made their way into our lives. Rhetoric for that much- ballyhooed political campaign, televised documentaries by Walter Cronkite and Charles Kuralt, and even the little *Weekly Readers* that enriched our formal educations introduced us to dilapidated shanties, hungry, hollow-eyed children, and strip-mine-ravished landscapes. On occasions when we would witness firsthand someone whose life appeared similar to widespread "Appalachian" images, I would probe the folks further about that curious place. Mom, who was always more blunt than Dad, occasionally uttered something about "poor white trash" under her breath and assured us those images were clearly "not us." Dad's response was similar, yet more gentle and reflective. Many times I recall him saying, "poor folks have poor ways." But, he invariably added, "save by the grace of God there goes I." Now that I know more about the hardships of his youth, I realize that was far more than just an expression.

On reflecting on my upbringing, I now know that my parents' actions bore a more enduring imprint on me than their words. No single act more typified the message they spread than their decision not to build the "big house overlooking the river." To be sure, they spent considerable money and energy upgrading the old house where they raised us boys and lived out their days. Their efforts clearly made the old place more comfortable, but even at its finest moment it was simple and better fit the surrounding community than would any new home they might have constructed. More important, that home symbolized a lifestyle my parents hoped their sons would emulate: investing one's time, energy, and effort into causes and needs greater than oneself. Gene and Katy Banker were far from perfect, but they never allowed their imperfections to keep them from investing their considerable talents in addressing the flaws and needs they saw in their world. Together they juggled many roles that reflected, by my standards, a truly Appalachian lifestyle. For all of their public commitments, my parents' most enduring legacies are in the lives of the countless young people they touched as parent, neighbor, teacher, Sunday school teacher, community activist, and scout leader. I only belatedly came to identify that habit as "regional stewardship," and although my parents never (as far as I know) related their many commitments to "Appalachia," I now know that worldviews and lifestyles like theirs were vital to the regional "awakening."

In wrapping up these insights, I must share one more family story that reflects "Appalachia's hold" on its children and illustrates the cultural context that proved so fruitful for the regional awakening. My aunt, Mary Banker Medema, was twenty years old in the middle of the Depression, when a young Dutchman came to board in the Banker household. Melvin Medema, a student from Fenn College in Cleveland, Ohio, was a co-op engineer at TVA's Norris Dam. After a whirlwind romance, he and Aunt Mary were married in 1939. Uncle Mel's deep commitment to the Christian Reformed tradition, and determination to raise his family in that environment, led the growing Medema family to move to Grand Rapids, Michigan in 1946. Aunt Mary's life in Grand Rapids was relatively comfortable, compared to that of many hardscrabble Appalachian out-migrants then moving to Detroit, Chicago, and other northern industrial centers. But she shared with her regional kinsmen a yearning for home and bouts of loneliness. Mary often laughed about being "just a hillbilly," but that seemingly self-deprecating line offered reassurance as well as relief. Regular and extended summer treks back home to East Tennessee and Uncle Gene's farm were one remedy for Mary's yearnings, and provided a way to pass her passion for East Tennessee to her four children. In spite of good-natured ribbing about "odd Yankee ways," my Michigan cousins inherited an affinity for family and place that geographical distance and removal by a generation only enhanced.

After Uncle Mel's death in 1990, Aunt Mary's trips to Tennessee became more frequent, and in her waning years her Tennessee ties became even more important. During one trip she joked with her sister Jo that she needed some "Tennessee dirt." Soon thereafter she received an ornamental jar filled with Tennessee red clay. For the rest of her life, Aunt Mary proudly displayed her memento in her Michigan living room. When she died in 1998, half of her "Tennessee dirt" was put in a plastic bag and placed in her coffin. The rest remains in the ornamental jar in the office of my cousin David in Grand Rapids. There, thanks to the wonders of the Internet, familiar music from East Tennessee radio station WDVX often fills the air.

Chapter Six

East Tennessee from Bad Times to Good Times (for Some), 1920–1965

As we have seen, Cades Cove by the early twentieth century had come to typify "traditional Appalachia." The Cove's setting and soils, to be sure, were better suited to human habitation than many hardscrabble areas of East Tennessee, but cultural patterns there mirrored many standard "Appalachian" images: simple, quaint, and far removed from modernity. Moreover, Cove residents experienced many of the upheavals that undermined the region during the nineteenth century, most notably the Civil War and its aftermath. Even though actual conditions there rebounded and differed markedly from what became popular notions about "Appalachia," authors such as Mary Noailles Murfree—and many outsiders—did not hesitate to make the Cove a setting for stereotypically nostalgic regional images.

The "death" of Cades Cove can only be understood in the context of otherwise positive developments that saw outsiders around the turn of the century discover the scenic beauty of the Great Smokies. No one played a greater role in the events leading to the creation of Great Smoky Mountains National Park than Knoxvillian David Chapman. Summer visits to the resort community of Elkmont stirred Chapman's affections for the mountains and awakened him to their potential as a tourist attraction. Chapman, head of a Knoxville pharmaceutical company and one-time University of Tennessee football player, was prominently involved in East Tennessee's nascent Auto Club and "Good Roads" movement, and he became director of Knoxville's Chamber of Commerce. When industrialist Willis P. Davis and his wife, Anne, returned to East Tennessee from a western vacation in 1923, they were convinced the nearby Smokies were as deserving of preservation as a tourist enclave as sites they had recently visited. The prominent Knoxville couple found Chapman a ready and capable ally.

To say that visions of profit motivated Chapman and his fellow Knoxville boosters is not to deny their attachment to the Smokies. Indeed, some of them were well-informed environmentalists. Young Knoxville attorney Harvey Broome, for example, began a lifelong commitment to protecting the Smokies from crass commercialism as Chapman's ally. But Chapman's credentials were a bit more suspect. Until he emerged as the chief promoter for a national park, he had apparently seen little of the mountains beyond Elkmont. In Chapman's defense, he learned quickly, and his characteristic energy and enthusiasm for the cause belied notions that he was insincere. Not all Elkmonters, however, shared Broome's environmental ethic or Chapman's enthusiasm for a park committed to "preserving" the Smokies. Attorney James Wright, who represented several still-powerful timber companies, expressed a clear preference for "conserving" the Smokies in a national forest that would be less restrictive of development of mountain resources than a national park. Park proponents, however, offered compelling evidence that existing national forests had done little to promote East Tennessee tourism, and with that goal as their mantra, Chapman and followers staved off Wright's efforts.

The fact that proposed boundaries for the park spilled over the Tennessee and North Carolina borders complicated promotional efforts. But by the mid-1920s, Knoxville- and Asheville-based boosters largely overcame this problem. In East Tennessee, school children (including my father and his siblings) contributed pennies, nickels, and dimes to the cause. Knoxville city officials displayed just how much a nearby mountain park meant to them when they voted to pay one-third ($91,000) of the purchase price to transfer more than 76,000 acres of Little River Lumber Company land to the proposed park. Strong support from Governor Austin Peay, who had a cabin and ties in Elkmont, strengthened the cause. Still, combined public and private efforts from Tennessee and North Carolina raised barely half of the $10 million necessary for purchasing land for the park. Only philanthropist John D. Rockefeller Jr.'s donation of the other $5 million enabled park promoters to meet the first important hurdle on the way to establishing the park.

Unlike earlier national parks, which had largely been carved from the public domain of western states, the proposed Great Smoky Mountains National Park included lands held by private business interests, seasonal residents of communities such as Elkmont, and descendants of the area's earlier settlers, many of whom still engaged in small-scale farming. Several large lumber companies were prominent among the first group, and by the mid-1920s, most of them had gleaned the most readily accessible stands of timber and profits; they needed little encouragement to sell their denuded slopes for whatever they could get.

Dealing with the Smokies' approximately four thousand human inhabitants proved more problematic. Cades Cove in 1928 had a population of six hundred. Although Cataloochee (on the park's proposed eastern boundary, with a population of around nine hundred) and the Cherokee reservation lay in the Tar Heel state, the bulk of the domain's permanent residents were East Tennesseans. Many long-established communities had churches, cemeteries, general stores, and federal post offices. In addition, by the late 1920s, the Appalachian and Wonderland Clubs in Elkmont had more than fifty seasonal cabins, a large "railroad hotel," a lodge, and an array of recreational facilities. Elkmonters were fewer in number but had more influence and political clout than their native neighbors. This was clearly evident in the selective, convenient, and occasionally deceitful depictions of the latter that Chapman and other park boosters offered. Pro-park publicity initially ignored the region's native inhabitants; when promoters such as Chapman acknowledged regional residents, they typically borrowed from prevailing nostalgia about "contemporary ancestors." This was hardly surprising. Such imagery still had wide appeal with the public. Indeed, Horace Kephart, one of the most vocal park promoters on the North Carolina side, had overcome personal misfortune and made a literary reputation perpetuating such portrayals. Moreover, many native residents initially joined forces with park promoters. Cades Cove patriarch John Oliver's tourist lodge introduced visitors from near and far to his beloved mountains (see photo page 157). Park rhetoric about preservation appealed to Oliver's progressive inclinations, and he befriended Chapman and other early boosters, including Carlos Campbell. When promoters brought John D. Rockefeller Jr. to the mountains to win his favor and dollars, they stayed in Oliver's lodge and introduced the philanthropist to the Cove's impressive leading citizen.

By the time President Calvin Coolidge signed legislation giving the go-ahead for a national park in 1926, rumors that at least some native residents might lose their homes were rampant. Tennessee senator (and Knoxvillian) Lawrence Tyson, a key promoter of the legislation, flatly denied that Congress had any intention (or power) to force such removal. The states of Tennessee and North Carolina, he conceded, however, might have other intentions. Soon thereafter, Tennessee governor Austin Peay asserted at a mass meeting at Elkmont that as long as he was a member of the park commission, mountaineers' homes were secure. Chapman, Campbell, and the Knoxville press vociferously repeated these denials. By the late 1920s, the soap opera reached fever pitch, when timber company lawyer and anti-park spokesman Jim Wright, in a last ditch effort to undermine the cause, offered a melodramatic, patronizing defense of "the mountain people." Concern and support for the mountain residents came from many corners, and some of it was surely genuine. But behind the scenes, wheeling and dealing reveal a more sordid story. Agreements in the Tennessee legislature left every substantial permanent (i.e., year-round) community in the area—other than Cades Cove—outside of the final park boundaries. By that time, National Park Service personnel were adamant: without inclusion of the scenic valley, there would be no park. Park backers resorted to degrading regional adjectives (such as "ignorant," "isolated," and "impoverished") to denigrate those whose lives their demands would disrupt. Ultimately, Cades Cove was included in the park, and Wright, his clients, and the Elkmont folks reached relatively beneficial arrangements with park planners. The story was, to be sure, very complex, but sufficient evidence exists to make Durwood Dunn's charge of "blatant deceit" credible and enduring.

Dunn's grandfather, John Oliver, awakened to that deceit only in 1927, after his support enabled the park movement to gain irrepressible headway. By then it was too late. Oliver, who did not give in without a fight, was not merely altruistic; his 337-acre farm, with its considerable improvements, held significant financial value, but the sentimental worth defied estimation. As for his neighbors, Oliver's leadership and integrity was their primary hope against a formidable foe. Maryville attorney Russell Kramer, with assistance from Oliver's son, Wayne, prepared a complex defense against Tennessee's assertion of eminent domain over Oliver's farm and the broader Cove community. Eventually, as Dunn recounts, "Oliver lost the war to save [his homeland], but even his critics were forced to concede his courage and tenacity."[1]

When John Oliver moved his last belongings from the family homestead on Christmas Day 1937, the once-vibrant Cove community was dead. A few neighbors, along with several other longtime residents of lands within the confines of the new park, reached lease agreements with the Park Service allowing them to remain on ancestral lands. This arrangement, however, proved less than satisfactory for most lessees, because it proscribed grazing livestock, hunting, fishing, and the gathering of firewood, wild fruits, and herbs—privileges they had enjoyed without restriction for more than a century. Rhetoric from park promoters that these mountaineer remnants (and the Cherokee on the North Carolina side of the Park) would become "a living museum" for curious tourists also proved illusory and demeaning. Five spinster sisters of the Little Greenbrier community (just over the ridge from Cades Cove) attempted to balance continuation of traditional ways with entertaining and educating visitors, but when the latter began to number more than three hundred a day, the Walker sisters informed park personnel that they no longer desired to serve as objects of attention for meddlesome tourists.

This is not to say that natives of areas absorbed into the park did not benefit at all from its creation. Younger, less traditional residents of Cades Cove used payments for their ancestral homes to acquire better farms or adjust happily to lives in urban or suburban settings. Other locals became tour guides and opened busi-

1. Dunn, *Cades Cove*, 250.

Cades Cove families packing up belongings after their legal fight against eviction from the Cove had failed in the mid-1930s. (Courtesy of Durwood Dunn.)

nesses in Gatlinburg, the most notable gateway community of the park's early era. The affable Wiley Oakley became Gatlinburg's "town character," the "Will Rogers of the Smokies." Oakley proved particularly adept at playing down to the expectations of tourists, who made his memoirs one of the most popular books about the region. His shrewd development of family lands in the Gatlinburg area left his children a valuable financial inheritance. Entrepreneurial efforts by other prominent mountain families, including the Reagans, Ogles, Huffs, and Whaleys, contributed to and benefited from the emergence of Gatlinburg as a tourist Mecca. Collectively, the experiences of these and other natives belie notions that outside shysters always victimized unsophisticated "hillbillies."

Shrewd natives were hardly the only locals to benefit from the coming of the park. Seasonal residents utilized their connections, skilled lawyers, and the greater clout and flexibility that accompany relative wealth to secure much better deals for their property than Oliver and most of his neighbors received. For example, an arbitration board awarded timber company attorney and prominent Knoxvillian Jim Wright $70,000 for property earlier appraised at $17,000. Among the weapons Wright cynically waged in this cause was "the plight of the poor mountain people." After much wrangling, most members of Elkmont's Appalachian and Wonderland Clubs agreed to sell their property for one-half

East Tennessee from Bad Times to Good Times (for Some)

of its appraised value in exchange for lifetime leases. Their connections with powerful people, and subsequent chicanery, enabled their heirs to continue this arrangement for most of the twentieth century. The Elkmonters' genuine love for their mountain haven (and in some cases for its native residents) did not lessen some locals' objections to the preferential treatment they received.

Longstanding rancor and ill will over Elkmont stemmed, no doubt, from the fact that not all former residents of parklands were as satisfied with their dealings with the National Park Service. The timing of the forced removal from the mountains was, of course, unfortunate. When John Oliver finally accepted courtroom defeat and departed his beloved home in 1937, the nation was still in the midst of the worst economic crisis in its history. Mountaineers were hardly unfamiliar with adversity,

Wiley Oakley in front of his Gatlinburg tourist shop in 1937. Oakley shrewdly used his mountain identity and persona to make a living by catering to tourists. Over the years, many other native entrepreneurs and entertainers have followed Oakley's example. (Great Smoky Mountains National Park Library and Archives.)

but creation of the park undermined the very family and community institutions and traditions that had enabled their survival in the face of earlier crises. The touching account of longtime mountain resident Dorie Cope's adjustment in her latter years to life in Knoxville clearly reveals the mountains' lingering hold on its children.

A brief glimpse into the Cades Cove's post-removal fate offers a useful transition to other concerns of this chapter. Even as they kept their vision under wraps, some early park backers planned to remove all dwellings and other evidence of human habitation from the Cove. The least inhibited boosters, including Knoxvillian David Chapman, envisioned damming Abrams Creek at the Cove's lower end to flood the valley floor and create a lake for tourists. When more farsighted folks, including environmentalist Harvey Broome and top Park Service officials, recognized the foolishness of that plan, it was jettisoned in the late

1930s. Ultimately after two extensive studies, the Park Service embarked upon a policy to create "a mountain culture museum" from some of the remaining Cove structures. Not surprisingly, the Park Service envisioned mountain culture as static and uniformly aberrant. Hence, only structures evoking a "pioneer life-style" (defined by park personnel as "pre-1890") were preserved. More modern structures and signs of progress (including telephones, electrical generators, and modern farm equipment) were removed or destroyed. To be sure, the Park Service's "Appalachia" fit prevailing assumptions about the region, but it bore more in common with the Cades Cove of the first John Oliver, the community's early-nineteenth-century patriarch. As the grandson of the later John Oliver writes, "It was as though, having destroyed the community of Cades Cove by eminent domain, the community's corpse was now to be mutilated beyond recognition."[2] Two decades later, as my brothers and I played among the abandoned cabins and split-rail fences of Cades Cove, I relished the rustic, the primitive. Cades Cove represented one of the "Appalachias" that I, as a child of the region, unwittingly embraced.

An Increased Federal Presence in East Tennessee

The coming of the National Park Service to East Tennessee in the Depression years was simply one facet of a grander regional story that continued for most of three decades. Just as the Public Works Administration, Civilian Conservation Corps, and other New Deal measures expedited development of the national park, these and a vast array of other federal efforts transformed the face of East Tennessee. Some endeavors, most notably the visionary Tennessee Valley Authority, were the product of considerable reflection and imagination in response to disheartening regional realities. But ultimately, global developments fortuitously transformed even that effort in ways that its instigators could never have imagined. Most important, World War II brought the top-secret Manhattan Project—and the most modern of sciences—to a once remote, overlooked, and traditional East Tennessee valley. The Depression and Second World War were over in 1945, but their long-range effects on East Tennessee endure even today.

From a historian's perspective, the Depression's impact on East Tennessee and southern Appalachia was similar in many ways to the impact of the Civil War. The two traumas increased national attention for a domain that Americans largely overlooked in more "normal" times. That attention, in turn, spurred an unprecedented federal presence that proved important and influential. Secondly, the Great Depression, like the Civil War, slowed and temporarily narrowed a

2. Ibid., 256.

widening gap between East Tennessee's more prosperous valley-urban areas and its hinterlands. Indeed, all but a few East Tennesseans suffered and succumbed to shared miseries from both of these traumatic events. Some observers misread these patterns and label the two eras as watersheds for the region. While understandable, that conclusion overlooks the fact that 1860s wartime and 1930s Depression-era realities spurred fortuitous developments that ultimately reaccelerated the gap between Knoxville and her hinterland neighbors. These developments assured Knoxvillians and many other more fortunate regional residents, including me, a "non-Appalachian" status; such was not the case for the depopulated, artificial, park-service-curated Cades Cove, or the less privileged residents of the painfully real communities of the Clearfork Valley. These mid-twentieth-century developments left East Tennesseans as a whole fragmented and without the cultural ballast that might help us come to terms with an elusive past and a future of bewildering change. Although it has taken a lifetime for me to recognize it, these developments made us "Appalachians all."

Many historians use the "three Rs"—relief, recovery, and reform—to make sense of the plethora of New Deal "alphabet agencies." I add a fourth "R" to emphasize what was President Franklin D. Roosevelt's greatest political gift: restoring confidence. FDR's memorable first inaugural address and his regular "fireside chats" over the radio proved as effective among East Tennesseans as they did many other Depression-wracked Americans. More than one visitor to East Tennessee during the 1930s observed pictures of the thirty-second president and Jesus Christ side by side on walls of simple regional homes. It is hardly surprising that the patronage and good intentions of FDR's Democrats made significant inroads in traditionally Republican East Tennessee during the era.

Relief programs that targeted primarily symptoms of the Depression (e.g., hunger, homelessness, and unemployment) typically gained approval from many regional residents during the decade's darkest times. To be sure, many proud and independent East Tennesseans only reluctantly accepted help from the public dole. But once many one-time coal miners and disappointed recent migrants to the region's towns and cites realized that returning to the family farm was not a satisfactory remedy for Depression woes, many of them at least temporarily accepted government aid. "Workfare" programs such as the PWA (Public Works Program) and WPA (Works Progress Administration) were typically more accepted than programs offering direct aid. The CCC (Civilian Conservation Corps) was by far the single most popular New Deal program in the region. This multi-faceted effort employed urban young men (a group particularly hard hit by unemployment) in an array of nature- and conservation-related activities, including trail building and construction of hiking lodges and other facilities in the new Great Smoky Mountains National Park.

The New Deal's initial "recovery" measures, the AAA (Agricultural Adjustment Act) and NIRA (National Industrial Recovery Act), enjoyed less success overall and produced only limited benefits in East Tennessee. Intended to jumpstart the nation's moribund economy, the two measures targeted agricultural and industrial overproduction. Large-scale wheat, cotton, and livestock producers were the primary beneficiaries of the AAA, and few East Tennessee farmers, other than some tobacco farmers from upper East Tennessee's wide valleys, were helped. The one NIRA-initiated effort intended to help out coal miners from locations such as the Clearfork Valley actually backfired. Long-overdue provisions to protect miners' rights to unionize were initially overruled in 1935, when the Supreme Court declared the NIRA unconstitutional, but reaffirmed when the Wagner Act was passed later that same year. This apparent victory, however, proved illusory, as coal operators responded to the resulting increase in operating costs by turning to machinery. The latter course reduced demand for handloading miners and made the work of the lucky few who retained jobs even more dangerous.

A Vision for "Life as It Ought to Be"

The original "third R" of FDR's New Deal connotes "reform" measures, and here Appalachia and East Tennessee took center stage. Intended to address and alleviate longstanding flaws in the national economy, reform efforts took measures so drastic that critics blasted them as "un-American." The aforementioned Wagner Act and Social Security Act, hallmarks of the 1935 second New Deal, were important reform measures, but the Tennessee Valley Authority, initiated during FDR's celebrated "first one hundred days," proved the most important and controversial. Plans for systematic regional development of the Tennessee Valley had preoccupied progressives since the time of World War I, and the perseverance of Nebraska Republican George Norris and the pragmatism of Franklin D. Roosevelt revived the idea in the Depression's darkest days. Headquartered in Knoxville, TVA was the first serious systematic attempt to address the intrastate rivalries and inherent geographical disadvantages that had always plagued the greater Appalachian region, of which the valley of the Tennessee and its tributaries are a major part. Construction of a network of dams was the centerpiece of a many-faceted scheme that created thousands of jobs, promised production of affordable hydroelectric power, initiated flood control and navigational improvement on the erratic Tennessee, and promised broad-based economic and social reforms for what in 1933 was one of the nation's poorest regions. My father's first "real job" was at Norris Dam, the first project in this visionary federal endeavor, which was hastily initiated in 1933.

The three-member board FDR appointed to head TVA reflected the president's pragmatism, but intra-TVA feuding became a major stumbling block for the agency's ambitious programs. Utopian engineer Arthur E. Morgan championed "life as it ought to be," drawing from missionary visions of the likes of John C. Campbell, as he promoted uplift for the entire region. Morgan's emphasis on "regional stewardship" targeted, in particular, the remote hinterlands, where decades of unwise farming practices and extractive industries left environmental havoc and economic disarray. TVA's other two directors—lawyer David Lilienthal, who headed the power division, and Harcourt Morgan, former president of the University of Tennessee, who oversaw programs related to agricultural development—rejected A. E. Morgan's vision. From the beginning, programmatic and philosophical differences produced rancor between the three directors, and by the mid-1930s, when Depression woes alleviated slightly, critics began to charge that TVA was "creeping socialism." Lilienthal and H. A. Morgan succeeded in isolating A. E. Morgan; consequently TVA's primary emphasis began to shift away from "regional stewardship" to construction of dams, power production, and farm programs proving most beneficial to large valley farmers and urban centers such as Knoxville. The ouster of A. E. Morgan in 1938 was only the coup de grace in a gradual shift away from programs that briefly promised attention for the greater region's most neglected residents.

Like the new national park, TVA benefited some East Tennesseans more than others. The celebrated Norris Dam project, which provided jobs for thousands, displaced more than three thousand mostly marginal farm families from longtime homes in the Clinch River basin. As in Cades Cove, they learned about eminent domain the hard way. In the difficult days of the Great Depression, the federal government could be as harsh as it could be generous. To justify the Norris removal efforts, TVA publicity echoed earlier missionary rhetoric, resorting to sweepingly negative "Appalachian" imagery that portrayed Appalachians as ignorant, backward, and poor. Thus the federals offered official imprimatur to longstanding regional stereotypes.

But the region's most downtrodden residents suffered even more when Lilienthal's "realist" idea for the agency triumphed. David Whisnant declared Lilienthal's victory "the cooptation of TVA." Agency officials found Whisnant's scholarship so inflammatory they pressured the University of Tennessee Press not to publish his book, *Modernizing the Mountaineer: People, Power, and Planning in Appalachia*, which Whisnant completed in 1975. Whether A. E. Morgan's emphasis on regional stewardship could have brought substantial benefit to East Tennessee's remote hinterlands cannot be decisively determined. But this much is certain: by 1938, when Morgan was ousted, Knoxville, where the infusion of federal funds was most immediate and effective, was pulling out of the

Depression. Simultaneously, the historic gap between the city and the hinterland areas, such as the Clearfork Valley and Smokies region, began to widen once again. Surely longstanding geographical conditions that had always advantaged the greater Tennessee Valley were the primary reason for this, but one cannot overlook how the assistance provided by TVA's massive infusion of federal dollars, and the immediate benefits of better flood control and ready access to cheap electricity, helped reinitiate East Tennessee's historic divisions.

Global Crises Challenge TVA and Change East Tennessee

Lilienthal's triumph over A. E. Morgan was neither the only nor the most important influence in TVA's shifting emphases and priorities. The rise of fascism in Germany, Italy, and Japan posed new global challenges. The latter, in turn, fostered domestic economic developments that alleviated Depression conditions in ways the New Deal had not. By the time war erupted in Asia and Europe in the late 1930s, even East Tennessee's most remote locales experienced economic resurgence. For East Tennesseans, the relationship of the Second World War to the Great Depression was comparable to connections between the Gilded Age's surge of industrialization and the Civil War. Just as the latter spurred reckless extractive industries, events related to World War II and the Cold War accelerated changes that deepened existing divisions between East Tennessee's three representative communities.

Like the nation as a whole, East Tennesseans mobilized quickly in the aftermath of the Japanese attack on Pearl Harbor. Once again, young mountain men rushed to enlist in the military, and like many "Alvin Yorks" before them, Tennessee Volunteers served valiantly in Europe and the Pacific. Thousands of other regional residents, particularly hinterland folk, migrated to urban centers where war industries mushroomed. The most common destinations for regional out-migrants were burgeoning industrial centers in the Midwest, most notably Cincinnati, Dayton, Chicago, and Detroit, but many also moved to Oak Ridge and Knoxville. The distinctive ways of the "hillbillies," their alleged clannishness, and their longing for home made them easy targets for the animosities Harriet Arnow so vividly recounts in her novel *The Dollmaker*, but their contributions to the war effort were significant. Wartime experiences for both GIs and civilians broadened many East Tennesseans' horizons and profoundly shaped their lives and home region. "After Paris," locales such as Clairfield, Cosby, and even Knoxville were never quite the same.

Not all East Tennesseans had to travel so far from home to contribute to the war effort or gain a grander view of the world. Instead, an unlikely and sudden sequence of events in 1942 brought thousands of regional residents (including my parents) and scores of outsiders—among them some of the world's most brilliant scientists—to a previously remote location thirty miles west of Knoxville. Within days of the arrival of droves of government surveyors and engineers in 1942, the War Department proclaimed eminent domain over more than 56,000 acres of Anderson and Roane county farmland. Wartime urgency made the removals of local farmers from Oak Ridge even more sudden, but no less traumatic, than the inconveniences "the greater good" had earlier imposed on residents of Cades Cove and the Norris basin.

The Oak Ridge story is told extensively elsewhere. The top-secret project that unfolded in the "city behind the fence" was important for America's World War II triumph and postwar hegemony; it also permanently changed the East Tennessee of my youth. As a permanent fixture in the United States' Cold War preparedness, Oak Ridge's laboratories also made vital contributions to nonmilitary and peacetime uses of nuclear energy. The unprecedented infusion of federal dollars and of workers, both outsiders and locals, dramatically changed the area north and west of Knoxville. Ultimately, these developments fortuitously affirmed a shift in TVA's priorities. Even before the agency's hydroelectric dams achieved peak production during the war years, TVA began constructing a network of coal-fired steam plants to fuel Oak Ridge. Consequently, the combined efforts of TVA and the Manhattan Project profoundly affected the vast part of the Appalachian region that still held significant coal reserves. Ironically, circumstances that enhanced "homeland security" and enabled many valley-urban East Tennesseans to achieve middle-class/mainstream status during the 1950s, sentenced neighbors in locales such as the Clearfork Valley to conditions many of us in following decades came to associate with yet another, less pleasant version of "Appalachia."

Golden Age America: An East Tennessee Perspective

Americans in the bewildering first decade of the twenty-first century look back longingly on the post–World War II era. Even historians who challenge the "happy days" image as nostalgic and oversimplified concede that the two decades after 1945 represented a "golden age." Postwar euphoria and anxieties paradoxically combined to restore the nation's confidence and foster unprecedented consensus. Simultaneously, fortuitous domestic and global developments gave rise to economic prosperity that furthered those impulses, allowing a generation raised on Depression and wartime sacrifices to indulge in a long-postponed splurge of materialistic consumerism. Within East Tennessee, Knoxville most nearly approximated these national trends.

Historian William MacArthur, whose mid-1970s work offered the first systematic scholarly analysis of Knoxville's history, emphasized that "three gigantic government institutions"—TVA, the Oak Ridge Laboratories, and a greatly strengthened University of Tennessee—became mid-twentieth-century Knoxville's "major reason for being." The economic benefits generated by the three agencies assured many residents of Knoxville and Valley East Tennessee a relatively non-"Appalachian" status. Recent analysis of Knoxville's past persuasively argues that the city on the surface enjoyed the resurgence in national prosperity and confidence of the nation's "golden age." "Material improvements, organizational developments, and plans encompassing public power, public housing authority, transportation reforms, and a new airport, coupled with the economic harvests of the wartime years," historian Bruce Wheeler writes, "appeared to have left Knoxville on the brink of a new era of development."[3] But *appeared* is the operative word in Wheeler's appraisal. To the city's great embarrassment, nationally prominent author John Gunther revealed in the widely read *Inside, USA* (1946) Knoxville's thinly disguised misfortunes. After citing several examples of Knoxville's parochial ways and dysfunctional traits, Gunther concluded that Knoxville possessed "an intense, concentrated, degrading ugliness" surpassing the unsightliness of all but a handful of cities he had known.[4] Gunther's charge spurred denials and denunciations, but even several leading Knoxvillians admitted both the physical and psychological condition of their city left much to be desired.

Manifestations of postwar Knoxville's ugliness were many and diverse: the city's envy of its progressive and innovative neighbor in nearby Oak Ridge; its pious clinging to anachronistic Blue Laws that shut down all nonreligious activities on Sunday; an increasingly rigid segregation along racial, social, and economic lines; McCarthyist narrow-mindedness at the University of Tennessee and in local public schools; and general foot-dragging as the civil rights crusade got underway. Of most importance for us here are the ways Knoxville's doldrums related to her regional identity. Sooty, unhealthy air, the product of continued reliance on cheap regional coal for heat and energy, was the most obvious sign that Knoxville was, to use Wheeler's oft-repeated term, an "Appalachian city." A large quantity of rural in-migrants among the city's population was even more important. For more than two decades, colorful grocer-politician and hillbilly demagogue Caswell Orton "Cas" Walker skillfully and cynically manipulated what Wheeler depicts as the reactionary provincialism of this large group of mostly blue-collar, newly urban East Tennesseans. Walker was true heir to Lee Monday (the city councilman who personally destroyed visionary city manager Louis Brownlow in the mid-1920s). The city's conservative and lethargic elite willingly allowed Walker to have his way, but Wheeler concludes it was Walker

3. Wheeler, *Knoxville, Tennessee,* 68.

4. Quoted in Wheeler, *Knoxville, Tennessee,* 61–62.

who "set the tone for a city unable to recapture its dynamic past and afraid to go forward into an uncertain and frightening future."[5] My own recollections of Walker's colorful antics, as portrayed on local television—and as I heard them described when I listened in on heated discussions at family gatherings—lend anecdotal credence to Wheeler's general charge. Yet, I also suspect Cas's populism was more a manifestation of than cause for Knoxville's doldrums. Much like his depiction of Lee Monday's role in the conservative backlash that rocked Knoxville in the 1920s, Wheeler's explanation for Knoxville's postwar doldrums rests, in part, upon tired notions that rural Appalachians were culturally uniform and static, frozen in a past fabricated by writers such as Mary Noailles Murfree and Horace Kephart.

Knoxville's doldrums and my parents' surprising journeys coincided symbolically in an issue that city residents debated vociferously in the mid-1950s. As young, ambitious Knoxvillians—like other Americans of their generation—fled to burgeoning suburbs, they left behind a dirty, depressed, and dying downtown. While once-vibrant Gay Street was the center of old Knoxville, Market Square, two blocks to the west, was the true soul of the city. Since the nineteenth century, regional farmers hawked produce and other wares there. The smells of distinct regional dishes often blended with less pleasant Market Square odors. At the end of many a long day, regional musicians gathered on the square to play music at once traditional and eclectic. And over the years, many a sidewalk preacher expounded on vices most commonly related to the same modernity that lured producers, shoppers, and other unwitting listeners to Knoxville's downtown landmark. As a young boy in the 1920s, my father sold potatoes there and developed affinities for "Appalachian" ways that neither two college degrees nor an administrative career in the "Atomic City" ever overcame. When Knoxville city officials debated the old Market House's future in the late '50s, Dad displayed much interest, even though he had not lived in Knoxville for more than a decade. Reactionary Cas Walker most ardently opposed demolishing the building, and in this debate Dad and the "old coonhunter" were strange bedfellows. When fire accidentally destroyed the Market House in 1960, Dad was greatly saddened, and over the last twenty-five years of his life, he watched with dismay as the city of his birth devised a host of less-than-satisfactory roles for a locale he and many other native East Tennesseans considered nearly sacred. Knoxville's uncertainty about Market Square reflected even greater uncertainty about its past and future and was rooted in misunderstandings of its place within greater East Tennessee and the Appalachian region. To better understand that ambiguity, we must now turn to the histories of our other two representative East Tennessee communities during this same traumatic era.

5. Wheeler, *Knoxville, Tennessee*, 60.

The Clearfork Valley in the Mid-Twentieth Century

America's golden age proved far from happy for most residents of the Clearfork Valley. From the days of Daniel Boone to the era of the Civil War, the Valley held little appeal for permanent settlers. Ambitious individuals seeking commercial pursuits passed the Clearfork in search of greener pastures. The experiences of those who settled there in the middle third of the nineteenth century largely confirmed those earlier negative appraisals of the Valley as isolated and economically disadvantaged. However, by the turn of the twentieth century, entrepreneurs harvested great fortunes from the Clearfork's forests and rich coal veins. When demands from World War I brought the coal industry to a peak, a string of populous company towns stretched along the winding Clearfork River. Many miners were descended from early independent settlers, and their agility in blending selective aspects of new ways with essential inherited traditions gave rise to a different, yet still distinctively "Appalachian" culture. But the Depression brought miseries and misfortunes that persisted even after World War II returned the nation to a general prosperity. Travails of a fickle coal industry and unprecedented demands from a distant federal government, mainstream consumers, and not so distant regional neighbors devastated the once pristine Clearfork environment, transforming descendants of once-sturdy pioneers and industrious miners into paupers. Out-migrants left the Clearfork in droves. Those who remained lived an existence more akin to a third-world country than to 1950s America. By the 1960s, their dilapidated homes, dependence on federal assistance, and grim determination captured public attention as a new generation of Americans again discovered "Appalachia."

From its latter nineteenth-century beginnings, boom and bust typified the Appalachian coal industry, but the sequence of circumstances that produced the Clearfork's mid-twentieth-century miseries intertwine so tightly not even a conspiracy theorist could have invented them. Again, unfortunate geography converged with even less fortunate historical timing. This combination proved particularly lethal to locales like eastern Kentucky, southern West Virginia, and East Tennessee's Clearfork Valley, where "coal was King"—and a despotic one.

Coal had been one of the "sick" industries of the 1920s, and grew only "sicker" in the following decade. Even apparent gains for miners, such as recognition of unions mandated by the 1935 Wagner Act, and deals with coal companies gained by autocratic UMWA leader John L. Lewis, ultimately proved harmful. World War II fortuitously spiked demand for coal and created a temporary shortage of laborers in the coalfields, but coal's resurgence in the 1940s proved even more illusory than earlier booms. Trends of the 1930s reappeared and worsened in the postwar era. For a few fortunate miners, the gains achieved by Lewis, and the advent of widespread mechanization of deep mining, brought higher wages and greater benefits. But the vast majority of young men who returned to locales such as the Clearfork after the war found that machines had replaced manual mining skills.

From a longer-range perspective, it was not decline, but a dramatic shift in the Appalachian coal industry that heightened misfortunes in the Clearfork Valley. Technology changed deep mining, but an even more extreme form of mechanization enabled coal operators to exploit seams of coal so near to the surface that deep mining them had been deemed too dangerous. New explosives and heavy machinery also proved advantageous for surface mining. In contrast to the increased capital demands for deep mining wrought by mechanization and recent labor gains, one could begin strip-mining with a minimal investment and just a handful of workers. For the few ambitious locals with access to funding—and for the relatively few workers employed to handle explosives, drive bulldozers, draglines, loaders, and coal trucks—strip-mining offered opportunities and benefits all too rare in locales such as the Clearfork in the 1950s. But major long-term costs for the broader community accompanied those short-term gains.

The most immediate spur to strip-mining was TVA's wartime decision to utilize regional coal to generate electricity for Oak Ridge and war industries emerg-

Strip mine in 1950's
near White Oak.
15mi N. of LaFollette

As this mid-1950s photo from White Oak in the Clearfork Valley reveals, powerful explosives and heavy equipment developed to wage global war spurred the transition to surface mining throughout coal Appalachia in the post–World War II era. The resulting economic devastation led to massive out-migration from Clearfork Valley coal towns in the years after World War II. (Courtesy of Campbell County Historical Society.)

East Tennessee from Bad Times to Good Times (for Some)

ing in Knoxville, Alcoa, Kingsport, and other East Tennessee settings. Cold War concerns meant that demand continued throughout the 1950s, but domestic developments created an equally voracious appetite for coal-generated electricity. As conspicuous consumption became the hallmark of "happy days" America, the nation's demand for electricity surged. In 1950, when television was rare and air conditioning and the "all-electric home" were still in the future, the average American home consumed 1,825 kilowatt hours of electricity per year, and the annual national consumption (for all purposes) was 329 billion kilowatt hours. Twenty years later, annual residential consumption had increased four times (to 6,863 kilowatt hours), and total U.S. electric consumption for the year 1970 exceeded 1.5 trillion kilowatt hours. Even as our fuel of choice for transportation shifted primarily to petroleum, demand for coal surged. In 1952, the nation's electricity-generating companies burned 92 million tons of coal; by 1970 the amount exceeded 321 million tons.[6]

Along with burgeoning demand, the other key to Appalachian strip-mining was the total absence of environmental concern. Those of us who came of age with the environmental ethic that emerged in the late 1960s and '70s often express dismay with this earlier attitude, but we forget it was another hallmark of the prosperous America of our youth. As electrical consumers, we only belatedly became aware of the long-range environmental and human costs behind the convenience of flipping the proverbial electrical switch to meet our burgeoning needs. For residents of the Clearfork Valley, scarred slopes, polluted streams, and shattered lives were a more immediate reality. But those folks, too, aspired to achieve the American Dream. For a fortunate few, strip-mining was the ticket to that end. Meanwhile, many of their neighbors experienced what can best called "an American nightmare." Nearly 90 percent of Clearfork's residents outmigrated in the quarter-century after World War II. Not only could they find jobs in distant cities, but they could also gain the benefits of modernity without witnessing the ugly mining methods that were making it possible.

Cades Cove and the Greater Smokies Region in the Mid-Twentieth Century

This chapter's trek through the history of East Tennessee in the middle years of the twentieth century now comes full circle. If one looks only at the melancholy experiences of the most disgruntled of the folks forced from their homes in Cades Cove, the story of this other "Appalachia" may equal that of the Clearfork for pathos. The transition to a tourist-driven economy came with traumas of its

6. Dwayne E. Walls, *The Kidwells: A Family Odyssey* (Durham: Carolina Academic Press, 1983), 193.

own, but serving the entertainment needs of "happy days" America was relatively less painful than feeding its demands for cheap energy. Even before creation of Great Smoky Mountains National Park, the National Park Service had a vague mandate emphasizing two conflicting agendas. In the middle years of the twentieth century, the NPS attempt "to conserve the scenery and natural and historic objects and wildlife [within the system's parks] and provide for the enjoyment of the same in such a manner as will leave them unimpaired for the enjoyment of future generations"[7] proved challenging. But this balancing act did not affect all East Tennesseans equally. From the park's earliest days, preservationists such as Harry Broome, and promoters of commercial tourism such as his fellow Knoxvillian, David Chapman, butted heads over a host of issues. The preservationists' aforementioned victory over a proposed dam of Abrams Creek that would have flooded Cades Cove was soon followed by an equally rancorous debate over a long-anticipated "skyline drive," which would have allowed automobile access to the park's highest reaches. In the 1940s, Broome and the preservationists prevailed in these skirmishes. Their efforts helped park flora and fauna overcome the ravages of the earlier logging era, saved the park from types of commercial development common in earlier-established western parks, and represented an important, if temporary, philosophical victory for "wilderness advocacy." Unfortunately, NPS preservation of the human history of the Great Smokies in this early era was less enlightened. Several studies called for saving selected "primitive" remnants from Cades Cove and other mountain homesteads to inform tourists about the "pioneer lifestyle." Meanwhile, a host of artifacts from homes the Park Service deemed unworthy of preservation were put in storage in the basements of park facilities with hopes they would eventually become displays in a "mountain culture museum." Longtime residents recently removed from the park's confines were notably missing from the Park Service "experts on Appalachian culture" who devised these plans. Budgetary constraints during the Depression years and World War II, however, prevented the plans' full implementation, and the ambitious schemes were themselves stored away and largely forgotten in NPS files. Consequently, much of the task of presenting regional culture to tourists fell by default to private, profit-motivated enterprises that appeared on the park's borders and throughout the greater Appalachian region.

The great prosperity of the postwar era created new opportunities and challenges for Great Smoky Mountains National Park and its burgeoning gateway communities. In the 1920s, boosters had projected the park's location near major eastern population centers would make it a popular tourist destination. With the ascension of America's auto culture in the 1950s, that prediction proved

7. From the National Park Service Act of 1916. Quoted in Pierce, *The Great Smokies*, 74.

prescient. Between 1941 and 1952, the number of visitors doubled, and most of the more than 2.4 million tourists visiting the park in 1954 arrived in private vehicles. During the following decade, advocates of tourist promotion held the upper hand over preservationists both in the NPS and in Great Smoky Mountains National Park. When the Eisenhower administration initiated an effort to fix problems in the parks in time for the fiftieth anniversary of the National Park Service in 1966, most of Great Smoky Mountains National Park's "Mission 66" funds were dedicated to road building and other projects catering to the needs of auto tourists. By then, the Smokies had become the country's most frequently visited national park. An improved "loop road" wound through Cades Cove, past a number of the "primitive" pioneer dwellings that had survived NPS scrutiny. John Oliver's once-vibrant community was by then sterile, yet another distorted image of "Appalachia" tourists could experience without even leaving their cars. By 1960, Cades Cove was the Smokies' single most popular destination, by itself hosting more visitors per year than most of the other parks in the national parks system.

Not even these efforts kept up with Great Smoky Mountains National Park's ever-increasing lure to "golden age" Americans. When "Mission 66" was implemented, park officials estimated that four million tourists would visit Great Smoky Mountains National Park in 1966; four years before that date, 5.2 million visitors had already crowded in.[8] By the anticipated fiftieth anniversary celebration, some observers realized Mission 66's reforms addressed only symptoms of the park's problems and actually worsened many of them. Once again, Harvey Broome led a crusade emphasizing that more systematic and intransigent causes underlay those outward crises, and that crusade reopened conflicts between tourism promoters and preservationists that have raged ever since. A host of challenges preoccupied park personnel in the mid-1960s: separating black bears from meddlesome tourists; dealing with threats to native flora and fauna from such imported exotics as the Russian boar and rainbow trout; and combating invasive fungi threatening dogwoods and Fraser firs. These and other new problems defied ready resolution. Even in the heady "no limits" 1960s, it was becoming obvious that conflicting demands—from hikers, horse riders, and auto tourists; from seasonal residents such as the Elkmont crowd and descendants of former park residents who flocked to Cades Cove, Cataloochee, and other locales for annual homecomings; and from the myriad of other visitors who loved the park in their own preferred fashion—posed unforeseen threats to the object of their attention and created challenges park boosters never imagined.

8. Margaret Lynn Brown, *The Wild East: A Biography of the Great Smoky Mountains* (Gainesville: Univ. Press of Florida, 2000), 216.

The success of Great Smoky Mountains National Park in keeping commercial tourist development beyond park confines created new opportunities and challenges for communities on the park's borders. From the creation of the national park, Cherokee on its North Carolina flank, and Gatlinburg in East Tennessee, were the park's primary gateway communities. By 1959, more than 40 percent of the park's 3.2 million visitors passed through Gatlinburg. A former farming community previously known as White Oak Flats, Gatlinburg had become a crafts center early in the twentieth century. Northern philanthropists, most notably the Pi Beta Phi sorority, heeded calls from the likes of Emma Bell Miles and John C. Campbell, and encouraged mountain women to regain skills such as spinning and weaving; soon their husbands and sons were carving objects and crafting "traditional" furnishings for tourists. Demand for these "primitive" offerings surged in the iconoclastic 1930s, supplementing meager farm incomes. The coming of the national park created a host of even more profitable new opportunities. Clever individuals such as the colorful Wiley Oakley (see photo page 176) catered to naïve notions about regional culture, and prominent local families spearheaded the town's early commercial development, profiting nicely from their efforts. As the park's popularity surged, a few locals continued to play prominent roles in the burgeoning tourist industry. In 1963, local families retained ownership of many of Gatlinburg's 47 restaurants and 153 motels. However, tourism's benefits for locals were never widespread. Year-round employment for regular folk was rare, and many of them had to supplement tourist-related income with farming and other, more conventional pursuits.

The connection between mountain tourism and regional identity is our particular concern here. By the burgeoning 1950s, a profound ambivalence most distinctly characterized that connection. Even as Gatlinburg itself took on the atmosphere of an "Aspen-style Swiss village," opportunistic entrepreneurs did not miss chances to gain profits from tourist demands for "authentic Appalachian" (as well as "authentic Cherokee") souvenirs and artifacts—even if they were made in Japan. At that time Americans were themselves ambivalent about "things Appalachian." That ambivalence was evident in the discrepancies between the Park Service's sterile, romanticized portrayal of regional culture at Cades Cove, the "hillbilly mementos" hawked in Gatlinburg shops, and the complex, contemporary Appalachians who owned and worked in those and other tourist enterprises. These discrepancies rarely disturbed casual tourists frequenting Gatlinburg's increasingly crowded streets.

Indeed, much like the problems that growth created for the national park next door, Gatlinburg's greatest challenge by the mid-1960s was too much "success." Set in a natural bowl between converging mountain slopes, Gatlinburg's useable space was limited. Thus tourism's blessings and burdens began a de-

Hillbilly Village (mid-1950s), one of the first tourist establishments in Pigeon Forge, unapologetically offered stereotypical Appalachian themes and images to attract customers. Today the sprawling tourist mecca dwarfs Hillbilly Village, but it and many other tourist-related businesses in Pigeon Forge and other Smokies gateway communities continue to attract tourists with an array of regional themes and "Appalachian appeal." (Courtesy of McClung Historical Collection.)

cade earlier to spill over into nearby Pigeon Forge. For most of my childhood, the main route between Knoxville and Gatlinburg was a two-lane highway running mostly through cornfields and cattle pastures. Signs advertising "live bears" and "real Cherokee Indians" alerted travelers to a handful of transient tourist establishments just ahead in the unincorporated village of Pigeon Forge. On one trip shortly after I learned to read, I spotted signs for "Hillbilly Village." Literacy, however, was hardly required to understand what I was being sold—the graphic images of poor, unrefined, and violent "hillbillies" said it all.

Regional scholars fiercely debate the marketing of hillbilly imagery. Some of them call the pervasive asphalt and general tackiness of present-day Pigeon Forge "strip-mining soul." But this response oversimplifies a complex reality. We Appalachians are adept at selective acculturation. As folklorist Michael Ann Williams points out: "people [often] make a living manipulating perceptions of their culture."[9]

Glimpses of New Realities

The East Tennessee developments explored in this chapter can only be understood in broader historical contexts. The 1920s witnessed the first full-scale

9. Michael Ann Williams, *Great Smoky Mountains Folklife* (Jackson: Univ. Press of Mississippi), 171.

triumph of American consumer capitalism. When the Great Depression nearly destroyed that very system, political responses modified it significantly. Some of those changes proved essential to the resurgence of consumer capitalism, which gave rise to America's golden age. This is not the place to debate the merits of consumer capitalism nor consider its many trade-offs. For the purposes of this study, one distinctive trait of the twentieth-century American economy stands out: the way it links and feeds upon the mutual needs of diverse elements of our nation's populace.

As this wider drama unfolded in the middle third of the twentieth century, the Appalachian region served the greater mainstream's needs for both energy and entertainment. Locales like East Tennessee's Clearfork Valley and Great Smokies provided mainstream America with coal and a national playground and were compensated for their contributions. Informed and conscientious observers disagree about the fairness of these transactions and whether Appalachia's diverse peoples benefited as much from their contributions as they should have. What complicates any discussion of this controversial topic is that East Tennessee in the middle years of the twentieth century was in many respects a microcosm of the United States as a whole. East Tennessee and the greater Appalachian region were far more diverse than imagined. Knoxville and surrounding valley areas—and certainly their most privileged residents—played the mainstream role. Like the nation as a whole, they benefited from Clearfork coal and found in the Smokies a haven from a modernity they at once cherished and disdained. More affluent and energetic residents of the Clearfork and the Smokies joined Knoxvillians and outsiders in these developments. Meanwhile, their less ambitious, or often simply less fortunate, neighbors benefited less from this unfolding drama. Some locals were forcibly removed from ancestral lands; others labored in dangerous industries for wages that did not merit risking one's life. While all of East Tennessee lies within geographical Appalachia and many residents of Knoxville and the valley region have rural roots, it was the two hinterland areas and their less fortunate residents who became "Appalachia." By the mid-twentieth century, Knoxvillians and more fortunate regional residents had in general bought into images that demeaned their neighbors—and of many of their forebears—as hopelessly out of touch with modernity. With few exceptions, these "successful" Appalachians—like the mainstream they emulated—distanced themselves from the "Appalachia" typified by the Clearfork Valley. Meanwhile, many of these same people selectively embraced romanticized elements of the Cades Cove "Appalachia" as an occasional alternative to modernity. Walking this cerebral tightrope bore important consequences for our regional sense of self.

Chapter Seven

Appalachia (Slowly) Awakens:
A Regional Overview, 1920–1975

Although I did not realize it at the time, the three East Tennessee communities that are substages for the regional drama presented here were important to my own upbringing. Of the three, Knoxville bore the most frequent and obvious influence on me. It was my father's hometown, residence of my paternal grandparents and several sets of cousins, and the economic-cultural hub of the East Tennessee of my youth. Among my earliest memories were Sunday dinners at Nanny and Pop Banker's. The trip from the farm on winding old Highway 70 in a car overcrowded with Banker brothers seemed interminable. When we finally approached the city's mushrooming western suburbs (now just west of the center of "greater Knoxville"), a mixture of awe and ambivalence took hold. My grandparents' home on East 5th Avenue in many ways typified 1950s Knoxville. A generation or two earlier that neighborhood had been a model of upper-middle-class respectability, but by the post–World War II era, the city's internal woes and dying downtown spilled over to a declining East 5th. My city cousins embraced the advantages of urban life with what seemed to me to be a sophisticated ease, which contrasted noticeably with my own awkwardness. In the heady days of America's "Golden Age," I sensed vaguely the way to the future ran through Knoxville. When the antennae on the hill behind the house cooperated, TV brought Knoxville and modernity in its even grander national forms into the living room of our humble old farmhouse. There were, to be sure, occasional contradictory messages. Residue on the seat of my pants after an afternoon playing on sooty Knoxville sidewalks was only the most obvious revelation of modernity's costs. More positively, Nanny Banker's chicken and dumplings and Pop's penchant for gospel hymns revealed enduring ties to a resilient rural past that even their disdain for Cas Walker failed to diminish. My parents' determination to raise us boys in the country tugged us in a very different direction. The six of us responded to this rural-urban tension in widely divergent ways. I confess that I leaned toward the urban end of that continuum.

When I began driving, the hectic pace of Knoxville's I-40 was both frightening and exciting. When I drove my senior prom date to a popular west Knoxville restaurant in Dad's 1967 Fairlane, I felt a great sense of accomplishment. A few months later I left for college with little doubt that life with all of its bounteous possibilities would carry me well beyond East Tennessee's provincial confines. I had outgrown even Knoxville, or so I thought.

Visits to Cades Cove and Great Smoky Mountains National Park were another influential childhood experience. I still recall my amazement when I read, for the first time, words from the sign at the entrance to the park. I had somehow presumed that "the Smokies" was our family's private name for the mountains my father so dearly loved. Before I even started school, a visit to the Cherokee Reservation on the park's North Carolina side sparked an enduring fascination and sympathy for America's aborigines; years later that impulse took me to New Mexico. The same latent antimodernism gave an allure to the frontier "Appalachian" culture preserved in Cades Cove. Split-rail fences and sterile shells of cabins, corncribs, and barns scattered throughout the Cove evoked a primitive, entrancing charm. At the same time, I found humor in "Hillbilly Village" and similar roadside businesses in Pigeon Forge and Gatlinburg. As best as I recall, these contradictory depictions of my own inherited culture caused no youthful consternation; for a credulous country boy, touristy glitz had an allure all its own. Only years later, while on a visit home from New Mexico, did it even begin to dawn on me that tourism entailed considerable costs.

My ties as a youth to the Clearfork Valley were less obvious. Travel on old US-25W surely brought me near the Valley on more than one occasion, but my most important ties to the Clearfork were less direct. One consequence of TVA's "coal decision" and the voracious energy demands of nearby Oak Ridge laboratories was construction of a massive coal-fired power plant in my hometown of Kingston. When completed shortly after my birth, it was "the world's largest steam plant." From then until my early days in college, I referred to that distinction proudly as I sparred with city cousins, Yankee roommates, and anyone else who questioned the relative merits of my humble hometown. TVA's "cheap electricity" benefited local consumers and further contributed to my obliviousness. Indeed, when I flipped on a light switch, mindlessly watched TV, or lingered in the shower, the belching row of stacks that were my hometown's claim to fame never came to mind. I was as oblivious of the trainloads of coal arriving each day at the TVA facility as I was to the environmental effects of extracting and burning that coal. As a "golden age" youth, I knew instinctively that the yoked federal agencies of TVA and Oak Ridge assured my family and the families of countless friends a middle-class existence. When new Interstate 75 crossed over and offered mountaintop vistas of the west end of the Clearfork Valley in the mid-1960s, I first heard about strip-mining's scars on the land. But even then I made no connection between those jagged landscapes and images of the unfortunate, benighted "Appalachia" that President Lyndon Johnson's "war on poverty" and the likes of Walter Cronkite and Charles Kuralt brought into our living room. Those realities in no way lessened the sense of pride the Kingston Steam Plant brought to me, nor its tangible benefits for my personal wellbeing. Twenty more years passed before I came to know the Clearfork and its people on a personal basis and I began to consider their costly contributions to my own good fortune. I was, of course, not alone in my late awakening. Since the earliest white settlements, American interest in "Appalachia" has ebbed and flowed in response to changing circumstances within the region and the shifting needs—physical and psychological—of the mainstream itself.

Roots of a Native Literary Awakening

The regional self-discovery was actually a re-awakening. The young "shoot" that broke through and saw the light of day in the 1960s grew from seeds this book explored earlier. One little-known agent of that ferment was Lincoln Memorial University, located in Harrogate, Tennessee, at the east end of the Clearfork Valley, and just south of the Kentucky border. In 1929, LMU alumni Jesse Stuart, James Still, and Don West all enrolled as graduate students at Vanderbilt University. There they came under the influence of the "agrarians," an interdisciplinary collection of intellectuals who boldly challenged prevailing literary practices and historical interpretations. The careers, concerns, and artistic efforts of the three young Appalachians diverged notably, but in the 1930s they shared a common anonymity. Only later would they, like Emma Bell Miles and John C. Campbell, receive just acclaim for the regional emphases of their works. But, unlike those earlier regional commentators, the LMU trio were insiders. James Still was an Alabama native, but like Stuart, made his home in, and became identified with, eastern Kentucky. West hailed from north Georgia's hills.

To date, East Tennessee native writers from the 1920s and '30s have received even less attention than Stuart, Still, and West. More thorough examination of the writings of Mildred Haun (a native of Cocke and Hamblen counties, she also studied with Vanderbilt's "agrarians") and Anne Armstrong (who moved to East Tennessee from Michigan as a child) could reveal more about native East Tennesseans and their largely futile efforts to assert a native voice in literature in the interwar years. Certainly Haun's *The Hawks Done Gone* (1940) and Armstrong's *This Day and Time* (1930) address the rural-urban encounters and conflicts that make East Tennessee's identity so elusive. While Armstrong wrote about her adopted hometown of Knoxville, the most profound insight into the city's identity crisis belonged to James Agee. Agee's *A Death in the Family* is a thinly disguised autobiographical account of his Knoxville childhood. Tensions between Agee's urban, Anglo-Catholic mother and his father, who hailed from East Tennessee's hinterlands, are the nexus of the novel. Agee's prolific career began nearly three decades before he posthumously received the Pulitzer Prize for *A Death in the Family* in 1958, but he was always known as a "southern"—and never an "Appalachian"—writer. The very similar story of Asheville's Thomas Wolfe suggests the degree to which students of American Literature, the general population, and most notably, atypical residents of our region, clung to (and in the latter case, distanced themselves from) popular images of "Appalachia" in the middle years of the twentieth century.

During the war-consumed 1940s, East Tennesseans and Appalachians in general, like all good Americans, became consumed with the crusade against the Axis, and later the Soviet Union. Those challenges exposed regional residents to broader horizons, heightened their expectations, and lured many of them temporarily from their roots. Consequently, "Appalachia" seemed far from the minds of most persons within and beyond the region. Yet the regional identity that concerns us here did not disappear in the 1940s, even if it was largely dormant. The blossoming of the careers of educator Cratis Williams and writer Harriet Arnow in the 1950s reveal the resilience and resurgence of that identity. Ashevillian Wilma Dykeman, who—thanks to her marriage to James Stokely—came to identify herself with East Tennessee as well as with her native western North Carolina, followed on the heels of Williams and Arnow in calling for and presenting more accurate and positive understandings of Appalachia. These literary developments were essential precursors for the better-known regional awakening of the 1960s.

Even Lesser-Known Incubators for Regional Awakening

Despite Lincoln Memorial University's role in Appalachia's literary renaissance, scholars have devoted almost no attention to contributions of institutions such as LMU to the mid-twentieth-century regional awakening. Around the turn of the century, Protestant mission schools, secular private institutions (including LMU), and public uplift agencies appeared throughout Appalachia, and meanwhile already extant educational institutions assumed new roles. The ostensible purpose of these regional schools was to usher aberrant Appalachians into the national cultural and religious mainstream. Henry Shapiro's assertion, that the first generation of home missionaries (most notably, Berea's W. G. Frost) created and perpetuated negative regional images, was one of the first volleys of the Appalachian studies revolution. To date, this valid insight blinds most observers to the efforts of John C. Campbell and other regional missionaries who defied popular images that all outsiders were inflexibly ethnocentric. When extended tenures in the region intersected with intellectual changes in the broader society, at least some "missionary longtermers" began to question and even replace their predecessors' simplistic, often demeaning images of "Appalachia." At the end of *Appalachia on Our Mind*, Shapiro celebrates Campbell's important contributions toward a more realistic understanding of Appalachia. Yet Shapiro's scholarly heirs have largely ignored (or worse, condemned) the second- and third-generation missionaries who quietly continued Campbell's cause in the decades after his untimely death. In recent years, general suspicion of religious matters among secular liberals and academics, and disdain for mainstream versions of Christianity by those who celebrate regional Christian culture, have accentuated this blindness. Yet revisionist accounts of several regional institutions, and new insights into the missionary enterprise in general, suggest that at least some do-gooders contributed, albeit not always intentionally, to the regional renaissance. East Tennessee's role in this broader drama has to date barely been examined.

In 1927, Henry S. Randolph, a native East Tennessean, took the reins of a struggling mission enterprise in the mountains of western North Carolina. For three decades, Presbyterians had sent outside educators and church leaders to uplift and transform "poor Appalachians" at Asheville Farm School and the denomination's broader network of "mountain schools." By the 1920s, changes in the region, dwindling denominational resources, and general unrest and a "spiritual malaise" in the broader society made it clear that approach was inappropriate. As a consequence, Presbyterian officials nearly abandoned their network of regional schools. In a desperate last-ditch effort to save that enterprise, Presbyterians turned to Henry Randolph. Raised on Coffee Ridge on the Tennessee–North Carolina border, and a product of a mission school in nearby Erwin, Tennessee, Randolph completed a doctorate at Columbia University and became an ordained Church of the Brethren minister. As Farm School's superintendent from 1927 to 1942, Randolph's seemingly disparate worlds merged. The self-proclaimed "hillbilly" applied concepts he learned at Columbia to challenges he had known as a youth. Randolph's gregariousness and infectious enthusiasm breathed new life into Farm School, and during the hard days of the 1930s, he attracted an unusually gifted faculty. Many of the latter became able "insider-outsiders," who saw the school through its 1960s transition into Warren Wilson College. Randolph's deftness in bridging two worlds is particularly relevant, as was his success in challenging prevailing notions about innate Appalachian deficiencies and presumptions about the homogenizing effects of acculturation. The native East Tennessean proved personally that "successful"

Appalachians need not discard their regional identity, nor be fossilized by the resilience of regional ways.

Conversations with Farm School and WWC alumni, and insights from revisionist studies of similar uplift efforts (for example provocative new accounts of Native American student life and cultural survival in missionary and government-sponsored schools), convince me that lessons many regional youths learned about their culture and identity at Farm School would have surprised the school's assimilationist founders. In other words, many Farm School-WWC students—and their mentors—became effective practitioners of the two-sided process of selective acculturation. By the time Warren Wilson evolved into a two-year college in the 1940s, bright, curious, and proud native young Appalachians came together with a corps of committed, sympathetic, often iconoclastic outsiders on the Swannanoa Valley campus. This combination nurtured regional assertiveness in the 1950s and fueled the awakening and activism that erupted in Appalachia of the 1960s.

Similar events transpired at Kentucky's Berea College during the critical middle decades of the twentieth century. Decades before William G. Frost transformed Berea into a school for deserving, disadvantaged Appalachian youths, it had been an important experiment in biracial education. Frost's stirring appeal on behalf of "our contemporary ancestors" brought donations from generous benefactors and won Berea national acclaim as "*the* Appalachian school." On the other hand, as Henry Shapiro shows so well, Frost's promotional efforts nurtured and perpetuated longstanding, sometimes enfeebling regional stereotypes. In recent decades, some Appalachian studies scholars, following Shapiro's lead, have associated those stereotypes with Berea College and dismissed its role in the awakening. In reality, Berea began moving away from some of Frost's more bombastic legacies soon after his retirement in 1920. Frost's successor, William J. Hutchins, was an insider-outsider who shared much in common with John C. Campbell. Like Campbell and Farm School's Randolph, Hutchins qualified the sweeping regional generalizations that were Frost's stock-in-trade and promoted more realistic understandings of Appalachia. "There is no such thing as truth about the mountains," Hutchins once observed. "What is true of one group or section is untrue of another."[1]

By World War II, Berea was well on its way to becoming what it is today: a four-year college committed to providing a practical, liberal arts education for mountain youths. Frost's successors have continued his effective fundraising efforts, and—with the help of compound interest—created an endowment al-

1. Shannon H. Wilson, *Berea College: An Illustrated History* (Lexington: Univ. Press of Kentucky, 2006), 128.

lowing Berea in the twenty-first century to continue its historic commitment to Appalachia's less-advantaged youth. One need consider only a handful of prominent Berea alumni to see connections between the college and the awakening. James Brown, who completed high school and undergraduate work at Berea in the 1940s, was a precursor of the Appalachian studies movement. During World War II and the early Cold War years, when both national and regional audiences largely overlooked Appalachia, Brown returned to eastern Kentucky from Harvard with a PhD in sociology and completed thorough ethnographic and genealogical studies of several communities in Clay County. Other notable Berea alumni included include Loyal Jones and Jim Wayne Miller, whose contributions to Appalachian studies (and the arguments of this book) are addressed elsewhere in this volume.

But what about native East Tennesseans who in the middle years of the twentieth century studied in the numerous schools and uplift agencies located within East Tennessee's geographical confines? Among these were church-affiliated schools and colleges, including Tusculum, Maryville, Hiwassee, Tennessee Wesleyan, Carson-Newman, and Milligan Colleges; secular private institutions, such as Lincoln Memorial University; and an array of public institutions, most notably the University of Tennessee in Knoxville. While official histories for each of these schools have been written (and in most cases updated in recent years) those studies offer little insight into the respective schools' relationships with the surrounding region during this period.

Limitations inherent to institutional histories doubtlessly contribute to this absence, but explanations for the oversight may also exist in the histories these books convey. First, the campuses of all but one of the institutions mentioned above are located in the greater Tennessee Valley; only Lincoln Memorial University is set in the hinterlands. Timing of the founding of these institutions was, of course, closely related to their locations. Tusculum and Maryville Colleges, and the educational effort that ultimately became the University of Tennessee, were all products of the early-nineteenth-century Second Great Awakening. As such, they were founded in East Tennessee's frontier era. Hiwassee, Tennessee Wesleyan, Carson-Newman, and Milligan were established in the Civil War era. This overall timeframe (ca. 1790–1870) unfolded before distinct "Appalachian" images took shape in the American mind. Indeed, by the late nineteenth century, when Americans were beginning to link "ignorance" with "Appalachia," these established institutions may have contributed to the divisions within East Tennessee society by generating negative regional images. The distancing of my maternal grandparents from their rural roots after their experiences at Milligan College appears, for example, to validate that contention. Finally, of these institutions, only Lincoln Memorial bore the imprint in its formative years of the latter-nineteenth-century home missionary ferment that shaped Farm School and Berea. In part for that reason, the Appalachian scholarship and the new mission history illuminating Warren Wilson and Berea's pasts are notably absent in the institutional histories of the other East Tennessee schools.

Antecedents of Regional Activism

Literary accomplishments were only one manifestation of the Appalachian awakening. An unprecedented activism in the late 1960s, most notably grassroots resistance to unregulated surface coal mining, also fueled the ferment. Yet, if we are to understand that activism, we must first return briefly to several unanticipated, largely overlooked developments from the interwar years. In particular, two institutions with East Tennessee ties that emerged in that era nurtured grassroots Appalachian activism three decades later.

The Council of the Southern Mountains was yet another product of the home missions' turn-of-the-twentieth-century mindset, which helped foster the persistent, pervasive image of "needy Appalachia" in the American mind. The Council of the Southern Mountains was the key agency in John C. Campbell's farsighted vision, and among other goals, encouraged more traditional-minded uplift agents to reconsider conventional approaches to the region. Annual summer conferences held in Knoxville from 1914 to 1925 (and sporadically thereafter) brought "mountain workers" together to share new, often progressive, sometimes controversial understandings of regional conditions. Among the most memorable of the latter were certainly Philander P. Claxton's chidings about "romantic and distorted notions about mountain culture," and his assertion that exploitation of mountain resources had caused "Appalachian" conditions. The host city's seeming lack of attention to the annual gathering is clearly relevant to this study, but that in no way lessens the early council's greater significance. What we do know about the CSM in those days suggests Campbell and Berea's William G. Frost engaged in a power struggle. The rivalry was apparently personal, but Campbell's more progressive stance also rankled Frost. This was David Whisnant's central contention when, more than thirty years ago, he suggested the eventual move of the council's headquarters to the Berea campus after Campbell's death coincided with a conservative shift in the council's outlook. It was, however, Whisnant's harsh portrayal of the council in the 1950s, when it was led by the amiable and progressive Perley Ayers, that rankled Loyal Jones and other Berea folk closely associated with Ayers.

These diverging interpretations of what was then recent history precipitated the aforementioned rancor that has for thirty years been pretty much the final word on the history of the Council of the Southern Mountains. One unfortunate consequence of this relative silence has been that observers on both sides of the debate have largely overlooked key persons and periods in the council's history during the interwar years that clearly kept Campbell's vision for Appalachia alive. For example, as editor of the CSM monthly newsletter, *Mountain Life and Work*, Berea sociologist Helen Dingman throughout the 1930s and '40s expressed views that echoed Claxton's earlier observations and anticipated heated regional rhetoric of the 1960s. Similarly, under the leadership of executive secretary Alva Taylor during the years of the Second World War, the council offered a view of Appalachia that links Campbell's earlier insights to the more overt regional awakening that erupted two decades later. Surely, further analysis of the progressive CSM under the influence of these individuals will reveal the awakening did not appear out of thin air in the 1960s.

As with the lesser-known Council of the Southern Mountains, the East Tennessee–based Highlander Center also made important contributions to the ferment of the interwar years. Although Highlander has been studied far more broadly, few of its present-day champions realize the same missionary impulses giving rise to the Council of the Southern Mountains initially nurtured it as well. In the summer of 1927, native Tennessean Myles Horton organized Bible schools for the Cumberland Presbyterian Church in the region around Ozone, Tennessee. Years of timbering and coalmining had devastated the hard-scrabble region where the Tennessee Valley and Cumberland Plateau merge, convincing the idealistic Horton that conventional religious responses to those ills were futile. After completing his bachelor's degree at Cumberland University the following year, Horton continued his formal education at New York's Union Theological Seminary, Columbia University, and the University of Chicago, where he came under the influence of Reinhold Niebuhr, John Dewey, and Jane Addams respectively. At the very historical moment when more conservative Christians were defining the fundamentals of their faith in the most narrow of terms, Horton and Highlander offered a radically different vision and response to Christ's message. The defection of the likes of Horton and folks at Highlander from the institutional church foreshadowed a broader secularizing trend among mid-twentieth-century American liberals. This divide and the historical amnesia it fosters still undermines American progressivism's response to our nation's culture wars. Of more immediate importance for this book, this divide keeps many present-day Appalachian scholars from fully understanding the beginnings of their movement.

During his formal education, Horton dabbled with socialism. But the Tennessean's innate independence and instinctive pragmatism made doctrines suspect. After completing his formal education, Horton traveled to Europe, where he found a vision for his mission in Denmark's folk schools. Upon returning to Tennessee in 1932, he joined forces with poet-activist Don West (the LMU and Vanderbilt alumnus) and founded Highlander Folk School near Monteagle, a few miles north of Tennessee's borders with Georgia and Alabama. As one historian of Highlander has emphasized, this was "no ordinary school." From its earliest days to the present, emphasis on adult education and faith that "ordinary people [could] build upon knowledge they had gained from experience and work collectively toward a more democratic and humane society" have been Highlander hallmarks.[2] As yet another commentator on the Highlander story notes poetically, Horton's vision "unearthed seeds of fire."[3] During the 1930s and '40s, Horton and Highlander worked with striking coal miners, timber workers, millhands, and government relief workers across the upper South; in 1937 they joined forces with what was then known as the Committee for Industrial Organization (CIO) and organized local textile workers. Highlander's visionary approach and insistence upon racial integration in all of its efforts created tensions with elements of the labor movement, and after World War II Highlander shifted its primary attention to the even more controversial challenge of racism. Residential workshops on nonviolent civil disobedience brought to the Highlander campus many future civil rights stalwarts, including Rosa Parks and Martin Luther King. In the late 1940s, Highlander-sponsored "Citizenship Schools" taught literacy skills to thousands of blacks in anticipation of voter registration drives. In the early '60s, idealistic youths—black and white—gathered at Highlander to explore tactics that ultimately became known as "sit-ins" and "freedom rides." And it was at Highlander that musicians created the anthem of the civil rights movement, adapting words from of the old spiritual "We Shall Overcome." Highlander, of course, paid a price for its leadership. Indeed, I vividly recall billboards along Tennessee highways and televised news reports during my childhood alleging that Highlander was a "communist training school." In 1962, the state of Tennessee revoked Highlander's charter and confiscated its property using an array of trumped up charges.

Fortunately, Highlander proved far more resilient than its detractors hoped. But attention to Highlander's civil rights efforts—and its subsequent involvement in an array of Appalachian activist causes in the 1960s and beyond—has obscured its role in developments that set the stage for the latter. There we see the reconvergence of two forces central to the Appalachian awakening. Despite

2. The phrase "no ordinary school" comes from the title of John M. Glen's *Highlander: No Ordinary School,* 2nd ed. (Knoxville: Univ. of Tennessee Press, 1996); the quotation regarding the school's purpose is from Glen's entry on Highlander in West, *The Tennessee Encyclopedia of History and Culture,* 423.

3. Frank Adams, *Unearthing Seeds of Fire: The Idea of Highlander* (Winston-Salem, NC: John F. Blair Publisher, 1975).

their alleged "conservatism," Perley Ayers and the reactivated Council of the Southern Mountains reached out from their base in Berea to regional activists, especially those involved in civil rights and in efforts that eventually merged into the "war on poverty." We still know little about this important moment in the Appalachian studies story. For too long, commentators have accepted categorization of the Berea-CSM crowd as "conservatives" and "disinterested academics," and Highlander folk as "rabid and impatient activists" without question and qualification. Indeed, representatives of the two groups occasionally engaged in "shouting match deliberations." But tensions can be creative and constructive, and that appears to be a more accurate description of CSM's efforts throughout the 1950s until the mid- to late 1960s. For example, a CSM/Berea-sponsored conference of church leaders in 1957 called for a more up-to-date and accurate profile of the region, and a grant from the Ford Foundation employed regional scholars to engage in that pursuit. The "Ford Survey," completed five years later, may have been too mild for many activists with Highlander credentials, but it represented an important benchmark on the path to increased regional activism.

The Awakening

As in American society at large, Appalachia's young people—from both the hinterlands and valley cities and towns—played vital roles in the growing unrest of the 1960s. On the campuses of private schools such as Berea, Warren Wilson, and Maryville Colleges—and at the burgeoning University of Tennessee—they encountered professors and mentors well versed in the ferment of this idealistic age. Involvement in, or at least sympathy for, the civil rights, antiwar, environmental, feminist, and youth movements made many of the region's youths natural allies for activist causes beginning to unfold in their home communities. Like angry blacks, Native Americans, Chicanos, gays, and other minorities, they yearned to know their own long-overlooked history. In turn, many sought more honest, if less becoming, accounts of our national saga.

All of these tensions, of course, found their way into what some observers have called "the Appalachian conversation." Throughout the 1950s and '60s, the revitalized version of John C. Campbell's Council of the Southern Mountains, which Perley Ayers and Berea College created, provided the most important forum for this dialogue. But as debates within and outside the region became more shrill, tensions between stereotypical "Berea folk" and "Highlander folk"— once creative and constructive—became more divisive and destructive. By the late 1960s, the activists gained ascendancy, but more moderate regional voices refused to relinquish control. These tensions erupted at the last two annual conferences of the council, at Fontana, North Carolina, in the spring of 1969 and a year later at nearby Lake Junaluska. There my personal journey fleetingly intersected with the regional saga. As a member of the council since its days as Asheville Farm School, Warren Wilson College had long sent a small contingent of regional students to the annual CSM meeting. In April 1970, I was chosen for this role, but I was not prepared for what I witnessed. My clearest recollections are of an angry, large woman shouting profanities at a slightly built man who, it seemed obvious, was supposed to be in charge of the proceedings. Like the proverbial "Dutch boy" with not enough fingers to plug a bursting dike, the man's only defense was goodwill, a lopsided smile, and a sense of humor. Many years passed before his life and mine again intersected, and I came to realize I was present at a historic moment in the Appalachian awakening.

With little help from this oblivious young East Tennessean, Perley Ayers's version of Campbell's council did not survive the showdowns at Fontana and Lake Junaluska. Strangely, the slow death of the Council of the Southern Mountains in the 1970s and 1980s enhanced the regional conversation. In 1977, an uneasy amalgam of academics and activists—and some with feet in both camps—found sufficient common ground to create the Appalachian Studies Association. Institutionalizing the "Appalachian conversation" has thankfully not ended the tensions that erupted in the 1960s. Indeed, disagreements among energetic activists and more reserved academics have doubtlessly become an ASA hallmark. Activists sometimes become impatient with academic findings that appear "less relevant" and more committed to objectivity than justice. Likewise, scholars sometimes chide the activists' subjectivity and impatience. Thus, the creative tensions that characterize the "Appalachian conversation" at its best continue to shape our ongoing regional saga. Less obviously, but of even greater importance to this study, the advent of Appalachian studies brought together two groups—sympathetic outsiders and successful Appalachian natives—who since the mid-nineteenth century had combined to perpetuate stereotypical images of "Appalachia."

Both the fruits and challenge facing the Appalachian studies community since 1990 will be apparent in chapters eight and nine. There we will explore in greater depth how the regional awakening in both its activist and literary-academic manifestations played out in this book's three representative East Tennessee communities. Reflecting on the broader regional, national, and global significance of developments in a region many still deem isolated, provincial, and unimportant will illuminate our regional elusiveness and reveal the challenges that make this endemic trait so enduring.

Chapter Eight

Coming Home to a New Appalachia: The Awakening in East Tennessee's Hinterlands, 1970–Present

"Part hoedown, part history lesson, part homecoming celebration"—my extended Banker family took advantage of Tennessee's *HOMECOMING '86* to plan a long overdue reunion. On the final weekend of June 1986, nearly seventy members of my extended clan gathered on the farm overlooking the forks of the Tennessee and Clinch rivers. Sooner than we would have preferred, Kathy, Tollie, and I returned to Albuquerque: contented, well fed, and eagerly anticipating the next family gathering. But that day came much sooner than we could have imagined. On Halloween Day 1986, my father, Luke Eugene Banker, had a homecoming of a more permanent sort. The day after Dad's memorial service, we flew home to New Mexico. For the next eight months I taught part-time at Albuquerque Academy and completed my University of New Mexico dissertation. Back in Tennessee, Mother made clear that she would not move from the rambling old farmhouse that had been her home since she was pregnant with me. Although I had years earlier abandoned notions of "coming home," six-year old Tollie's only wish was to have a horse, and Kathy convinced me that our future plans should consider both our daughter's and Mom's needs. So at Christmas we told Mother that we would return to the farm.

This was hardly, however, the case of a country boy yearning to return to his roots. Indeed my mood bordered between melancholy and morose as I wondered if there was "life after New Mexico" and if I "could go home again." With respect to Thomas Wolfe, I have discovered that "going home" is more complicated than imagined. First, I did not really know the "home" to which I was returning. At age thirty-six, I had spent half of my life elsewhere and was hardly the same person who left East Tennessee as an eager eighteen-year-old, oblivious to surroundings so familiar that I took them for granted. Indeed, twelve years in New Mexico prepared me in ways that I could never have planned for the homecoming I never anticipated. Moreover, the nation, East Tennessee, and greater Appalachia had all changed dramatically during the years I was away.

Of greatest importance here, my 1987 homecoming converged with the cresting of the first wave of the Appalachian awakening.

This chapter and the one that follows explore the varied ways the "Appalachian awakening" unfolded in this book's three representative East Tennessee communities in the years leading up to and since my 1987 homecoming. Told separately, these stories offer evidence of the dynamism and diversity that are the most important revelations of the thirty years of regional scholarship. These "kaleidoscopic consequences" leave many observers so bewildered that some regional scholars consciously question the appropriateness of the distinction "Appalachia." Such questioning allows less intentional observers to simply dismiss our region as "unique," a truly misleading distinction that really means odd, curious, and undeserving of serious attention. We Appalachians know this status well, but it is hardly "unique" to us. Herein lies the value of telling the stories of the three communities side by side and restoring them to broader contexts. This three-sided, integrative approach offers further clues and glimpses into how *real* "Appalachian" conditions came to be, why popular explanations that attribute those conditions to regional peculiarities are so enduring, and why we need to set aside those tired old images and reimagine Appalachia. This perspective affirms the insight of the late Jim Wayne Miller: Appalachia is more nearly universal than unique.

The Awakening in "Coal Appalachia" and the Clearfork Valley

It is neither surprising nor insignificant that the regional awakening appeared in the Clearfork Valley before it reached this book's other two representative communities. The early wake-up calls for the more general regional awakening—Jack Weller's *Yesterday's People*, Harry Caudill's *Night Comes to the Cumberlands*, Michael Harrington's *The Other America*, and televised exposés offered by Walter Cronkite and Charles Kuralt—all focused on Appalachia's coalfields. Similarly, John F. Kennedy's personal shock at conditions he witnessed while campaigning in West Virginia in 1960 stirred national attention to the region. Five years later, his successor fired one of the first shots in the "war on poverty" from the front porch of a miner's cabin in eastern Kentucky. The Clearfork Valley was little more than rifle's range away, becoming one of many targets for that unprecedented federal effort.

As earlier chapters have shown in detail, coal in general—and surface-mining in particular—brought both blessings and burdens to the region. But by the 1960s, the burdens were more obvious. Crises in the coalfields converged with the broader national mood to bring a newfound fervor for change. The anti-strip-mining army enlisted strange bedfellows. Old timers, whom casual observers might label "conservative," were at the forefront of the crusade. One observer calls Jink Ray, Old Dan Gibson, the Widow Combs, and Joe Begley and other early foes of strip-mining "reactionary rebels." Among their most sympathetic allies were outsiders, particularly idealistic, impatient youths, often derided as "tree huggers" and "hippies." Highlander Center played a critical, if not always successful, role in keeping this unlikely coalition together. Myles Horton's insistence that newcomers listen to natives and tailor their responses to local needs became the model for effective and enduring Appalachian activism. Nonetheless, even now many self-styled, genuinely sympathetic liberals fail to adequately appreciate the deep pride and identification with "King Coal" prevalent among many coalfield residents.

From the vantage point of nearly forty years, it is apparent that the upheavals in the coalfields enjoyed only limited success. A mixture of protests and lobbying produced important, if less than perfect, efforts to rein in unregulated strip-mining. Among these were the federal Surface Mining Control and Reclamation Act (1977) and eastern Kentuckians' success in the following decade in abolishing the broad form deed that had long allowed strip miners to menace neighbors and ravage their land. Of course, coal operators resisted these efforts and devised means to circumvent them. Meanwhile, Mother Nature often exacerbated the long-term effects of mining by inflicting floods and other "natural" disasters on locales throughout coal Appalachia. Finally, innate and long-standing natural disadvantages assuring the region's perennial peripheral status in the capitalist system undermined attempts to initiate alternative economic efforts. Consequently, in spite of the awakening concerning us here—and the unprecedented federal "war on poverty"—coal Appalachia remains a backwater, and for many observers, the essence of the region. On a micro scale, all of these patterns appear in the last half-century of the Clearfork Valley's history.

As a result of decades of destructive mining, by around 1960 the Clearfork Valley was in many ways a third-world island within a first-world sea. Between the end of World War II and around 1970, more than 90 percent of the Valley's residents joined the great regional diaspora. Some relocated to Knoxville or to burgeoning cities on the fringe of the region, such as Nashville and Atlanta; many others relocated to midwestern and northern industrial cities. Meanwhile, seemingly insurmountable obstacles blocked hope for change and impeded unprecedented federal uplift efforts in the 1960s. Within the Valley, native "wildcatters" (independent strip-miners driven by the immediate bottom line), locals fortunate enough to secure strip-mining jobs, and opportunistic politicians in several county seats took advantage of exhausted—some say fatalistic—neighbors and effectively co-opted those federal efforts. Meanwhile, consumers of "cheap TVA electricity" (including many of us not so far away) were covertly complicit. As John Gaventa suggests, this was more than just a local matter, for it represented "the tension between the energy and economic demands of the industrial society and the development needs of the rural hinterland."[1]

Yet even in those most dismal days, Clearfork locals fought back. Valley native and longtime schoolteacher Tilda Kemplen devoted her life to improving childcare, education, health, nutrition, and economic and agricultural development. Kemplen enjoyed strong support and encouragement from CORA (the Commission on Religion in Appalachia) and several agencies from outside the Valley. Longtime Clairfield postmaster Louise White Adams, who was "born and raised in the holler," was another local unafraid to challenge the status quo. At the post office, Louise daily heartened discouraged neighbors. She was a veteran of World War II, as was yet another local, Shelby York. Like most Valley males, the one-time deep miner was initially reluctant to become engaged in controversial efforts promoted by outsiders and the likes of Kemplen and Adams. However, when the latter insisted his support was vital to their cause, York told his wife, "Well they're bent on me getting involved, I might as well . . . really get up there and do something."[2] When Highlander Center shifted its focus to Appalachia in the mid-1960s, its staff shared its organizational expertise with these struggling efforts in the Clearfork Valley. Valley folk joined SOCM (Save Our Cumberland Mountains, a grassroots group drawing membership from several of East Tennessee's coal counties). These ties brought energy and inspiration to the Clearfork cause and linked it to ferment from greater Appalachia, as well as to the exhilarating national and global impulses of the '60s. Their problems, Valley residents learned, were not as unique as they imagined. Indeed, they could share with others strategies to alleviate endemic "Appalachian" ills.

The arrival of Marie Cirillo in 1967 was a turning point in Clearfork history. The diminutive, modest Cirillo continued the vital tradition of insider-outsider modeled by the likes of John C. Campbell and Emma Bell Miles. A Brooklyn native with Italian and Kentucky roots, Marie was a devout Catholic who joined the Glenmary Sisters after completing high school. In the four years prior to her 1967 arrival in the Clearfork, Marie served in Chicago's uptown Appalachian ghetto. As she recalls, "I knew . . . of the migration of Appalachians to the cities . . . [but] I couldn't understand why mountain people, who loved the land more than anything else, were forced to move into dirty, industrial cities . . . . Why

1. John Gaventa, *Power and Powerlessness: Quiescence and Rebellion in an Appalachian Valley* (Urbana: Univ. of Illinois Press, 1982), 135.

2. Helen M. Lewis and Monica Appleby, *Mountain Sisters: From Convent to Community in Appalachia* (Lexington: Univ. Press of Kentucky, 2003), 189.

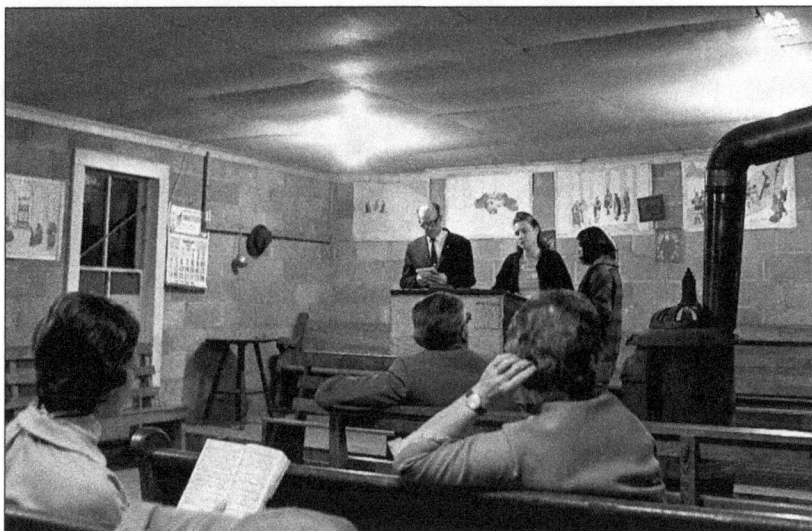

Marie Cirillo (back to the camera on last pew) at gathering in Clearfork Valley Church (ca. 1970). This photo captures the characteristic patient, low-key approach to activism that has made Marie's work effective. (Courtesy of Jack Corn and Clearfork Community Institute.)

did they have to leave? I wanted to find out."[3] Probing this query, along with an array of divisive social and ecclesial issues, convinced Marie and approximately two-thirds of the Glenmary Sisters to leave the order. Still devout Christians committed to the spirit of their vows, forty-four of these one-time nuns formed FOCIS (Federation of Communities in Service) and pledged to continue to work among Appalachians in communities in West Virginia, Virginia, and Tennessee, and in urban ghettoes in the North and Midwest.

These developments coincided with Marie's long-anticipated relocation to the heart of Appalachia. With assistance from a Catholic bishop and contacts with an OEO director,[4] she took a position as "community developer" in Clairfield in the Clearfork Valley. There, with encouragement and support from Postmaster Adams, she finally had the opportunity to address firsthand the query she pondered in Chicago. Thirty years later, Marie acknowledged that she was "just beginning to get a grasp on" that elusive question.[5] This frank conclusion reveals much about a remarkable human being and the place to which she

---

3. Ibid., 39.

4. OEO was the Office of Economic Opportunity and the frontline agency of the Great Society's "war on poverty."

5. Lewis and Appleby, *Mountain Sisters,* 39.

devoted her good life. It also helps explain the modest success of so many of the programs she helped initiate.

Internecine community tensions were only the first of many obstacles to Marie's efforts. When she assumed the position in Clairfield, the OEO supervisor warned her about deep political factions in the community. Rooted in the petty, personal differences that sharply conflicting local responses to strip-mining exacerbate, these divisions still impede efforts in the Clearfork today. Moreover, Marie's Catholicism and status as a woman provoked hostility and resistance (sometimes violent) from a few of her overwhelmingly Protestant and patriarchal neighbors. Yet Marie, much like Highlander's Myles Horton, knew outside altruists have long contributed to the sad tragedy of coal Appalachia, and that even modest success demands that locals define their needs and develop strategies to ameliorate them.

Marie also knew instinctively that the Clearfork Valley was not isolated. Scars from recently removed veins of coals were only the most obvious evidence that someone else benefited from the Valley's misfortunes. But Marie also knew outsiders might bring benefits to the Clearfork cause. In 1973, she hosted sixteen-year-old Caroline Kennedy at her home on Roses Creek, while Kennedy and several other students were doing oral histories exploring the coal industry and its effects. Twenty years later, the adult daughter of the slain president recalled the experience fondly. Marie, she observed, "was very strong but very gentle . . . [and] genuinely loves the area and people."[6] Earlier that same year, a young Ralph Nader wrote a ten-page letter to Sir Denys Flowerdew Lowson, chairman of the Board of Directors of the British company American Association, Ltd, which still owned approximately 85 percent of the land and most of the mineral and timber rights in the Valley. Nader concluded a scathing overview of the association's role in the Valley's history with nine suggestions that might transform the association "from a hostile aggressor to a more responsible, constructive citizen."[7] Nader did not mention Marie Cirillo in the letter, but her shadow is obvious.

Marie's friendships, however, have never been limited to celebrities. Knoxville's Sequoyah Hills Presbyterian Church is only one of many institutions from East Tennessee's leading city to support the Clearfork cause. Marie's open invitation to students from Vanderbilt University in the late 1960s, and to students from near and far ever since, brought benefits, immediate and long-

6. Fred Brown, "Caroline Kennedy recalls a summer at Roses Creek," *Knoxville News-Sentinel*, Jan. 31, 1993.

7. I stumbled across a copy of Nader's 1973 Letter to the American Association in the vertical files of the Children's Museum of Oak Ridge (TN).

range, to the Valley that even she could not have envisioned. Indeed, this book would likely never have been written had Marie not extended the same generous welcome to a "bunch of smart, rich kids" and their teacher from a Knoxville prep school in the mid-1990s.

Marie's most enduring legacies are the array of nonprofits that emerged from dialogue among her neighbors about pressing community needs. Tilda Kemplen, Louise Adams, and other locals initiated some of these efforts before Marie's arrival. For example, a community health clinic had been established, and responses to a number of community-based educational needs were already underway. Marie had the good sense to encourage continuation while also bringing about greater coordination of these efforts. Her influence was particularly evident in convincing men of the community, led by Shelby York, to address an array of economic concerns. These collective concerns eventually took the name Model Valley Development Corporation. Devising alternatives to extractive industries and expensive commutes to low-paying jobs in distant towns and cities proved problematical. Together, Marie and York convinced a local resident to sell forty acres of timberland, hoping local wood would furnish raw materials for a pallet factory. The plan envisioned employing community men and pumping needed cash into the local economy. That effort failed, but in characteristic Clearfork fashion, York and Cirillo transformed this failure into several successes. Land closest to Highway 90 offered space for Model Valley's headquarters, the community health clinic, and a community center that has served an evolving array of needs. Remaining land became available for home sites for regional natives who had long been orphans in their own domain. After ten years of persistent effort, a safe and reliable community water system was established. In 1977, an even more visionary effort, Woodland Community Land Trust, emerged. With support from churches and many individuals, Woodland acquired 101 acres in Roses Creek Hollow. Land trust families followed a Habitat for Humanity–like approach to constructing modest homes, defraying costs by relying on neighborly cooperation and utilizing native materials. Most recently, Clearfork locals, with help from outside volunteers, renovated the dilapidated Eagan School House to make room for the Clearfork Community Institute, which as envisioned will serve many community needs.

Scholars Discover the Clearfork Valley

The same ferment motivating activism in the Clearfork Valley in the 1960s and '70s also spurred academic and literary efforts seeking to capture and preserve the region's stories. In John Gaventa, activism and academics are one and the same. Son of African missionaries, Gaventa came to the Clearfork on a Vanderbilt

The renovation of the old Eagan Schoolhouse and its transformation into the Clearfork Community Institute has been one of the most ambitious grassroots efforts in the Clearfork Valley. Begun in the 1990s, the project is nearing completion as this book goes to press. The new community center is a testimony to the hard work, faith, and vision of community residents, Marie Cirillo, and outside supporters. (Courtesy of Clearfork Community Institute.)

University research project in 1971. The juxtaposition of "power and powerlessness" that he found to be the Valley's most distinctive and disturbing trait intrigued the idealistic young student. Gaventa made the Clearfork the target of an extensive study, which used sociological, economic, and political science theories to analyze abundant statistical evidence along with conventional research and anecdotal accounts from the valley's past.

At the same time Gaventa was probing the economic and sociological causes for Valley misfortunes, University of North Carolina journalism professor Dwayne E. Walls was hard at work on a very different, yet equally important, Clearfork study, *The Kidwells: A Family Odyssey*. Extensive interviews with Clearfork natives Doc and Bess Kidwell—and with their ten adult children—provide the nucleus for Walls's study. The experiences of those second-generation Kidwells varied widely, but they shared common experiences with many of their Valley neighbors: out-migration to an array of northern and midwestern cities, hostility from new neighbors in those settings, myriad social problems (e.g., poverty and dependence on public assistance, alcoholism, gambling and marital conflicts), unrealistic yearnings for "home," and occasional returns to the Clearfork, where limited opportunities and unpleasant realities compounded depression and hardships.

Recent Developments in the Clearfork Valley

Those who cling to popular notions of an isolated "Appalachia" frozen in time need only consider developments in this supposedly remote and static valley since my 1987 Tennessee homecoming. These developments remind us that the Clearfork story has never occurred in a vacuum. Today our nation's voracious energy appetite may again cost folks of this supposedly isolated locale dearly. Crippling dependency on Middle East oil makes domestic coal an attractive energy alternative, and some coal champions point to mountaintop removal as a "cheap" means of solving this truly national dilemma. Activists decry the environmental harm the very name implies. Other critics point to connections between burning coal and global warming. Knowing energy extraction has always been precarious, Marie Cirillo and other Clearfork folk call for more sustainable economic alternatives.

As Clearfork moves into the future, its residents will be wise to consider models offered by neighbors within coal Appalachia. One appealing alternative is heritage and eco-tourism. The restored Barthell Coal Camp (just north of the Tennessee-Kentucky border), and the Kentucky Coal Museum (farther north and east in Benham-Lynch, Kentucky) offer ways of preserving and presenting the rich history of coal Appalachia. Even closer is the Coal Creek Watershed Foundation, headquartered in Knoxville. As an economic complement to coal, which the organization recognizes will remain an economic mainstay for the area, the foundation promotes an array of venues and approaches for celebrating the rich, colorful history of this small part of coal Appalachia.

In closing, it is important to recognize the problems persisting in today's Clearfork Valley are not all new. All of the hard work and goodwill in the world can never overcome the steep hillsides, thin soils, and distances to markets that have hampered existence in the Clearfork since Europeans arrived two centuries ago. Despite recent gains, outsiders still control most Valley land and resources. In the twenty-first century, these old disadvantages continue to leave the Valley on global capitalism's fringes. These difficulties, in turn, give rise to problems of substance abuse, which has become the Clearfork's "primary self-inflicted destroyer." Marie Cirillo and her neighbors would be the last to declare today's Clearfork Valley utopia. A chapter in the recently published history of FOCIS's "mountain sisters" likens the efforts of Marie and her neighbors to a "journey." It is, to be sure, a journey that deserves to be better known and restored to broader contexts. The destinies of Clearfork residents and countless persons from beyond this supposedly isolated valley—including many of their East Tennessee neighbors—have long been and remain intertwined.

The Awakening in Cades Cove and Timber-Tourism Appalachia

The Appalachian awakening also came to Cades Cove and the greater Smokies region, but developments in this other East Tennessee hinterland over the past half-century have not mirrored those in the Clearfork Valley and coal Appalachia. Overall, the awakening in the Smokies, in both its activist and literary forms, arrived later and has been more subtle and subdued. However, developments now underway hint that a more strident form of activism may yet emerge in the normally calm Smokies.

The main distinction between Cades Cove and the Clearfork Valley is that the former died as a living community in 1937. The National Park Service, which oversaw that execution, quickly embalmed the corpse of once-vibrant Cades Cove by preserving sterile remnants of Cove farmsteads. Ever since, countless Cove visitors have embraced and carried home images of a static, homogenous "Appalachia" that are reassuringly misleading. Meanwhile, beyond the confines of the national park, the gateway communities of Gatlinburg, Pigeon Forge, Sevierville, and Townsend have engaged tourism's Faustian offerings with mixed sentiments and success. A profound, at best pragmatic, ambivalence toward "things Appalachian" undergird the marketing ploys they offer. Though less apparent than the Clearfork's crises, the challenges facing the national park and "tourist Appalachia" at the dawn of the twenty-first century are real and defy easy remedies. Perhaps even less obviously, outsiders—including residents of this book's other two representative East Tennessee communities—play important roles in the Smokies' dramatic crises.

In the turbulent 1960s, the one notable incident of activism in this quiet East Tennessee hinterland was, ironically, a reaction against Highlander Center's efforts to extend its influence here. In the summer of 1963, Highlander secured property adjacent to Great Smoky Mountains National Park for a camp bringing together young northern and southern whites with black teens who had recently participated in civil rights activities in Alabama. Soon after the camp convened, the Blount County sheriff and deputies conducted a warrantless midnight raid, hauling the twenty-nine participants and their adult leaders off to the county jail. The next day, eight students faced charges of disorderly conduct, and several others were charged with possession of liquor. Authorities charged the two adults with contributing to the delinquency of minors. Several days before the trial in Blount County Court, the camp cabin and several tents mysteriously burned. Even as the presiding judge refused to hear charges that the mostly circumstantial evidence had been obtained without warrant, and that the raiders had trespassed on private property, he convicted all but one of those as charged. Highlander's lawyer, Blount County native Edwin Lynch, appealed the case to the Tennessee Supreme Court. Recognizing the weakness of their case, Blount officials voided the convictions. But that did not end the turmoil. Several days later, Lynch and Highlander head Myles Horton were assaulted in a Maryville restaurant. Faced with threatened disbarment, Lynch left Blount County and relocated to New York. Soon thereafter, Highlander abandoned its work in the Smokies.

Another indication of quiescence in the Smokies in the middle years of the twentieth century was the relative acceptance by most Smokies natives of Elkmont's continued privileged status. When Great Smoky Mountains National Park included that seasonal community within its confines, most owners of Elkmont cabins accepted half of the assessed value for their summer residences in return for lifetime leases on their property. When the majority of Elkmonters in 1952 again used powerful political and Park Service connections to trade in their nearly expired lifetime leases for twenty-year leases, there was some grumbling but no groundswell of local opposition. Of course, the expiration of those leases in 1972 coincided with the peaking of sixties ferment and grassroots activism in Appalachian locales such as the Clearfork Valley. Elkmont folk again utilized connections to renew one more round of twenty-year leases, but this time they faced greater resistance. Many dispossessed landowners and their descendants informed a sympathetic park official that "continued use of the cabins as a private resort was a grave injustice against the poor who had to leave."[8] Environmental activists also opposed the agreement. Thus strange bedfellows, as so often typify Appalachian activism, began to coalesce in the Smokies. Their influence in convincing park officials to terminate the Elkmont leases in 1992 was only one indication that the sixties arrived, albeit belatedly, in this other East Tennessee hinterland.

8. Lipsey, "The Elkmont Cabins in the Great Smoky Mountains National Park," 17.

What explains the relative absence of grassroots activism in this area in the turbulent 1960s and beyond? The persistent stereotype that Appalachians are too fatalistic and independent to act in concert rests on an element of truth. Appalachian studies pioneer Loyal Jones's frank concession that "our independence keeps us from getting involved, from creating a sense of community, cooperation, and devotion to social causes"[9] certainly applies to Smokies folk, and is significant for this story. Many 1960s activists of the Highlander ilk failed to appreciate the stubborn independence, distrust of outsiders (particularly "do-gooders"), and reverence for traditional values that distinguish these and many other residents of rural East Tennessee. Even when reformers have joined forces with such residents (as they did to end Elkmont's privileged status in 1992) the alliance was uneasy. Persistent yeoman values also contribute to rural East Tennesseans' longstanding identification with the Republican Party. Long-forgotten and misunderstood Civil War–era legacies and commitments to religion, private property, and other traditional values help explain why many less-affluent regional residents in our own times have embraced the conservatism of Ronald Reagan and George W. Bush against what some consider their economic self-interest. In dismay, self-professed liberals often dismiss locals as ignorant and uninformed. Such attitudes have clearly impeded grassroots activism in Smokies communities.

Yet another reason for this relative calm is the nature of economic development in the Smokies. With the exception of a few choice locations, such as Cades Cove, farming was rarely profitable in the subregion, and by the time the park was founded, timbering had played out. For many locals, tourism represented the only means of entering the cash-consumer economy while remaining in (or near) ancestral homes. By some definitions, the coming of the park and tourism to the gateway communities can be considered "extractive," but that label is overly academic and irrelevant for people struggling to make ends meet. Transition to a tourist economy created crises more gradual and less threatening than simultaneous developments in coal Appalachia. Even Pigeon Forge's acres of asphalt are less destructive than strip-mining. Before the park was established, opportunistic locals (including Cades Cove patriarch John Oliver) encouraged and benefited from tourism. From the post–World War II economic boom to the 1970s, prominent Gatlinburg families (such as the Ogles, Whaleys, and Reagans) were among the biggest winners from the tourist bonanza. Colorful Wiley Oakley was only the best known among scores of everyday, local folk who found larger incomes from tourist-related employment than from anything they had previously done. "Playing hillbilly" was hardly imposed on locals by heart-

9. Loyal Jones, *Appalachian Values* (Ashland, KY: Jesse Stuart Foundation, 1994), 135.

less outsiders. As a drive down Pigeon Forge's strip reveals, Smokies tourism today is multifaceted, and some believe "hillbilly tourism" has diminished and become less offensive in this era of Dolly Parton. Nonetheless, much like their Cherokee neighbors across the mountains, most Smokies residents find tourism a precarious, if profitable, balancing act. One prominent player in Pigeon Forge's recent boom often tells my students that "we have created a beast . . . and we must continue to feed it."[10]

Recent developments in the Smokies reveal why conventional, melodramatic accounts of Appalachia's story often distort more than they clarify. The earliest warnings about overuse of the national park and calls to constrain "the beast" running amok in the gateway communities came from "meddlesome outsiders" whom locals often demeaned. By the 1950s, a few sympathetic nonnatives began to raise concerns about the park's popularity and what they perceived as the Park Service's preferences for recreation over preservation. By the 1960s, these calls became more frequent and strident. Some youthful Elkmonters, smitten by 1960s idealism and environmentalism, joined the crusade. But journalists from Knoxville's dailies offered more persistent and influential voices of concern. Among these were the *News-Sentinel*'s folksy and nostalgic Bert Vincent and Don Whitehead; Vic Weals, whose regular columns in the *Knoxville Journal* revealed that fascination with colorful "Appalachian ways" still sold; and long-time *News-Sentinel* columnist Carson Brewer, who balanced genuine interest in distinct mountain traditions with concerns that fans of the park were "loving it to death." When Wilma Dykeman, an Asheville native and acclaimed novelist and historian, joined the *News-Sentinel*'s editorial staff in the 1960s, general East Tennessee readers saw their first foreshadowing of the Appalachian awakening. Dykeman's and Brewer's columns addressed an array of environmental issues, including devastation from invasive species. They were also among the first to announce that the Smokies had become even hazier than their name implied. They cautiously related air pollution to the automobiles that made the park so popular and tourism so profitable. They also hinted that burning regional coal to serve the increasingly comfortable lifestyles of mid-twentieth-century Americans—including many of us "successful" East Tennesseans—also contributed to this new challenge. Regional scholars soon affirmed these assertions. This book's three-sided emphasis and call for restoring our East Tennessee story to broader contexts emerged from and echoes those early warnings.

National Park Service personnel also played an important, if little recognized, role in setting off the Smokies' alarm. In the eyes of some natives and

---

10. Ken Maples has expressed this view on several occasions when speaking at student and teacher workshops I have organized. He served for a number of years as Sevier County's assistant county executive.

many early Appalachian studies scholars, NPS personnel were uniformly arrogant and distant from locals and their interests. Much like popular perceptions of earlier home missionaries, such notions were not completely unfounded, but they are also misleading. Like any large bureaucracy, the Park Service in the middle years of the twentieth century was sometimes lethargic, but also diverse, and not even the NPS was immune to the ferment of the times. By the mid-1960s, observers such as Knoxville lawyer Harvey Broome and the aforementioned Knoxville journalists joined forces with park employees smitten with the environmental impulse then in its infancy. Their calls for greater attention to preservation and restrictions on development unleashed debates still raging among park personnel and friends. Some Smokies natives were among the most vocal critics of this farsighted effort.

Rediscovering Cades Cove's and the Smokies' Pasts

While the academic/literary awakening to the crises of coal Appalachia came initially and primarily from sympathetic outsiders, descendants of several prominent Cades Cove families first challenged longstanding romantic, nostalgic, and misleadingly vague accounts of the Smokies' past. By 1940, several Park Service studies called for creation of a "living museum" in the Cove that would preserve for tourists elements of an allegedly "dying" Appalachian culture. Some advocates called for employing locals to demonstrate "traditional" farming methods, crafts production, and musical/dance routines. However, tight budgets and other demands combined to prevent full implementation of this plan. A modified version resulted in construction of a one-way paved loop road and the decision to preserve log cabins, barns, and other structures "representative of [the Cove's] pioneer past." More common frame structures (with the exception of several church houses and one residence) were razed, as were most other signs of modernity. Soon opportunities to view these nostalgic dwellings, the Cove's scenic vistas, and bear, deer, and other wildlife without even leaving the comfort of private autos made Cades Cove the most popular GSMNP site. This was, of course, the Cades Cove that first introduced me to "Appalachian" culture. Official bulletins for travelers on the increasingly congested loop road and accounts in the popular media referred to isolated, rugged, self-sufficient pioneers. Not surprisingly, neither A. Randolph Shield nor Durwood Dunn, who first challenged these popular depictions of their ancestral home, fit the Park Service's portrayal of their forebears.

First published in 1977 by the Great Smoky Mountains Natural History Association, A. Randolph Shields's *The Cades Cove Story* remains popular today in park bookstores. Like Dunn, Shields's family roots lay within the Cove. The bulk of Shields's attention focused on the Cove community, including sections on home life, religion, communications, and education. Considering his past as a ranger-naturalist in the park, his academic orientation as a PhD biologist, the time in which his book took form, and the venue that distributed it, it is not surprising that Shields mentions the coming of the national park only in passing. His assertion that the Cove was "secluded—though not isolated" and his brief histories of the varied, diverse, and often innovative and progressive Cove families anticipated several essential insights into Appalachian culture uncovered by the regional awakening. The book's final two paragraphs acknowledge the National Park Service's efforts to preserve selected aspects of the Cove community. But, Shields writes politely, "[We] can never really recreate life as it was for the owners and settlers of this valley . . . [nor really know the families] who walked here." Only if we "let our imaginations carry us back to another century," Shields concludes, can "we feel the presence of these people."[11] Randolph Shields understood that past better than his own era. Even as he wrote these words, a regional renaissance was underway. Soon thereafter, his cousin Durwood Dunn published his more detailed, scholarly account, which carried the Cove's history into the twentieth century. In turn, outstanding studies bringing Cades Cove, Great Smoky Mountains National Park, and East Tennessee mountain tourism into the first decade of the twenty-first century have followed. Two outstanding accounts of the history of Great Smoky Mountains National Park (Daniel Pierce's *The Great Smokies* and Margaret Lynn Brown's *The Wild East*), a pathbreaking work on regional environmental history (Donald Davis's *Where There Are Mountains*), and the first scholarly investigation of "mountain tourism" (C. Brenden Martin's *Tourism in the Mountain South*) all rely heavily on Dunn's *Cades Cove*. But perhaps two efforts recently pitched to popular audiences are even more important legacies: Noel Fisher's *The Civil War in the Smokies* is a highly readable account of its subject, while Steve Cotham's *The Great Smoky Mountains National Park* (in the Images of America series) offers a wonderful collection of park photos along with a succinct narrative that incorporates many insights from Dunn.

A Burst of Activism in the Smokies

The appearance of exemplary, balanced historical accounts of developments in the Smokies has coincided in recent years with an increasingly strident, albeit multifaceted activism. Within the park, shrinking budgets—combined with

11. A. Randolph Shields, *The Cades Cove Story* (Gatlinburg, TN: Great Smoky Mountains Natural History Association, 1977), 103.

ever-increasing numbers of visitors—have created unprecedented challenges. Park Service personnel are often castigated with sweeping denigration, but many of these public servants strive courageously to balance the competing demands and challenges facing Great Smoky Mountains National Park. Tourism and resort-related developments have also forced at least some locals to abandon their legendary independence and cautiously join forces with park officials and supportive "outlanders."

Diversity distinguishes the array of organizations that have emerged in the last two decades to protect the national park and neighboring communities from rampant development. Members of the "Friends of the Smokies" are overwhelmingly middle and upper class. Many of the organization's members reside in locales distant from the mountains they love, the largest percentage having addresses in Knoxville. Since 1993, Friends of the Smokies has raised more than $24 million to help preserve and protect Great Smoky Mountains National Park.

In contrast, the Cades Cove Preservation Association, organized in 2001, has a more local flavor. Persons "who left the Cove as children, but . . . cling to precious memories of home sites, relationships, and events" still lead the CCPA, but, as "real" old-timers have declined, new and outside influences have grown. This is particularly evident at "Old Timers Days," a twice-annual event that evolved several decades ago from more spontaneous homecomings and reunions of Cove descendants. Youthful antimodernists, particularly fans of recently fashionable old-time and bluegrass music, have become an ever-larger presence at "Old Timers Days."

The Friends group, CCPA, and NPS officials cooperate in maintaining Cades Cove structures and in keeping its history alive, but like most marriages of convenience, this one sometimes grows frazzled.

Indeed, even when Smokies folk concur that a concern demands attention, they often wrangle about a proper remedy. Such is the case currently in Townsend, the national park's "other" gateway community. Located midway between Maryville and Cades Cove, the one-time logging center has long prided itself as being "the peaceful side of the Smokies." But in recent years its residents have reached no consensus on how best to retain that distinction.

Conclusion

Finally, during the years in which I have been actively engaged in writing this book, debates over proper development of mountain lands outside the park have become increasingly rancorous. Wealthy outsiders who can afford the exorbitant cost of a mountain view ally with opportunistic native-born developers, and together they sanctimoniously assert the sacredness of private property and

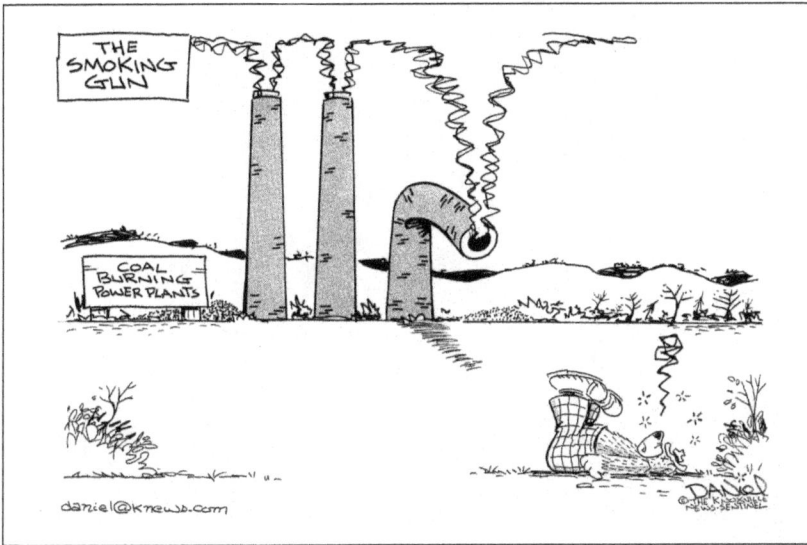

While communities of "coal Appalachia" and "Timber-Tourism Appalachia" have often been harmed by actions of outside interests and residents of "Valley-Urban Appalachia," economic activities in these hinterland areas often, in fact, prove mutually harmful. (Cartoon courtesy of Charlie Daniel.)

proclaim how "investment" benefits the surrounding community. In response, environmentalists and some descendants of longtime mountain residents join voices in decrying scars upon the land that are Smokies' tourism's version of strip-mining. Indeed, Marie Cirillo's cry from the Clearfork Valley—"no second homes for anyone until everyone has a first one"—now echoes in the Smokies.

Increased self-awareness and an array of activist efforts are two more traits that these two long-overlooked East Tennessee hinterlands share in common. Yet, as *Knoxville News-Sentinel* cartoonist Charlie Daniel graphically reminds us, the crises and challenges that the Clearfork Valley and the greater Smokies region face in the early twenty-first century cannot be separated. Like the protagonists in Greek tragedies, both of these two "victims" contribute to their mutual misfortunes. At the start of a new millennium, Daniel's own Knoxville was equally ensnared in this persistent Appalachian nexus.

Chapter Nine

The Awakening in East Tennessee's Leading City and an Ongoing Homecoming, 1970–Present

I came home to the family farm just outside the small town of Kingston in 1987. For twenty years now, the half-hour drive to and from Webb School on Knoxville's western outskirts has allowed me to reflect on the issues and concerns that ultimately found their way into this book. Only gradually have I come to realize how much residents of East Tennessee's leading city contributed to the broader history of East Tennessee and to my own homecoming. In 1987, neither my Knoxville friends (new or old) nor I glimpsed, even dimly, the idea that this book's title conveys. As students enrolled in my regional history elective remind me each fall, Knoxvillians are still puzzled with my assertion that East Tennesseans are "Appalachians all." Yet circumstances underway even before I headed west for New Mexico in 1976 changed East Tennessee's preeminent city and challenged Knoxvillians to reconsider and temper their characteristic ambivalence for things Appalachian. These admittedly uneven developments are still unfolding. Where they will lead is unclear, but this much is certain: the events, issues, and themes explored in this final chapter are very important for Knoxville, its East Tennessee neighbors, and this elusive place we call Appalachia.

The World Comes to Knoxville

Freewheeling discussions in the office of Knoxville Mayor Kyle Testerman in the mid-1970s gave rise to one of the most important and symbolic events in East Tennessee's history. Determined to stimulate a "quantum leap" that would end decades of lethargy and revitalize the city's downtown, the energetic mayor unveiled plans for a "Knoxville International Energy Exposition." Soon renamed "Expo '82," the event ultimately became known as "Knoxville's World's Fair." From May to October 1982, eleven million fairgoers came to Knoxville, surpassing the goals of Mayor Testerman and his band of boosters. The popular response to the fair surprised many observers and dismayed a few others, and a recent twenty-fifth anniversary celebration reveals that "the fair" still engenders controversy among city residents. This is not the place to assess the fair's broader effect; suffice it to say that Knoxville's 1982 World's Fair brought both benefits and costs to the host city and greater East Tennessee that did not end when the fair left town.

How did the fair affect and reflect Knoxville's relationship with its neighbors and the greater Appalachian region? Downtown development was clearly the fair promoters' top priority, but when quizzed about what they most enjoyed, casual fairgoers offered an array of responses. The fair's official theme, "Energy Turns the World," and unprecedented, impressive exhibits and pavilions from nineteen nations gave the fair a contemporary, cosmopolitan atmosphere. Yet accounts (official and otherwise) suggest many visitors passed quickly (if at all) through the high-tech exhibits, flocking instead to displays of traditional arts in the various national exhibits. Even greater numbers reportedly visited the fair's popular Folklife Festival. Funded by East Tennessee–based Stokely–Van Camp Corporation, the festival highlighted music, dance, artifacts (including a "working moonshine still"), and foodways from a region "defined as primarily South-Central Appalachia." To broaden appeal, the festival also invited performers and offered exhibits from areas of the deeper South associated with the blues tradition and all of Tennessee.

Like the fair itself, the folklife festival evoked debate. When initially approached about the idea, leading Knoxvillians responded ambivalently. Fears that they might appear "a step or two behind modern society to visitors from around the world" sparred with characteristic East Tennessee pride and echoed self-doubts that have characterized Knoxvillians since the days of William Blount. Still, the festival proved extremely popular among the scores of outsiders, East Tennesseans, and Knoxvillians who passed through the fair's turnstiles. Among other things, this popularity revealed that a fascination with Appalachia, real and imagined, retained power near the end of the twentieth century. As the fair wound down, backers erected a downtown billboard proclaiming, "The Scruffy Little City Did It!" A response to a pre-fair prediction in the *Wall Street Journal,* the retort revealed a defensiveness that has long defined East Tennessee's leading city. That attitude also helps explain Knoxvillians' clearly ambivalent responses to the Folklife Festival and to Appalachia in general.[1]

1. Richard Van Kleeck, "Reflections on the 1982 World's Fair," *Tennessee Folklore Society Bulletin* 49, no. 1 (Spring 1983): 2; Wheeler, *Knoxville, Tennessee,* 162.

An Identity Crisis?

As this book's three-sided emphasis reveals, Knoxville has been East Tennessee's political, economic, and cultural hub since Europeans arrived in the region in the late eighteenth century. Knoxville's relationship with this book's other two representative communities, the Clearfork Valley and Cades Coves, helped make those places decidedly "Appalachian." Conversely, those connections helped Knoxville largely escape an "Appalachian" fate. While extractive exploitation of hinterland resources contributed most obviously to this pattern, important intra–East Tennessee demographic changes should not be overlooked.

Although the nature of American censuses makes it impossible to determine exactly how many Knoxvillians at any moment in-migrated from the hinterlands or were descendants of such persons, anecdotal accounts, like my own family's history, suggest the percentage has always been high. Moreover, studies of rural-to-urban migration elsewhere suggest the energetic and talented are often the first to relocate, a finding with significant implications for both Knoxville and its hinterland neighbors. Indeed, official uncertainty about the exact origins of many Knoxvillians of regional background is itself strangely symbolic. Many of the city's most powerful political figures of the past half-century either in-migrated or were children of in-migrants. The widely divergent styles, priorities, perspectives, political persuasions, and accomplishments of Cas Walker, John Duncan Sr. and Jr., Kyle Testerman, Randy Tyree, Jake Butcher, and Chris Whittle offer proof of our region's diversity, while also warning against sweeping portrayals of Knoxville's population of native in-migrants.

That reality alone demands caution from anyone daring to comment on Knoxville's sense of identity. Surely the city's self-perception is complex, sometimes confused. As the popular response to the 1982 World's Fair folk life exhibit revealed, Knoxvillians are often both proud and embarrassed about their heritage and condition. One reason for this dilemma is that Knoxvillians often allow outsiders to do the defining. Countless visitors to the city since John Gunther's scathing portrayal of Knoxville in 1947 have offered less-than-flattering images of East Tennessee's leading city. To be sure, some criticism has always been merited. Moreover, there is value, as Robert Burns suggests, in "seeing ourselves as others see us." Between simply hanging their heads in shame and responding with blind, exaggerated defensiveness, Knoxvillians have left untried many alternative responses to their critics that might be appropriate. Ambivalence need not be considered a sign of weakness; it can be a source of strength.

Knoxville's troubled self-identity ebbs and flows throughout the history we have already examined, as the city had been buffeted by events both outside and inside East Tennessee. The era between the end of World War II and around

1970 was, overall, a dysfunctional and unhappy time for Knoxville. In contrast, Knoxvillians in recent years appear to be more comfortable with themselves. Yet, as perceptive journalist Jack Neely often suggests, peace comes from grappling with and coming to terms with, not avoiding, the city's elusive history. The cultural ferment that gave rise to Knoxville's recent progress in self-discovery simultaneously nurtured the Appalachian awakening that is our greater concern. Yet that awakening came more slowly to Knoxville than it did to our other two representative communities. Indeed, a prominent Appalachian studies scholar suggested to me early in this project that Knoxville is "a city without a soul." Perhaps Phil Obermiller should be dismissed as yet another outside observer. But his diagnosis that Knoxville's ills stemmed from the city's reluctance to embrace its Appalachian identity resonates with the rest of this book.

Knoxville finds itself at the nexus of numerous dichotomies: the North-South divide, rivalry with long-dominant Middle and West Tennessee, and, of course, rural-urban differences. Knoxville since its beginnings has always tended to dominate and distinguish itself from rural neighbors. When the idea of "Appalachia" appeared in the latter nineteenth century, Knoxville residents understandably placed their rural neighbors in that category. Thus Knoxville's struggle with its identity is simply one link in a long chain of mutual denigration, our own regional version of one of humanity's less admirable but predictable games. I often joke with my students that "everybody's somebody's redneck." Those of us who are formally educated prefer to think the simple explanations offered by these dichotomies hold particular appeal for more simple, less sophisticated folk. My own experience, and Knoxville's history, suggest otherwise. Indeed those of us who think ourselves "sophisticated" are often the most blind to "the beam in our own eye" and the mysterious dependencies that accompany modernity.

When the large number of Knoxvillians with roots in rural East Tennessee and southern Appalachia grapple with their identity, they typically follow one of two broad patterns. Those who I define as "successful" Appalachians tend to distance themselves from and often deny their roots; yet, even then, many individuals from this group retain modified aspects of their cultural inheritance, such as selected facets of traditional religion, music, and foodways. My parents' 1950 decision to move to the farm represents an extreme version of this response. On the other hand, my maternal grandmother (though she lived in Bristol rather than Knoxville) typified the successful Appalachian's tendency to disassociate from the region. Of particular importance here, both sub-camps of successful Appalachians are notably missing from the most recent, sophisticated account of Knoxville's history, Bruce Wheeler's *Knoxville, Tennessee: A Mountain City in the New South*.

On the other hand, in-migrants to Knoxville who are less successful in making the rural-urban transition sometimes resent their status and actively resist "haughty" treatment from their self-proclaimed "superiors." Because these individuals cling to family ties, inherited religious practices, and traditional foodways and musical preferences, they define themselves as "conservative" while other observers portray them as "reactionary." But recent Appalachian scholarship and studies of other arenas of cultural interaction reveal that these individuals (like their rural cousins who resist the city's lure) rarely reject outright all aspects of the new culture. Instead they more typically retain modified versions of vital inherited traditions by selectively embracing aspects of the new culture. Thus, the radio became the venue for country music and Bible-thumping preachers; the auto the preferred means of "running moonshine"; and the Internet a medium for "fighting back" against strip-mining or problems facing rural ghetto dwellers. By whatever means, cultural resistance becomes particularly pronounced in hard economic times and is often outwardly "conservative." This helps explain how opportunistic demagogues, such as Lee Monday in the 1920s and Cas Walker in the twentieth century's middle third, effectively played upon and manipulated marginal, often provincial Knoxville constituencies. Bruce Wheeler's aforementioned recent history of Knoxville attributes the city's lack of energy and foresight from around 1945 to the late 1960s (which promoters of the '82 World's Fair sought to ameliorate) to an unlikely alliance between Walker and the city's business elite. According to this take on Knoxville's history, traditional powerbrokers allegedly abhorred Walker and his "redneck legions." But a mutual suspicion of change wedded the unlikely partners. This dysfunctional relationship, Wheeler concludes, bore lasting misfortunes for East Tennessee's leading city. While this assertion is undeniable, one should not overlook that 1950s America also produced Joseph McCarthy. Populist demagoguery was hardly unique to Knoxville and East Tennessee.

Hindsight notwithstanding, I must confess that my parents, one-time residents of Knoxville who remained concerned about developments there after moving to the farm, viewed Cas Walker's colorful antics, the heated debates over Market Square discussed in chapter six, and many other East Tennessee–wide developments of my childhood through the same prism as Wheeler. I was, of course, oblivious to most of this. But in my limited, youthful view, they were black-white issues. That is why I became puzzled when Walker (the "bad guy") supported the "good cause" (i.e., preserving Market Square). Of even more importance to many other fellow successful East Tennesseans of the era was the matter of musical preferences—specifically, a disdain for country music. Indeed, most of "Knoxville's finest" initially dismissed Roy Acuff (a rural in-migrant, but lifelong Knoxville resident) as a "hillbilly entertainer" until late in his career.

Only when outsiders praised Acuff did some of his fellow Knoxvillians claim him. Similarly, when early bluegrass performers, such as Lester Flatt and Earl Scruggs, offered a new, appealing musical style on Cas Walker's locally produced and regionally distributed television show in the 1950s, a few respectable Knoxvillians began to reconsider their disdain. Even more alluring was a buxom, blond vocalist from Sevier County. Cas Walker may have "discovered" the youthful Dolly Parton, but that could not keep many who disapproved of the "Old Coonhunter" from embracing the music and musicians he promoted. Music, more than demagogic politicians, began to narrow Knoxville's historic social divide by the time I left East Tennessee in 1969. Still, a profound ambivalence lies at the heart of an identity crisis many successful Knoxvillians and other East Tennesseans cannot escape. A subtle, and by all means less than complete, shift toward greater self-acceptance was the Appalachian awakening's greatest legacy for Knoxville.

Yet another factor that influenced East Tennessee's broader climate and contributed to this ambivalence in the mid-twentieth century was the important federal presence in the region. In the antebellum era, the region's yeoman outlook led most East Tennesseans to embrace the Jeffersonian-Jacksonian ideals of limited government and states rights. But in Knoxville, Hamiltonians and Whigs always challenged that impulse as they sought government aid in combating their region's relative isolation. Republican political leanings after the Civil War heightened this impulse. In the twentieth century, Depression, global war, and the impulses giving rise to the Great Society dramatically increased the federal presence in East Tennessee, and Knoxville in particular. By the era of concern here, discrepancies between East Tennesseans' inherited Republicanism (with its embrace of "limited government") and the dependence of Knoxville and surrounding areas on federal and state funds were obvious. TVA, Oak Ridge's labs, Alcoa, and the University of Tennessee are hardly exemplars of unencumbered free enterprise. Indeed the impetus for the quantum leap World's Fair backers sought in the 1970s was securing increasingly scarce federal monies. Rhetoric about our region's rugged independence at the fair's folk life exhibit was only one manifestation of Knoxville's futile attempt to disguise this not-so-well-kept secret. Effective political leaders, such as the two John Duncans who have represented Knoxville in Congress for half a century, former U.S. senator Howard H. Baker, and current senator Lamar Alexander, instinctively understand these complex realities and deftly manage their contradictions. Approval from their constituents suggests many East Tennesseans accept this pragmatic view.

An Uncertain Awakening

Knoxville writers and thinkers may have been slow to respond to the Appalachian awakening, but they grappled with their city's identity problem long before that stirring erupted. Although most city residents initially refused to respond directly to John Gunther's 1947 charges about the city's "ugliness," several prominent journalists eventually addressed the issue. Bert Vincent and Don Whitehead, veteran, generally folksy reporters for the *Knoxville News-Sentinel,* were themselves in-migrants to the city. Shortly after fire destroyed Knoxville's old Market House in 1959, Vincent—a native of rural Virginia who had been with the Knoxville paper since the Depression—wrote a nostalgic piece decrying plans to replace it with a new, modern facility. In assessing why so many city residents would miss the old place, Vincent exposed one of Knoxville's best-kept secrets. "You see," he wrote, "we are country folks in Knoxville. Most of us are only one and two jumps out of the briar patches and red gullies."[2]

Vincent's admission fortuitously coincided with a resurgence of national attention to Appalachia, and his colleague Whitehead did not fail to comment on the latter. Raised in Campbell County not far from the Clearfork Valley, the journalist reflected several times on unbecoming stereotypes accompanying the "war on poverty" in the region. "I pretend no expertise on mountaineers," Whitehead wrote, "but I do know that even in poverty there is personal pride and that mountain people have the same hopes, fears, loves, good qualities, and bad qualities [as other people]."[3] Many Knoxvillians doubtlessly found Vincent and Whitehead's views reassuring, but the journalists' "Appalachian" forthrightness also threatened to expose much that Knoxville residents, particularly those I have described as "successful," had long kept hidden about themselves and their rural neighbors.

By the mid-1960s, two young journalists joined these two veterans at the *News-Sentinel* and echoed their sentiments. In one of her first columns for the paper, a youthful Wilma Dykeman decried outsiders' stereotypical views of "Appalachia." "Provincialism," she opined in her closing paragraph, "is not always confined to rural areas."[4] Carson Brewer, as we have seen, was another *News-Sentinel* writer who commented often on local history and culture. When a *Washington Post* columnist—around the time of the World's Fair—wrote a disparaging account of life in Sunbright (a small town about an hour north of Knoxville),

2. Bert Vincent, "Strolling," *Knoxville News-Sentinel,* Dec. 20, 1959.

3. Don Whitehead, "Don Whitehead Reports—On Mountain Folks," *Knoxville News-Sentinel,* Jan. 25, 1972.

4. Wilma Dykeman, "Rural Areas Are Misrepresented," *Knoxville News-Sentinel,* Jan. 14, 1965.

Brewer blasted the *Post's* "parochial" view.[5] With the exception of Dykeman, these Knoxville-based journalists never became formally involved in the Appalachian awakening. But this did not keep them from offering advice to those who did. "Maybe—just maybe—with the new interest in Appalachia," Don Whitehead wrote, "there will emerge a more rational view of what [the region] really is with its treasures of raw materials, beauty, mountain customs, history and human resources—along with its splotches of ugliness and its shortcomings."[6]

Whitehead's vision echoed sentiments of John C. Campbell and Emma Bell Miles and foretold much that Appalachian studies has achieved. But the challenge was greater than he or anyone else imagined. Today, nearly forty years after Whitehead's prophetic appeal, the fruits and insights of Appalachian studies are still little known beyond activist and literary-academic circles. Nowhere in East Tennessee is this more true, and with greater consequence, than in the Appalachian city where Whitehead wrote for a living. It is tempting to explain Knoxville's reluctance to embrace the Appalachian awakening by pointing to the city's instinctive, conservative aversion to what many perceived to be "Highlander Center radicalism." Perhaps we should also blame Appalachian scholars for not making their message more accessible to general readers. But even collectively, these plausible explanations fall short of fully explaining the complicated reality so vital to this book.

Additional considerations compounded Knoxville's ambivalence. First, early Appalachian scholars focused on two major themes: origins of the idea of "Appalachia," and how and why the region's most hardscrabble areas had come to their existing crises. Unmasking longstanding ideas about "Appalachia" and debunking unquestioned explanations for rural Appalachia's misfortunes demanded great intellectual effort, leaving little time for addressing urbanization within the region. At best, locales such as Knoxville were simply omitted from the new regional history. Secondly, the anger and outrage typifying much early Appalachian studies scholarship evoked denials from some Knoxvillians, for whom defensiveness was almost instinctive. "Outsiders" may have been the primary target of Henry Shapiro, Ron Eller, and John Gaventa, but they and other early regional scholars also pointed accusatory fingers at regional elites, implying hostility for *successful* Appalachians. Many Knoxvillians, of course, objected to "academic elitists" accusing them of being villains.

In spite of these impediments, new perspectives on the region found their way to East Tennessee's leading city. In the years before and immediately after

5. Carson Brewer, "Washington Post—A Parochial View?" *Knoxville News-Sentinel,* Aug. 16, 1982.

6. I found "Don Whitehead Reports—On the End of an Era in Appalachia" in the Whitehead file at the McClung Collection's vertical files. The undated clipping is clearly from the *News-Sentinel;* the context suggests that it was written in the late 1960s.

my 1987 return to East Tennessee, this was evident in depictions and perceptions of Appalachia offered by Knoxville's media and popular culture; in Knoxvillians' responses to regional needs; in activist efforts seeking to ameliorate them; and in literary-academic attempts to capture and convey the regional story. New attitudes and the passage of time have tempered, but never completely eradicated, Knoxville's characteristic ambivalence for "things Appalachian." Like so much else we have considered, that attitude is remarkably resilient. As the twentieth century drew to a close, Knoxvillians still relied on regional resources for energy and continued to flock to regional havens for escape and entertainment. At best, some city residents today appreciate these privileges more than their forebears. Of greater concern, the Appalachia many Knoxvillians embrace is nostalgic and romanticized. The view from 2010 is hazy at best. But, as paradoxical as it may seem, one senses that acceptance of certain, more popular aspects of the regional renaissance in the twentieth century's final decades may have inoculated some Knoxvillians from more virulent forms of that same awakening.

Awakening from Ambivalence

Throughout the twentieth century's final decades, Carson Brewer and Wilma Dykeman continued to make Knoxville readers aware of the richness of regional culture and ever more vigilant against unregulated strip-mining, overdevelopment of the Smokies, and other threats to the region. By the mid-1980s, two younger writers joined them on the pages of *Knoxville News-Sentinel,* writing regional articles reflecting even more clearly Knoxville's mixed mind about Appalachia. Fred Brown's genuine concern for the region was evident, for example, in his series of 1993 articles introducing *News-Sentinel* readers to Marie Cirillo and the challenges of life in the Clearfork Valley. But even as he occasionally penned similar articles about other regional topics, Brown often focused on quaint, exotic themes that mimicked earlier light, "Appalachian" fare. Sam Venable, a fifth-generation southern Appalachian, conveyed similarly mixed images as he served the *News-Sentinel* in a variety of capacities and authored a number of books on regional themes. Venable's sense of humor placed him in line with a host of native voices dating to the antebellum era, assuring him a wide regional readership. Both Brown and Venable struck a balance between educating and entertaining their readers. But in the latter role, they sometimes echoed local colorists from a century before. If their accounts more clearly reflected the needs and anxieties of their mostly Knoxvillian readers than regional realities, that is hardly a new pattern in Knoxville's relationship with its neighbors.

Of course, by the time the Appalachian awakening was underway, the print media was not the only, nor even the most influential, purveyor of regional images. From the time television became widespread from the mid-1950s to the 1980s, programs created and circulated on the national networks, such as *Andy Griffith, The Beverly Hillbillies,* and *Hee Haw*—as well as local shows filmed live in the studios of Knoxville's NBC and CBS affiliated stations—conveyed images confirming distinct regional stereotypes. Cas Walker's crudely produced half-hour shows conveyed his colorful, controversial views on everything from religion to politics, displaying cornball humor at its worst. Yet, a number of fine musical performers owed their starts to "the Cas show." By the 1970s, much of this type of programming waned, but continuous syndicated reruns on Knoxville stations revealed Appalachian images retained their appeal.

Ironically, a desire to counter these images helped spur the advent of Appalachian studies. Yet many of us in that movement who are heirs to successful Appalachians often fail to appreciate our neighbors' attachments to Cas's show, Mayberry, or even the tomfoolery of Jed Clampett and his kin. The resulting popular perception that "we are getting above our raisin'" may help explain why our quests are so elusive and incomplete, and why so few Appalachians beyond academic circles recognize our efforts.

These same contradictions are evident in what has doubtlessly been the most popular locally produced television program of the past two decades. What became *The Heartland Series* first aired in 1984 on Knoxville's WBIR Channel 10 to celebrate the fiftieth anniversary of the founding of Great Smoky Mountains National Park. The series initially ran brief, five-minute clips. Since its beginning, more than one thousand short features and over one hundred half-hour specials have been produced; Tennessee- and Texas-educated Bill Landry has served as the program's voice, host/narrator, and coproducer. In these capacities, he has won the hearts of countless viewers and guests. The late Smoky Mountains matriarch, Lucinda Oakley Ogle, "loved Bill like a son."[7] She was not alone. The show's Web site states that its purpose is to "celebrate the people and land of the entire Appalachian region." "Celebrate" is the key word. The program occasionally addresses melancholy aspects of regional stories, such as the forced removals that made way for Great Smoky Mountains National Park, Oak Ridge, and TVA dams. But those stories invariably end on a pleasant note or, at least, with an air of predestined finality. Landry's "celebrations" typically avoid controversial subjects, such as strip-mining or how some regional people have benefited at the expense of their neighbors.

If a pollster asked contemporary Knoxvillians about the sources of their regional images, the Museum of Appalachia would vie with Landry's *Heartland*

7. Linda James, untitled columns, *[Pigeon Forge] Tennessee Star Journal* (Dec. 8–14, 2004 and Aug. 16–22, 2002).

Series for top honors. Located in Norris, sixteen miles north of Knoxville, the museum grew out of John Rice Irwin's penchant for collecting regional artifacts. The descendant of early settlers of the area and a longtime public servant, Irwin began in the 1960s to assemble today's "living history farm and village of sixty-five acres, thirty-five historic structures, and a quarter of a million items."[8] Although it is certainly more alive than the National Park Service's depiction of Cades Cove, Irwin's spread of log cabins, barns, and other primitive outbuildings evokes a similar nostalgia frozen from an earlier era. Many persons from outside the region visit the museum as they travel up and down nearby Interstate 75 and carry away enduring "Appalachian" images. But conversations with neighbors, acquaintances, and many of my students reveal that locals do the same. To suggest the museum causes East Tennessee residents to misunderstand their history would be unfair, but it no doubt confirms notions that Appalachia is frozen in the nineteenth century.

Curiously primitive log structures, whether viewed in person or on a five-minute television clip after the evening news, hold special appeal for at least some folks residing in comfortable, modern homes in Knoxville and its suburbs. The human penchant for nostalgia and romance is, of course, universal and not by its nature harmful, and it will not soon disappear. But perhaps one reason images of static, homogenous, sanitized "Appalachia" hold such appeal is that they deflect attention from less pleasant realities: strip-mined slopes and down-and-out folks in places such as the Clearfork Valley, seasonal workers eking out a marginal existence in asphalt-covered Pigeon Forge, and environmental-economic challenges linking all East Tennesseans under a yoke as unprecedented as it is unpleasant. Did not local-color literature a century ago mask similarly unpleasant realities of America's Gilded Age? This irreverent query has important implications for other facets of the regional awakening and how they played out in Knoxville and among other successful Appalachians.

Knoxvillians and Appalachian Activism

Throughout their history, Knoxvillians have preferred established practices to abrupt change and moderation to extremism. That alone should reassure the city's often-insecure citizens that they are reasonably normal. When crises related to strip-mining nurtured grassroots outbursts in the coalfields in the late 1960s, only a few "agitators" in Knoxville (mostly clustered around UT, with ties to Highlander) showed more than casual interest. Civil Rights concerns in the

---

8. Misty Yeager, "Museum of Appalachia," in Abramson and Haskell, *Encyclopedia of Appalachia*, 1496.

early 1960s—and later objections to the Vietnam War—demanded practically all of the energy and passion potential activists could expend. Moreover, youthful potential rebels in Knoxville have been reluctant to embrace the old-timers and "reactionary rebels" taking up arms in the coalfields. The urbanite's instinctive disdain for rural folk and liberals' self-righteous tendency to distance themselves from those who do not share their "enlightened" views may also have impeded cooperation that would have advanced the protests. Knoxvillians, however, were not completely missing from grassroots movements emerging from the Appalachian awakening. But responses in the city to the challenges drawing activists to the hinterlands were, in general, subdued. More important, activist efforts in East Tennessee's leading city defy simple generalizations and assumptions associated with the labels "liberal" and "conservative."

While organizations such as Highlander Center and SOCM (Save Our Cumberland Mountains) had a presence in Knoxville, their influence was not widespread. Much more common, particularly after the wave of 1960s angst ran its course, were "respectable" middle-class, nonpartisan/nonideological efforts reaching out to deserving causes in the hinterlands. Indeed, many "good Knoxville Republicans" belong to "Friends of the Smokies" and support many other worthwhile regional causes. Similarly, Marie Cirillo's calls for help for the Clearfork Valley attract an eclectic array of Knoxvillians. When "Highlander folk" and idealistic UT students and faculty join forces with typically more moderate volunteers from Sequoyah Hills Presbyterian Church and my own gang from Webb School, Marie's true gifts become apparent, and important changes become reality.

When the federal government retreated from the "war on poverty" in the 1970s, more systematic, private uplift efforts appeared, and many of them set up headquarters in Knoxville. These organizations also reflect a diversity defying simplistic generalizations. No doubt the most widely known and touted effort is "Mission of Hope." Since 1996, this organization served those who "live in the depths and despair of poverty stricken areas of rural Appalachia."[9] Though it has no denominational affiliation, the mission's core support comes from conservative Evangelicals. Like some early home missionaries and other altruists of a century ago, Mission of Hope addresses many needs unmet by government and other private agencies. However, their promotional efforts, particularly televised spots seeking donations for their Christmas campaign, use stereotypical depictions of Appalachians at their worst to win sympathy and support from more advantaged Knoxvillians. Consequently, these activities perpetuate images of a static, homogenous "Appalachia" that sometimes demean regional residents and

9. Mission of Hope publicity.

obscure why these conditions exist. Mission of Hope's tendency to encourage Knoxvillians to donate dollars without actually engaging directly with their less affluent regional neighbors is particularly dismaying.

However, many (less well-known) Knoxville and East Tennessee Christians share with earlier "missionary longtermers" preferences for the "social gospel" and pluralism that are often overlooked. They support regional self-help efforts as individuals, congregations, and through loose-knit regional organizations. Since 1965, many progressive East Tennessee Christians have supported CORA (the Commission on Religion in Appalachia), the interdenominational agency headquartered in Charleston, West Virginia, which works for justice in a land where it sees mountaintop removal as just the latest injustice. Among CORA's recent East Tennessee commitments have been support for renovating the old Eagan schoolhouse and furthering Marie Cirillo's vision for the Clairfield Community Institute. CAM (the Coalition for Appalachian Ministry) with its more narrow, Reformed denominational base, seeks to "make a positive impact wherever the Reformed tradition and Appalachian culture come together." Recently, CAM headquarters moved from Knoxville to a site in Wears Valley, where it shares space with an ambitious effort to market local crafts and inform Christians from East Tennessee and beyond about Appalachian issues and relevant scholarly understandings of the region. Finally, since 1987, the Knoxville-based Appalachian Community Fund has distributed more than $5 million "for community organizing and social change in the region."[10]

Knoxville and the Regional Renaissance

Sneering cosmopolitans often mock Knoxville's parochial ways, but their ignorance of the city's impressive cultural achievements validates Wilma Dykeman's assertion that "provincialism is not always confined to rural areas." Unfortunately, many Knoxvillians still accept outsiders' appraisals. Nothing illustrates this better than the saga of James Agee and his acclaimed novel *A Death in the Family*. Like many youthful Knoxvillians, the mercurial Agee struggled with an identity rooted in both urban and rural worlds. That neither he nor his most famous novel—which revolves around this inner struggle—were ever labeled "Appalachian" is revealing. Knoxville in our own times has produced a number of other outstanding writers, including David Madden, Richard Marius, Cormac

10. Information and quotations are taken from the Web sites of the Council on Religion in Appalachia (http://www.geocities.com/appalcora/), the Coalition for Appalachian Ministry (http://www.appalachianministry.org/), and the Appalachian Community Fund (http://www.appalachiancommunityfund.org/).

McCarthy, and Wilma Dykeman. Novels by the first three offer grimy, unbecoming images of East Tennessee's leading city, which affirm negative views. They are "Appalachia" only for those with an agenda to demean the region, and none of the three writers identified with the Appalachian awakening. In contrast, Dykeman, a prolific writer of fiction and nonfiction, understood perhaps better than any other regional figure how much the blessings and burdens of her adopted hometown connect to East Tennessee's hinterlands. Not surprisingly, she was the only one of Knoxville's most acclaimed authors of the post–World War II generation to become actively involved in Appalachian studies.

The View from "Rocky Top"

Of course, one cannot comment on Knoxville's literary-cultural-academic reputation without addressing the University of Tennessee. Indeed, the city's profound ambivalence about "things Appalachian" is more evident on "the Hill" than in any other Knoxville institution. Several years ago, when I offered the course that became the basis for this book at UT's Evening School, I joked with my students that we should market a ("big orange") bumper sticker with the message *UT: Rocky Top Yes . . . Rednecks No*. In reality, UT's relationship with the surrounding region is much more complicated than my rather poor attempt at humor suggests.

As in earlier chapters in its history, many dedicated educators with a genuine commitment to Appalachia have graced UT's Knoxville campus in recent years. Nonetheless, UT's collective response to the region has, at best, been ambivalent. Several concerted efforts to establish an Appalachian center and even faculty efforts to initiate a regional-sudies major have failed. Compared to the state universities of Kentucky and West Virginia, smaller regional schools in Western North Carolina, and even such small private institutions as Berea College, UT's reluctance to embrace Appalachia stands out. Within Tennessee, UT by default allowed Johnson City's East Tennessee State University to become *the* state school identified with the region.

My suggested bumper sticker aside, a variety of factors contributed to UT's institutional reluctance to embrace Appalachia. As *the* state university of a political entity that spans more than five hundred miles east to west, UT has obligations to Tennesseans beyond its nearest neighbors. Moreover, disciplinary turf wars and inter- (as well as intra-) departmental rancor (neither unique to UT) have undermined these efforts. Indeed the status of Appalachian studies as a proverbial "red-headed step child" in UT's dysfunctional family lends credence to the old adage about "herding cats." Hence "stars" that might have enhanced Appalachian interests never "aligned" on the Knoxville campus.

Although this book has demonstrated that malevolent motives have rarely been the sole causes of East Tennessee's past misfortunes, several developments at UT demand at least brief attention. For example, in 1975 UT Press succumbed to pressure from TVA when it reneged on a contract to publish David Whisnant's controversial *Modernizing the Mountaineer.* Members of UT's History Department were also apathetically unsupportive of Durwood Dunn's Cades Cove dissertation. An understandable preference among the department's southern specialists for the "flatland South" and uncertainty about how to deal with the new, provocative scholarship dealing with the region's "uplands" doubtlessly contributed to this lack of enthusiasm. Still, it is not insignificant that the department failed to recognize what became one of the most important Appalachian studies works. Finally, the history of Knoxville that UT historians William Bruce Wheeler and Michael McDonald completed in 1983 (and Wheeler's 2005 revision of the same) offers further evidence of the department's characteristic distancing from Appalachia. Paradoxically, that history and Wheeler and McDonald's 1986 essay, "The Communities of East Tennessee," are among the most important "Appalachian" works ever completed by UT-based scholars. The general dearth of references to Appalachian scholarship in their bibliographies might make this assertion seem dubious. But the efforts of these two UT historians illumine and illustrate the riddle of greater concern here: Knoxville's enduring ambivalence for "things Appalachian." Behind that ambivalence lies either a lack of awareness or a disapproval of more than thirty years of regional scholarship. Moreover, one suspects that consideration of recent insights into the intertwining of urban/rural demographic and economic patterns might have modified the authors' conclusions about Knoxville's and East Tennessee's "Appalachian deficiencies."

This critique should, however, end on a positive note. Bruce Wheeler and his late colleague made important contributions to an "Appalachian conversation" that is ongoing, and I am personally indebted to them. Their scholarly efforts and the epiphanies they evoked awakened me as I too struggled to grasp hard and unpleasant realities. The 1987 essay, in particular, led me to envision the three-sided emphases that carried over into this book. That, in turn, made me realize that a more complete and honest account of East Tennessee's past could not leave out Knoxville, its identity crises, and its complex relationships with its neighbors. As historians, Wheeler and McDonald no doubt knew that important human endeavors often emerge from "unintended consequences" and that scholarship advances when bold, flawed ideas are challenged. That same fate no doubt awaits this present book and historian.

Recent Developments in Knoxville

For Knoxville, even more than this book's other two representative communities, history is relentless. I share the following thoughts on recent developments in Knoxville, East Tennessee, and the greater Appalachian region fully aware that future commentators will see them more clearly. Indeed my views may even be outdated before they are in print.

For the sake of clarity, recent changes and challenges for Knoxville can be sorted into three categories: demographic, economic, and environmental. However, these artificial groupings overlap and intertwine with one another even as they link Knoxville inextricably with its East Tennessee neighbors, greater Appalachia, and the four corners of our modern globalized earth. Even a casual Rip Van Winkle who went to sleep in East Tennessee in 1970 and awakened today could not help but notice a dramatic change in local eating establishments. I am not referring to the bevy of chain fast-food joints that have mushroomed in even my own little hometown. Nor am I talking about the high-scale restaurants recently appearing in West Knoxville's fashionable new Turkey Creek development. Instead I am talking about small, typically modest, ethnic eateries. When I first traveled to Latin America in the late 1960s, Knoxville had one (very bad) Mexican restaurant. Out here in Kingston, we did not know how to pronounce, much less eat, enchiladas, guacamole, and so forth. In Knoxville today one can eat almost every kind of cuisine, from Middle Eastern to Indian to Mexican in establishments ranging from "Mom and Pop" to upscale. In the hinterlands our choices are more limited, but within fifteen minutes of home I can find good Chinese, Vietnamese, Thai cuisine, and several varieties of Mexican food. East Tennessee may still be more homogenous than many parts of the nation, but Knoxville has always had a more varied populace than most folks imagine. Only now it is more proud of that variety. To be sure, we have nativist moments, and our congressional leaders did not distinguish themselves with enlightened contributions to recent immigration debates. But once again we were not alone in our shortsightedness.

Other contributors to Knoxville and East Tennessee's diversity are the increasing number of American mainstreamers who arrive here from outside the region. Some come for employment, others for retirement, but many come voluntarily, drawn here by a mythical, sanitized, "Appalachian" allure. As a one-time newcomer to New Mexico, I understand that many recent arrivals to East Tennessee genuinely embrace "native" ways. This embrace is understandably selective, but that in no ways lessens its importance in bringing yet another perspective to debates over an ever-more diverse and dynamic "Appalachian" identity. For example, while our less-advantaged folk tend to live in mobile homes of varying quality, a booming log home business caters both to new arrivals and successful insiders. "Humble" homesteads mirroring Cades Cove cabins on the outside hide inside the latest appliances and technologies, even as two-car garages enshroud upscale autos. Indeed, East Tennessee's own version of what my Santa Fe friends call "primitive *chic*" is evident in eclectic musical tastes with distinct "bluegrass" tones and "comfort food" served at chain eateries such as Cracker Barrel. An insatiable penchant for quilts, dulcimers, and countless other "homemade" items are the ultimate sign that country is indeed cool.

Mast General Store, an upscale retailer of outdoor and regional "stuff," opened shop on Knoxville's Gay Street in 2008. Across Gay Street one can visit the new headquarters for WDVX-FM. From humble beginnings in a Norris, Tennessee, camping trailer, WDVX has become a musical powerhouse with a cult following. Thanks to the wonders of the World Wide Web, WDVX streams its quirky down-home flavor to the corners of the globe. All of this suggests that selective acculturation continues in an East Tennessee that is more diverse and dynamic than we imagine. Collectively, this new demographic mix and related cultural trends and preferences assure that "Appalachia," both real and imagined, will be an important part of the mix shaping Knoxville and East Tennessee's elusive culture and identity for the foreseeable future. To be sure, the lure of nostalgia explains in part the attraction of these and other local venues. Fortunately, those attracted to these offerings can embrace more complete and realistic views on our regional past at several recently opened exhibits in downtown Knoxville.

For example, one may visit the Knoxville Museum of Art's new permanent exhibit, "Higher Ground: A Century of the Visual Arts in East Tennessee." The museum's curator observed that "the public will be surprised to see that Knoxville has a rich art history that stretches back more than 100 years," adding that "we should be the place where people come to get that story."[11] Many one-time Knoxvillians, like James Agee and maybe even my parents, would be among those surprised to discover our region's long-unrecognized creativity. But I suspect Wilma Dykeman would not. Wilma would also surely be delighted with the East Tennessee Historical Society's newest permanent exhibit, "Voices of the Land: The People of East Tennessee." The 8,300-square-foot exhibit, which opened in September 2008, combines valuable artifacts and the latest of museum technologies. The exhibit creators drew from recent largely unknown fields of scholarship, including Appalachian studies.

11. Doug Mason, "A 'Higher' Level: Knoxville Museum of Art assembles local works of past 100 year in permanent exhibit," *Knoxville News-Sentinel*, June 22, 2008.

One sign of Knoxville's recent Appalachian Awakening has been the phenomenal success of "East Tennessee's own WDVX." This scene from the station's popular "Blue Plate Special" conveys the station's commitment to presenting traditional music in new, unorthodox ways. (Photo copyright 2007, Robert J. Goodwin.)

Economics, of course, has always been one our region's greatest challenges. Overall, Knoxville's economy during the 1980s and '90s largely mirrored broader patterns: a prosperity we hardly appreciated in the 1990s, and less prosperous trends in recent years. Focusing too closely on those patterns, however, blinds us to more fundamental concerns. First, present-day East Tennessee faces widening economic-social divisions. I see this each day as I drive to work. The status of many of my neighbors, who benefited in many ways during America's "golden age," had begun to stall by the time I returned to the farm. Twenty years later, "stagnate" is more appropriate. On the other hand, a host of newcomers have come into our midst. Large, sprawling homes and upscale autos and rivercraft suggest these folks are prospering. The divide is more apparent when I arrive at Webb School, and even more so when I take my mostly privileged students on service outings to the Clearfork Valley. While most Webb families have absorbed escalating tuitions since my arrival there, folks in Clairfield have experienced a stagnation that only the specter of mountaintop removal appears likely to ameliorate—and then for only a few. Indeed, the East Tennessee divide that Bruce Wheeler and Mike McDonald described in 1987 has grown much wider.

The Awakening in East Tennessee's Leading City

Two other hallmarks distinguish Knoxville's twenty-first-century economy. Many longtime industries, particularly textiles, have "gone offshore." Those that survive have adapted to new realities, often shrinking their workforce. As elsewhere, farsighted entrepreneurs have embraced new high-tech and service industries. County and city officials strive to find a balance between old and new in enterprise and the public sector. Government at all levels still plays a huge role in the regional economy, but balancing shifts in public priorities and shrinking federal funds with our regional independence (both real and rhetorical) demands agile public leadership.

The other, less obvious, but potentially more important, influence on the regional economy is environmental. *Knoxville News-Sentinel* op-ed columns and letters to the editor reveal that East Tennesseans are (true to form) opinionated and divided about global warming and other environmental issues. But perhaps our equally characteristic realism will lead us to important adjustments. Here the central premise of this book perhaps becomes most valid. Air and water pollution do not stop at city or county lines, or at the walls of affluent, gated communities.

In 1999, a number of progressive East Tennesseans initiated a "visioning process" bringing together leaders and "regular folk" from throughout greater East Tennessee to identify common challenges and opportunities. Over the next five years, 3,600 East Tennesseans offered 8,827 ideas in countless public meetings. Many critics decried "Nine Counties. One Vision" as just another top-down endeavor that would produce interesting, but impractical, blueprints for the future. But more than six hundred volunteers and community leaders have already committed themselves to prioritizing the results and transforming the energy into realistic goals, and twenty-six task forces have developed strategies for implementation. "Nine Counties. One Vision" emphasized, in particular, the need for greater cooperation across East Tennessee, the importance of addressing shared environmental concerns, and the need to improve public education.

In 2004, a coalition of Knoxville business leaders initiated "Jobs Now!" to stimulate job creation, wage growth, and capital investment in Knoxville and greater East Tennessee. A nationwide survey of corporate officials to determine executive impressions of the Knoxville, Oak Ridge, and Smoky Mountain areas began the effort. Not surprisingly, stereotypical perceptions of "mountain people" and a sense that East Tennessee's various entities lacked cohesion were cited as impediments to the development the business leaders sought to promote. Armed with these results, "Jobs Now!" developed a regional marketing plan and set the following five-year goals: 35,000 net new jobs, $2.5 billion in non-residential capital investment, and improved wages by an overall average of $5,000 per job. By its third year, the effort was well on its way to achieving the first two goals, and had made slower, but still significant, progress on the wage front.

Knoxville public officials strongly supported both "Nine Counties. One Vision" and "Jobs Now!" Throughout the time I have been engaged in this project, community organizers and business leaders in the Clearfork Valley, officials of Great Smoky Mountains National Park, and an array of persons interested in promoting regional tourism and other forms of development have unanimously proclaimed City Mayor Bill Haslam's progressive and far-sighted leadership. On the first anniversary of his 2004 election, Mayor Haslam attributed revitalization of Knoxville's downtown to joint city-county efforts and cooperation with UT, the Knoxville Area Chamber of Commerce, Oak Ridge, and the state of Tennessee. The same forces, he might have added, brought greater East Tennessee many benefits. The recent conference, "Plain Talk for Quality Growth," offers further reason for optimism. Knox County Mayor Mike Ragsdale, U.S. Secretary of Transportation Mary Peters, U.S. Representative John Duncan Jr., and Mayor Haslam joined a host of other government leaders, urban planners, and community representatives to encourage public dialogue about a myriad of development and planning issues.Their aim was to "dispel the inherent resistance to change in the region and inspire local residents to envision opportunities for cooperation and action."[12] It is too early to know the full effects of these developments, but no one can doubt that Knoxville and East Tennessee in the twenty-first century's first decade are finding common ground in unprecedented ways.

Considering my earlier criticism of the University of Tennessee, I would be remiss if I did not mention several developments on the Knoxville campus that reflect a greater and more genuine institutional interest in the surrounding region. The Great Smoky Mountains Project is an ongoing effort of the John C. Hodges Library, which is creating a "massive annotated bibliography" of materials related to the Smokies. The Library has also hosted a speaker's series and a series of regional films and documentaries to highlight this project and related efforts of university personnel. During the 2006–07 academic year, UT's "Ready for the World Program" conducted a year-long "Celebration of Appalachian Peoples and Cultures." As on many campuses, student-initiated efforts at UT sometimes push university officials to address issues they might prefer to avoid. In the spring of 2007, SPEAK (Students Promoting Environmental Action in Knoxville) initiated a campaign against the university's purchasing of strip-mined coal. Most recently (September 2008), the university hosted the world premiere of a new, four-part regional documentary, *Appalachia: A History of Mountains and People*.

12. Elisha Sauer, "East Tennessee Conference Strategizes Regional Growth," Knoxville Voice (Apr. 2007).

Several prominent members of the UT community made notable contributions to the documentary, and its producer, Jamie Ross, commented that "Knoxville is the incarnation of some of the best values of the region—smarts, independence, energy and diversity."[13]

Across campus, the UT Institute for Secure and Sustainable Environment's Community Partnership Center coordinates student involvement in an array of regional service activities. One of their most impressive recent projects was a comprehensive effort in cooperation with an array of federal, state, local, and private organizations to promote water quality in the Little River Watershed. Center Director Tim Ezzell has also worked with students involved in the Appalachian Teaching Project, which has received funding from the Appalachian Regional Commission since 2001. As one of thirteen regional institutions engaged in ATP, UT has sent students to selected East Tennessee communities, where they work with local people to "build on community assets to shape a positive future for Appalachia."[14] Finally, three floors below the Community Partnership Center, the University of Tennessee Press retains its strong reputation as one of the leading academic publishing houses in the field of Appalachian studies. Recent acclaim for the superb *Encyclopedia of Appalachia* reaffirms that standing.

A Lingering Ambivalence

Despite all of these notable advances, Knoxvillians' characteristic ambivalence about "things Appalachian" has not completely disappeared. Remnants of this mixed outlook are evident in debates among leading Knoxvillians about the future of Elkmont, the place of Appalachian coal in America's energy future, and proper responses to the challenges facing the Smokies. No one who watches local TV news or the *Heartland Series* can doubt Knoxvillians' genuine love of place, but "quaint Appalachian" images cannot hide regional ills nor Knoxvillians' complicity in them. Advocates of "tough" love occasionally counter those who prefer more pleasant, nostalgic views of our region. The same contradictory impulses are evident in the pages of the *Knoxville News-Sentinel*. Articles lament the ravages of strip-mining and rampant tourism and decry misleading "Appalachian" images; at the same time, stories from Scripps-Howard and locals' letters to the editor perpetuate tired, old notions about our region. Columnists identifying

13. "UT to Host World Premiere of Appalachia Documentary," Univ. of Tennessee press release, Sept. 11, 2008.

14. Tim Ezzell, "Building Sustainable Partnerships," *Appalachian Journal* 34, nos. 3–4 (Spring/ Summer 2007): 354. This is part of "Appalachian Teaching Project," a larger article authored by Alice Sampson and Roberta Herrin.

themselves as "native East Tennesseans" and "Appalachians" appear more regularly in *News-Sentinel* op-ed pages than ever before. That they often express very different responses to such controversial concerns as mountaintop removal and ridgetop development in the Smokies, and range from "Reagan Republicans" to "raging radicals," are yet further indication that Knoxvillians are of many minds on most regional issues.

The fall 2006 issue of the University of Tennessee alumni magazine offers perhaps the most graphic indication that Knoxville's ambivalence about Appalachia persists. Intended to celebrate publication of the long-awaited *Encyclopedia of Appalachia* by UT Press, the issue highlighted contributions of past and present UT faculty to reimagining the region. Yet the cover of the magazine, and four pages of black and white photos by a UT alumnus who has documented "the people and places of Appalachia for forty years," graphically subverts the nearly forty years of regional scholarship informing the *Encyclopedia*. The "Appalachia" of this montage is indeed "black and white": stereotypically homogenous, rural, old-fashioned, poor, and just a little bit bizarre.

While all of the above may be important, the best known—and for this book most revealing—UT story of late involved what is truly Knoxville and East Tennessee's other "religion": Volunteer football. When all-time fan-favorite Peyton Manning fell short in his bid for the Heisman trophy in 1996, many Vol faithful charged that the cable-TV giant ESPN had unfairly promoted his rival. The UT-ESPN feud festered for several years. In 2000, the network promoted an upcoming game and tried to have a little fun at the expense of thin-skinned Vol diehards at the same time. UT's Athletic Department and "Big Orange Legions" failed to see humor in commercials portraying a hefty, gingham-clad lady in curlers clutching a pig named "Rocky Top." Yet when the *News-Sentinel's* front page triumphantly proclaimed "ESPN drops ad mocking UT devotees," few people grasped what I believe is the story's greater message. To be sure, UT football draws support from all types of Tennesseans and pulls together our often-fragmented community in much the way the Roman Catholic Church once united European Christians. (Outsiders may think this an exaggeration, but an autumn Saturday in Knoxville would teach them otherwise.) Yet, one would have to look hard among the 110,000 orange-clad fanatics who regularly fill Neyland Stadium to its brim to find the gingham-clad lady. Vol partisans, at least those who attend games, are mostly successful folks. To be sure, this sweeping assertion includes a wide array of peoples, from my mostly privileged Webb School students and their parents to members of the working middle class. But, other than those who hawk concessions, few less-advantaged folk can afford the hefty price of a ticket. The large lady with her friendly pig appeared on ESPN more often in two weeks in August 2000 than she might have visited Neyland Stadium over an entire lifetime.

This anecdote reveals an important reality we East Tennesseans have long overlooked to our own detriment. We "successful" Appalachians are often so adept at intragroup distinction that we unwittingly become ensnared in the very stereotypes good fortune and adeptness at selective acculturation have enabled us to overcome. When it comes to belittling (or celebrating) "poor old Hillbillies," outsiders, as David Hsiung argues and ESPN so recently proved, take their cues from us.

A Confession and the Long Way Home

Lest I appear overly critical and self-righteous, a confession is due. Along with the story that follows, this admission reveals that my "homecoming" was more circuitous and unlikely than even I imagined. Bruce Wheeler and Mike McDonald's "Communities of East Tennessee" was published in the 1986–87 issue of the *East Tennessee Historical Society's Publications;* during the same months, my father passed away, and I left New Mexico to return to East Tennessee. Had I read Wheeler and McDonald's essay during my first year back home, I confess I would have found nothing in it objectionable. If anything, my newly minted PhD made me even more blind to "what I did not know" about East Tennessee and southern Appalachia than I had been as a youth. This blindness was particularly inexcusable, for (as I shared earlier) I actually witnessed firsthand a pivotal moment in the "Appalachian awakening." As an oblivious eighteen-year-old, I had no idea that the seemingly chaotic events I saw at Lake Junaluska in April 1970 were memorable. History rarely looks like "history" when it occurs— particularly to a brash and budding young historian who was unaware of what he did not know.

The return to family and farm awakened me ever so slightly to my own personal and regional stories. By the end of my first year at Webb School, following my East Tennessee homecoming, several colleagues saw through my attempts to disguise my new interests in my own personal and regional stories, and urged me to attend UT's Stokely Institute. After I learned that my PhD overqualified me for that opportunity, a friend told me about the Summer Appalachian Workshop for Teachers at Kentucky's Berea College. I could not help but notice the unusual given name of the program's director. Only after seeing him and overhearing several conversations during my first several days at Berea did I realize I had seen Loyal Jones before. His lopsided smile, sense of humor, and genuine good nature were unmistakable. The frenzied man I had seen in 1970 at Lake Junaluska was much more relaxed eighteen years later. After his attempt to save the Council of the Southern Mountains from a self-inflicted death proved futile, Loyal Jones, in characteristic "Appalachian" fashion, landed on his feet. He returned to his alma mater to create one of the nation's first and most effective Appalachian centers. The summer course for teachers was only one of many programs Loyal spearheaded that continues to produce valuable results for our region today.

Together Loyal, historian Richard Drake, and writer extraordinaire Wilma Dykeman offered a gift that welcomed me back home. At the time, the gift was barely a seed. But, just as good farmers share only good seeds, Loyal, Dick, and Wilma chose their offerings well. I am grateful to a mysterious and generous Creator that their seeds found fertile ground. Twelve wonderful years in New Mexico had stirred in me unusual interest in the matter of human identity. Living and learning in the Land of Enchantment taught me about cultural resilience and persistence and gave me distinct perspectives on the complex dynamics of cultural interaction. The real New Mexico, not the Chamber of Commerce's tri-cultural utopia, taught me that diversity inevitably engenders tensions, but that those tensions can be creative. The Southwest's Native Americans, *Hispanos,* and Anglos offered me a vision and hope that the peoples of valley Appalachia and upland Appalachia, rural Appalachia and urban Appalachia, traditional Appalachia and modern Appalachia can not only coexist but, indeed, thrive from their diversity. New Mexicans of all persuasions welcomed this outsider in a way we Appalachians would do well to embrace our own "foreigners." As one Pueblo elder put it, "if you inhale and exhale here, you are one of us." Perhaps most important for this book, twelve years in the Southwest taught me that "successful" regional residents impoverish and diminish their lives if they do not embrace and learn from their diverse and varied neighbors and the rich cultural inheritance that make's New Mexico so enchanting.

With one foot on the farm and small-town East Tennessee and the other at suburban Webb School—and New Mexico fresh in my mind—I began to glimpse insights on the diverse geographical settings and human inclinations that make this place we call "Appalachia" so elusive. Gradually I began to unlearn what I thought I knew about "Appalachia," my home, and myself. In time, new information and ideas gave rise to new understandings of my homeland. In the years since, sound, provocative scholarship, and insightful, generous and understanding friends, colleagues, and students helped me discern the insights and generalizations about our region that I have shared here. My hope is that these more realistic glimpses of our past will prepare us better for our future. "Coming home" is truly a journey, not a destination. Writing this book makes me aware of how truly blessed my journey has been.

Epilogue

Reimagining Appalachia and Ourselves

*And the end of all of our exploring will be to arrive where we
started and know the place for the first time.*

—*T. S. Eliot*

My personal Appalachian saga affirms T. S. Eliot's often-repeated assertion, and
I hope this book will help other East Tennesseans and Appalachians engage in a
similarly fruitful self-discovery. Yet I must confess that coming home has been
a gradual, often arduous journey that is still underway. Even the most recent leg
of this sojourn, the writing of this book, has consumed more time and energy—
and generated far more questions—than ever I imagined when the year off from
my teaching duties in 2005–06 formally initiated a process that actually began
much earlier.

Throughout this endeavor, treks to my parents' cemetery bench have been
a constant. Moments of reflection from that lofty vantage point enabled me to
glimpse stories from a personal past and the broader East Tennessee story that
were largely unknown to me twenty-one years ago when unforeseen circumstances brought me home. In the years since, this special place nurtured the
words and insights that you have just read. Yet, while we historians arbitrarily
determine a time to end our investigations, history itself is relentless. Hence,
Pop and Mom's bench has also served as my vantage point for witnessing and
reflecting upon the never-ceasing events of East Tennessee's ongoing saga.

Some developments of late were readily apparent from my cemetery perch.
For example, last year as I looked north, a new "scrubber" emerged in the shad-
ows of the two towering smokestacks of TVA's steam plant in the foreground.
TVA officials reported that the $500 million project would reduce the plant's
emissions of sulfur dioxide by 98 percent. Yet from my parents' bench, I knew
that considerable costs accompanied this obvious good news. Surely no one could
question the value of reducing air pollution, but—considering the nation's energy

and environmental dilemmas—I wondered about unintended consequences of this advance. Even though much of the coal burned at the Kingston plant comes from western states, increased TVA demand for coal could bring needed cash and jobs to hardscrabble locales like the Clearfork Valley. But at what cost? Ostensible effects of mountaintop removal for such locations and recognition that Knoxville and the Smokies surely share in the harmful effects—as well as the benefits—that accompany mining and burning coal give me pause.

Of course, other changes are occurring in the Clearfork Valley and beyond that I cannot discern from my parents' bench. I am speaking about ongoing work by Marie Cirillo and Clearfork folks and efforts like the Coal Creek Cooperative that I explored in chapter eight. Other, more recent developments also demand attention. TVA, for example, has installed a network of towering wind turbines on Buffalo Mountain about thirty miles to the northeast, just beyond the horizon from my parents' bench. At present this is the only operating "wind farm" in the southeastern United States and represents the first half of a twofold TVA strategy that calls for expanding renewable energy sources and a return to the nuclear program that the agency abandoned in the 1980s. A prominent East Tennessee environmentalist recently praised the Buffalo Mountain project and TVA's new emphasis on wind power and other renewable energy sources and its increased commitment to conservation. In response, Tennessee's senior senator decried the project and advocated more conventional forms of energy production. Although vague, his plan certainly includes coal and forms of extracting it that cause the aforementioned short-term environmental damage and potentially interminable long-term costs for all East Tennesseans.

The view south and east from my cemetery perch, up the Tennessee Valley and beyond to the Smokies and Blue Ridge, is more limited than the view north. But one peering upriver today might reasonably be more optimistic than even a few years ago. Overall the advent of environmentalism has reduced urban pollution coming downriver from Knoxville, and the Tennessee River today is much cleaner than when I swam in it as a youth. A number of projects underway in Knoxville and in other upriver communities promise continued progress on this front. One example is the Little River Watershed project that is introducing UT students to a regional environmental ethic and encouraging them to consider careers in related fields. New models for eco- and heritage tourism emerging in Townsend and in the Coal Creek Watershed and a new generation of leadership at the Great Smoky Mountains National Park also offer hope for a more positive future. Perhaps most encouraging of all are increased commitments to intraregional cooperation among Knoxville officials as they support endeavors like "Nine Counties. One Vision" and "Jobs Now!" Whether these will prove that East Tennessee's more privileged residents truly envision an enlightened self-interest, only the future will tell. Doubtless one key to the regional stewardship envisioned in this book will be the response(s) of we "successful" Valley residents to aforementioned issues in coal and timber-tourism Appalachia.

A few days before Christmas 2008, when an earlier draft of this manuscript sat in the offices of the University of Tennessee Press awaiting a copyeditor's final review, a mishap less than two miles from my home and my cemetery refuge, offered a poignant reminder of just how much the fortunes—and misfortunes—of all East Tennesseans intertwine. From the early days of TVA's Kingston power plant in the 1950s, disposal of coal ash that remains behind as electricity is generated has been a problem for TVA. Over the years, the agency devised an array of schemes for recycling this material, but a variety of developments rendered those plans illusory. Paradoxically, the agency's responses to air quality concerns exacerbated its dilemma, and over the years the "temporary" response was to place the ash in containment ponds where mixing it with water keeps the former from becoming airborne. In the more than a half century since Kingston's TVA plant and I were born, the containment ponds steadily expanded and unofficially became the "permanent" response to the coal ash problem. Pride in being home to "the world's largest steam plant" and addiction to a lifestyle dependent upon "cheap electricity," left most of us living nearby largely oblivious as the containment pond walls grew ever higher.

Then, on the night of December 22, unusually heavy rains and sharply fluctuating, below-freezing temperatures combined to create a break in a wall of one cell of the pond. What happened next was eerily similar to the settlement pond spills that have periodically devastated mining towns throughout the greater Appalachian region. Amazingly this spill claimed no human lives, but it did destroy three homes nearby and damage twenty-three others. The massive discharge of coal sludge spilled into the Emory River and spread across more than three hundred acres of adjoining land. Shortly below the spill site, the Emory flows into the Clinch River, which two miles farther downstream—and less than a half-mile from my home—flows into the Tennessee. In the months since, local and regional media have provided almost daily coverage that reflects diverse responses to community and even global consequences of the spill.

Although fierce debates continue to rage, several points of general consensus at this present juncture are clear. After initial evasion, TVA's local and federal officials agreed with its critics that approximately 5.3 million cubic yards of sludge spilled from the site. In May, the Environmental Protection Agency joined TVA in assuming responsibility for the cleanup, and as of this writing, officials from the two federal entities do not dispute estimates that the full cost of a cleanup that will require years—not months—to complete may exceed $1 billion. Of course, residents of the nearby Swan Pond community witness daily the magnitude of the debacle, but just when those of us who live a bit farther away were about to succumb to the proverbial obliviousness that contributed to the misfortune, heavy spring rains flushed debris from the site downstream into the Clinch and Tennessee rivers, a reminder that the costs of coal are widely shared and will not end anytime soon. Beyond these basic facts, the one certainty—now and for the foreseeable future—is controversy. We who reside in the vicinity hope that the immediately negative effects on our property values will be temporary, but only time will reveal if those expectations are realistic. Outside commentators and activists with much grander agendas have entered the fray, and advocates of "clean coal" spar with those who see the spill as only one facet of our national debate over fossil fuels and climate change. Predictably the spill's local and immediate human consequences are often overlooked in these debates.

As I write in June 2009, this much is certain: coal-bearing regions of East Tennessee and southern Appalachia, including the Clearfork Valley, will be critical to American energy policy for the foreseeable future. The coal ash spill simply affirms this book's fundamental premise that developments in East Tennessee's three representative parts intertwine inextricably. Knoxville and the Smokies have not to this point paid the price that we in the shadow of TVA's Kingston power plant have, but they—and the scores of East Tennessee communities that they represent in this study—share in the benefits and harmful effects associated with America's addiction to "cheap energy." Long before the Kingston spill, rates for asthma and other respiratory illnesses in Knoxville were well above the national average, runoff from surface mining sites fed into streams that feed into the Tennessee River system, and depletion of the ozone level and acid rain threatened our beloved Smokies. All of these conditions can be attributed in part to mining and burning coal. Now, increased monthly bills for TVA-generated electricity to pay for the Kingston cleanup will provide a more immediate, yet recurring reminder to a broad range of East Tennesseans that we are indeed "Appalachians all."

For me, at least, insights from my parents' bench leave no doubt that the time has arrived for those of us who reside in East Tennessee and the greater Appalachian region to reimagine ourselves. As the coal ash spill reminds us, not even our most successful residents escape costs that geographical and historical forces have forged. Ambivalence about Appalachia exacerbates those costs for all of us. I am not, however, so optimistic nor single-minded to presume that I have convinced all of those who read these words that we East Tennesseans are, in fact, "Appalachians all." Nor do I believe our people can become whole—nor even address present challenges—simply by chanting that mantra as we hold hands and sing "Kumbaya" together. I am asking that all take an honest view of how our region came to its present juncture, that we recognize the diversity and

This photo taken shortly after the December 22, 2008, coal ash spill reflects the extent of its damage. (Courtesy of *Roane County News*.)

dynamism that has always existed here, and that we refrain as much as possible from the understandable, but destructive, habit of dehumanizing whole groups of our neighbors as a means of elevating ourselves and justifying our own fortunes—however beneficial or harmful they may be.

Some readers may conclude that we should abandon the elusive, tired, and worn-out "Appalachian" label all together. The track record of African and Native Americans and all the other "others" who attempted to rename themselves in the optimistic 1960s leads to my preferences for sticking with—but reimagining—our old name and label. As the recently released documentary *Appalachia: A History of Mountains and People,* forcefully argues, mother earth is the common ground on which our complex drama has been played. A geographical definition of our region acknowledges intraregional diversity and dependency that more self-serving cultural definitions of Appalachia obscure. Moreover, within a greater American society that has always been mobile, dynamic, and diverse, the old static and uniform cultural definitions of our region diminish both Appalachia and the nation. A reimagined Appalachia can offer a more cordial welcome to newcomers who, for whatever reason, come into our midst. Conversely, as Jeff Biggers suggests in *The United States of Appalachia,* reimagining our region can also allow us to reclaim both well- and little-known individuals with roots in our region, many of whose accomplishments can be attributed at least in part to hard work, self-reliance, humility, common sense, and other attributes long associated with Appalachia. A more honest understanding of who we are can provide ballast for both those who are stereotypically "Appalachian" and those whose "successful" fulfillment of the American Dream breeds anomie. While results from the 2008 presidential election may reveal that the Appalachian South is the reddest part of a shrinking "red America," those of us in the "blue minority" need to be responsible in our minority status and heed lessons about the cyclical and enfeebling costs of intragroup distinction.

An old adage reminds us that one may pick friends but not family. Similarly I believe recognition of the intertwined destinies of our diverse East Tennessee family is essential to our collective wellbeing and future. Yes, there will always be tensions between East Tennessee's disparate parts and peoples, but those tensions need not enfeeble us. Whatever we call ourselves is less important than that we begin to acknowledge that East Tennesseans—and Appalachians in general—are a diverse, ever-changing lot, whose destinies have always intertwined. Cultivating creative, constructive tensions from our diversity is our greatest hope for a better future.

Is this vision realistic? I will end with two stories close to my heart that offer assurance that simply striving for this end can, at the very least, bring certain benefits to us all. For many summers, my neighbors Imogene and Fred Pogue Jr. have operated "Honesty Fruit Stand." Set in a wide curve on James Ferry Road and in clear view of the old cemetery so essential to this book, the produce stand offers local clientele tomatoes, cucumbers, an array of squashes, and other seasonal produce on an "honor basis." A sign indicates prices and instructs customers to leave their payment in a slot in the fruit stand counter. The Pogues' commitment to the old-time value of personal integrity, however, should be considered neither nostalgic nor naïve. Some visitors, they know, take advantage of their trust. Fred and Imogene's willingness to continue operating the stand in light of that reality and their faith in a value that moderns so often violate and ridicule explains why this and other regional ways have been so resilient. The persistence of traditional values in our very nontraditional times and into the future will depend on similar behavior from others who share the wisdom and faith of my good neighbors.

Finally, a month after the Kingston coal ash spill, Clearfork residents and a group of Webb students joined together to celebrate Martin Luther King's birthday and learn more about their common interests. The highlight of our day was coming together on that blustery, snowy afternoon to plant four, 80-percent-American, blight-resistant chestnut saplings on property in Roses' Creek adjacent to the Clearfork Community Land Trust. The spring before another group of locals and Webb students planted four similar saplings on what was once strip-mined land; we hope to continue this tradition into the future. Under this arrangement, Webb students raise monies to purchase the saplings; several locals assume responsibility for tending and watering them through the vulnerable weeks after the planting; but the planting itself is a collective effort. Bringing together representatives of two of East Tennessee's disparate communities in an effort that may yield benefits long after we are no longer here symbolizes a spirit that has too often been absent in Appalachia.

I am mindful, however, that Webb students—and other "successful Appalachians" and antimodernist intellectuals whom I presume will be among my readers—are particularly inclined to embrace romanticized images of "Appalachia." Homogenously idyllic images of our region, the history just recounted suggests, have often been as inaccurate and potentially harmful as notions of a uniformly negative "Appalachia." My sincerest hope is that Webb ventures to Clearfork *and* this book elicit neither pity nor reverie. Rather, I hope introduction to the likes of the Pogues and Clearfork folks fosters a genuine appreciation of peoples who are trying to make do in a complicated, puzzling world with the resources at their disposal. As such, they are not so different from the rest of us, and because they are often of more than one mind about these matters, they (again like the rest of us) are more diverse and dynamic than long-popular stereotypes suggest. At their best, findings from Appalachian studies affirm this

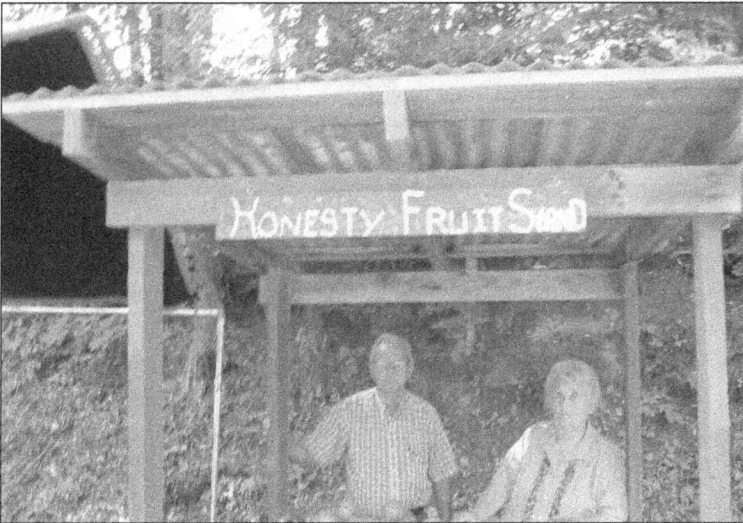

The author's neighbors, Fred and Imogene Pogue, in front of their "Honesty Fruitstand." (Photo by author.)

Reimagining Appalachia and Ourselves

Webb School students and Clearfork residents engaged in chestnut project, January 2009. (Photo by Bindy Sefton, Webb School Class of 2009.)

reality. To those representatives of our field and other, antimodernist intellectuals who object that this "reimagined Appalachia" deprives Appalachians of their legitimate uniqueness, I echo Jim Wayne Miller's bold assertion that "the regional is universal." That which is deemed "unique," I might add, may fascinate, but it is typically dismissed as unimportant and unusual.

Lest rhetoric about unique and universal attributes overwhelm my argument, I offer one other, sober observation that has profound implications for reimagining our region and ourselves. Scholars, who in recent years have offered "new" insights into the workings of the human mind, remind us that we humans instinctively prefer simple dichotomies to complex realities. Seemingly wired to distinguish between "me and you" and "us and them," we prefer to define ourselves by that which we are not. Overcoming the negative implications of these largely unconscious processes is the work of religion, philosophy, literature, and (yes!) education and history. Frightening challenges that we collectively face in our present historical chapter complicate and hinder these efforts but make addressing them even more important. Compared to global inequities, terrorism, climate change, systemic economic challenges, and other great issues of our time, the matter of one's identity as an "East Tennessean" or "Appalachian" is admittedly minor. But for those of us who make our homes here, it is fundamental. Indeed, I believe that, at least for our youths, coming to terms with the matter of regional identity is prerequisite to addressing other greater issues. The concern that emphasizing one's familial/regional stories may lead to "redneck chauvinism" or "rural Balkanism" is valid, but it is also misleading and limiting. "The challenge," as the clergyman William Sloane Coffin wisely observes, "[is] to recognize the need for roots while insisting that the point of roots is to put forth branches." "Human beings," Coffin continues, "are fully human only when they find the universal in the particular, [and] when they recognize that all people have more in common than in conflict."[1] As we "reimagine" and prepare East Tennessee and Appalachia for that type of future, we need full and complete understandings of our past—its burdens and its beauties and everything in between. If this book helps even a few readers avoid self-demeaning denigration and idyllic, nostalgic nonsense, it will be worthwhile.

1. William Sloane Coffin, *A Passion for the Possible: A Message to U.S. Churches* (Louisville, KY: Westminster/John Knox Press, 1993), 7–8.

Notes on Sources

For the full facts of publication for books, as well as those for encyclopedia, journal, and magazine articles, see the bibliography. The dates of newspaper articles are included within this section.

Prologue: East Tennessee Insights into Elusive Appalachia

A good starting point for getting a handle on Appalachian stereotypes is David Hsiung's chapter in Tyler Blethen and Richard Straw's *High Mountains Rising: Appalachians in Time and Place.* The editors' introduction to this book is also helpful on this front. Provocative treatment of regional stereotyping is the forte of Dwight Billings, Gurney Norman, and Katherine Ledford, editors of *Confronting Appalachian Stereotypes: Back Talk from an American Region.*

The origins of the word "Appalachia" are discussed briefly in David S. Wall's entry in Abramson and Haskell's *Encyclopedia of Appalachia.*

Karl Raitz and Richard Ulack offer a detailed account of cartographical differences in defining Appalachia in *Appalachia: A Regional Geography: Land, People, and Development.*

Ron Lewis's "Beyond Isolation and Homogeneity: Diversity and History of Appalachia" offers an excellent overview of the evolution of Appalachian studies. Alan Banks, Dwight Billings, and Kathleen Blee offer provocative reflections on current and future directions of our field in "Appalachian Studies, Resistance, and Postmodernism."

Complementing the Appalachian surveys by Richard Drake and John Alexander Williams is the late journalist John O'Brien's *At Home in the Heart of Appalachia,* an overview that incorporates many insights from thirty years of regional scholarship and presents them in accessible prose.

Completion of the *Encyclopedia of Appalachia* was a monumental achievement that will benefit our region for years to come. Editors Rudy Abramson (recently deceased) and Jean Haskell deserve accolades and appreciation for this notable achievement.

A more complete description of the course "History of East Tennessee and Southern Appalachia" is presented in my contribution to Sandra Hayslette and

Chad Berry's "AppalJ Roundtable Discussion: A Conversation About Teaching Appalachian Studies."

A particularly provocative work that affirms my preference for reimagining Appalachia, and which offers a refreshingly revisionist view of the diverse, dynamic dimensions of our region's culture and history, is journalist Jeff Biggers's *The United States of Appalachia: How Southern Mountaineers Brought Independence, Culture, and Enlightenment to America*.

After completely ignoring the region's urban enclaves for most of the past twenty-five years, Appalachian studies scholars are waking up to this important topic. See, for example, Emily Satterwhite's "Seeing Appalachian Cities." Phillip Obermiller and Michael Maloney's "Urban Appalachian Experience" insightfully discusses this important topic and points regional scholars in important new directions.

Durwood Dunn's *Cades Cove: The Life and Death of a Southern Appalachian Community, 1818–1937* is an outstanding example of the second phase of Appalachian studies and vital to my own efforts. Unique, personal insights from a descendant of longtime Cove residents are presented in Randolph Shields's *The Cades Cove Story*. Among the sources that helped me fill in the holes in the histories of Cades Cove and its neighboring Smokies communities are Ronald Lewis's *Transforming the Appalachian Countryside: Railroads, Deforestation, and Social Change in West Virginia, 1880–1920* and Michael Ann Williams's *Great Smoky Mountains Folklife*. Williams's insights into the complexities of tourism are particularly valuable.

John Gaventa's provocative insights into the devastating effects of the coal industry for the Clearfork Valley are presented in *Power and Powerlessness: Quiescence and Rebellion in an Appalachian Valley*, a book vital for parts 1 and 3 of this book. For a more general introduction to the Valley, see Bonnie Page's *Clearfork and More (History and Memories)*. For general insights into the effects of the coal industry, see Ron Eller's *Miners, Millhands, and Mountaineers: Industrialization of the Appalachian South, 1880–1930*, particularly chapters 4–6. Crandall Shifflett's *Coal Towns: Life, Work, and Culture in Company Towns of Southern Appalachia, 1880–1960* offers more positive views of the coal industry.

University of Tennessee historians Bruce Wheeler and (the late) Mike McDonald offered the first scholarly recounting of Knoxville's history in *Knoxville, Tennessee: Continuity and Change in an Appalachian City*. Wheeler completed a revised edition of the book in 2005 under the title *Knoxville, Tennessee: A Mountain City in the New South*. Wheeler and McDonald's essay "The Communities of East Tennessee, 1850–1940: An Interpretive Overview" is particularly relevant to the basic premises of this book. Often humorous insights into Knoxville's past can be found in journalist Jack Neely's regular "Knoxville's Secret History" columns in *Metro Pulse* and in his small volumes, *Knoxville's Secret History* and *Secret History II,* compiled from those pieces. His short piece "Who Are We?" (*Metro Pulse,* Feb. 26, 1993) offers a witty but forthright discussion of Knoxville's identity crises.

Several works sharpened my thinking on the intertwining of East Tennessee's various parts and influenced my contention that the whole is greater than the sum of its parts. Although William Cronon's *Nature's Metropolis: Chicago and the Great West* deals with a city and hinterland much grander than Knoxville and East Tennessee, his insights into how urban and rural areas relate (and do *not* relate) to one another helped clarify my thinking. Regarding rural and urban distinctions, Cronon observes that they are "labels for a single region and the relationship that defined it." By "erasing the false boundaries between themes," he asserts, we can begin to recover "their common pasts." Cynthia Duncan's *Worlds Apart: Why Poverty Persists in Rural America* also confirmed much of my thinking about how attitudes of more "successful Appalachians" can exacerbate—or ameliorate—economic and social conditions in a given region.

I first considered the concept of selective acculturation while engaged on my University of New Mexico doctoral dissertation, which focused on "cultural interaction in the Southwest." Rebecca Bailey's "'I Never Thought of My Life as History': A Story of the Hillbilly Exodus and the Price of Assimilation" introduced me to intragroup distinction. Subsequent conversations with Rebecca and other southwestern and Appalachian scholars have convinced me of the value of these concepts and of their relevance to this study, and have increased my general interest in cultural interaction.

Michael Montgomery's "Myths: How a Hunger for Roots Shapes Our Notions About Appalachian English," is also relevant to this discussion. At the time Montgomery wrote this piece, he was well on his way to completing the acclaimed *Dictionary of Smoky Mountain English,* begun by the late Joseph S. Hall. The dictionary is a virtually career-long work of particular significance to this study.

For a discussion of the divide between academic historians and genealogists, see Elizabeth Shown Mills's insightful essay, "Genealogy in the 'Information Age': History's New Frontier?" Mills, past president of the American Genealogical Society and immediate past editor of the *NGS Quarterly,* quotes several notable academic historians who share her belief that scholars and genealogists would mutually benefit from moving beyond longstanding differences.

In integrating my personal stories and attempting to share scholarly insights with more general readers, this book aspires to emulate John O'Brien's *At Home in the Heart of Appalachia.* However, readers familiar with that superb book should be mindful of notable differences between the two. Most important, O'Brien came to terms with his roots after years of hardship and personal angst. For me—and for most of my forebears—the opposite is true: our misfortune was good fortune.

I found encouragement and reassurance for my attempt to make this book accessible to a general audience in the writing of Patricia Nelson Limerick, a leading light in the history of the American West. Limerick addresses this issue with humor, wisdom, and conviction in part 5 of *Something in the Soil: Legacies and Reckonings in the New West* (319–43). Limerick's essay "What on Earth Is the New Western History?" reflects how much new trends in my PhD field of emphasis have influenced my understanding of Appalachia.

Part I. Before There Was an Appalachia

The word myth has, of course, many meanings. As my narrative suggests, I use myth as an idea that holds deep cultural significance for those who adhere to it, and that is rooted in fact. For provocative insight into this topic, see William H. McNeill's "Mythistory, or Truth, Myth, History, and Historians."

My account of my Grandmother Thomas's Morris/Brumit lineage draws from records passed down to me from my mother and from the following entries from *Carter County, Tennessee and Its People, 1796–1993:* entry 837, Edward Morris, Sr.; entry 095, David Vaughn Brumit, Sr.; entry 099, Brumit-Francis. I am indebted to Ginger Dillon, Archivist at Milligan College (my maternal grandparents' alma mater), for assisting me in the search for my Morris/Brumit roots.

Among the important general regional studies of preindustrial Appalachia appearing in recent years that have provided historical context for the experiences of my forebears and other antebellum East Tennesseans are Paul Salstrom's *Appalachia's Path to Dependency: Rethinking a Region's Economic History;* Wilma Dunaway's *The First American Frontier: Transition to Capitalism in Southern Appalachia;* and Durwood Dunn's *Cades Cove: Life and Death of a Southern Appalachian Community, 1818–1937,* which is the most thorough study of an East Tennessee community to date and invaluable for my efforts. Dunn's chapters 1–4 focus on the antebellum era. Analyses of the preindustrial era in other Appalachian subregions can be found in excerpts from broader works by Tyler Blethen and Curtis Wood (western North Carolina), Ronald Lewis and John Alexander Williams (West Virginia), and Dwight Billings and Kathleen Blee (eastern Kentucky), and in the aforementioned essays in *Appalachia in the Making.* In part 1, I draw from these broader Appalachian sources to fill holes and offer plausible explanations for developments that East Tennessee scholars have yet to explore adequately.

My account of my Grandmother Banker's Gibbs lineage draws from records my father passed down to me, and from pertinent sections from the genealogical guide, *Nicholas Gibbs and His Descendants, 1733–1977.* Mark Groover's *An Archaeological Study of Rural Capitalism and Material Life: The Gibbs Farmstead in Southern Appalachia, 1790–1920* is the most detailed study to date of an East Tennessee–Appalachian family and its property. Groover utilizes cutting-edge regional scholarship in his analysis of the physical remains of the Gibbs homestead. The book was a revelation to me, especially since many of my forebears are its primary focus.

My mother's first cousin, Aline Hardwick, genealogist extraordinaire, kindly shared with me letters written by Mitch Thomas, as well as much other valuable Thomas-family information. Thanks to my brother Tom, I became reacquainted with my mother's distant cousins, Val and John Green, when I returned to East Tennessee in 1987. Val and John each spent more than ninety years in a house at the foot of Brierpatch Mountain, just down the hill from the abandoned home of our mutual and distant grandfather, Wesley Thomas. As a historian, I should probably attempt to validate their story about Mitch refusing to sign an oath of allegiance to the United States, but to date I am content with the story as it is. Perhaps it is just as well that the facts not get in the way of a good story.

My account of my father's Banker ancestors draws from records he and my mother gathered on a trip to Michigan in the 1980s, and on genealogical information from the time his forebears settled in East Tennessee.

1. East Tennessee Beginnings

Ronald Satz's *Tennessee's Indian Peoples: From White Contact to Removal* offers a brief, general account of its subject. For insights into Cherokee history, I am particularly indebted to John Finger. His essays "Cherokee Accommodation and Resilience in the Southern Appalachians" and "Tennessee Indian History: Creativity and Power"—as well as portions of his book *Tennessee Frontiers*—insightfully analyze the complexities of Cherokee encounters with Europeans. Finger, in turn, is very much indebted to Richard White's book *The Middle Ground: Indians, Empires, and Republics in the Great Lakes Region, 1650–1815* for developing a theme essential to his work and to mine. Another author who contributed much to our understanding of Cherokee-white relations was the late William McLoughlin, whose *Cherokee Renascence in the New Republic* is particularly relevant to this discussion. Much has been written about Cherokee removal and the Trail of Tears. An accessible, popular account focusing on intratribal divisions between "progressives" and "traditionalists" is John Ehle's *Trail of Tears: The Rise and Fall of the Cherokee Nation.*

The introduction to Colin Calloway's *First Peoples: A Documentary Survey of American Indian History* offers a succinct introduction to recent developments in Indian historiography. For a provocative account offering many insights applicable to Appalachian studies, see Fergus Bordewich's *Killing the White Man's Indian: Reinventing Native Americans at the End of the Twentieth Century.* Bordewich, a journalist, makes the "new Indian history" accessible to nonscholarly audiences even as he challenges the political correctness of some of that scholarship.

For Cherokee legacies and influences on the emerging Appalachian culture, see the various aforementioned offerings of John Finger. Also see Donald Davis's *Where There Are Mountains: An Environmental History of the Southern Appalachians,* particularly chapters 5 and 6.

American fascination with the trans-Appalachian frontier is obviously part of our greater fascination with "the West." Frederick Jackson Turner's monumental 1893 essay, "The Significance of the Frontier in American History"—and the voluminous responses to it—explore this theme. This study's suggestions regarding "the mythical west" draw from Henry Nash Smith's venerable *Virgin Land: The American West as Symbol and Myth.* Richard Etulain, one of my University of New Mexico mentors, offers a superb recent update on the theme in *Re-Imagining the American West: A Century of Fiction, History, and Art.*

A solid general introduction to the question of Appalachian ethnicity is H. Tyler Blethen's "Pioneer Settlement" in *High Mountains Rising.* Blethen has also written extensively on Scots-Irish influences on Appalachian culture. See, for example, his essay "The Scotch-Irish Heritage on Southern Appalachia." James Webb's *Born Fighting: How the Scots-Irish Shaped America,* a recent account of the broader Scots-Irish imprint on the United States, makes scholarly insights accessible to popular audiences. For a provocative analysis of one distinct aspect of Scots-Irish (or "Celtic") influence on regional culture, see Forrest McDonald and Grady McWhiney's "The Antebellum Southern Herdsman: A Reinterpretation."

For a general discussion of the complexities of antebellum culture and economy, see chapters 7 and 8 of Finger (2001). John Solomon Otto provides many useful insights into what he calls the "stockman-farmer-hunter economy of the upland South" in "The Migration of the Southern Plain Folk: An Interdisciplinary Synthesis." Much has been written about the Appalachian log cabin. Two sources particularly relevant to my treatment of this topic are Terry Jordan and Matti Kaups's *The American Backwoods Frontier: An Ethnic and Ecological Interpretation* and John Morgan's *The Log House in East Tennessee.*

A standard account of frontier East Tennessee is John Caruso's *The Appalachian Frontier: America's First Surge Westward.* Recent emphasis on the role of land speculation in the region's early history is evident in the first several chapters of Finger (2001) and in Wilma Dunaway's "Speculators and Settler Capitalists: Unthinking the Mythology of Appalachian Landholding, 1790–1860." Dunaway expands on this theme in *The First American Frontier: Transition to Capitalism in Southern Appalachia, 1700–1860*. Pudup, Billings, and Waller's "Taking Exception with Exceptionalism: The Emergence and Transformation of Historical Studies of Appalachia" explores how insights from Appalachian studies challenge popular understandings of the region in the nineteenth century.

Part 2 of Deborah Vansau McCauley's *Appalachian Mountain Religion: A History* offers provocative insight into the roots and development of religion in antebellum Appalachia.

For a general introduction to early political developments in what became the state of Tennessee, see Finger (2001) and Paul Bergeron, Stephen Ash, and Jeanette Keith's *Tennesseans and Their History*. For general discussion of East Tennessee's frontier and antebellum economy and the question of isolation, see chapter 8 of Finger (2001). For a more focused analysis, see David Hsiung's "How Isolated Was Appalachia? Upper East Tennessee, 1780–1835." Other important recent studies of the antebellum Appalachian economy are Dunaway (1996) and Paul Salstrom's *Appalachia's Path to Dependency: Rethinking a Region's Economic History, 1730–1940*. Kevin Barksdale's recently published *The Lost State of Franklin: America's First Secession* fills an important void by addressing the puzzling political developments in 1780s East Tennessee.

Among the early commentators to emphasize Appalachia's yeoman origins was John C. Campbell in *The Southern Highlander and His Homeland*. Among Appalachian studies pioneers, Richard Drake has consistently emphasized a "yeoman thesis" in an array of publications and presentations. Drake offers a more qualified version of the yeoman thesis in his recently published *A History of Appalachia*. Wilma Dunaway's (1996) criticism of the yeoman thesis and of many popular notions about life in antebellum Appalachia is the most systematic and strident. An application of Dunaway's premises to East Tennessee can be found in Christopher Baker's "East Tennessee within the World Economy, 1790–1850: Pre-Capitalist Isolation or Peripheral Capitalism?" More balanced analyses are Blethen's "Pioneer Settlement"; appropriate portions of Finger (2001); Bergeron, Ash, and Keith (1996); and Lee Soltow's "Land Inequality on the Frontier: The Distribution of Land in East Tennessee at the Beginning of the 19th Century."

William J. MacArthur, *Knoxville's History: An Interpretation* is still the best scholarly introduction to Knoxville's early history. Also see Folmsbee and Deaderick's "The Founding of Knoxville." Popular, informative sources on Knoxville's early history are chapters 1–6 of Betsey Beeler Creekmore's *Knoxville!* Although dated, the essays in part 1 of Mary U. Rothrock's *The French Broad–Holston Country: A History of Knox County, Tennessee* are also useful. John

Finger (2001) discusses Knoxville's early development in the context of broader Tennessee patterns. Also see Samuel Cole Armstrong's "George Roulstone: Father of the Tennessee Press."

University of Tennessee anthropologist Charles Faulkner and his students have immensely increased knowledge about early life in Knoxville. See, for example, Faulkner's "'Here Are Frame Houses and Brick Chimneys': Knoxville, Tennessee in the Late Eighteenth Century" and "Knoxville and the Southern Appalachian Frontier: An Archaeological Perspective."

Many developments in early Knoxville fit general patterns for frontier cities that Richard Wade insightfully examines in the introductory chapter of *The Urban Frontier: Pioneer Life in Early Pittsburgh, Cincinnati, Lexington, Louisville, and Saint Louis*. Wade emphasizes, for example, that frontier cities preferred the grid layout to distinguish themselves from rural locales.

Jack Neely describes Blount's and White's real estate schemes in "Knoxvilles That Never Were" (*Metro Pulse*, Oct. 9, 1997). Scholars have largely ignored this colorful incident. Alice B. Keith devotes some attention to it in "Three North Carolina Blount Brothers in Business and Politics, 1783–1812."

Almost all accounts of early Knoxville recount the visit of Louis Philippe. Jack Neely offers a particularly colorful version of that story in "Bathing in the Holstein" (*Metro Pulse*, Apr. 24–May 1, 1997), as does Carson Brewer in "Distinguished Visitors. . . ." (*Knoxville New-Sentinel*, undated clipping, Brewer—1978 Articles, vertical file, McClung Collection, Knox County Public Library, Knoxville [hereafter abbreviated as MC]).

An outstanding examination of East Tennessee's conflicts with Middle and West Tennessee is Eric Russell Lacy's *Vanquished Volunteers: East Tennessee Sectionalism from Statehood to Secession*. LaReine Warden Clayton's "East Tennesseans Begin to Advertise" provides interesting snippets about early Knoxville's economy. A colorful account of the droving business is found in Edmund Cody Burnett's "Hog Raising and Hog Driving in the Region of the French Broad River." For that topic, also see McDonald and McWhiney (1975) and Donald Buckwalter's "Effects of Early Nineteenth Century Transportation Disadvantage on the Agriculture of Eastern Tennessee," which offers sober analysis of a topic too often distorted by exaggeration.

A firsthand account of Knoxville's 50th birthday celebration is presented in the *Knoxville Post*, Feb. 16, 1842 (a transcription is available in Knoxville History Through 1866, vertical file, MC). Journalist Barbara Aston-Walsh provides a recent, colorful account of that event in "Knoxville Partied at 50 . . ." (*Knoxville News-Sentinel*, October 3, 1991).

The first significant account of Cove life was Randolph Shields's "Cades Cove in the Great Smoky Mountain National Park." His *The Cades Cove Story* is more complete. Outstanding local historian Inez Burns also wrote several solid accounts of Cove life in "Settlement and Early History of the Coves of Blount County, Tennessee." For firsthand insights into antebellum Cove life, see A Mountaineer in Motion: The Memoir of Dr. Abraham Jobe, 1817–1906, edited by David C. Hsiung, and the unpublished memoir "The Hatcher Papers (1793–1898)," a photocopy of which is preserved (along with a copy of Dr. Jobe's original memoir) in the vertical file of the Library of Great Smoky Mountains National Park.

My account of the initial settlement and life in the Cove up to the Civil War draws primarily from chapters 1–4 of Dunn's *Cades Cove*. Also see "Early Iron Works Flourished Till 1840s in the Smokies" (*Knoxville News-Sentinel*, May 27, 1956).

A wide body of scholarship has examined the discrepancies in the self-identification of Appalachian residents and standard geographical definitions of the region. See, for example, Raitz and Ulack (1984). Michael Montgomery, a fellow East Tennessean, reflects on this influence on his broader concerns about the nature of "Appalachian English" in his essay, "Myths" (2000, 7–13).

John Gaventa's (1982) scholarly analysis of the Clearfork Valley informs latter parts of this study. Reflecting the state of scholarship when he completed that work (the late 1970s), Gaventa did not question notions about "pioneer Appalachia." Bonnie Page's compilation, *Clearfork and More*, is a valuable source for this entire project. The extended quote on page 30 is from her introduction. Another similar source, which largely affirms traditional assumptions about the region's pioneer era, is Miller McDonald's three edited volumes, *Campbell County, Tennessee USA: A History of Places, Faces, Happenings, Traditions, and Things*.

Paul Salstrom's contributions to our understanding of mid-nineteenth-century Appalachia are notable. For specific aspects of his thesis relevant to this chapter, see his essays, "The Agricultural Origins of Appalachian Dependency" and "Newer Appalachia as One of America's Last Frontiers." These and other ideas are more fully developed in his book, *Appalachia's Path to Dependency*.

Critics of the "yeoman thesis" utilize methods and perspectives developed by the "new social history." Wilma Dunaway has been the most vocal and general of these critics. Others who have focused on specific Appalachian locales have more or less shared her skepticism and raised valid objections to the "yeoman thesis" as an explanation for Appalachian development. These scholars (and the subregions they have examined) include Robert Mitchell and Warren Hofstra (Virginia's Shenandoah Valley), Tyler Blethen and Curtis Wood (western North Carolina), and Tyrel Moore and Mary Beth Pudup (eastern Kentucky). Durwood Dunn and David Hsiung express concerns about applying the "yeoman thesis" to East Tennessee. The introduction to the volume *Appalachia in the Making* summarizes revisionist objections to the "yeoman thesis." The same volume contains essays by many of the scholars mentioned above.

Richard Drake's career-culminating survey, *A History of Appalachia* (2001), offers a nuanced yet determined response to revisionist thinking on the yeoman thesis. Another recently completed regional survey, John Alexander Williams's *Appalachia: A History* (2002), offers a balanced stance that artfully avoids the extremes on both sides of this debate. John Finger's *Tennessee Frontiers* (2001), the most thorough and informed history of frontier East Tennessee, offers a similar view.

David Hsiung's *Two Worlds in the Tennessee Mountains: Exploring the Origins of Appalachian Stereotypes* offers valuable insights into perceptions and self-perceptions of East Tennesseans from the Revolutionary era to the mid-nineteenth century and persuasively argues that although Appalachian images occasionally circulated in this era, neither outsiders nor regional residents embraced them. To a significant extent, Dunaway's *First American Frontier* affirms that assessment.

2. Mid-Nineteenth-Century Crises

Although he is not typically identified with Appalachian studies, John Solomon Otto was one of the first scholars to deal systematically with the region in its frontier and antebellum eras. He commented on the harmful effects of partible inheritance in "The Migration of the Southern Plain Folks" (196). Appalachian scholars who have attributed the region's pre–Civil War woes to partible inheritance include Wilma Dunaway, Richard Drake, John Alexander Williams, and Paul Salstrom.

Groover uses the term "rural patrimony" to describe the tactics used by the likes of Nicholas and Daniel Gibbs to maintain cohesion in their families and retain ownership of family-owned lands. I have drawn in particular from chapters 3 and 10 of his *An Archaeological Study of Rural Capitalism* in my treatment of the Gibbs family. For an insightful study of changes in regional architecture that reflected aspirations to appear more modern, see Charles E. Martin's *Hollybush: Folk Building and Change in an Appalachian Community.*

Dunn explores demographic trends in pre–Civil War Cades Cove in chapter 3 of *Cades Cove.*

Salstrom introduces "newer Appalachia" and discusses the crises it faced in the years immediately before and after the Civil War in chapters 1 and 2 of *Appalachia's Path to Dependency.*

For general comments on antebellum East Tennessee's proclivities for mobility, see John Finger's *Tennessee Frontiers* (particularly chapters 7 and 10) and Bergeron, Ash, and Keith's *Tennesseans and Their History*, chapter 5.

A good introduction to the Tennessee-Texas connections can be found in the essays in Herbert L. Harper's *Houston and Crockett: Heroes of Tennessee and Texas*. East Tennessee native Crockett had, of course, relocated to West Tennessee before going to Texas in 1835.

Hugh Heiskell's edited diary was published—with an introduction by Edward Steel—as *A Forty-Niner from Tennessee*. Jack Neely offers a lighthearted yet informative introduction to Heiskell in "The Forty-niner" (*Metro Pulse*, Apr. 22, 1999).

Western scholars have devoted far more attention to Walker's career than have Tennessee writers. See, for example, Bil Gilbert's *Westering Man: The Life of Joseph Walker*. A brief account from a Tennessee writer is Ed Hopper's "The Mountain Man from Tennessee" (*Tennessee Star Journal*, Feb. 22–28, 2002).

General discussion of economic modernization and the market revolution in the antebellum United States can be found in all standard U.S. history survey texts. Two I have used in recent years are Alan Brinkley's *The Unfinished Nation: A Concise History of the American People* (chapters 10 and 11 in particular) and James West Davidson's *Nation of Nations: A Concise Narrative History of the American Republic—Volume I: to 1877* (245–68). A dated but still valuable and more detailed account is Douglas C. North's *The Economic Growth of the United States, 1790–1860*.

Ron Lewis's overview essay, "Industrialization," in Blethen and Straw's *High Mountains Rising* is a solid introduction to general economic developments in mid-nineteenth-century Appalachia. Wilma Dunaway's *First American Frontier* offers the most thorough, if controversial, account of Appalachia's mid-nineteenth-century economic misfortunes. See, for example, pages: 80–81; 87–121; 258–62; and 288–89.

A dated but useful overview of economic developments in antebellum East Tennessee is presented in chapters 7, 8, and 9 of Rothrock's *The French Broad–Holston Country*.

Many scholars have commented in recent years on growing inequities in antebellum East Tennessee. In addition to Dunaway, also see: Lee Soltow (1981); Fred A. Bailey's "Tennessee's Antebellum Common Folk"; and Robert Tracy McKenzie's "Wealth and Income: The Preindustrial Structure of East Tennessee."

For a general discussion of early manufacturing and extractive industries in East Tennessee, see Rothrock (1946, chapter 8) and Finger (2001, chapter 8).

Susanna Delfino offers more detailed coverage in two insightful essays, "Many Souths: Changing Social Contexts and the Road to Industrialization in Antebellum East Tennessee" and "Antebellum East Tennessee Elites and Industrialization."

The contributions of altruistic reform rhetoric to what eventually became negative images of rural East Tennesseans foreshadowed the effect of Home Missionary promotional literature that I examine in part 2, and which Henry J. Shapiro suggested was a key influence on the Appalachian stereotypes that emerged in the era around 1870–1920.

For general scholarly accounts of East Tennessee's steamboat era, see: Finger (2001); Rothrock (1996); Jack Neely's "The Port of Knoxville" (*Metro Pulse*, Apr. 11–18, 1996); Fred Brown's "Knoxville's First Steamboat Made Town Happy, Hopeful" (*Knoxville New-Sentinel*, undated clipping, Fred Brown, 1994–96, vertical file, MC); and Ray Brooks's "Steamboat 'Round the Bend" (*Knoxville Journal*, Apr. 28, 1940).

Scholars have devoted considerable attention to East Tennessee railroad promotion. See, for example: Finger (2001, 201–2); MacArthur (1978, 18–20); and Hsiung (1997, 158). The standard, but dated, account is Stanley J. Folmsbee's "The Beginnings of the Railroad Movement in East Tennessee."

Hsiung's *Two Worlds in the Tennessee Mountains* is also an excellent source for information on how regional elites contributed to Appalachian stereotypes. A shorter version of his argument, with greater emphasis on regional stereotypes (and less attention on East Tennessee), can be found in his chapter on stereotypes in Straw and Blethen's *High Mountains Rising*. Dunaway's assertions regarding Appalachia's growing economic divisions in the pre–Civil War era nicely complement and confirm Hsiung's contentions.

For a general account of Tennessee politics in this era, see chapter 5 of *Tennesseans and Their History* (Bergeron, Ash, and Keith 1996). Solid analyses of East Tennessee's conflicts with Middle and West Tennessee, and its role in the broader issues of sectionalism, can be found in *Vanquished Volunteers* (Lacy 1965), especially chapters 2–5. Other insights on political developments from an East Tennessee perspective are offered by: MacArthur (1978, 16–18); and Rothrock (1946, 38–40). Two scholars who offer more in-depth coverage of East Tennessee antebellum politics are Jonathan Atkins and Craig Brashear. See, for example, Atkins's "Politicians, Parties, and Slavery: The Second Party System and Decision for Disunion in Tennessee"; and Brashear's "The Market Revolution and Party Preference in East Tennessee."

The pioneering Appalachian studies work on slavery and racism in the mountain South was a volume of essays edited by William Turner and Edward Cabbell, *Blacks in Appalachia*. John Inscoe of the University of Georgia has done more than any other scholar to probe many of the issues raised in that pathbreaking volume, and to encourage other scholars to explore regional slavery and racism. Inscoe's *Mountain Masters: Slavery and the Sectional Crisis in Western North Carolina* is *the* model study of Appalachian slavery. Since publication of that work, Inscoe has made many notable contributions to the debate he helped initiate. His introduction to *Appalachians and Race: The Mountain South from Slavery to Segregation,* and the essays he edited for that volume, are essential to the insights offered here. Wilma Dunaway recently offered her provocative insight in *Slavery in the American Mountain South.*

Specific knowledge about slavery in East Tennessee is spotty and sketchy. See, for example, Finger's *Tennessee Frontiers* (2001), Lacy's *Vanquished Volunteers* (1965), and the edited volumes on East Tennessee by Rothrock (1946) and Deaderick (1976). John Cimprich offers the most thorough scholarly discussion of the topic in *Slavery's End in Tennessee, 1861–1865.*

Richard Drake, a notable Appalachian studies pioneer, devoted much attention to Appalachian antislavery efforts before the topic became fashionable. In an updated version of his classic essay, "Slavery and Anti-Slavery in Appalachia," Drake devotes considerable attention to the complexities of East Tennessee antislavery. Also see Lawrence B. Goodheart's "Tennessee's Antislavery Movement Reconsidered: The Example of Elihu Embree."

The inclination of many non–slave holding southerners to support the "peculiar institution" is explored in practically every U.S. history textbook. See, for example, Brinkley (2004, 289–91) and Davidson (1998, 333–35).

The most thorough one-volume account of Tennessee's antebellum politics is Jonathan Atkins's *Parties, Politics, and Sectional Conflict in Tennessee, 1832–1861.* For more general accounts, see Lacy's *Vanquished Volunteers* and chapter 5 of Bergeron, Ash, and Keith (1996).

Informative biographies of Andrew Johnson and Parson Brownlow can be found in Hans L. Trefousse's *Andrew Johnson: A Biography* and E. Merton Coulter's *William G. Brownlow: Fighting Parson of the Southern Highlands.* Also see Thomas B. Alexander's "Strange Bedfellows: The Interlocking Careers of T. A. R. Nelson, Andrew Johnson, and W. G. (Parson) Brownlow." For a more general account of Tennessee Politics in the tumultuous 1850s, see chapter 5 of Bergeron, Ash, and Keith (1996).

General accounts of the 1860 election and secession crisis in Appalachia and East Tennessee can be found in: McKinney's "Civil War and Reconstruction"; Drake's *A History of Appalachia* (293–95); Bergeron, Ash, and Keith's *Tennesseans and Their History* (132–35); and Lacy's *Vanquished Volunteers* (170–77).

Digby Seymour's *Divided Loyalties: Fort Sanders and the Civil War in East Tennessee* is *the* standard account of military and political aspects of the Civil War in East Tennessee. Seymour provides extensive coverage of the war in the

Cumberland Gap. For more on the war in that area (including the Clearfork Valley), see Gregory Miller's *The Civil War in Campbell County*. The "Campbell County" vertical file in the McClung Collection contains a series of articles Guy Easterly wrote for *The LaFollette Press* at the time of the Civil War centennial, which provide details about fighting in and around the Clearfork Valley.

A number of more recent works have refined Seymour's treatment of the war in East Tennessee and focus on more than just military matters. Among these, three of the most important are Charles F. Bryan's "The Civil War in East Tennessee: A Social, Political, and Economic Study"; W. Todd Groce's *Mountain Rebels: East Tennessee Confederates and the Civil War;* and Shannon Wilson and Kenneth Noe's *The Civil War in Appalachia*.

General accounts of the Greeneville Convention and the Bridge Burner activities can be found in Bergeron, Ash, and Keith (139–41). Also see David Madden's "Unionist Resistance to Confederate Occupation: The Bridge Burners of East Tennessee" and Cameron Judd's *The Bridge Burners: A True Adventure of East Tennessee's Underground Civil War*.

A superb overall assessment of the war's economic and emotional impact can be found in Robert Tracy McKenzie's "'Oh! Ours is a Deplorable Condition': The Economic Impact of the Civil War in Upper East Tennessee." McKenzie's *Lincolnites and Rebels: A Divided Town in the American Civil War* offers a thorough scholarly analysis of the war's many facets in Knoxville.

The siege of Knoxville and the war's overall impact on the emerging hub city of East Tennessee is recounted in many places, but nowhere in more depth than in Seymour's *Divided Loyalties*. The McClung Collection's vertical files on the Civil War contain many informative clippings describing the siege of Knoxville from an array of partisan perspectives. A superb firsthand account is "The Siege of Knoxville: Graphic Description of the Siege," written by Union Captain Fred W. Smith of Detroit (undated clipping, Knoxville History Through 1929). Smith describes the days leading up to Longstreet's assault on Ft. Sanders, the assault itself, and its aftermath from the perspective of the "everyday soldier" he considered the conflict's true heroes.

A superb general account of guerilla activity in Civil War East Tennessee is Noel C. Fisher's *War at Every Door: Partisan Politics and Guerilla Violence in East Tennessee, 1860–1869*. Durwood Dunn vividly recounts the war's effects on Cades Cove and particularly the pervasive guerilla activities there in chapter 5 of *Cades Cove*. Fisher has done the same for the Smokies in his book, *The Civil War in the Smokies*. Readers who prefer fiction can find many informative and generally accurate accounts of guerilla activities along the East Tennessee–Western North Carolina border country in Wilma Dykeman's *The Tall Woman*, Charles Frazier's *Cold Mountain* (also made into an acclaimed film), and Sharyn McCrumb's *Ghost Riders*.

Notes on Sources

General introductions to Reconstruction are offered in all standard U.S. history texts. See, for example, chapter 15 of Brinkley (2004) and chapter 17 of Davidson (1998). Eric Foner's *Reconstruction: America's Unfinished Revolution, 1863–1877* offers a needed corrective to many of the most negative (largely pro-southern) assessments of Reconstruction, but no scholar has yet attempted to apply those important revisionist insights to the Reconstruction drama as it played out in East Tennessee and southern Appalachia. For standard accounts of the latter, see Drake (2001, 112–15); McKinney (2004); and chapter 7 of Bergeron, Ash and Keith (1996).

The assertion that geographical limitations and the practice of partible inheritance contributed even more than the Civil War to East Tennessee's postwar woes is persuasively argued in McKenzie (2001, 208–25). Salstrom makes the same argument in *Appalachia's Path to Dependency*.

Part II. Appalachia Discovered

I return several times to the themes of "urban," "invisible," and "successful" Appalachians. At this point, a few brief comments beyond what I said in these notes at the end of the "Prologue" section will suffice. First, for most readers, the words "urban Appalachians" are contradictory. Scholars, on the other hand, have used the term since the 1980s, but until very recently "urban Appalachian" referred to regional residents who relocated to large urban centers in the North and Midwest from the early days of World War II until around 1970. The term also refers to their descendants, who remain in places like Cincinnati, Dayton, Chicago, and Detroit today.

The classic study of the discovery of Appalachia is Henry Shapiro's *Appalachia on our Mind: The Southern Mountains and Mountaineers in the American Consciousness, 1870–1920.* Shapiro thoroughly examines the contributions of home missions, promotional materials, and local color literature in creating distinctive "Appalachian" images in the American mind at the turn of the century.

A good starting place for understanding the formal education my grandparents were exposed to in the early twentieth century are the early chapters of Lawrence Cremin's *American Education.* The Bristol that became my grandparents' home is the 1920s is one of the foci of Tom Lee's *The Tennessee-Virginia Tri-Cities.*

Anthony Harkins's *Hillbilly: A Cultural History of an American Icon* thoroughly examines Paul Webb's "mountain boy" cartoons.

Phil Obermiller, who has devoted his career to exploring the experiences of Appalachian out-migration, offered valuable insight into the process of intragroup distinction when he observed that "the strongest negative images of Appalachians are held by middle class persons of Appalachian origins" (1987, 39–40). Although Obermiller was speaking specifically about "urban Appalachian" residents of cities in the Midwest and North, I believe his observation is relevant to the behavior of my grandparents and to many other "successful" Appalachians.

The process of selective acculturation offers strikingly new insights into the complex dynamics of cultural interaction and deserves more attention from scholars and the general public than it has received. I became aware of it when I completed my doctoral work at the University of New Mexico and explored the experiences of Native Americans and *Hispanos.*

The related process of intragroup distinction is also very relevant for this discussion. Rebecca Bailey's provocative essay "I Never Thought of My Life as History" first made me consider how intragroup distinction has influenced the course of Appalachian history and helps explain the experiences of "successful Appalachians" such as my own forebears.

3. Queen City of the Mountains

Knoxville's postwar miseries and resurgence are recounted in many places. See, for example, Alfred Grey and Susan Adams's chapter on government in Deaderick's *Heart of the Valley.* Jack Neely's columns in *Metro Pulse* offer vivid insights into little-known aspects of Knoxville's history. The 1867 flood is the focus of "The Turbid Waters" (Mar. 21, 2002); Neely mentions the 1869 fire in "From Their Own Green Hills," a column on the city's Irish population (Mar. 13, 2003). Neely also offers insights into Knoxville's turn-of-the-century optimism. See, for example, "Concentrate" (May 15–22, 1997) and "Century's Start: A Colorful Walk Through the Streets of Knoxville c. 1900" (Dec. 9, 1999).

The phrase "Queen City of the Mountains" was just one of many catchy titles utilized by Knoxville's late nineteenth-century boosters. Jennifer Brooks examines these promotional efforts and their effects in "'One Grand United Hymn': Boosterism in Knoxville, Tennessee at the Turn of the Century."

Of the many commentators on Knoxville's history during this important era, William MacArthur most clearly saw the importance of the city's economic ties with outlying areas, which he addresses briefly and speculatively in *Knoxville's History* (23–45). MacArthur completed that extended essay in 1978, just as Appalachian studies scholars were beginning to examine economic developments in rural settings, such as East Tennessee's hinterlands. Unfortunately no one has since explored the connections MacArthur suggested were critical to Knoxville's economic surge.

Wheeler and McDonald's essay "The Communities of East Tennessee" is particularly relevant to concerns about connections between Knoxville and East Tennessee hinterlands raised in chapters 3 and 4.

I have noted elsewhere the longstanding neglect by Appalachian studies scholars of urban centers within the Appalachian region and of Knoxville in particular. Phil Obermiller and Michael Maloney (2006) offer evidence that this is beginning to change. Tom Lee's *The Tennessee-Virginia Tri-Cities: Urbanization in Appalachia, 1900–1950* offers proof of the importance of urbanization within the Appalachian region and provides a model for examining it.

The standard assessment of American antimodernism is T. J. Jackson Lears's *No Place of Grace: Anti-Modernism and the Transformation of American Culture, 1880–1920*. Other works relevant to that topic will be cited in chapter 5.

My probing into the rural-urban dichotomy led to an array of provocative works, including Raymond Williams's *The City and the Country;* Leo Marx's *The Machine in the Garden: Technology and the Pastoral Ideal in America;* Robert M. Potter and Tim Unwin's *The Geography of Urban-Rural Interaction in Developing Countries;* Michael M. Bell's "The Fruit of Difference: The Rural-Urban Continuum as a System of Identity"; and David Hummon's "City Mouse, Country Mouse: The Persistence of Community Identity."

I am most indebted to William Cronon for *Nature's Metropolis: Chicago and the Great West.* Potter and Unwin (1989) affirm Cronon's insights. "All too often," they write, "urban and rural have been dealt with as if they denote entirely dichotomous categories." "In reality," they conclude, "they are but two sides of the same coin."

Alan Batteau's *The Invention of Appalachia* elaborated on many of the ideas first offered by Shapiro.

The statistics regarding Knoxville's population growth are drawn from the U.S. Census: 1880, 1890, 1900, 1910, 1920, as presented by Jennifer Brooks (1991, 8–102). Also see table 1, "Population Trends, 1795–1970," and table 3, "Knoxville and Knox County Population Change" in Gray and Adams (1976).

Rothrock (1946, 220–32) offers a general account of Knoxville's post–Civil War economy. Kathleen Johnson offers a more detailed and sophisticated account of the economic surge of the 1880s in "'The City of Tomorrow with the Spirit of the Past': Bankrolling the Industrial Development of Knoxville, Tennessee, 1875–1907" (42–46).

For general introduction to the subject of the "New South," see Brinkley (2004, 419–26). The classic detailed study of the subject is C. Vann Woodward's *The Origins of the New South, 1877–1913*. A provocative recent account is Edward Ayers's *The Promise of the New South*. As his subtitle suggests, Bruce Wheeler's

Knoxville, Tennessee: A Mountain City of the New South emphasizes Knoxville's development as a "New South city."

The history of the array of railroad lines that came to Knoxville and East Tennessee in the latter nineteenth century is complex and confusing. MacArthur (1978, 43–44) offers a good introduction. Also see Rothrock (1946, 227–33); Patton's "Transportation Development"; and Briscoe's "Commerce and Industry."

Chapter 16 (C. E. Allread, "Farming from 1860 to 1900," 186–202), from Rothrock's *The French Broad–Holston Country* offers an excellent discussion of East Tennessee's agricultural resources in the latter nineteenth century. Chapter 18 of that same volume (C. P. White, "Commercial and Industrial Trends since 1865," 220–25) and Briscoe (1976) address East Tennessee's timber and mineral resources and related extractive industries.

The careers of Knoxville's Gilded Age entrepreneurs have been told in many places. For general accounts, see appropriate sections of MacArthur (1976), Rothrock (1946), Deaderick (1976), Creekmore (1991), and Wheeler (1983). For exhaustive treatment of McGhee's career, see William MacArthur's "Charles McClung McGhee: Southern Financier." Perez Dickinson's career is recounted thoroughly by Creekmore (1991). The careers of Sanford, Albers, William and Hiram Chamberlain, and Peter Kern are addressed briefly by MacArthur (1978, 32–33) and by Wheeler (1983, 14–17). A brief summary of Kern's notable career is presented in the appendix of Rothrock (1946, 436–37).

Bruce Wheeler explores the ideological outlook of Knoxville's elite (1983, 17). Kathleen Johnson (1994) emphasizes the cautious, conservative nature of leadership of Knoxville's Mechanics' National Bank. See, for example, her conclusion and particularly page 72.

Secondary resources addressing Knoxville's demographics and, in particular, rural in-migration to the city include Rothrock (1946, 221); Wheeler (1983, 22–27); and Wheeler and McDonald (1986, 27–29). An interesting contemporary assessment of these developments is found in the articles "Tendency of People is to Go to Cities" and "East Tennessee Outstrips other Grand Divisions" (author unknown, *Knoxville Sentinel,* December 11, 1910, vertical file, MC).

The best general account of Knoxville's post–Civil War economic development is MacArthur (1978, 30–45). For more details, see Rothrock (1946, 220–32), and Wheeler (1983, 18).

Knoxville's responses to the challenges of urbanization are recounted in many places. Brooks (1991) exhaustively examines debates regarding the city's water services. Mark V. Wetherington offers a fascinating and perceptive overview in "Streetcar City: Knoxville, Tennessee, 1876–1947." For a more general account, see Rothrock (1946, chapter 23). Religious developments in Knoxville are explored in Rothrock (1946, chapter 22).

Educational developments in Knoxville are explored in Rothrock (1946, chapter 21) For an interesting account of the University of Tennessee's leadership in educational reform, see: James Montgomery's "The Summer School of the South." For the development of Knoxville's public library system, see Rothrock (1946, chapter 20). The history of Staub Opera House and the appearance of other theaters in the city are explored by G. Allan Yeomans and Paul L. Soper, "The Theatre." Also see John K. Thomas's "The Cultural Reconstruction of an Appalachian City: Knoxville, Tennessee and the Coming of the Movies."

The attitudes of Knoxvillians toward their rural neighbors is explored by Joe Cummings in "Community and the Nature of Change: Sevier County, Tennessee, in the 1890s." Cummings relates Knoxvillians' tendency to look disparagingly on hinterland residents' response to the broader effects of the progressive impulse, and he cites Robert Wiebe's highly acclaimed *The Search for Order* to support that contention.

Jack Neely describes the "million dollar fire" and Knoxvillians' response to it in "The Fire of 1897" (*Metro Pulse,* Apr. 3–9, 1997).

Wheeler and McDonald are the most vocal critics of the leadership of the second generation of Knoxville's post–Civil War business leadership. See, in particular, Wheeler (2005, 29–33). William MacArthur (1978, 60) and Kathleen Johnson (1994) call for a more nuanced understanding of Knoxville's gradual decline in the first decades of the twentieth century.

To date, no scholar has devoted significant attention to the "Prophet of Smokies." But journalists have often told his story. See Jack Neely's "The Prophet" (*Metro Pulse,* Oct. 4, 2001); Fred Brown's "Prophet of Smokies" (*Knoxville News-Sentinel,* July 19, 1992); and Robert Williams's "Judge Bob Recalls . . ." (*Knoxville News-Sentinel,* Mar. 30, 1947).

Robert Lukens has extensively investigated Knoxville's expositions. His essay "The New South on Display" examines, in particular, the Appalachian Expos of 1910 and 1911. As the title suggests, his "Portraits of Progress in New South Appalachia: Three Expositions in Knoxville, Tennessee, 1910–1913" focuses on all three of the expos.

James Burran's "A Labor Conflict in Urban Appalachia: The Knoxville Street Car Strike of 1919" examines labor unrest in Knoxville in the post–World War I era. There are many accounts of the Gay Street race riot of 1919. Robert Booker's *Heat of a Red Summer: Race Mixing, Race Rioting in 1919 Knoxville* is a brief, accessible, still-thorough account. Also see, Lester C. Lamon's "Tennessee Race Relations and the Knoxville Race Riot of 1919." For a perceptive analysis of the broader contexts and legacies of the riot, see John H. Stanfield's "The Sociohistorical Roots of White/Black Inequality in Urban Appalachia: Knoxville and East Tennessee."

Oliver was outspoken in his criticism of Knoxville's shortsighted business leadership. See Wheeler (2005, 32). For interesting commentary on a youthful James Agee's disdain for his home city, see Jack Neely's "Knoxton High" (*Metro Pulse*, undated clipping, Newspaper Columnist: Neely, Jack, vertical file, MC).

Louis Brownlow was a distant relative of Civil War–era firebrand "Parson Brownlow." His tirade against Monday reveals that he shared some of the Parson's penchant for fiery prose. Brownlow's harsh view of Knoxville's rural in-migrants is presented in his autobiography and is recounted in Wheeler (2005, 27). The same book presents a lengthy account of the clash between Brownlow and Monday—from a decidedly pro-Brownlow perspective (39–44).

4. New South Realities

Although it is admittedly one-sided, chapter 6 from Ron Eller's *Miners, Millhands, and Mountaineers* offers an informed introduction to Gilded Age Appalachian entrepreneurs: their backgrounds, business practices, worldviews, and attitudes toward regional natives. For a more positive view of the "coal barons," see Crandall Shifflett's *Coal Towns.*

A persuasive analysis of the various ways regional residents adapted to and sometimes resisted these developments is found in Dwight Billings, Kathleen Blee, and Louis Swanson's "Culture, Family, and Community in Preindustrial Appalachia."

A solid, insightful examination of Appalachian studies scholarship since the seminal work of Ron Eller can be found in Ron Lewis (1999).

Longtime Knoxville journalist Vic Weals deserves much credit for recounting and saving many stories from the region's past. He was particularly interested in the pre–national park culture in the Smokies. Two of his articles, "Cove Lumber Plentiful" (*Knoxville Journal,* Jan. 7, 1982) and "Oak and Yellow Poplar Eldorado's Gold" (*Knoxville Journal,* Jan. 14 1982), offer useful insights into lumbering by Cades Cove residents. For more scholarly treatment, see Dunn (1988, 225–27).

A good introduction to timbering in the Clearfork region is presented in "Some of the Country's Finest Virgin Timber Came from Duff," collected in Miller McDonald (1991–93, vol. 3: 9–14).

Logging in the Smokies has received much attention from both scholars and popular observers. A good, brief overview is presented by Janet Winters in "Logging Important Prior to the Park," *Maryville Daily Times,* (Feb. 24, 1984). Ronald Schmidt and William Hooks deserve special accolades for *Whistle over the Mountain: Timber, Tracks, and Trails in the Tennessee Smokies.* Hook's informative and accessible narrative—and an array of photos and Schmidt's pen-

and-ink illustrations—make this an invaluable book for anyone interested in the intricacies of this topic.

Robert S. Lambert offers the most extensive scholarly analyses of Smokies timbering. See, for example: "Logging on the Little River, 1890–1940" and "Logging in the Great Smokies, 1880–1930." Two other useful sources available in the national park library's vertical file are: Randy Cullom's "Early Logging in the Great Smoky Mountain National Park: Little River Lumber Company" and Lee Barnes's "Appalachian Logging."

Olin Watson and former Great Smoky Mountain National Park historian Ed Trout offer a particularly human face to the timbering story in their contributions to *The Gentle Winds of Change: A History of Sevier County, Tennessee, 1900–1930.*

Florence Cope Bush's *Dorie: Woman of the Mountains* is particularly informative about the Smokies timber industry and its costs. Dorie, the author's mother, grew up in the Smokies during this important transitional era. Her husband, Fred Cope, was a Little River employee, and they lived together in several of the company's timber camps. Bush's detailed and forthright description of her parents' (and grandparents') experiences make this a valuable book.

An accessible overview revealing how timbering in the Smokies fit into broader, forest-related matters in greater Appalachia is Barry Buxton and Malinda Crutchfield's *The Great Forest: An Appalachian Story.*

Most of the information about the routine and daily life of loggers is from chapter 5 of *The Gentle Winds of Change,* and from articles by Vic Weals, which can be found in the "Logging" and "Vic Weals" vertical files of the McClung Collection. A collection of Weals's articles were published in *The Last Train to Elkmont: A Look Back at Life on Little River in the Great Smoky Mountains.*

Almost all accounts of the Little River Lumber Company's relationships with its employees suggest the latter were overall very contented with their lot. See, for example, Schmidt and Hooks (1994, 139) and Bush (1992).

Townsend's relationship with wealthy Knoxvillians and the circumstances that led to the advent of tourism in Elkmont are controversial topics that have received much, rather contradictory, attention from scholars and others. More detailed citations will accompany treatment of these topics and the broader theme of antimodernism in chapter 5. A recent balanced and objective account is Mary Fanslow's "From Timbering to Tourism."

For a clear and objective account of the complex transactions leading to the creation of Great Smoky Mountains National Park, see Virgil F. Carmichael's "The Acquisition of Land in the Creation of the Great Smoky Mountains National Park."

Appalachian studies scholars have examined the timber industry in a number of broader contexts, and these studies overall suggest the situation in the Smokies was not unique. For a good general overview, see Davis (2000). Ron Lewis (1998) offers a thorough analysis of the effects of logging in West Virginia.

Growing support for "conservation" and the movement to create Great Smoky Mountain National Park have received considerable attention in recent years. Two thorough studies are Daniel Pierce's *The Great Smokies: From Natural Habitat to National Park* and Margaret Lynn Brown's *The Wild East: A Biography of the Great Smoky Mountains.*

For general information regarding Tennessee's early coal industry, see James Fickle's "Mining." Ron Eller (1982, 127–32) outlines the defining characteristics of the first phase of Appalachian coal mining. A fascinating firsthand account from the pioneer era is reported by Major E. E. McCroskey in "Our Coals: An Exhaustive Paper Before the Chamber of Commerce" (*Knoxville Daily Tribune,* Apr. 17, 1892) McCroskey, an early coal promoter, offers his views on the state of the industry and its future. An informative, more recent article is James B. Jones Jr.'s "Coal Mining in the Cumberland Plateau, 1850–1920."

Even though few Tennesseans know the colorful and important story of the Coal Creek Rebellion, it has received considerable attention from both popular writers and scholars. Perry Cotham offers a solid, brief account of the rebellion in *Toil, Turmoil, and Triumph: A Portrait of the Tennessee Labor Movement* (56–79). Also see A. C. Hutson Jr.'s "The Overthrow of the Convict Lease System in Tennessee." For a clearly pro-miner account that includes many firsthand comments from locals and descendants of participants in the rebellion, see Fran Ansley and Brenda Bell's "Miner's Insurrections / Convict Labor." The most thorough academic analysis of the rebellion is Karin Shapiro's *A New South Rebellion: The Battle Against Convict Labor in the Tennessee Coalfields.*

The activities of the American Association and the rise and fall of Middlesboro are examined in Eller (1982, 81–85) and Gaventa (1982, 7–86).

The historiography of Appalachian coal during the industrial era is vast, as the bibliographies of any of the following books will reveal. Gaventa (1982) is the most in-depth study of the industry in the Clearfork Valley, but one should note that only the initial chapters of the book address the era that is the focus of this chapter. Eller (1982) is still among the best general accounts of the subject. David Corbin's *Life, Work, and Rebellion in the Coal Fields: The Southern West Virginia Miners, 1880–1922* is another early work focusing on the state that has borne the greatest influence from the coal industry. Shifflett (1991) remains the most outstanding revisionist account of the industry. Even though Shifflett barely addresses East Tennessee mining or the Clearfork Valley, and is overly sympathetic to the coal industry, his general premises, I believe, are still valid, a needed corrective to scholars' failure to consider the industry's perspectives.

For a good general account of the miner's work routine, see Eller (1982, 175–98). An excellent firsthand account from the Clearfork Valley is provided by Cecil Winchester's "Clearfork," in *Clearfork and More (History and Memories)*, edited by Bonnie Page (64–69). He also discusses the shifting fortunes for coal in the Clearfork Valley.

The disasters at Fraterville and Cross Mountain have been recounted many times in books and newspaper articles. See, for example, Vic Weals's "Coal Miners' Farewell Notes . . ." (*Knoxville Journal*, December 27, 1979). A more recent account by columnist Don Williams is "1911 mine disaster still haunts" (*Knoxville News-Sentinel* Oct. 7, 2005). Alan Gratz poignantly captures the Fraterville story in his play *Measured in Labor: The Coal Creek Project*, which enjoyed an extended run at Knoxville's Black Box Theatre in 2004.

For a broader, New South perspective on Appalachian coal mining and its many hazards, see Edward Ayers (1992, 115–23).

For general information on the circumstances leading to the decline of the Appalachian coal industry, see Eller (1982, 156–60).

The West Virginia Coal Mine War, and particularly the "Matewan Incident" and the Battle of Blair Mountain have attracted attention from scholars and popular commentators. Corbin (1982) offers a standard account. The documentary *Even the Heavens Weep* (produced in the mid-1980s by the West Virginia Humanities Council and WPBY-TV in Huntington), Denise Giardina's outstanding novel *Storming Heaven*, and the acclaimed John Sayles film *Matewan* make these colorful stories accessible to broad and diverse audiences.

Coal mine violence in Harlan, Kentucky, in the 1930s is examined in Linda Ann Ewen's *Which Side Are You On?* The Wilder Strike is briefly explored in Cotham (1996, 99–125). Knoxville librarian Loletta Clouse's historical novel, *Wilder,* presents a realistic, fictional account of that little-known chapter in Tennessee history.

5. APPALACHIA ON THEIR MINDS

Henry Shapiro's *Appalachia on Our Mind* and Alan Batteau's *The Invention of Appalachia* are standard works on Appalachian identity. In addition to David Hsiung's essential contributions to my take on this topic, I have also benefited from such recent works as Anthony Harkins's *Hillbilly* and Jerry Williamson's *Hillbillyland*, and from the essays in Billings, Norman, and Ledford's *Confronting Appalachian Stereotypes*. For a documentary assault on regional stereotypes, Herb E. Smith's *Strangers and Kin* is dated but still very informative.

For an insightful discussion of similarities and differences in the experiences of Appalachians and other American minorities, see Phillip J. Obermiller's "The Question of Appalachian Identity."

My understanding of new scholarly insights into human identity was very much illuminated by Manuel Cassells's *The Power of Identity* and Craig Calhoun's *Social Theory and the Politics of Identity*. Emily Satterwhite, who introduced me to this scholarship, is one of the first Appalachian scholars to recognize the importance of these works for our field.

Two dated (but classical) accounts of developments on the broader national stage during the timeframe for this chapter are Robert Wiebe's *Search for Order*, on progressivism, and William Leuchtenburg's *The Perils of Prosperity, 1914–1932*, on the 1920s. Also see David Noble's "The Paradox of Progressivism."

My take on American antimodernism draws heavily from three provocative essays: John Higham's "The Reorientation of American Culture"; Roderick Nash's "The American Cult of the Primitive"; and F. H. Matthews's "The Revolt against Americanism: Cultural Pluralism and Cultural Relativism as an Ideology of Liberation." The most extensive study of American anti-modernism is T. J. Jackson Lears's *No Place of Grace: Anti-Modernism and the Transformation of American Culture, 1880–1920*.

For brief introductions to the several genres of Appalachian literature and authors mentioned in this section, general readers would do well to turn to the recently published *Encyclopedia of Appalachia*. The following entries are relevant to topics addressed in these pages: Grace Toney Edwards and Theresa Lloyd's introduction to the section on literature (1035–39); Lloyd's "Humor in Appalachian Literature" (981–83); Allison Ensor's "Local Color" 1069–70); Nancy Carol Joyner's "Mary Noailles Murfree" (1077); and Aaron Davis's "John Fox, Jr." (1059–60). For Civil War–era images of Appalachia and East Tennessee and their impact, see Drake (2001, 93–115) and Hsiung (1997, 121–23).

The best general introduction to Appalachian local color writing is still Shapiro's "The Local Color Movement and the Discovery of Appalachia" chapter from *Appalachia on Our Mind*.

For insight into the career of Mary Noailles Murfree and extensive commentary on one of her most popular stories ("The Star in the Valley"), see Shapiro (1978, 18–26). For less critical accounts, see Nathalia Wright's introduction to *In the Tennessee Mountains* and Allison Ensor's "What Is the Place of Mary Noailles Murfree Today?" Dunn's critique of Murfree is presented on pages 161–63 of *Cades Cove*.

For general insights into Fox's career and works, see Shapiro (1978, 30–31; 70–76). For very critical views of Fox from Appalachian insiders, see Don Askins's "John Fox, Jr.: A Reappraisal; or With Friends Like That, Who Needs Enemies?"

and Darlene Wilson's "A Judicious Combination of Incident and Psychology: John Fox Jr. and the Southern Mountaineer Motif." Fox's ties to the Jellico area of East Tennessee are explored in "John Fox, Jr.—Famed Author Wrote of Life, Times in Campbell County," an unsigned newspaper article reprinted in Miller McDonald (1991–93, vol. 1: 175–78).

A number of outstanding studies offer insight into "the great era of Protestant missions" and the broader context in which the mainstream "discovery of Appalachia" occurred. See, for example, Sidney Ahlstrom's *A Religious History of the American People;* Robert Handy's *A Christian America: Protestant Hopes and Historical Realities;* and Colin B. Goodykoontz's *Home Missions on the American Frontier.*

Shapiro (1978) remains the best starting point for understanding home missionaries' role in the "discovery of Appalachia." See, in particular, "Protestant Home Missions and the Institutionalization of Appalachian Otherness" (chapter 2). Thereafter throughout *Appalachia on our Mind,* Shapiro frequently discusses missionary contributions to emerging Appalachian images. Deborah Vansau McCauley's outstanding *Appalachian Mountain Religion* is unabashedly critical of the home missionary enterprise. See, in particular, chapter 17, "A Christian American and the Appalachian *Problem.*"

New insights into the Appalachian home missions enterprise are presented in recent histories of several of the schools discussed in this chapter that evolved into four-year liberal arts colleges. See Shannon Wilson's *Berea College: An Illustrated History;* P. David Searles's *A College for Appalachia: Alice Lloyd on Caney Creek;* and *Warren Wilson College: A Centennial Portrait,* which I wrote with my dear, late friend, Reuben A. Holden.

Treatment of missionary and other altruistic work in southern Appalachia has evolved with the climate of public opinion. Prior to the 1960s, most accounts accepted the altruists on their own merits and treated their efforts as one of the fruits of progress. Beginning with Shapiro's contention in 1978 that many Appalachian images (particularly negative ones) emerged from missionary rhetoric, a generation of scholars castigated what they portrayed as "misguided do-gooders." David Whisnant's *All That Is Native and Fine* and Deborah McCauley's *Appalachian Mountain Religion* are two of the finest, most articulate examples of this view. A more recent round of revisionism has sought to present a more balanced account, emphasizing positive contributions from "missionary longtermers." See the recent institutional histories cited earlier of schools that are products of this era of Protestant missions. Also see Helen Lewis and Monica Appleby's *Mountain Sisters: From Convent to Community in Appalachia.* My own essay, "Of Missionaries, Multiculturalism, and Mainstream Malaise," places the topic in broader contexts.

Robert Taylor Jr. explores the career and outlook of William Rule in "Mainstreams of Mountain Thought: Attitudes of Selected Figures in the Heart of the Appalachian South" (chapter 2). A more cogent account is Taylor's "The New South Mind of a Mountain Editor: William Rule." That Taylor completed these works several years before Appalachian studies scholarship became well known makes his insights particularly impressive. The quotes from the *Daily Chronicle* are taken from these two pieces.

Jack Neely comments on the place of Market Square in the early development of country music in "Deconstructing Market Square" (*Metro Pulse*, Feb. 22, 2001). Regarding the growth of Pentecostalism in Knoxville, see Rothrock (1946, 299–300). Deborah McCauley discusses this trend more generally in *Appalachian Mountain Religion*.

See notes from chapter 4 for sources on the Coal Creek Rebellion. The White Cap chapter in Sevier County history has often been a source of embarrassment to county residents, and that has made fully analyzing the complex events of that era difficult. A selection entitled "Terror of the Whitecaps" in *Sevier County Tennessee and Its Heritage* (p. 41) starts with this line: "There is a big black spot in the otherwise wonderful history of Sevier County." Sharon Hurst presents a brief account in "Days of Terror." For scholarly analysis, see Joseph Lewelling's "The White Caps of Sevier County: Economic and Cultural Perspectives" and William J. Cummings's outstanding "Community, Violence, and the Nature of Change: Whitecapping in Sevier County, Tennessee During the 1890s."

Appalachian feuding and violence have received extensive attention from popular commentators and scholars. An exhaustive analysis of the literature on the subject is presented by Altina Waller in "Feuding in Appalachia: Evolution of a Cultural Stereotype." Waller is also the author of *Feud: Hatfields, McCoys, and Social Change in Appalachia, 1860–1900.* Also see Gordon B. McKinney's "Industrialization and Violence in Appalachia in the 1890s." Stereotypes of "violent Appalachia" are one target of Dwight Billings, Gurney Norman, and Katherine Ledford's *Confronting Appalachian Stereotypes.* The awarding of a Pulitzer Prize in 1992 to Robert Schenkkan's *The Kentucky Cycle* was a major impetus leading the editors to compile this volume.

The best introduction to Emma Bell Miles's life and artistic work are Roger D. Abraham's foreword and David Whisnant's introduction to the 1975 reprint of *The Spirit of the Mountains.* The contemporary comments are from entries in the recently released *Encyclopedia of Appalachia:* Richard Blaustein, "East Tennessee Public Folklore" (859); Grace Toney Edwards, "Emma Bell Miles" (1074). Also see Edwards's "Emma Bell Miles: Feminist Crusader in Appalachia." East Tennessee's Cumberland County Playhouse several years ago made Miles's provocative story accessible to broader audiences with a musical production based on *The Spirit of the Mountains.*

For insight into the career of Samuel Tyndale Wilson and an introduction to the history of Maryville College, a good starting point is Harold M. Parker Jr.'s "A School of the Prophets at Maryville." Also see Carolyn Blair and Arda Walker's *By Faith Endowed: The Story of Maryville College.* For a critical view of Wilson and *The Southern Mountaineers,* see McCauley (1995, 409–11). Wilson, of course, did not escape the perceptive eye of Henry Shapiro; see pages 100, 158–59, and 189 of *Appalachia on our Mind.*

Presently Eric Lovik's entry on "John C. and Olive Dame Campbell" in the *Encyclopedia of Appalachia* (1528–29) and Rupert Vance's brief and dated foreword to the 1969 reprint of *The Southern Highlander and His Homeland* are the best starting points for exploring Campbell's important career. Fortunately, historian Penny Messinger is well into research on a provocative new analysis of the Council of the Southern Mountains and the important work of the Campbells. This (presently unnamed) manuscript will build upon her doctoral dissertation, "Leading the Field in Mountain Work: A History of the Conference of Southern Mountain Workers."

The annual meetings of the "Conference of Southern Mountain Workers" are nowhere to be found in either popular (e.g., Creekmore) or more scholarly (MacArthur, Wheeler) accounts of Knoxville's history. Even more perplexing is the fact that the East Tennessee Historical Society's massive clippings files has no folder devoted to the work of the Council of the Southern Mountains or its "Teacher Conferences," which met annually in Knoxville between 1914 and 1925 (and sporadically thereafter). This is particularly telling when one considers the large number of topics (many of which I believe are historically less important than the CSM) that have merited the attention of the faithful archivists and volunteers who have created and maintained that valuable collection. Claxton's provocative messages to the CSM are recorded by Whisnant (1994, 6).

At the risk of redundancy, I emphasize that Kephart deserves more attention from historical observers than he has received. At present, the single best source on his career is George Ellison's introduction to *Our Southern Highlanders.*

See notes from chapter 4 regarding the "Prophet of Great Smokies" and Knoxville's 1910, 1911, and 1913 expos.

For information on antimodernism and Elkmont, see earlier notes from this chapter and chapter 4. I bring the Elkmont saga up to the present in part 3.

Dunn examines Oliver's commitment to progressivism and his fight against the plan to incorporate Cades Cove in Great Smoky Mountains National Park in *Cades Cove,* chapters 9 and 10.

No topic in East Tennessee's early twentieth-century history has received more historical scrutiny than the Scopes Trial of 1925. Two very solid accounts are Ray Ginger's *Six Days or Forever? Tennessee v. John Scopes* and George Webb's *The Evolution Controversy in America*. Jeanette Keith considers how rural East Tennesseans viewed the trial in *Country People in the New South: Tennessee's Upper Cumberland*.

Joseph Wood Krutch and several other members of his talented family deserve more attention than they have received. After his 1925 assignment in Dayton, Krutch became a nationally prominent writer and philosopher. Jack Neely recounts Krutch's response to the Scopes Trial in "Bigotry, Militant, and Sincere" (*Metro Pulse*, July 2, 1993).

For provocative insight into the importance of positive relations between more affluent and less fortunate members of marginalized regions and societies, see Cynthia Duncan's *Worlds Apart*.

PART III. APPALACHIA, EAST TENNESSEE, AND MODERN AMERICA

Regional scholars have devoted surprisingly little attention to John C. Campbell, and no one has addressed his decision to use the term "Southern Highlanders" to describe the peoples who were the object of his career and enduring tome. The fact that Horace Kephart used the same label raises doubts about my contention about why Campbell substituted "Highlander" for "Appalachian." This will remain a puzzle until some future scholars examines it in the detail it deserves. Shapiro's final chapter of *Appalachia on Our Mind* is the best effort to date that explores Campbell's thinking on these matters.

Twenty-five years ago, Phil Obermiller explored issues related to the minority status of Appalachian people in "The Question of Appalachian Ethnicity." I challenge regional scholars to devote more attention to this dimly understood topic.

Two excellent introductions to life in Manhattan Project–era Oak Ridge are Charles Johnson and Charles Jackson's *City Behind the Fence: Oak Ridge, Tennessee, 1942–1946* and James Overholt's *These Are Our Voices: The Story of Oak Ridge 1942–1970*. Over the years, I have benefited from insights of many people (in addition to my parents) who shared their firsthand experiences about early Oak Ridge. I particularly appreciate insights from my aunt, Jo Pierce, and dear, longtime neighbor, Marnie Shields.

6. EAST TENNESSEE FROM BAD TIMES TO GOOD TIMES (FOR SOME)

The related stories of the creation of Great Smoky Mountains National Park and the forced removal of Cades Cove residents from their ancestral home have been told many times. Fortunately for this book, two solid monographs recently appeared that offer slightly different, but equally valuable perspectives on the park's formation. Margaret Lynn Brown's eloquently written *The Wild East* offers particularly significant human and environmental insights into the story. Dan Pierce's *The Great Smokies* focuses more directly on administrative and institutional aspects of the park's creation and evolution. No author to date has matched Durwood Dunn (1988) in capturing the pathos of the forced removal of the Cades Cove residents. Dunn's touching account of his own grandfather's role in this saga may not be objective, but it is credible and persuasive. Dunn's epilogue and final chapter, "Death by Eminent Domain," should be required reading for all of the tens of thousands of auto tourists who drive the Cove's loop road each year and leave the park without fully understanding the Cove's tragedy and the complexities of our elusive regional culture.

Brown and Pierce offer useful views of the role of Knoxvillians in the creation of GSMNP, with Brown portraying the city's park boosters in somewhat more negative light. Betsy Beeler Creekmore's *Knoxville!* offers an informative, if uncritical, account from the perspective of East Tennessee's leading city.

My primary concern here, of course, is with the removal of East Tennessee residents from lands absorbed into the park. General insight into how residents of North Carolina's Cataloochee Valley and Cherokee Reservation fared with removal by park forces can be found in Michael Ann Williams's *Great Smoky Mountains Folklife.*

A full and objective account of the Elkmont story and of the roles of David Chapman, Governor Austin Peay, and other Elkmonters in the creation of the park has not yet been written. Former East Tennessean—and regular Elkmont visitor—Eleanor Dickinson has been working on a sympathetic account of that saga for years, and thanks to assistance from Lynn Faust, Ms. Dickinson shared with me a draft of that manuscript. Scholars in general have been far more critical than these observers of the Elkmonters, and the vertical files at GSMNP Archives are filled with reports (official and otherwise) generally portraying the Elkmont connection negatively. Mary Fanslow's recent essay, "From Timbering to Tourism," offers a rare balanced account of one facet of this important chapter in the greater saga of the Smokies.

Brown and Pierce offer insights into the experiences of the Walker sisters, Wiley Oakley, and Gatlinburg's native entrepreneurs.

Florence Cope Bush's *Dorie* should be another "assigned reading" for those who visit the park and for residents of Knoxville (and other East Tennessee communities) whose forebears abandoned rural homes and moved to the city in this traumatic era.

As already noted, Dunn's final chapter and epilogue offer firsthand perspectives on the sad removal of Cades Coves' long-term residents. A. Randolph Shields offers another native view in *The Cades Cove Story.*

Copies of the several park service plans for development of Cades Cove, and records related to the aborted plans to dam Abrams Creek and transform the Cove into a lake, can be found in the vertical files of the library and archives of GSMNP. Brown and Pierce offer valuable insight into these matters.

For general accounts of the Depression and New Deal in Appalachia, see Drake (2001, 162–68) and Williams (2002, 281–306). In chapters 5–7 of *Appalachia's Path to Dependency,* Paul Salstrom offers a provocatively critical appraisal of the New Deal's impact on the region, with relevant implications for Tennessee. Jerry Bruce Thomas's *An Appalachian New Deal: West Virginia in the Great Depression* is the most thorough study to date of the impact of the Depression and the New Deal on an Appalachian subregion. Thomas's conclusions appear relevant to East Tennessee, and his approach and methodology should prove useful for future scholars.

The popularity of the Civilian Conservation Corps (CCC) among East Tennesseans is evident in clippings from the *Campbell Countian* 13, no. 2.

Historical literature on TVA is extensive. Among general works are Phillip Selznik's *TVA and the Grassroots: A Study in the Sociology of Formal Organization* and David Lilienthal's *TVA: Democracy on the March.* More specialized studies include Edwin Hargrove and Paul Conkin's *TVA and 50 Years of Grass-roots Bureaucracy;* Hargrove's own *Prisoners of Myth: The Leadership of the Tennessee Valley Authority, 1933–1990;* and Walter L. Creese's *TVA's Public Planning: The Vision, the Reality.*

Among the studies of TVA most relevant to this work is Michael J. McDonald and John Muldowny's *TVA and the Dispossessed: The Resettlement of Population in the Norris Dam Area.* The book offers sympathetic insight into the plight of the Norris Dam removals and provides a generally critical view of TVA's handling of that matter. A more friendly response toward TVA is Michael Rogers's "TVA Population Removal: Attitudes and Expectations of the Dispossessed at the Norris and Cherokee Dam Sites."

The saga of David Whisnant's controversial *Modernizing the Mountaineer: People, Power, and Planning in Appalachia* reveals as much about the legacies of TVA's evolution as it does about the events Whisnant recounts. Four years after TVA officials pressured the University of Tennessee Press not to publish Whisnant's manuscript, the Appalachian Consortium Press published it. Whisnant's "Reflections on the New Edition," which UT Press published in 1992 (xxiii–xxxvi), offers the author's perspectives on the publication history of his controversial book.

Both Richard Drake and John Alexander William explore the impact of World War II on the Appalachian region at various places in their general histories of the region. Bergeron, Ash, and Keith do the same for Tennessee in *Tennesseans and their History* (279–85).

Phil Obermiller is widely recognized as the leading authority on Appalachian out-migration. His chapter in Blethen and Straw's *High Mountains Rising* offers a solid introduction to the topic, as well as a bibliography. Another good place to start is Phil Obermiller and Michael E. Maloney's introduction to the section "Urban Appalachian Experience" in the *Encyclopedia of Appalachia*. Harriet Arnow's novel, *The Dollmaker*, is a classic of the World War II out-migration experience, often likened to *The Grapes of Wrath*. Hollywood's mid-1980s version of Arnow's book brought a somewhat sanitized version of its tragic story to broader audiences.

The general story of Oak Ridge has been told often and well. Among the best works are Charles W. Johnson and Charles O. Jackson's *City Behind a Fence, Oak Ridge, Tennessee 1942–1946;* Overholt's *These Are Our Voices: The Story of Oak Ridge;* and Russell B. Olwell's *At Work in the Atomic City: A Labor and Social History of Oak Ridge, Tennessee.* Each of these fine works touches upon the encounter between outsiders and natives that is a primary concern of this work, but that important topic still awaits exhaustive analysis. An interesting, brief account by a native of the region is Clifford Seeber's "Acorns to Atoms: A Grass Roots History of Oak Ridge."

The literature on post–World War II America is extensive. Standard U.S. history textbooks are a good place to start, including appropriate chapters in Brinkley's *The Unfinished Nation* and Davidson's *Nation of Nations.* Among the many solid texts focusing on the post–World War II years, a notable volume is William H. Chafe's *The Unfinished Journey: America Since World War II.* For a particularly insightful and more popular account by a British native who has lived most of his adult life in the U.S., see Michael Elliott's *The Day Before Yesterday: Recovering the American Past, Rediscovering the Present.* In describing the aberrant nature of the post–World War II era, Elliot bluntly calls America of that era "a great freak."

University of Tennessee historians Bruce Wheeler and Michael McDonald explore the causes and consequences of the gap between East Tennessee's valley-urban communities and its hinterlands in "The Communities of East Tennessee."

For a general overview of Cas Walker's entrepreneurial and political careers, see Ajay Karla's "Cas Walker." Wheeler (2005, chapter 2–4) offers the most extensive coverage of Walker's long, colorful, and controversial career. Wheeler also offers extensive coverage of John Gunther's caustic portrayal of Knoxville and popular responses to it on pages 61–63 of *Knoxville, Tennessee.*

Exactly how many (or what percentage) of Knoxville residents (at any moment in time) are descendants of native East Tennesseans who migrated into the city is difficult to determine. Census records indicate state of birth but not exact city, town, or location within a state. My own random sampling from groups of students and other groups I have spoken to in the city and other anecdotal evidence suggests that both the number and percentage is high.

The file "Market Square" in the McClung Collection's vertical files contains numerous clippings and reminiscences regarding Market Square, the controversies surrounding its demise, and debates over use of that space ever since. Wheeler (2005, 115–18) explores these same topics.

For general information about the coal industry in this era, see appropriate sections of Drake (2001) and Williams (2002) and chapters 5 and 6 of Eller (1982). Eller explores the travails of the coal industry in the Great Depression on pages 237–42. Salstrom (1991) does so in chapter 5.

The shift to surface (strip) mining is explored in Chad Montrie's *To Save the Land and People: A History of Opposition to Surface Mining in Appalachia.* For the coming and effects of strip-mining in the Clearfork Valley in particular, see Winchester (1986) and chapter 4 of Dewayne Walls's *The Kidwells: A Family Odyssey.*

For a highly critical (and controversial) account of TVA's "coal decision," see Whisnant (1994, chapter 2).

The early history and competing demands on the National Park Service are recounted in many places. A solid, general account particularly relevant to this study can be found in chapter 2 of Pierce (2000).

Margaret Lynn Brown (2000) and Pierce both ably describe the history of the GSMNP. My treatment of the park's early history and the tensions between preservationists (led by Harvey Broome) and promoters of tourism (such as David Chapman) draws primarily from these two fine sources.

Copies of the several park plans for Cades Cove are preserved in the vertical files of the library of GSMNP.

For GSMNP in the years since around 1950, Brown's (2000) account is the most extensive and thorough. In particular, she discusses "Mission 66" and the 1950s emphasis on promotion of auto tourism in chapters 6 and 7.

Both Pierce and Brown offer brief accounts of the histories of Gatlinburg and Pigeon Forge as they relate to the history of GSMNP. For more detailed coverage, see C. Brenden Martin's *Tourism in the Mountain South: A Double-Edged Sword.*

For a thoughtful discussion of the tradeoffs associated with a tourist economy, see Michael Ann Williams (1995, chapter 9). More extended commentary on the broader phenomenon of regional crafts and the "preservation of Appalachian culture" can be found in Whisnant (1983) and in Jane Becker's *Selling Tradition: Appalachia and the Construction of an American Folk, 1930–1940.* Jim Wayne Miller's classic poem, "The Brier Loses Touch with His Traditions," offers cogent, nuanced insight into this very controversial topic. Gnomon Press of Frankfort,

Kentucky, recently published many of Miller's best-loved poems under the title *The Brier Poems*.

As I noted previously, much information about the controversial Elkmont saga is available, but a definitive history still awaits an able chronicler. See earlier comments in this chapter.

Ron Eller, a pioneer in Appalachian studies, made an important contribution to the field—and particularly the final four chapters of this book—with the recent publication of *Uneven Ground: Appalachia Since 1945*.

7. APPALACHIA (SLOWLY) AWAKENS

A contemporary account of TVA's mammoth steam plant at Kingston is recorded in "Kingston Steam Plant Is World's Largest" (*Harriman Record*, October 24, 1957).

For general information about the Appalachian awakening that unfolded in the first two decades of the twentieth century, see chapter 5 and its sources.

The involvement of the three Lincoln Memorial alumni in the 1930s Appalachian literary awakening is explored by Ted Olson in his chapter on Appalachian literature in Blethen and Straw's *High Mountains Rising*. Also see the entries about each of the three authors in the *Encyclopedia of Appalachia*.

New insights into revisionist studies of Native American experiences in the early decades of the twentieth century reveal the "reawakening" examined here was hardly unique to Appalachia. See, for example, Frederick E. Hoxie's *Talking Back to Civilization: Indian Voices from the Progressive Era*.

For information on Mildred Haun and Anne Armstrong, see Sandra L. Ballard's entry on Haun and Linda Behrend's entry on Armstrong in the *Encyclopedia of Appalachia*. I owe special thanks to former University of Tennessee English professor Allison Ensor for sharing his insights into these two relatively little-known East Tennessee authors.

Agee and Wolfe have, of course, been targets of considerably more scholarly attention. See, for example, Ross Spears and Jude Cassidy's *Agee: His Life Remembered* and David Herbert Donald's *Look Homeward: A Life of Thomas Wolfe*.

Chapter 2 of Shapiro (1978) is the key scholarly analysis on home missionary influences on evolving Appalachian stereotypes. Shapiro's comments on John C. Campbell on pages 264–65 of the same volume are particularly important for my appraisal of that "missionary longtermer."

A particularly provocative example of the "new mission history," which influenced and affirmed my thinking on this topic is Lian Xi's *The Conversion of Missionaries: Liberalism in American Protestant Missions in China, 1907–1932*.

For general histories of Asheville Farm School and Warren Wilson, see my *Toward Frontiers Yet Unknown: A 90th Anniversary History of Warren Wilson College, 1894–1984* and *Warren Wilson College: A Centennial Portrait.*

Randolph left Farm School in 1942 to assume a top-echelon position with the Presbyterian Board of National Missions. Thereafter he served the church in many capacities and locations. Although he did not return permanently to East Tennessee, Randolph never "got above his raisin'" nor his East Tennessee and Appalachian roots.

New scholarship exploring Native American interaction with the greater American mainstream has greatly influenced my take on both missionary activity and the Appalachian experience. See for example K. Tsianina Lomawaima's *They Called It Prairie Light* and Michael C. Coleman's *American Indian Children at School, 1850–1930.* Another provocative recent work is Bonnie Sue Lewis's *Creating Christian Indians: Native Clergy in the Presbyterian Church.*

Chapters 4–6 of Shannon Wilson's *Berea College* focus on the presidencies of Frost and his successors during a timeframe when Berea's response to Appalachia evolved in important ways.

Loyal Jones and Jim Wayne Miller deserve more acclaim and appreciation than either the present generation of Appalachian scholars or I could ever give them. For basic details about their lives, see Harry Robie's entry on Jones and Ricky Cox's entry on Miller in the *Encyclopedia of Appalachia.* A brief synopsis of Billy Edd Wheeler's life and career as writer and performer is found on page 1219 of the same volume.

I know personally the constraints and concerns that typically shape and limit institutional histories. Certainly, familiarity with Appalachian studies has never been a major consideration in selecting authors for such projects at the East Tennessee schools of concern here. Indeed, I confess that I was totally unfamiliar with the field when I wrote my first Warren Wilson history in 1984. Several flaws and glaring omissions from that volume are now obvious to me.

The investigations of James S. Brown, who passed away in 1999, are known collectively as "the Beech Creek studies." Brown's efforts laid the foundation for investigations by several generations of subsequent scholars. Dwight Billings and Kathleen Blee, authors of the recently published and provocative *The Road to Poverty: The Making of Wealth and Hardship in Appalachia,* clearly state their debt to Brown and describe his nearly fifty-year relationship with Beech Creek families as "a model of perceptive, sensitive, and ethical ethnographic research." Shannon Wilson kindly shared information about Brown's career.

Examples of recent institutional histories of several of the East Tennessee schools discussed here include Blair and Walker's *By Faith Endowed: The Story of Maryville College;* Joseph T. Fuhrmann's *The Life and Times of Tusculum*

College; James Riley Montgomery, Stanley Folmsbee, and Lee S. Greene's *To Foster Knowledge: A History of the University of Tennessee, 1794–1970;* and Joseph Suppiger's *Phoenix of the Mountains: The Story of Lincoln Memorial University.* The authors of these volumes have impressive scholarly credentials, but none of them was particularly familiar with the field of Appalachian studies.

James Montgomery (1963) offers a useful overview of the University of Tennessee's "Summer School of the South." That program and the career of Philander Claxton, its primary promoter and later U.S. Commissioner of Education, await further probing by Appalachian studies scholars.

I am particularly indebted to Tom Hood, a retired UT sociology professor, for introducing me to William Cole and his role as a native East Tennessean at the university in an important chapter of its history. Dr. Hood provided me with a copy of university historian Dr. Milton Klein's tribute to Dr. Cole ("William E. Cole: An Exemplary Social Servant") and a copy of Cole's reminiscences about his Carter County upbringing, *Tales from a Country Ledger.*

Debates about the rancorous events of the early 1970s unfolded in the pages of the then recently inaugurated *Appalachian Journal.* The two protagonists— David Whisnant and Loyal Jones—were two of the earliest pioneers in the nascent field of Appalachian studies; they have since become stalwarts of the discipline. Whisnant's essay, "Controversy in God's Grand Division: The Council of the Southern Mountains," offered the first volley in the exchange. Jones responded two issues later with "Problems in Revisionism: More Controversy in God's Grand Division." In the same issue, Jones's Berea Colleagues, Thomas Parrish and A. H. Perrin, further criticized Whisnant's take on the history (181–89) in letters to the editor. Immediately following their letters, Whisnant responded to his critics (189–91) with a letter of his own. Over the next thirty years, Appalachian scholars largely avoided this volatile topic.

Fortunately, this is changing even as I write these words. In 2003, *Appalachian Journal* briefly revisited this controversy in Logan Brown, et al., "Where Have We Been? Where Are We Going? A History of the Appalachian Studies Association." The same volume includes "Early Voices in the Appalachian Conversation," a valuable response from Richard Drake, participant in the events of concern here and longtime Berea colleague of Jones. As mentioned in the notes on sources to chapter 5, historian Penny Messinger is revisiting the history of the Council of the Southern mountains, in particular the contributions of Helen Dingman, Alva Taylor, and Perley Ayers to the council's evolving relationship with the Appalachian region. See, for example, her "Restoring the Woman Reformer: Helen Hastie Dingman and the Conference of Southern Mountain Workers, 1918–1952." Still, the fact that none of these individuals (who were all associated with Berea College) merited an entry in the new, comprehensive *Encyclopedia of Appalachia* reveals that much work still needs to be done. In addition to Messinger's manuscript on the council's history, historian John Glen is exploring the council's last days, as it fragmented and its remnants eventually evolved into the Appalachian Studies Association. Also see Tom Kiffmeyer's recently published *Reformers to Radicals: The Appalachian Volunteers and the War on Poverty.* While the council became relatively insignificant after the Fontana and Lake Junaluska conferences, a final vestige of it did not "officially" die until 1989.

Highlander has received much attention from scholars and popular observers, including several individuals intimately involved in its exciting and controversial history. Historian John Glen offers a brief account of the Highlander saga in two entries in *The Tennessee Encyclopedia of History and Culture.* Glen's *Highlander: No Ordinary School* is the most thorough scholarly account of Highlander's story. Longtime Highlander insider Candie Carawan composed the Highlander entry for the *Encyclopedia of Appalachia.* Horton's colleague, Frank Adams, offers a more extensive, inside account in *Unearthing Seeds of Fire: The Idea of Highlander.* Chapter 8 of Cotham (1996) focuses, in particular, on Highlander's labor activities.

Essays in Stephen Fisher's *Fighting Back in Appalachia* explore many different manifestations of the broader issue of Appalachian activism. Within that volume, John Glen's "Like a Flower Slowly Blooming: Highlander and the Nurturing of an Appalachian Movement" explores Highlander Center's shift to—and continued efforts to improve—its Appalachian emphasis.

General accounts of developments on the national stage during the 1960s can be found in any good U.S. survey text. See, for example, chapters 31 and 32 in Brinkley (2004).

General accounts of the "the Appalachian Conversation" can be found in the two recently published regional surveys by Richard Drake and John Alexander Williams. In addition to the 2003 *AJ* essay on the origins of the Appalachian Studies Association, see Alan Banks, Dwight Billings and Karen Tice's "Appalachian Studies, Resistance, and Post-Modernism."

Chapter 8 will explore more fully findings from Appalachian studies that offer particular insights into this book's "three representative communities." For more general overviews of important themes in Appalachian studies scholarship from a turn-of-the-twenty-first-century perspective, see John Inscoe's "The Discovery of Appalachia: Regional Revisionism as Scholarly Renaissance" and Ronald Lewis's "Beyond Isolation and Homogeneity: Diversity and the History of Appalachia."

8. Coming Home to a New Appalachia

The two recently published regional overviews by Drake (2001) and Williams (2002) offer valuable general insights into the Appalachian awakening, as well as general accounts of the "war on poverty" in Appalachia. Chad Montrie's *To Save the Land and People* offers particular insight into grassroots resistance to strip-mining. Sociologist Helen Lewis allegedly coined the term "reactionary rebels."

Gaventa offers much more detail on the awakening in the Clearfork Valley in *Power and Powerlessness,* in addition to providing valuable insights into how local forces co-opted federal efforts in the Valley.

Tilda Kemplen published her autobiography, *From Roots to Roses,* in 1992. The roles of Louise White Adams and Shelby York are presented in Lewis and Appleby (2003, 93, 149, 189).

Chapters from Steve Fisher's *Fighting Back in Appalachia* explore the work of SOCM and Highlander's decision to refocus its attention on Appalachia in the mid-1960s. One of the most important results of the efforts of these two organizations was an extensive study of landownership in the Appalachian region. John Egerton explored and commented on this study in "Appalachia's Absentee Landlords."

Although she shuns attention, Marie Cirillo has been the focus of many newspaper and magazine accounts. See, for example, Fred Brown's series of articles, led by "Miracle at Rose's Creek" (*Knoxville News-Sentinel,* Jan. 31, 1993). Ten years later, Jennifer Osha penned "Marie Cirillo: Helping the People of Appalachia Regain Control over Their Communities and Lives." Publication that same year of Lewis and Appleby's *Mountain Sisters* introduced even wider audiences to Marie in the context of the broader work of the Glenmary Sisters and FOCIS.

The various Clairfield non-profits are explored throughout *Mountain Sisters.* For Model Valley Community Development Corporation, see pages 182–93. For Woodland Community Land Trust, see pages 166–67;196; 205–6; 236.

For more information about alternative models for development in coal Appalachia, see the following Web sites: Kentucky Coal Museum, www.kingdomcome.org/museum; Barthell Coal Mining Camp, www.barthellcoalcamp.com; and Coal Creek Watershed Foundation, Inc., http://www.coalcreekaml.com.

As a child in the 1930s, the late Sonny Koger often visited Barthell with his father, who was an employee of Stearnes Coal Company. Given the opportunity to purchase the site in his retirement, Sonny employed researchers from the University of Kentucky to lay out plans for restoration of Barthell to its heyday status. Today, his widow, Marilyn, and his son and daughter-in-law, Richard and Donna, thankfully keep his dream alive in this superb combination museum and bed and breakfast. The efforts of the Coal Creek Watershed foundation have apparently set well with many local politicians. Lake City Mayor Buck Wilson recently advocated expending public funds for a coal museum. The mayor also advocates restoring the town's name to "Coal Creek." See Clayton Hensley, "Tapping Tourist Dollars," *Knoxville News-Sentinel* (June 5, 2007).

No issue generates more emotion in Appalachia today than strip-mining, and more specifically, mountaintop removal. Compared to West Virginia and eastern Kentucky, East Tennessee has thus far seen little of this controversial mining method. However, growing demands for alternatives to imported petroleum have led to an increase in this practice, and there is presently some evidence that a mountaintop removal project may be in the making for Clearfork Mountain. SOCM, Highlander, and several new environmental groups active in East Tennessee will surely join many Clearfork residents in resisting this project. Concern about mountaintop removal has nudged scholars and activists to put away their differences and cooperate, much like they did in the 1960s, when observers first awakened to the impact of unregulated strip-mining. Indeed, no single topic received more attention at the 2008 Appalachian Studies Conference than mountaintop removal. The winner of this year's conference prize for nonfiction was Shirley Stewart Burns's *Bringing Down the Mountains: The Impact of Mountaintop Removal on Southern West Virginia Communities.*

For their part, the coal companies have responded by touting the merits of "clean coal" with persuasive commercials on television and lobbying efforts in Congress and in the legislatures of the various coal states that proclaim the merits of "clean coal."

Highlander's efforts in Blount County in 1963 are explored in Adams (1975, 201–3).

[The Elkmont saga is still controversial and awaits a definitive scholarly examination. For a relatively balanced overview, see C. McCurdy Lipsey's "The Elkmont Cabins in the Great Smoky Mountains National Park: A Social History."]

For historical background on East Tennessee Republicanism, see Gordon McKinney's *Southern Mountain Republicans.*

The most recent and thorough examination of Smokies tourism is C. Brenden Martin's *Tourism in the Mountain South.* For a somewhat different perspective, see appropriate portions of Michael Ann Williams's *Great Smoky Mountains Folklife.*

Clippings from Knoxville journalists Bert Vincent, Don Whitehead, Vic Weals, Carson Brewer, and Wilma Dykeman about the GSMNP, tourism, Appalachian culture, and so on may be found in the vertical files of the McClung Collection, a branch of the Knox County Public Library located in the East Tennessee History Center.

Margaret Lynn Brown and Daniel Pierce explore changes in NPS outlook in their recently published histories of the GSMNP. An important primary source, "Mission 66 for Great Smoky Mountains National Park," may be found in the GSMNP Library.

Copies of the 1939 and 1941 plans for Cades Cove are also preserved in the GSMNP Library. For harsh criticism of those plans and their ultimate implementation, see T. Young's "False, Cheap, and Degraded: When History, Economy, and Environment Collided at Cades Cove, Great Smoky Mountains National Park."

An assortment of Cades Cove guides and bulletins can be found in the GSMNP Library. Articles from the *Tennessee Conservationist* include Bart Leiper's "Time Stands Still in Cades Cove" (Dec. 1957); Arthur Green's "Cades Cove: Tourist Mecca" (July 1962); and Vera T. Dean's "Where the Drama Really Began" (Sept./October 1979). U.S. Supreme Court Justice William O. Douglas's "The People of Cades Cove" appeared in *National Geographic* in July 1962. I must confess the first book on the Appalachian region that I read after my 1987 return to East Tennessee was Horace Kephart's *Our Southern Highlanders.*

Park official John O. Morrell prepared "A History of the Cottages in the Vicinity of the Former Town of Elkmont: The Appalachian Club and the Wonderland Club" for the National Park Service in 1976. His bold assertion that "one word: *politics*" could explain why private individuals continued at that time to own dwellings within park confines infuriated the Elkmont folks. For insights into their perspective on this controversial (and ongoing) matter, I am indebted to Lynn Faust and Eleanor Dickinson.

During the time I have been engaged in writing this book, the NPS finished up a prolonged assessment of the Elkmont situation and reached a compromise plan calling for preserving "18 buildings as a museum community with exhibits that interpret the Elkmont story from its days as a logging camp through its history as a summer resort" (Morgan Simmons, "Compromise Saves 18 Elkmont Buildings," [*Knoxville News-Sentinel,* Feb. 7, 2007, A-1]). GSMNP Superintendent Dale Ditmanson said the compromise "strikes a balance between preserving natural and cultural resources," but many of the parties in this ongoing dispute have expressed objections to this plan. I have a file folder filled with editorials, letters to the editor of the *Knoxville News-Sentinel,* and a host of other items suggesting the issue will not be resolved soon. Meanwhile, it is a topic begging for a serious academic study.

Further information regarding Friends of the Smokies may be found at http://www.friendsofthesmokies.org. Former Friends director Charles Maynard has been a supporter of this project and a source for useful information.

Further information regarding the Cades Cove Preservation Association is available in the files of the GSMNP Library and at the Web site: http://cadescovepreservationtn.com. Information about the "Old Timer Days" is found in Williams (1995, 150–54). I am indebted to Dave Post, president of CCPA, for sharing information and insights into that organization and its ongoing efforts.

Evidence of the tensions that inevitably appear and sometimes undermine efforts to "protect and preserve" locations such as Cades Cove are readily apparent in the flyer "Cades Cove in Crisis: A National Treasure is Dying . . . A Wake Up Call for Those Who Care"; a copy of this flyer is preserved in the Cades Cove file in the vertical file collection in the GSMNP Library.

For a more dated and somewhat more objective perspective on Townsend and the controversies related to mountain development in general see "Battlefield: East Tennessee" (*Metro Pulse,* Feb. 3, 2000).

My clippings file on "Great Smokies—Development Debates" has filled up in recent months. For various perspectives, see the following columns and editorials from the *Knoxville New-Sentinel:* Roger Harris, "New Wave in Sevier" (Nov. 6, 2005) and "Citizen vs. Developers on Cove Mountain" (Feb. 8, 2006); Greg Johnson, "Cove Mountain Compromise" (Aug. 8, 2006) and "Doomsday Development Denied" (May 11, 2007); and Jessica Davis, "Raised on a Ridge" (June 24, 2007). The latter two columnists, both East Tennessee natives and self-professed "conservatives," have very different views of the matter in question. Ms. Davis's caustic column came in response to "Madness in the Mountains," a news article by the *News-Sentinel's* Tom Benning (June 1, 2007), which highlighted the objections of another heir to a longstanding Sevier County family to intensive "ridge top development." Johnson most recently expressed dismay about developments in his home county in "Tough Times for Sevier Families" (*Knoxville News-Sentinel,* October 23, 2008). As with Elkmont, this saga shows no sign of abating and may end up as heated as debates over mountaintop removal in Appalachia's coal country.

9. The Awakening in East Tennessee's Leading City

For a general accounts of Knoxville's World's Fair, see Bruce Wheeler's "Knoxville's World's Fair of 1982." For more details, see either of the two editions of Wheeler's history of Knoxville. Joe Dodd, former UT political scientist and active opponent of the fair as it was being debated in the 1980s, offers a highly critical account of many questionable aspects of the fair's history and legacies in *World Class Politics: Knoxville's 1982 World's Fair, Redevelopment and the Political Process.* Inman Majors recently published *The Millionaires,* a thinly disguised fictional account of the role of East Tennessee's Butcher brothers in the fair's successes and less commendable results.

Practically the entire issue of the Spring 1983 edition of the *Tennessee Folklife Society Bulletin* (vol. 49, no. 1) is devoted to the fair's "Folklife Festival." Articles by the festival's director, by a musician participant who is also prominently involved in Appalachian studies at East Tennessee State University, a sampler of press coverage of the exhibit, and a debate about the festival's effects (including views from UT historians Bruce Wheeler and Michael McDonald, who had recently completed the first edition of their history of Knoxville) make this issue invaluable.

Wheeler and McDonald comment in several places on Knoxvillians' responses to John Gunther. For a sampling of commentary on other less than becoming views of Knoxville offered by outsiders, see Jack Neely's "Ol' Man River" (*Metro Pulse*, Apr. 4, 1996) and "The Whole Elephant" (*Metro Pulse*, Sept. 27, 2001); and Sam Venable's "So We're 'Strange'? Awesome!" (*Knoxville News-Sentinel*, Aug. 16, 2005).

Phil Obermiller, recent past president of the Appalachian Studies Association, and widely recognized as *the* authority on the Appalachian out-migrant experience, shared his dismal appraisal of Knoxville with the author in the fall of 2005. Interestingly, he had written earlier (1987, 39–40) that he had never seen more rampant anti-Appalachian stereotypes than among successful out-migrants from the region.

The political careers and antics of Lee Monday and Cas Walker are addressed earlier in this book and in Wheeler's history of Knoxville. The assertion that Knoxville's business elite allied with Walker to impede change in Knoxville from the 1940s to around 1970 is a major theme of Bruce Wheeler's writings on Knoxville.

Practically every commentator on twentieth-century Knoxville (including William J. MacArthur, Michael McDonald, and Bruce Wheeler) emphasizes the federal presence in East Tennessee.

I cannot help but wonder if Dykeman had readers from Knoxville in mind when she charged that provincialism was not limited to rural areas. I became well acquainted with Wilma after my return home in 1987, and I have little doubt she included many Knoxvillians among the provincial. But I also believe Wilma was too generous and wise to be so blunt.

A review of the *Knoxville News-Sentinel* from around 1980 to the present will reveal the many and varied regional interests of Dykeman, Brewer, Brown, and Venable. Fred Brown's series on the Clearfork Valley appeared in January 1993. Venable reflected, in typical lighthearted fashion, on the evolution of his views of his home region in "I See the Light—Appalachia R Us—the people."

For general overviews of evolving media images of Appalachia, see Williams (1995) and Harkins (2004).

Nostalgic recollections of "The Cas Walker Show" are presented in Matt Lakin's "On With the Cas Show" (*Knoxville News-Sentinel*, October, 26 2006).

For general information on the *Heartland Series*, see the Web site http://www.wbir.com/life/programming/local/heartland/b_landry.aspx. Columnist Linda James reflects on the series and particularly Landry's relationship with Lucinda Ogle in the *[Pigeon Forge] Tennessee Star Journal* (Dec. 8–14, 2004).

For general information on the Museum of Appalachia, see the "Museum of Appalachia" entry by Misty Yeager in the *Encyclopedia of Appalachia,* 1496, and the museum's own Web site: http://museumofappalachia.com. Interestingly, Irwin often offers his own take on misleading views of Appalachia. See, for example, "Society's Typical view of Appalachia is 'totally erroneous,' Irwin Believes" (*Knoxville News-Sentinel,* November 28, 1993).

See the following Web sites for more details about the various agencies and their efforts to address East Tennessee ills: http://www.missionofhope.org; http://appalcora.org; http://www.appalachianministry.org; and http://appalachiancommunityfund.org.

For brief biographies and assessments of the work of James Agee, Richard Marius, Cormac McCarthy, and Wilma Dykeman, see the *Tennessee Encyclopedia of History and Culture* for entries on these Knoxville authors by, respectively, Robert Coles, Edwin S. Gleaves, Robert Benson, and Carroll Van West. A good introduction to David Madden and his work can be found in a collection of essays edited by Randy J. Hendricks and James A. Perkins titled *David Madden: A Writer for All Genres.*

From the time I first became engaged in Appalachian studies, UT's mixed views toward the region and hesitance to embrace it intrigued me. I discussed the matter with Wilma Dykeman at Berea in the summer of 1988, after she offered a provocative lecture on Appalachian literature. I revisited that conversation with her several times thereafter. As this project unfolded, a number of UT veterans and one newcomer to the faculty shared with me their views on the matter. They include Charles Faulkner, Lynn Champion, Tom Hood, Allison Ensor, Frank Harris, Bill Dockery, Tim Ezzell, and Ernie Freeburg.

James Horne offers an exhaustive analysis of the program of the Stokely Institute in "Personal Renewal and Professional Growth for Teachers: A Study of Meaningful Learning in an Interdisciplinary Environment."

David Goldfield (1984) and Bradley Rice's (1985) reviews of Wheeler and McDonald's *Knoxville, Tennessee* suggest the authors had not adequately placed Knoxville's story in broader historical contexts. Reviewers of Wheeler's second edition include Chris Baker (2006) and Charles W. Crawford's (2005). Baker, an

Appalachianist, offers an overall positive appraisal, but he criticizes Wheeler's failure to utilize recent regional scholarship. Crawford, a non-Appalachianist, offers a glowing review and accepts, without qualification, Wheeler's depiction of harmful "Appalachian influences" on Knoxville's development. I believe his appraisal is pretty representative of the views of non-academic East Tennesseans to Wheeler's scholarship. *Knoxville News-Sentinel* columnist Ina Hughes praised Wheeler's record and scholarly contribution at the time of his retirement in "Under Construction" (Dec. 18, 2005). She mentions, in particular, Wheeler's "homestead in the backwoods of Wears Valley" and his penchant for "old harp music."

Over the years, Wheeler has been very gracious about speaking to area civic groups and general audiences. Consequently, his take on Knoxville's past has become pervasive. Periodically his influence appears in the *News-Sentinel*'s letters to the editor section, as it may have on September 6, 2004, when a writer blasted present-day "parochial" Knoxvillians who opposed funding a new library. His explanation follows Wheeler's thesis in detail.

Regular readers of the *Knoxville News-Sentinel* have seen plenty of evidence in recent years of Knoxville's growing diversity and particularly the growing Hispanic presence in our region. See, for example: "Now You're talking—in 45 different ways" (Apr. 4, 2005); "City Streets flooded in sea of red and white" (Apr. 11, 2006); and the editorial "Communities must deal with racism" (May 29, 2005). Scholars have also begun to take notice of East Tennessee's growing diversity. See, for example, Chris Baker and Brandy Zmich-Latno's "Hispanic Migration and Changing Institutions in Rural East Tennessee"; Marcos McPeek Villatoro's interview with Jim Minick; and Rajini Srikanth's "Identity and Admission into the Political Game: The Indian American Community Signs." The latter essay explores the failed 1994 campaign of Ram Uppuluri for Tennessee's third district seat in the U.S. Congress.

Knoxville News-Sentinel columnists' series "The New Homesteaders: How Rural East Tennessee is Changing" in the mid-1990s offers many valuable insights into recent new arrivals to Knoxville and other dimensions of the city's and East Tennessee's growing diversity.

Knoxville's economic challenges and responses to them are recorded regularly in the pages of the *News-Sentinel*. For a general overview that is mostly positive, see Calvin Johnson's "Why Business (and Pleasure) is Booming in East Tennessee," which appeared in the in-flight magazine *AirTran Arrivals*.

Again, perusal of the last twenty years of the *News-Sentinel* will provide plenty of evidence of the various environmental challenges facing Knoxville and how those challenges link the city to greater East Tennessee. University of Tennessee philosophy professor and activist John Nolt offers a frightening assessment in *A Land Imperiled: The Declining Health of the Southern Appalachian Bioregion.*

"Nine Counties. One Vision" received extensive coverage in the *Knoxville News-Sentinel.* See the following articles: "New Coalition Will Enhance Arts" (Jan. 11, 2004); "ET Population Older, Working More—Study Finds" (Jan. 13, 2004); "Road to Improvement Begins with Summit" (Jan. 26, 2004); "As '9 Counties. One Vision' Ends, Organizers Hope Process Won't" (Dec. 29, 2004); "Sunset, Sunrise: '9 Counties' Paves Way" (Jan. 2, 2005); and "Public Invited to Celebrate '9 Counties' Accomplishments" (Jan. 16, 2005). A more extensive, multi-page assessment of the program may be found in the *Sentinel*'s "Perspective Section" (Jan. 23, 2005).

"Jobs Now!" also received much attention from the *Knoxville News-Sentinel.* See the following articles: "Executive Perception" (Jan. 8, 2004); "Jobs Now Rolls Out Marketing Concept" (Dec. 1, 2004); and "Jobs Now! Delivering on What Its Creators Hoped" (June 21, 2006).

The meeting billed as "Plain Talk for Quality Growth" is recounted in Elisha Sauers's "East Tennessee Conference Strategizes Regional Growth" (*Knoxville Voice,* Apr. 5, 2007). Former Knoxville mayor Bill Haslam kindly shared information about this meeting as well as his thoughts on it. Bill offered his own views on the developments in Knoxville at the end of his first year in office in "Cooperative Spirit Moving Knoxville into Bright Future" (*Knoxville News-Sentinel,* Dec. 26, 2004).

The *Knoxville News-Sentinel* offers regular updates on UT developments and the university's relationship with the region. See especially the following articles: "UT to Catalog Smokies Material" (Sept. 26, 1998) and "Students Push for Coal Buying Limits" (Mar. 30, 2007). The September 27, 2006, issue of the *UT Daily Beacon* (the student newspaper) announced the "Ready for the World Celebration of Appalachian Peoples and Cultures." At the past two Appalachian Studies conferences, representatives from the "Community Partnership Center" have shared their efforts in panels on student volunteerism. At the spring 2007 conference at Maryville College, they focused on the Little River Watershed Program. Also see Alice V. Sampson and Roberta T. Herrin's "Appalachian Teaching Project."

The special issue of *Tennessee Alumnus* 86, no. 4 (Fall 2006), highlighted publication of the *Encyclopedia of Appalachia,* and the issue reported on recent scholarship by geographer John Rehder and anthropologist Benita Howell. Howell also provided a "Who's Who? An Appalachian Roll of Honor" of UT personnel. The annotated list reveals that a wide variety of people who do not fit conventional regional stereotypes have served the university. The photo collection is from the works of Don Dudenbostel, who enrolled at UT from 1967 to 1971.

Again the *News-Sentinel* offers a regular reading on Knoxville's pulse, which reveals its continued ambivalence toward "things Appalachian." Writers Venable and Brown continue to write about the region with a mixture of realism and romance. Columnist Ina Hughes offered her own take on the perpetuation of regional stereotypes in "Weird Stories, Silly Jokes" (Jan. 25, 2007). In 2005, Scott Barker began a series called "Man and the Mountains," which highlighted how "humans have ravaged and restored the East Tennessee landscape." For a short time, the Friday *News-Sentinel*'s op-ed page offered very divergent perspectives from two sparring Appalachians, Greg Johnson and Don Williams.

The UT-ESPN feud was recorded in detail in the pages of the *Knoxville News-Sentinel* over a stretch of several weeks in late August 2002. Columnist Don Williams offered a particularly interesting response in "We Hillbillies Shouldn't Take the Media So Seriously" (Aug. 30, 2002). For a serious assessment of the importance of UT footfall to the Knoxville-East Tennessee community long before the feud with ESPN, see Carson Brewer's column in the *News-Sentinel* of September 12, 1999. The Volunteers of General Robert Neyland, Brewer writes, were "the first . . . anything to achieve greatness in East Tennessee in modern times."

EPILOGUE: REIMAGINING APPALACHIA AND OURSELVES

Information about the new scrubbers at TVA's Kingston power plant can be found in "Looming Scrubber Means Cleaner Air" (*Roane County News,* Apr. 27–29, 2007).

TVA's Buffalo Mountain Project is described in "Winds of Change," (*Knoxville News-Sentinel,* June 1, 2007). Three weeks later, (June 23, 2007) the same paper carried columns from environmentalist-activist Steve Smith and U.S. Senator Lamar Alexander about TVA's new venture.

There are hopeful signs that Knoxvillians' interest in the greater East Tennessee and Appalachian region is more widespread and persistent than in earlier times. The independent newspaper *Metro Pulse* recently ran a feature story on mountaintop removal (Feb. 28, 2008). Debates over Appalachia's role in the 2008 presidential primaries stirred a mixed outpouring of articles and letters to the editor of the *Knoxville News-Sentinel.* A column by Jerry Dobson (regional native, now professor of geography at the University of Kansas) titled "Everybody's favorite minority joke: Us" (June 1, 2008) is particularly relevant to this book.

The TVA-Kingston coal ash spill generated much discussion in local and national news outlets, including the Roane County News, the Knoxville News-Sentinel, and the Metropulse. One early, generally objective, account that won approval from a diverse lot of players in this ongoing controversy is Sean Flynn's "Black Tide," Gentlemen's Quarterly (June 2009).

Bibliography

Abramson, Rudy, and Jean Haskell, eds. *Encyclopedia of Appalachia.* Knoxville: Univ. of Tennessee Press, 2006.

Adams, Frank. *Unearthing Seeds of Fire: The Idea of Highlander.* Winston-Salem, NC: John F. Blair Publisher, 1975.

Ahlstrom, Sidney. *A Religious History of the American People.* New York: Image Books, 1975.

Alexander, Thomas B. "Strange Bedfellows: The Interlocking Careers of T. A. R. Nelson, Andrew Johnson, and W. G. (Parson) Brownlow." *East Tennessee Historical Society's Publication* 51 (1979): 54–77.

Allread, C. E. "Farming from 1860 to 1900." In Rothrock, *The French Broad–Holston Country,* 186–202.

———, et al. *Economic and Social Study of Tennessee: Part IIA, Comparative Study of the Counties.* University of Tennessee Extension Series, vol. 1, no. 5. Knoxville: Univ. of Tennessee Extension Service, 1924.

Ansley, Fran, and Brenda Bell, eds. "Miners' Insurrections/Convict Labor." *Southern Exposure* 1, nos. 3 and 4 (1974): 144–59.

Askins, Don. "John Fox, Jr.: A Re-Appraisal; or With Friends Like That, Who Needs Enemies?" In *Colonialism in Modern America: The Appalachian Case,* edited by Helen Lewis, Linda Johnson, and Don Askins, 251–57. Boone, NC: Appalachian Consortium Press, 1978.

Atkins, Jonathan. *Parties, Politics, and Sectional Conflict in Tennessee, 1832–1861.* Knoxville: Univ. of Tennessee Press, 1997.

———. "Politicians, Parties, and Slavery: The Second Party System and the Decision for Disunion in Tennessee." *Tennessee Historical Quarterly* (Spring 1986): 21–39.

Ayers, Edward. *The Promise of the New South: Life after Reconstruction.* New York: Oxford Univ. Press, 1992.

Bailey, Fred A. "Tennessee's Antebellum Common Folk." *Tennessee Historical Quarterly* (Spring 1986): 41–55.

Bailey, Rebecca. "'I Never Thought of My Life as History': A Story of the Hillbilly Exodus and the Price of Assimilation." *Journal of Appalachian Studies* 3, no. 2 (1997): 231–39.

Baker, Chris. Review of *Knoxville, Tennessee: A Mountain City in the New South,* by Bruce Wheeler. *Appalachian Journal* 33, no. 2 (Winter 2006): 226–29.

Baker, Chris, and Brandy Zmich-Latno. "Hispanic Migration and Changing Institutions in Rural East Tennessee." Paper presented at the annual Appalachian Studies Conference, Radford, VA, March 18, 2005.

Baker, Christopher. "East Tennessee within the World Economy, 1790–1850: Precapitalist Isolation or Peripheral Capitalism?" Master's thesis, Univ. of Tennessee, 1991.

Ballard, Sandra L. "Mildred Haun." In Abramson and Haskell, *Encyclopedia of Appalachia*, 1065–66.

Banker, Mark T. "Of Missionaries, Multiculturalism, and Mainstream Malaise: Reflections on the 'Presbyterian Predicament.'" *Journal of Presbyterian History* 81 (Summer 2003): 77–102.

———. *Toward Frontiers Yet Unknown: A 90th Anniversary History of Warren Wilson College, 1894–1984*. Swannanoa, NC: Warren Wilson College, 1984.

———. "We're ALL Appalachian." *Appalachian Journal* 29, no. 4 (2002): 418–21.

Banker, Mark T., and Reuben A. Holden. *Warren Wilson College: A Centennial Portrait*. Swannanoa, NC: Warren Wilson College, 1994.

Banks, Alan, Dwight Billings, and Karen Tice. "Appalachian Studies, Resistance, and Post-Modernism." In Fisher, *Fighting Back in Appalachia*, 283–302.

Barksdale, Kevin T. *The Lost State of Franklin: America's First Secession*. Lexington: Univ. Press of Kentucky, 2008.

Barnes, Lee. "Appalachian Logging." *Katuah Journal* (Fall 1992): 4–6.

Batteau, Allen W. *The Invention of Appalachia*. Tucson: Univ. of Arizona Press, 1991.

Becker, Jane. *Selling Tradition: Appalachia and the Construction of an American Folk, 1930–1940*. Chapel Hill: Univ. of North Carolina Press, 1988.

Behrend, Linda. "Anne W. Armstrong." In Abramson and Haskell, *Encyclopedia of Appalachia*, 1044–45.

Bell, Michael M. "The Fruit of Difference: The Rural-Urban Continuum as a System of Identity." *Rural Sociology* 57, no. 1 (1992): 65–82.

Benson, Robert. "Cormac McCarthy." In West, *The Tennessee Encyclopedia of History and Culture*, 581–82.

Bergeron, Paul H., Stephen V. Ash, and Jeanette Keith. *Tennesseans and Their History*. Knoxville: Univ. of Tennessee Press, 1996.

Biggers, Jeff. *The United States of Appalachia: How Southern Mountaineers Brought Independence, Culture, and Enlightenment to America*. Emeryville, CA: Shoemaker & Hoard, 2006.

Billings, Dwight, and Kathleen Blee. *The Road to Poverty: The Making of Wealth and Hardship in Appalachia*. New York: Cambridge Univ. Press, 2000.

Billings, Dwight, Kathleen Blee, and Louis Swanson. "Culture, Family, and Community in Preindustrial Appalachia." *Appalachian Journal* 13 (Winter 1986): 154–70.

Billings, Dwight, Gurney Norman, and Katherine Ledford, eds. *Confronting Appalachian Stereotypes: Back Talk from an American Region*. Lexington: Univ. Press of Kentucky, 1999.

Blair, Carolyn and Arda Walker. *By Faith Endowed: The Story of Maryville College, 1819–1994*. Maryville, TN: Maryville College Press, 1994.

Blaustein, Richard. "East Tennessee Public Folklore." In Abramson and Haskell, *Encyclopedia of Appalachia*, 859–60.

Blethen, H. Tyler. "Pioneer Settlement." In Blethen and Straw's *High Mountains Rising*, 17–29.

———. "The Scotch-Irish Heritage on Southern Appalachia." In *Appalachia Inside Out: A Sequel to* Voices from the Hills; Volume 1: *Conflict and Change*, edited by Robert J. Higgs, Ambrose N. Manning, and Jim Wayne Miller, 2–8. Knoxville: Univ. of Tennessee Press, 1995.

Blethen, H. Tyler, and Richard Straw, eds. *High Mountains Rising: Appalachians in Time and Place.* Urbana: Univ. of Illinois Press, 2004.

Booker, Robert J. *The Heat of a Red Summer: Race Mixing, Race Rioting in 1919 Knoxville.* Danbury, CT: Rutledge Books, 2001.

Bordewich, Fergus M. *Killing the White Man's Indian: Reinventing Native Americans at the End of the Twentieth Century.* New York: Anchor Books, 1996.

Brashear, Craig. "The Market Revolution and Party Preference in East Tennessee: Spatial Patterns of Partisanship in the 1840 Presidential Election." *Appalachian Journal* 25 (Fall 1997): 8–29.

Brinkley, Alan. *The Unfinished Nation: A Concise History of the American People.* 4th ed. New York: McGraw Hill, 2004.

Briscoe, W. Russell. "Commerce and Industry." In Deaderick, *Heart of the Valley,* 410–13.

Brooks, Jennifer. "'One Grand United Hymn': Boosterism in Knoxville, Tennessee at the Turn of the Century." Master's thesis, Univ. of Tennessee, 1991.

Brown, Logan, Theresa Burchett-Anderson, Donavan Cain, Jinny Turman Deal, and Howard Dorgan. "Where Have We Been? Where Are We Going? A History of the Appalachian Studies Association." *Appalachian Journal* 31, no. 1 (Fall 2003): 30–85.

Brown, Margaret Lynn. *The Wild East: A Biography of the Great Smoky Mountains.* Gainesville: Univ. Press of Florida, 2000.

Brownlow, Louis. *The Autobiography of Louis Brownlow: A Passion for Anonymity.* Chicago: Univ. of Chicago Press, 1958.

Bryan, Charles F. "The Civil War in East Tennessee: A Social, Political, and Economic Study." PhD diss., Univ. of Tennessee, 1978.

Buckwalter, Donald. "Effects of Early Nineteenth Century Transportation Disadvantage on the Agriculture of Eastern Tennessee." *Southeastern Geographer* 27, no. 1 (May 1978): 18–37.

Burnett, Edmund Cody. "Hog Raising and Hog Driving in the Region of the French Broad River." *Agricultural History* 20 (1946): 86–103.

Burns, Inez. "Settlement and Early History of the Coves of Blount County, Tennessee." *East Tennessee Historical Society's Publications* 24 (1952): 44–67.

Burns, Shirley Stewart. *Bringing Down the Mountains: The Impact of Mountaintop Removal on Southern West Virginia Communities.* Morgantown: West Virginia University Press, 2007.

Burran, James. "A Labor Conflict in Urban Appalachia: The Knoxville Street Car Strike of 1919." *Tennessee Historical Quarterly* 38, no. 1 (1979): 62–78.

Bush, Florence Cope. *Dorie: Woman of the Mountains.* Knoxville: Univ. of Tennessee Press, 1992.

Buxton, Barry, and Malinda Crutchfield, eds. *The Great Forest: An Appalachian Story.* Boone, NC: Appalachian Consortium Press, 1985.

Calhoun, Craig, ed. *Social Theory and the Politics of Identity.* Oxford: Blackwell, 1994.

Calloway, Colin. *First Peoples: A Documentary Survey of American Indian History.* Boston: Bedford/St. Martin's, 1999.

Campbell, John C. *The Southern Highlander and His Homeland.* New York: Russell Sage, 1921.

Carawan, Candie. "Highlander Research and Education Center." In Abramson and Haskell, *Encyclopedia of Appalachia,* 1535–37.

Carmichael, Virgil F. "The Acquisition of Land in the Creation of the Great Smoky Mountains National Park." *Smoky Mountain Historical Society Journal and Newsletter* 25, no. 1 (Spring 1999): 2–10.

Caruso, John Anthony. *The Appalachian Frontier: America's First Surge Westward.* Indianapolis: Bobbs-Merrill, 1959.

Cassells, Manuel. *The Power of Identity.* Maiden, MA: Blackwell Publishers, 1997.

Chafe, William H. *The Unfinished Journey: America Since World War II.* 6th ed. New York: Oxford Univ. Press, 2003.

Cimprich, John. "Slavery's End in Tennessee." In Inscoe, *Appalachians and Race,* 189–98.

———. *Slavery's End in Tennessee, 1861–1865.* Tuscaloosa: Univ. of Alabama Press, 1985.

Clayton, LaReine Warden. "East Tennesseans Begin to Advertise." *Tennessee Historical Quarterly* 39, no. 2 (1980): 149–65.

Clouse, Loletta. *Wilder.* Nashville: Rutledge Hill Press, 1990.

Coffin, William Sloane. *A Passion for the Possible: A Message to U.S. Churches.* Louisville, KY: Westminster/John Knox Press, 1993.

Cole, William E. *Tales from a Country Ledger.* Acton, MA: Tapestry Press, 1990.

Coleman, Michael. *American Indian Children at School, 1850–1930.* Jackson: Univ. Press of Mississippi, 1993.

Coles, Robert. "James Agee." In West, *The Tennessee Encyclopedia of History and Culture,* 3–4.

Corbin, David. *Life, Work, and Rebellion in the Coal Fields: The Southern West Virginia Miners, 1880–1922.* Urbana: Univ. of Illinois Press, 1982.

Cotham, Perry. *Toil, Turmoil, and Triumph: A Portrait of the Tennessee Labor Movement.* Nashville: Providence House Publishers, 1996.

Cotham, Steve. *Images of America: The Great Smoky Mountains National Park.* Charleston, SC: Arcadia Press, 2006.

Coulter, E. Merton. *William G. Brownlow: Fighting Parson of the Southern Highlands.* With a New Introduction by Stephen V. Ash. Knoxville: Univ. of Tennessee Press, 1999.

Cox, Ricky. "Jim Wayne Miller." In Abramson and Haskell, *Encyclopedia of Appalachia,* 1074-76.

Crawford, Charles W. Review of *Knoxville, Tennessee: A Mountain City in the New South,* by Bruce Wheeler. *Journal of East Tennessee History* 77 (2005): 102–3.

Creekmore, Betsey Beeler. *Knoxville!* Knoxville: East Tennessee Historical Society, 1991.

Creese, Walter L. *TVA's Public Planning: The Vision, the Reality.* Knoxville: Univ. of Tennessee Press, 1990.

Cremin, Lawrence A. *American Education: The Metropolitan Experience, 1876–1980.* New York: Harper & Row, 1988.

Cronon, William. *Nature's Metropolis: Chicago and the Great West.* New York: W. W. Norton, 1991.

Cullom, Randy. "Early Logging in the Great Smoky Mountain National Park: Little River Lumber Company." Paper prepared for Geography 6420, Univ. of Tennessee, Spring 1983.

Cummings, Joe. "Community and the Nature of Change: Sevier County, Tennessee, in the 1890s." *East Tennessee Historical Society's Publications* 58–59 (1986–87): 67–88.

Cummings, William J. "Community, Violence, and the Nature of Change: Whitecapping in Sevier County, Tennessee, During the 1890s." Master's thesis, Univ. of Tennessee, 1988.

Davidson, James West, Gordon M. Wardlaw, William E. Gienapp, and Christine Leigh Heyrman. *Nation of Nations: A Concise Narrative History of the American Republic; Volume I: To 1877.* New York: McGraw Hill, 1996.

Davis, Donald Edward. *Where There Are Mountains: An Environmental History of the Southern Appalachians.* Athens: Univ. of Georgia Press, 2000.

Deaderick, Lucille, ed. *Heart of the Valley: A History of Knoxville, Tennessee.* Knoxville: East Tennessee Historical Society, 1976.

Delfino, Susanna. "Antebellum East Tennessee Elites and Industrialization: The Examples of the Iron Industry and Internal Improvements." *East Tennessee Historical Society's Publications* 56–57 (1984–85): 102–19.

———. "Many Souths: Changing Social Contexts and the Road to Industrialization in Antebellum East Tennessee." *Southern Studies* 22, no. 1 (1983): 82–96.

Dodd, Joe. *World Class Politics: Knoxville's 1982 World's Fair, Redevelopment and the Political Process.* Salem, WI: Sheffield Publishing, 1988.

Dodds, Gordon B. "Joseph Reddeford Walker." In *The Reader's Encyclopedia of the American West,* edited by Howard Lamar, 1233. New York: Thomas Y. Crowell and Company, 1977.

Donald, David Herbert. *Look Homeward: A Life of Thomas Wolfe.* Boston: Little, Brown, 1987.

Drake, Richard. "Early Voices in the Appalachian Conversation." *Appalachian Journal* 31, no. 1 (Fall 2003): 86–87.

———. *A History of Appalachia.* Lexington: Univ. Press of Kentucky, 2001.

———. "Slavery and Anti-Slavery in Appalachia." In Inscoe, *Appalachians and Race,* 16–26.

Dunaway, Wilma A. *The First American Frontier: Transition to Capitalism in Southern Appalachia, 1700–1860.* Chapel Hill: Univ. of North Carolina Press, 1996.

———. *Slavery in the American Mountain South.* New York: Cambridge Univ. Press, 2003.

———. "Speculators and Settler Capitalists: Unthinking the Mythology of Appalachian Landholding, 1790–1860." In Pudup et al., *Appalachia in the Making,* 50–75.

Duncan, Cynthia M. *Worlds Apart: Why Poverty Persists in Rural America.* New Haven: Yale Univ. Press, 1992.

Dunn, Durwood. *Cades Cove: The Life and Death of a Southern Appalachian Community, 1818–1937.* Knoxville: Univ. of Tennessee Press, 1988.

Dykeman, Wilma. *The Tall Woman.* New York: Holt, Rinehart and Winston, 1962.

Edwards, Grace Toney. "Emma Bell Miles: Feminist Crusader in Appalachia." In *Appalachia Inside Out: A Sequel to* Voices from the Hills. Volume 2: *Culture and Custom,* edited by Robert J. Higgs, Ambrose N. Manning, and Jim Wayne Miller, 709–13. Knoxville: Univ. of Tennessee Press, 1995.

Egerton, John. "Appalachia's Absentee Landlords." *The Progressive* 45, no. 6 (June 1981): 42–45.

Ehle, John. *Trail of Tears: The Rise and Fall of the Cherokee Nation.* New York: Anchor Books, 1988.

Eller, Ronald D. *Miners, Millhands, and Mountaineers: Industrialization of the Appalachian South, 1880–1930.* Knoxville: Univ. of Tennessee Press, 1982.

———. *Uneven Ground: Appalachia Since 1945.* Lexington : University Press of Kentucky, 2008.

Elliott, Michael. *The Day Before Yesterday: Reconsidering America's Past, Rediscovering the Present.* New York: Simon and Schuster, 1996.

Ellison, George. Introduction to Kephart, *Our Southern Highlanders,* ix–xlviii.

Ensor, Allison. "What Is the Place of Mary Noailles Murfree Today?" *Tennessee Historical Quarterly* 47 (1988): 198–205.

Etulain, Richard. *Re-Imagining the American West: A Century of Fiction, History, and Art.* Tucson: Univ. of Arizona Press, 1996.

Ewen, Linda Ann. *Which Side Are You On? The Brookside Mine Strike in Harlan County, KY.* Chicago: Vanguard Press, 1979.

Ezzell, Tim. "Building Sustainable Partnerships." *Appalachian Journal* 34, nos. 3–4 (Spring/Summer 2007): 379–83.

Fanslow, Mary. "From Timbering to Tourism: The Wonderland Hotel's Early Years." *Journal of Appalachian Studies* 9, no. 2 (Fall 2003): 433–49.

Faulkner, Charles H. "'Here Are Frame Houses and Brick Chimneys': Knoxville, Tennessee, in the Late Eighteenth Century." In *The Southern Colonial Backcountry: Interdisciplinary Perspectives on Frontier Communities,* edited by David Allen Crass, Crass, David Colin, Steven D. Smith, Martha A. Zierden, and Richard D. Brooks, 137–61. Knoxville: Univ. of Tennessee Press, 1998.

———. "Knoxville and the Southern Appalachian Frontier: An Archaeological Perspective." *Tennessee Historical Quarterly* 59 (Fall 2000): 158–72.

Fickle, James. "Mining." In West, *The Tennessee Encyclopedia of History and Culture,* 627–28.

Finger, John R. "Cherokee Accommodation and Resilience in the Southern Appalachians." In Pudup et al., *Appalachia in the Making,* 25–49.

———. *Tennessee Frontiers: Three Regions in Transition.* Bloomington: Indiana Univ. Press, 2001.

———. "Tennessee Indian History: Creativity and Power." *Tennessee Historical Quarterly* 54, no. 4 (Summer 1995): 285–305.

Fisher, Noel C. *The Civil War in the Smokies.* Gatlinburg, TN: Great Smoky Mountains Association, 2005.

———. *War at Every Door: Partisan Politics and Guerilla Violence in East Tennessee, 1860–1869.* Chapel Hill: Univ. of North Carolina Press, 1997.

Fisher, Stephen L., ed. *Fighting Back in Appalachia: Traditions of Resistance and Change.* Philadelphia: Temple Univ. Press, 1993.

Folmsbee, Stanley J. "The Beginnings of the Railroad Movement in East Tennessee." *East Tennessee Historical Society's Publications* 5 (1933), 81–104.

———. "Growth of Knox County to 1861." In Rothrock, *The French Broad–Holston Country,* 34–41.

Folmsbee, Stanley J., and Lucille Deaderick. "The Founding of Knoxville." *East Tennessee Historical Society's Publications* 13 (1941): 3–21.

Foner, Eric. *Reconstruction: America's Unfinished Revolution, 1863–1877.* New York: Harper & Row, 1998.

Frazier, Charles. *Cold Mountain.* New York: Atlantic Monthly Press, 1997.

Fuhrmann, Joseph T. *The Life and Times of Tusculum College.* Greeneville, TN: Tusculum College, 1986.

Gaventa, John. *Power and Powerlessness: Quiescence and Rebellion in an Appalachian Valley.* Urbana: Univ. of Illinois Press, 1982.

Giardina, Denise. *Storming Heaven: A Novel.* New York: W. W. Norton, 1987.

Gilbert, Bil. *Westering Man: The Life of Joseph Walker.* Norman: Univ. of Oklahoma Press, 1983.

Ginger, Ray. *Six Days or Forever? Tennessee v. John Thomas Scopes.* New York: Oxford Univ. Press, 1958.

Gleaves, Edwin S. "Richard Marius." In West, *The Tennessee Encyclopedia of History and Culture,* 572–72.

Glen, John M. "Highlander Folk School." In West, *The Tennessee Encyclopedia of History and Culture,* 423–24.

———. *Highlander: No Ordinary School.* 2nd ed. Knoxville: Univ. of Tennessee Press, 1996.

———. "Like a Flower Slowly Blooming: Highlander and the Nurturing of an Appalachian Movement." In Fisher, *Fighting Back in Appalachia,* 31–56.

Goldfield, David. Review of *Knoxville, Tennessee: Continuity and Change in an Appalachian City,* by Bruce Wheeler and Michael McDonald. *American Historical Review* 89, no. 3 (June 1984): 880–81.

Goodheart, Lawrence B. "Tennessee's Antislavery Movement Reconsidered: The Example of Elihu Embree." *Tennessee Historical Quarterly* 41, no. 3 (1982): 224–38.

Goodykoontz, Colin B. *Home Missions on the American Frontier.* Caldwell, Idaho: Caxton Printers, 1939.

Grey, Alfred, and Susan Adams. "Government." In Deaderick, *Heart of the Valley,* 68–144.

Groce, W. Todd. *Mountain Rebels: East Tennessee Confederates and the Civil War, 1860–1870.* Knoxville: Univ. of Tennessee Press, 1999.

Groover, Mark. *An Archaeological Study of Rural Capitalism and Material Life: The Gibbs Farmstead in Southern Appalachia, 1790–1920.* New York: Plenum, 2005.

Handy, Robert. *A Christian America: Protestant Hopes and Historical Realities.* New York: Oxford, 1984.

Hargrove, Erwin C. *Prisoners of Myth: The Leadership of the Tennessee Valley Authority, 1933–1990.* Princeton, NJ: Princeton Univ. Press, 1994; repr., Knoxville: Univ. of Tennessee Press, 2001.

Hargrove, Erwin C., and Paul K. Conkin, eds. *TVA, 50 Years of Grass-roots Bureaucracy.* Urbana: Univ. of Illinois Press, 1983.

Harkins, Anthony. *Hillbilly: A Cultural History of an American Icon.* New York: Oxford Univ. Press, 2004.

Harper, Herbert L., ed. *Houston and Crockett: Heroes of Tennessee and Texas; An Anthology.* Nashville: Tennessee Historical Commission, 1986.

Hayslette, Sandra, and Chad Berry, eds. "AppalJ Roundtable Discussion: A Conversation About Teaching Appalachian Studies." *Appalachian Journal* 29, no. 4 (2002): 416–41.

Heiskell, Hugh Brown. *A Forty-Niner from Tennessee: The Diary of Hugh Brown Heiskell.* Edited by Edward M. Steel. Knoxville: Univ. of Tennessee Press, 1998.

Hendricks, Randy J., and James A. Perkins, eds. *David Madden: A Writer for All Genres.* Knoxville: Univ. of Tennessee Press, 2005.

Higham, John. "The Reorientation of American Culture in the 1890s." In *Writing American History: Essays on Modern Scholarship,* edited by John Higham, 73–102. Bloomington: Indiana Univ. Press, 1970.

Horne, James. "Personal Renewal and Professional Growth for Teachers: A Study of Meaningful Learning in an Interdisciplinary Environment." *Teacher Development* 3, no. 2 (1999): 263–89.

Hoxie, Frederick E., ed. *Talking Back to Civilization: Indian Voices from the Progressive Era.* Boston: Bedford/St. Martin's Press, 2001.

Hsiung, David C. "How Isolated Was Appalachia? Upper East Tennessee, 1780–1835." *Appalachian Journal* 16 (1989): 336–49.

———. "Stereotypes." In Blethen and Straw, *High Mountains Rising*, 101–13.

———. *Two Worlds in the Tennessee Mountains: Exploring the Origins of Appalachian Stereotypes.* Lexington: Univ. Press of Kentucky, 1997.

———, ed. *A Mountaineer in Motion: The Memoir of Dr. Abraham Jobe, 1817–1906.* Knoxville: Univ. of Tennessee Press, 2009.

Hummon, David. "City Mouse, Country Mouse: The Persistence of Community Identity." *Qualitative Sociology* 9, no. 1 (Spring 1986): 3–25.

Hurst, Sharon. "Days of Terror." *Our Smokies Heritage* 22 (September 1980): 284–85.

Hutson, A. C., Jr. "The Overthrow of the Convict Lease System in Tennessee." *East Tennessee Historical Society's Publications* 51 (1979): 92–113.

Inscoe, John C., ed. *Appalachians and Race: The Mountain South from Slavery to Segregation.* Lexington: Univ. Press of Kentucky, 2001.

———. "The Discovery of Appalachia: Regional Revisionism as Scholarly Renaissance." In *A Companion to the American South,* edited by John B. Boles, 369–386. Malden, MA: Blackwell Publishers, 2002.

———. *Mountain Masters: Slavery and the Sectional Crisis in Western North Carolina.* Knoxville: Univ. of Tennessee Press, 1989.

Johnson, Calvin. "Why Business (and Pleasure) is Booming in East Tennessee." *AirTran Arrivals* (April/May 1998): 47–51.

Johnson, Charles W., and Charles O. Jackson. *City behind a Fence: Oak Ridge, Tennessee, 1942–1946.* Knoxville: Univ. of Tennessee Press, 1981.

Johnson, Kathleen. "'The City of Tomorrow with the Spirit of the Past': Bankrolling the Industrial Development of Knoxville, Tennessee, 1875–1907." Master's thesis, Univ. of Tennessee, 1994.

Jones, James B., Jr. "Coal Mining in the Cumberland Plateau, 1850–1920." *The Courier* 28, no. 3 (June 1990): 4–6.

———. "Convict Lease Wars." In West, *The Tennessee Encyclopedia of History and Culture,* 204–5.

Jones, Loyal. *Appalachian Values.* With photography by Warren E. Brunner and an introduction by John B. Stephenson. Ashland, KY: Jesse Stuart Foundation, 1994.

———. "Old-Time Baptists and Mainline Christianity." In Williamson, *An Appalachian Symposium,* 120–30.

———. "Problems in Revisionism: More Controversy in God's Grand Division." *Appalachian Journal* 2, no. 3 (Spring 1975): 175–80.

Jordan, Terry G., and Matti Kaups. *The American Backwoods Frontier: An Ethnic and Ecological Interpretation.* Baltimore: Johns Hopkins Univ. Press, 1989.

Judd, Cameron. *The Bridge Burners: A True Adventure of East Tennessee's Underground Civil War.* Johnson City, TN: The Overmountain Press, 1996.

Karla, Ajay. "Cas Walker." In Abramson and Haskell, *Encyclopedia of Appalachia,* 544–45.

Keith, Alice B. "Three North Carolina Blount Brothers in Business and Politics, 1783–1812." PhD diss., Univ. of North Carolina, 1940.

Keith, Jeanette. *Country People in the New South: Tennessee's Upper Cumberland*. Chapel Hill: Univ. of North Carolina Press, 1995.

Kemplen, Tilda. *From Roots to Roses: The Autobiography of Tilda Kemplen*. Edited by Nancy Herzberg. Athens: Univ. of Georgia Press, 1992.

Kephart, Horace. "Horace Kephart by Himself." *North Carolina Library Bulletin* 5 (June 1922): 49–52

———. *Our Southern Highlanders: A Narrative of Adventure in the Southern Appalachians and a Study of Life Among the Mountaineers*. With an introduction by George Ellison. Knoxville: Univ. of Tennessee Press, 1976.

Kiffmeyer, Thomas. *Reformers to Radicals: The Appalachian Volunteers and the War on Poverty*. Lexington, KY: Univ. Press of Kentucky, 2008.

Lacy, Eric Russell. *Vanquished Volunteers: East Tennessee Sectionalism from Statehood to Secession*. Johnson City, TN: East Tennessee State Univ. Press, 1965.

Lambert, Robert S. "Logging in the Great Smokies, 1880-1930." *Tennessee Historical Quarterly* 21 (December 1961): 350–63.

———. "Logging on the Little River, 1890-1940." *East Tennessee Historical Society's Publications* 33 (1961): 32–42.

Lamon, Lester C. "Tennessee Race Relations and the Knoxville Race Riot of 1919." *East Tennessee Historical Society's Publications* 41 (1969): 67–85.

Lears, T. J. Jackson. *No Place of Grace: Antimodernism and the Transformation of American Culture, 1880–1920*. New York: Pantheon Books, 1981.

Lee, Tom. *The Tennessee-Virginia Tri-Cities: Urbanization in Appalachia, 1900–1950*. Knoxville: Univ. of Tennessee Press, 2005.

Leuchtenburg, William E. *The Perils of Prosperity, 1914–1932*. 2nd ed. Chicago: Univ. of Chicago Press, 1993.

Lewelling, Joseph. "The White Caps of Sevier County: Economic and Cultural Perspectives." *Tennessee Anthropologist* 11, no. 2 (Fall 1986): 156–73.

Lewis, Bonnie Sue. *Creating Christian Indians: Native Clergy in the Presbyterian Church*. Norman: Univ. of Oklahoma Press, 2001.

Lewis, Helen M., and Monica Appleby. *Mountain Sisters: From Convent to Community in Appalachia*. Lexington: Univ. Press of Kentucky, 2003.

Lewis, Ronald L. "Beyond Isolation and Homogeneity: Diversity and the History of Appalachia." In Billings et al., *Confronting Appalachian Stereotypes*, 21–43.

———. "Industrialization." In Blethen and Straw, *High Mountains Rising*, 59–73.

———. *Transforming the Appalachian Countryside: Railroads, Deforestation, and Social Change in West Virginia, 1880–1920*. Chapel Hill: Univ. of North Carolina Press, 1998.

Lian Xi. *The Conversion of Missionaries: Liberalism in American Protestant Missions in China, 1907–1932*. University Park: Pennsylvania State Univ. Press, 1997.

Lilienthal, David E. *TVA: Democracy on the March*. New York: Harper, 1944.

Limerick, Patricia Nelson. *Something in the Soil: Legacies and Reckonings in the New West*. New York: W. W. Norton, 2000.

———. "What on Earth Is the New Western History?" In *Trails: Toward a New Western History*, edited by Patricia Nelson Limerick, Clyde A. Milner II, Charles E. Rankin, 85–86. Lawrence: Univ. Press of Kansas, 1991.

Lipsey, C. McCurdy. "The Elkmont Cabins in the Great Smoky Mountains National Park: A Social History." Paper presented at the annual meeting of the Southern Sociological Society, Atlanta, GA, April 6, 1995.

Lomawaima, K. Tsianina. *They Called It Prairie Light: The Story of Chilocco Indian School.* Lincoln: Univ. of Nebraska Press, 1994.

Lukens, Robert. "The New South on Display: The Appalachian Expositions of 1910 and 1911." *Journal of East Tennessee History* 69 (1997): 1–28.

———. "Portraits of Progress in New South Appalachia: Three Expositions in Knoxville, Tennessee, 1910–1913." Master's thesis, Univ. of Tennessee, 1996.

MacArthur, William J. "Charles McClung McGhee: Southern Financier." PhD diss., Univ. of Tennessee, 1977.

———. *Knoxville's History: An Interpretation.* Knoxville: East Tennessee Historical Society, 1978.

Madden, David. "Unionist Resistance to Confederate Occupation: The Bridge Burners of East Tennessee." *East Tennessee Historical Society's Publications* 52–53 (1980–81): 22–39.

Majors, Inman. *The Millionaires.* New York: W. W. Norton, 2009.

Maloney, Michael E., and Obermiller, Phillip J. "Urban Appalachian Experience." In Abramson and Haskell, *Encyclopedia of Appalachia,* 347–52.

Martin, C. Brenden. *Tourism in the Mountain South: A Double-Edged Sword.* Knoxville: Univ. of Tennessee Press, 2007.

Martin, Charles E. *Hollybush: Folk Building and Change in an Appalachian Community.* Knoxville: Univ. of Tennessee Press, 1982.

Marx, Leo. *The Machine in the Garden: Technology and the Pastoral Ideal in America.* New York: Oxford Univ. Press, 1964.

Matthews, F. H. "The Revolt against Americanism: Cultural Pluralism and Cultural Relativism as an Ideology of Liberation." *Canadian Review of American Studies* 1, no. 1 (Spring 1970): 4–31.

McCauley, Deborah Vansau. *Appalachian Mountain Religion: A History.* Urbana: Univ. of Illinois Press, 1995.

McCrumb, Sharyn. *Ghost Riders.* New York: Dutton, 2003.

McDonald, Forrest, and Grady McWhiney. "The Antebellum Southern Herdsman: A Reinterpretation." *Journal of Southern History* 41, no. 2 (May 1975): 147–66.

McDonald, Michael J., and John Muldowny. *TVA and the Dispossessed: The Resettlement of Population in the Norris Dam Area.* Knoxville: Univ. of Tennessee Press, 1982.

McDonald, Miller, comp. *Campbell County, Tennessee USA: A History of Places, Faces, Happenings, Traditions, and Things.* LaFollette, TN: County Services Syndicate, 1993–1994.

McKenzie, Robert Tracy. *Lincolnites and Rebels: A Divided Town in the American Civil War.* New York: Oxford Univ. Press, 2006.

———. "'Oh! Ours Is a Deplorable Condition': The Economic Impact of the Civil War in Upper East Tennessee." In Noe and Wilson, *The Civil War in Appalachia,* 199–226.

———. "Wealth and Income: The Preindustrial Structure of East Tennessee in 1860." *Appalachian Journal* 21 (Spring 1994): 260–79.

McKinney, Gordon B. "Civil War and Reconstruction." In Blethen and Straw, *High Mountains Rising,* 46–47.

———. "Industrialization and Violence in Appalachia in the 1890s." In Williamson, *An Appalachian Symposium*, 131–44.

McLoughlin, William. *Cherokee Renascence in the New Republic*. Princeton, NJ: Princeton Univ. Press, 1986.

McNeill, William H. "Mythistory, or Truth, Myth, History, and Historians." *American Historical Review* 91, no. 1 (Nov. 1986): 1–10.

Messinger, Penny. "Leading the Field in Mountain Work: A History of the Conference of Southern Mountain Workers." PhD diss., The Ohio State Univ., 1998.

———. "Restoring the Woman Reformer: Helen Hastie Dingman and the Conference of Southern Mountain Workers, 1918-1952." Paper presented at the annual Appalachian Studies Conference, Dayton, Ohio, March 2006.

Michaux, François A. *Travels to the Westward of the Allegheny Mountains* (1802). Reprinted in vol. 3 of *Early Western Travels, 1748–1846*, translated and edited by Reuben Gold Thwaites. New York: AMS Press, 1966.

Miles, Emma Bell. *The Spirit of the Mountains*. With a foreword by Roger D. Abrahams and an introduction by David E. Whisnant. Knoxville: Univ. of Tennessee Press, 1975.

Miller, Gregory. *The Civil War in Campbell County*. Jacksboro, TN: Action Printing, 1992.

Miller, Jim Wayne. *The Brier Poems*. Frankfort, KY: Gnomon Press, 1997.

Mills, Elizabeth Shown. "Genealogy in the 'Information Age': History's New Frontier?" *National Genealogical Society Quarterly: Centennial Issue* 91 (Dec. 2003): 260–77.

Montgomery, James Riley. "The Summer School of the South." *Tennessee Historical Quarterly* 22, no. 4 (1963): 361–81.

Montgomery, James Riley, Stanley Folmsbee, Lee S. Greene. *To Foster Knowledge: A History of the University of Tennessee, 1794–1970*. Knoxville: Univ. of Tennessee Press, 1984.

Montgomery, Michael. "Myths: How a Hunger for Roots Shapes Our Notions About Appalachian English." *Now and Then: The Appalachian Magazine* 17, no. 2 (Summer 2000): 8.

Montgomery, Michael, and Joseph S. Hall. *Dictionary of Smoky Mountain English*. Knoxville: Univ. of Tennessee Press, 2004.

Montrie, Chad. *To Save the Land and People: A History of Opposition to Surface Coal Mining in Appalachia*. Chapel Hill: Univ. of North Carolina Press, 2003.

Morgan, John. *The Log House in East Tennessee*. Knoxville: Univ. of Tennessee Press, 1990.

Murfree, Mary Noailles. *In the Tennessee Mountains*. With an introduction by Nathalia Wright. Knoxville, Univ. of Tennessee Press, 1970.

Nash, Roderick. "The American Cult of the Primitive." *American Quarterly* 18 (1966): 517–37.

Neely, Jack. *Knoxville's Secret History*. Knoxville, TN: Scruffy City Publishing, 1995.

———. *Secret History II: Stories About Knoxville, Tennessee*. Knoxville, TN: Scruffy City Publishing, 1998.

Nicholas Gibbs Historical Society. *Nicholas Gibbs and His Descendants, 1733–1977*. Knoxville: Nicholas Gibbs Historical Society, 1977.

Noble, David. "The Paradox of Progressivism." American Quarterly 5 (Fall 1953): 201–12.

Noe, Kenneth. *Southwest Virginia's Railroad: Modernization and the Sectional Crisis.* Urbana: Univ. of Illinois Press, 1994.

Noe, Kenneth W., and, Shannon H. Wilson, eds. *The Civil War in Appalachia: Collected Essays.* Knoxville: Univ. of Tennessee Press, 2001.

Nolt, John. *A Land Imperiled: The Declining Health of the Southern Appalachian Bioregion.* Knoxville: Univ. of Tennessee Press, 2005.

North, Douglass C. *The Economic Growth of the United States, 1790–1860.* New York: W. W. Norton, 1966.

Obermiller, Phillip J. "Labeling Urban Appalachians." In Obermiller and Philliber, *Too Few Tomorrows,* 35–42.

——. "The Question of Appalachian Identity." In *The Invisible Minority: Urban Appalachians,* edited by William W. Philliber and Clyde McCoy, 9–19. Lexington: Univ. Press of Kentucky, 1981.

Obermiller, Phillip J., and Michael E. Maloney, eds. *Appalachia: Social Context Past and Present.* 4th ed. Dubuque, IA: Kendall Hunt, 2002.

Obermiller, Phillip J., and William W. Philliber, eds. *Too Few Tomorrows: Urban Appalachians in the 1980s.* Boone, NC: Appalachian Consortium Press, 1987.

O'Brien, John. *At Home in the Heart of Appalachia.* New York: Alfred A. Knopf, 2001.

Olson, Ted. "Literature." In Blethen and Straw, *High Mountains Rising,* 171.

Olwell, Russell B. *At Work in the Atomic City: A Labor and Social History of Oak Ridge, Tennessee.* Knoxville: Univ. of Tennessee Press, 2004.

Osha, Jennifer. "Marie Cirillo: Helping the People of Appalachia Regain Control over Their Communities and Lives." *Orion* 67 (January/February 2003).

Otto, John Solomon. "The Migration of the Southern Plain Folk: An Interdisciplinary Synthesis." *Journal of Southern History* 51, no. 2 (May 1985): 184–200.

Overholt, James, ed. *These Are Our Voices: The Story of Oak Ridge 1942–1970.* Oak Ridge, TN: Children's Museum, 1987.

Page, Bonnie. *Clearfork and More (History and Memories).* Lake City, TN: B. M. Page, 1986.

Parker, Harold M., Jr. "A School of the Prophets at Maryville." *Tennessee Historical Quarterly* 34 (1975): 72–90.

Patton, Edwin P. "Transportation Development." In Deaderick, *Heart of the Valley,* 178–236.

The People of Carter County, Tennessee. *Carter County, Tennessee and Its People, 1796–1993.* Elizabethton, TN: Carter County History Book Committee, 1993.

Pierce, Daniel S. *The Great Smokies: From Natural Habitat to National Park.* Knoxville: Univ. of Tennessee Press, 2000.

Potter, Robert M., and Tim Unwin, eds. *The Geography of Urban-Rural Interaction in Developing Countries.* London: Routledge Press, 1989.

Pudup, Mary Beth, Dwight B. Billings, and Altina L. Waller. *Appalachia in the Making: The Mountain South in the Nineteenth Century.* Chapel Hill: Univ. of North Carolina Press, 1995.

——. "Taking Exception with Exceptionalism: The Emergence and Transformation of Historical Studies of Appalachia." In Pudup et al., *Appalachia in the Making,* 270–96.

Raitz, Karl B., and Richard Ulack. *Appalachia: A Regional Geography; Land, People, and Development.* Boulder, CO: Westview Press, 1984.

Rice, Bradley. Review of *Knoxville, Tennessee: Continuity and Change in an Appalachian City,* by Bruce Wheeler and Michael McDonald. *The Journal of Southern History* 51, no. 1 (Feb. 1985): 129–30.

Robie, Harry. "Loyal Jones." In Abramson and Haskell, *Encyclopedia of Appalachia,* 985–86.

Rogers, Michael. "TVA Population Removal: Attitudes and Expectations of the Dispossessed at the Norris and Cherokee Dam Sites." *Journal of East Tennessee History* 67 (1995): 89–105.

Rose, Patricia Gaultney. "The Murrays Move West." *The Campbell Countian* 11, no. 2 (July–September 2000): 26–27.

Rothrock, Mary U., ed. *The French-Broad Holston Country: A History of Knox County, Tennessee.* Knoxville: East Tennessee Historical Society, 1946.

Salstrom, Paul. "The Agricultural Origins of Economic Dependency, 1840–1880." In *Appalachian Frontiers: Settlement, Society and Development in the Preindustrial Era,* edited by Robert D. Mitchell, 261–83. Lexington: Univ. Press of Kentucky, 1991.

———. *Appalachia's Path to Dependency: Rethinking a Region's Economic History, 1730–1940.* Lexington: Univ. Press of Kentucky, 1994.

———. "Newer Appalachia as One of America's Last Frontiers." In Pudup et al., *Appalachia in the Making,* 76–102.

Sampson, Alice V., and Roberta T. Herrin. "Appalachian Teaching Project: An Opportunity for Academic-Community Activism." *Appalachian Journal* 34, nos. 3–4 (Spring/Summer 2007): 352–83.

Satterwhite, Emily. "Seeing Appalachian Cities." In Obermiller and Maloney, *Appalachia,* 104–8.

Satz, Ronald N. *Tennessee's Indian Peoples: From White Contact to Removal, 1540–1840.* Knoxville: Univ. of Tennessee Press, 1979.

Sayles, John. *Matewan.* Cinecom Pictures, 1987. DVD: Santa Monica, CA: Lions Gate, 2001.

Schmidt, Ronald G., and William S. Hooks. *Whistle over the Mountain: Timber, Tracks, and Trails in the Tennessee Smokies.* Yellow Springs, OH: Graphicon Press, 1994.

Searles, P. David. *A College for Appalachia: Alice Lloyd on Caney Creek.* Lexington: Univ. Press of Kentucky, 1995.

Seeber, Clifford. "Acorns to Atoms: A Grass-Roots History of Oak Ridge." *Antioch Review* 12 (September 1952): n.p.

Selznick, Philip. *TVA and the Grassroots: A Study in the Sociology of Formal Organization.* New York: Harper and Row, 1966.

Sevier County Heritage Book Committee. *Sevier County, Tennessee and Its Heritage.* Waynesville, NC: Walsworth Pub., 1994.

Seymour, Digby. *Divided Loyalties: Fort Sanders and the Civil War in East Tennessee.* 3rd ed. Knoxville: East Tennessee Historical Society, 2002.

Shapiro, Henry D. *Appalachia on Our Mind: The Southern Mountains and Mountaineers in the American Consciousness, 1870–1920.* Chapel Hill: Univ. of North Carolina Press, 1978.

Shapiro, Karin A. *A New South Rebellion: The Battle Against Convict Labor in the Tennessee Coalfields, 1871–1896.* Chapel Hill: Univ. of North Carolina Press, 1998.

Shields, A. Randolph. "Cades Cove in the Great Smoky Mountain National Park." *Tennessee Historical Quarterly* 24 (Summer 1965): 103–20.

———. *The Cades Cove Story.* Gatlinburg, TN: Great Smoky Mountains Natural History Association, 1977.

Shifflett, Crandall A. *Coal Towns: Life, Work, and Culture in Company Towns of Southern Appalachia, 1880–1960.* Knoxville: Univ. of Tennessee Press, 1991.

Smith, Henry Nash. *Virgin Land: The American West as Symbol and Myth.* Cambridge, MA: Harvard Univ. Press, 1950.

Smith, Herb. E. *Strangers and Kin: A History of the Hillbilly Image.* DVD. Appalshop Films, 1984.

Smoky Mountain Historical Society. *The Gentle Winds of Change: A History of Sevier County, Tennessee, 1900–1930.* Sevierville, TN: Smoky Mountain Historical Society, 1986.

Soltow, Lee. "Land Inequality on the Frontier: The Distribution of Land in East Tennessee at the Beginning of the 19th Century." *Social Science History* 5, no. 3 (Summer 1981): 275–91.

Spears, Ross, and Jude Cassidy, eds. *Agee: His Life Remembered.* New York: Holt, Rinehart and Winston, 1985.

Srikanth, Rajini. "Identity and Admission into the Political Game: The Indian American Community Signs Up." *Amerasia Journal* 25, no. 3 (1999): 59–80.

Stanfield, John H. "The Sociohistorical Roots of Black/White Inequality in Urban Appalachia: Knoxville and East Tennessee." In *Blacks in Appalachia,* edited by William Turner and Edward Cabbell, 133–44. Lexington: Univ. Press of Kentucky, 1985.

Suppiger, Joseph. *Phoenix of the Mountains: The Story of Lincoln Memorial University.* Harrogate, TN: Lincoln Memorial University Press, 2001.

Taylor, Robert, Jr. "Mainstreams of Mountain Thought: Attitudes of Selected Figures in the Heart of the Appalachian South, 1877–1903." PhD diss., Univ. of Tennessee, 1971.

———. "The New South Mind of a Mountain Editor: William Rule, 1877–1898." *East Tennessee Historical Society's Publications* 47 (1975): 100–117.

Tennessee Valley Authority, Department of Regional Planning Studies. *The Population of the Tennessee Valley.* Knoxville: Tennessee Valley Authority, 1937.

Thomas, Jerry Bruce. *An Appalachian New Deal: West Virginia in the Great Depression.* Lexington: Univ. Press of Kentucky, 1998.

Thomas, John K. "The Cultural Reconstruction of an Appalachian City: Knoxville, Tennessee and the Coming of the Movies." *Journal of East Tennessee History* 65 (1993): 34–52.

Trefousse, Hans L. *Andrew Johnson: A Biography.* New York: W. W. Norton, 1989.

Turner, William, and Edward Cabbell, eds. *Blacks in Appalachia.* Lexington: Univ. Press of Kentucky, 1985.

Van Kleeck, Richard. "Reflections on the 1982 World's Fair OR Mainlining in Knoxville." *Tennessee Folklore Society Bulletin* 49, no. 1 (Spring 1983): 1–6.

Vance, Rupert B. Foreword. In *The Southern Highlander and His Homeland,* by John C. Campbell, vii–ix. Lexington: Univ. Press of Kentucky, 1969.

Venable, Sam. "I See the Light—Appalachia R Us—the people." *Tennessee Alumnus* (Fall 2006): 46.

Villatoro, Marcos McPeek. "Latino Hillbilly: An Interview with Marcos McPeek Villatoro." By Jim Minick. *Appalachian Journal* 28, no. 2 (2001): 204–20.

Wade, Richard C. *The Urban Frontier: Pioneer Life in Early Pittsburgh, Cincinnati, Lexington, Louisville, and St. Louis.* Chicago: Univ. of Chicago Press, 1969.

Wall, David S. "Appalachia." In Abramson and Haskell, *Encyclopedia of Appalachia*, 1006–7.

Waller, Altina L. *Feud: Hatfields, McCoys, and Social Change in Appalachia, 1860–1900*. Chapel Hill: Univ. of North Carolina Press, 1988.

———. "Feuding in Appalachia: Evolution of a Cultural Stereotype." In Pudup et al., *Appalachia in the Making*, 347–76.

Walls, Dwayne E. *The Kidwells: A Family Odyssey*. Durham: Carolina Academic Press, 1983.

Watson, Olin, and Ed Trout. "Lumber and Logging." In *The Gentle Winds of Change: A History of Sevier County, Tennessee, 1900–1930*, by the Smoky Mountain Historical Society, 103–28. Sevierville, TN: Smoky Mountain Historical Society, 1986.

Weals, Vic. *The Last Train to Elkmont: A Look Back at Life on Little River in the Great Smoky Mountains*. Knoxville: Olden Press, 1991.

Webb, George Ernest. *The Evolution Controversy in America*. Lexington: Univ. Press of Kentucky, 1994.

Webb, James. *Born Fighting: How the Scots-Irish Shaped America*. New York: Broadway Books, 2004.

West, Carroll Van. "Wilma Dykeman." In West, *The Tennessee Encyclopedia of History and Culture*, 581–82.

———, ed. *The Tennessee Encyclopedia of History and Culture*. Nashville: Rutledge Hill Press/Tennessee Historical Society, 1998.

Wetherington, Mark V. "Streetcar City: Knoxville, Tennessee, 1876–1947." *East Tennessee Historical Society's Publications* 54–55 (1982–83): 70–110.

Wheeler, Bruce. *Knoxville, Tennessee: A Mountain City in the New South*. 2nd ed. Knoxville: Univ. of Tennessee Press, 2005.

———. "Knoxville's World's Fair of 1982." In West, *The Tennessee Encyclopedia of History and Culture*, 513–14.

Wheeler, Bruce, and Michael McDonald. "The Communities of East Tennessee, 1850–1940: An Interpretive Overview." *The East Tennessee Historical Society's Publications* (1986): 3–38.

———. *Knoxville, Tennessee: Continuity and Change in an Appalachian City*. Knoxville: Univ. of Tennessee Press, 1983.

Whisnant, David E. *All That Is Native and Fine: The Politics of Culture in an American Region*. Chapel Hill: Univ. of North Carolina Press, 1983.

———. "Controversy in God's Grand Division: The Council of the Southern Mountains." *Appalachian Journal* 2, no. 1 (Fall 1974): 7–45.

———. *Modernizing the Mountaineer: People, Power, and Planning in Appalachia*. Rev. ed. Knoxville: Univ. of Tennessee Press, 1994.

C. P. White. "Commercial and Industrial Trends since 1865." In Rothrock, *The French Broad–Holston Country*, 220–25.

White, Richard. *The Middle Ground: Indians, Empires, and Republics in the Great Lakes Region, 1650–1815*. New York: Cambridge Univ. Press, 1991.

Wiebe, Robert H. *The Search for Order*. New York: Hill and Wang, 1967.

Williams, John Alexander. *Appalachia: A History*. Chapel Hill: Univ. of North Carolina Press, 2002.

Williams, Michael Ann. *Great Smoky Mountains Folklife*. Jackson: Univ. Press of Mississippi, 1995.

Williams, Raymond. *The Country and the City.* Oxford: Oxford Univ. Press, 1973.

Williams, Samuel C., ed. "Journal of Events (1825–1873) of David Anderson Deaderick." *East Tennessee Historical Society's Publications* 8 (1936): 121–37.

Williams, Samuel Cole. "George Roulstone: Father of the Tennessee Press." *East Tennessee Historical Society's Publications Series* 17 (1945): 51–60.

Williamson, J. W. *Hillbillyland: What the Movies Did to the Mountains and What the Mountains Did to the Movies.* Chapel Hill: Univ. of North Carolina Press, 1995.

———, ed. *An Appalachian Symposium: Essays Written in Honor of Cratis D. Williams.* Boone, NC: Appalachian State Univ. Press, 1977.

Wilson, Darlene. "A Judicious Combination of Incident and Psychology: John Fox Jr. and the Southern Mountaineer Motif." In Billings et al., *Confronting Appalachian Stereotypes,* 98–118.

Wilson, Shannon H. *Berea College: An Illustrated History.* Lexington: Univ. Press of Kentucky, 2006.

Winchester, Cecil. "Clearfork." In *Clearfork and More (History and Memories),* edited by Bonnie Page, 67–69. Lake City, TN: B. M. Page, 1986.

Woodward, C. Vann. *The Origins of the New South, 1877–1913.* Baton Rouge: Louisiana State University, 1951.

Wright, Nathalia. Introduction to Murfree, *In the Tennessee Mountains,* v–xxxiii.

Yeager, Misty. "Museum of Appalachia." In Abramson and Haskell, *Encyclopedia of Appalachia,* 1496.

Yeomans, G. Allan, and Paul L. Soper, "The Theatre," in Deaderick, *Heart of the Valley,* 457–81.

Young, T. "False, Cheap, and Degraded: When History, Economy, and Environment Collided at Cades Cove, Great Smoky Mountains National Park." *Journal of Historical Geography* 32 (2006): 169–89.

Index

Index

union(ists), 21-22, 36, 49, 64-71, **67**, 84, 88, 92-93, 100, 126, 129, 134, 270
U.S. Bureau of Mines, 130
U.S. Postal Service, **79**
University of Tennessee Knoxville (UTK), 74n, 76, 98, 165, **166**, 171, 183, 199, 228
University of Tennessee Press (UT Press), **20**, 151, 180, 237, 243-44, 249 286
University of Tennessee Institute for Secure and Sustainable Environment's Community Partnership Center, 241, 300
University of Tennessee "Ready for the World Celebration," 300
University of Tennessee History Department, 237
University of Tennessee Volunteer Football, 244
urban Knoxville, 87
urbanization, 62, 86-87, 96, 99, 133, 230, 273-74; within Appalachia, 87

Vanderbilt University, 195, 202, 210-11
Venable, Sam, 297
Vietnam War, 234
Vincent, Bert, 217, 229, 229n, 294
Voices of the Land (exhibit of East Tennessee Historical Society), 239
Volunteer Football, 244

Wagner Act, 179, 285
Walden's Ridge, Tennessee, 144
Walker Sisters, 174, 185
Walker, Caswell Orton ("Cas"), 184, 193, 225, 227-28, 232, 287, 297-98
Walker, Joseph R., **54**
Walland, Tennessee, 112, 114, 117
Walls, Dwayne E., 187n
War of 1812, 29, 41, 45, 52, 55-56, 60-61, 69
War on Poverty, 11, 168, 203, 206-7, 229, 234, 292-93
Warren Wilson College, 139n, 197, 204, 281, 290
Warren Wilson Junior College, 147
Watauga, 18, 26, 31
Watauga Association, 18, 31
WDVX-FM Radio, 170, 239, **240**
Weals, Vic, 119n, 217, 276-77, 279, 294

Webb, Paul, 80, **81**, 144, 271
Webb School of Knoxville, 6, 223, 234, 240, 244-46, **254**
West Tennesseans, 61, 66
West Tennessee, 38, 40, 52, 57-58, 60-61, 90, 98, 226, 264, 268
West Virginia, 124, 131, 140, 142, 157, 161, 185, 206, 209, 235-36, 258, 260, 278-79, 286, 294
West, Don, 195, 202
Wheeler, Billy Edd, 290
Wheeler, William Bruce, 237
Whig, 61, 64-66, 83, 228
Whisnant, David, 145n, 180, 200, 237, 281-83, 286, 288, 291
White Caps, 143-44, 282
White Lily Flour Mills, 91
White, Hugh Lawson, 38, 61
White, James, 34, 41, 58, 91
White's Fort, **36**
Whitehead, Don, 217, 229, 229n, 230, 230n, 294
wholesale business, 38, 58, 83, **86**, 88, 91, 93, 95
Wilder, Tennessee, 131, 157, 279
Williams, Cratis, 45, 196
Williams, Elizabeth, 147
Wilson, Samuel Tyndale, 148, 153, 283
Wilson, Shannon, 270, 281, 290
Wilson, Woodrow, 104
Wolfe, Thomas, 196, 205, 289
women missionaries, 147
Wonderland Club, 175
Wonderland Park Company, 122
Woodland Community Land Trust, 211, 293
World War I, 89, 98, **103**, 104, 106, 113, 117, 120, 139-31, 152, 179, 185
World War II, 10, 53, 77, 127, 132, 177, 181-82, 185, **186**, 187-88, 193, 198-99, 202, 207-8, 216, 225, 271, 286-87
Wright, James (Jim), 172-73, 175

yeomen, 7, 32, 41, 46
YMCA, 97, 129
York, Shelby, 208, 211, 293
youthful Dolly Parton, 228

www.ingramcontent.com/pod-product-compliance
Lightning Source LLC
Chambersburg PA
CBHW021848020426
42334CB00013B/241